Great Traditions In Ethics

Fourth Edition

Great Traditions In Ethics

Fourth Edition

Ethel M. Albert
Northwestern University

Theodore C. Denise
Sheldon P. Peterfreund
Syracuse University

D. VAN NOSTRAND COMPANY

New York Cincinnati Toronto London Melbourne

D. Van Nostrand Company Regional Offices:
New York   Cincinnati

D. Van Nostrand Company International Offices:
London   Toronto   Melbourne

Published by D. Van Nostrand Company
135 West 50th Street, New York, N.Y. 10020

10   9   8   7   6   5   4   3   2   1

Preface

The Fourth Edition of *Great Traditions in Ethics* is based largely on suggestions and comments we have had from professors and reviewers. The new edition strengthens our representation of ethical theories with two new chapters: "Morality and Sentiment" and "*Prima Facie* Duty." In the first of these, our selections are taken from David Hume's *An Enquiry Concerning the Principles of Morals;* in the second, from W. D. Ross's *The Right and the Good.* We believe that the absence of Hume from the previous editions was unfortunate and we are pleased to have this opportunity to set matters aright. By adding Ross, we gain both a notable extension of Kant and provide a counterbalance to many contemporary theories. We have also added a few pages to the Spinoza selection to make it more complete. The chapter on "Situation Ethics" has been omitted in favor of the two new chapters.

In view of the diversity of theories and points of view in ethics, we have thought that the fairest way to introduce the subject to those who have no previous acquaintance with it is to direct them to representative primary sources. To lessen somewhat the difficulty of the original writings, without sacrificing accuracy or reducing the challenge of ethics, we have subjected the material to some internal editing. By this means, we have eliminated what we regard as extraneous to the central argument, and, through rearranging the components of some of the theories, we believe we have clarified the major lines of their arguments. The brief biographies and introductions at the beginning of each chapter suggest, respectively, something of the theorists' personal and historical backgrounds and of their general philosophical positions as they bear on ethical theory. In short, we hope that we have provided a guide to ethical theory for the beginning student.

As far as we were able, we presented each theory in its best light and followed as closely as possible what we believe the author intended. Beyond the exercise of judgment in the selection of writers and of passages to be used, and apart from our statements in the introductory chapter and epilogue, we have endeavored to keep our own views and interests from prejudicing the presentation of the theories we treated. We have sought to put forward material which can serve as a basis for classroom work, not as a substitute for lectures and discussions.

Completeness has not been our goal. It is not within the compass of a single volume to contain even in brief form all the ethical theories which may deserve to be called classics. Moreover, it was not feasible to present any theory in its entirety. We made no attempt at the delicate and tenuous task of classifying types of ethical theory, but rather, we adopted a simple historical arrangement of chapters. Each chapter is an independent unit — although there are occasional cross-references — since it is desirable to leave the decision of a suitable order of treatment to the users of the book.

For the reader, we have undertaken to make the classical theories of ethics more readily accessible. On the assumption that comprehension is a necessary precondition of intelligent criticism, we have been interested primarily in the exposition of points of view which are important in the history of ethical theory, leaving for a later stage of ethical inquiry their analysis, criticism, comparison, and interpretation. Within each chapter, the constituent ideas of the theory treated have been set off from each other, and connecting passages introduced to serve both as transitions and as explanations of important concepts. In addition, where we deemed it necessary, we have given definitions of technical terms.

At the close of each chapter we have included a list of questions, a Key to selections, and a Guide to Additional Reading.

There is a A Study Guide written by Professors Erwin J. Franco and Alex Bell.

E. M. A.
T. C. D.
S. P. P.

Contents

Great Traditions In Ethics

Fourth Edition

CHAPTER 1

Introduction

"The Unexamined Life Is Not Worth Living."

The unexamined life is not worth living." In these terms, Socrates — the first great moral philosopher of western civilization — stated the creed of reflective men and set the task of ethical theory. To seek, with the aid of reason, a consistent and correct ideal of life is the traditional goal of moral philosophers. Yet, to search for basic moral principles and to attempt to solve problems concerning the good and the bad, the right and the wrong, is not the exclusive province of philosophers. Writers and statesmen, historians, and ordinary citizens also conduct ethical inquiry, although they may not call it that. Aristotle's *Nichomachean Ethics*, Shakespeare's *Hamlet*, Lincoln's *Gettysburg Address*, and Adam Smith's *Wealth of Nations*, as well as discussions at the bridge table and in college dormitories, exemplify at various levels the same questing spirit and desire for wisdom.

Flowing beneath every human action is the current of ethical significance, and in all ages and places, questions about moral conduct and moral principles are posed and answers attempted. "To be or not to be?" is at its heart a question of ethics. And "Whether 'tis nobler in the mind to suffer the slings and arrows of outrageous fortune, or to take arms against a sea of troubles, and by opposing end them" — this is, indeed, a difficult decision. In this, Hamlet's dilemma is typical of the problems that confront the ethical theorist and the sensitive layman alike. They are among the most subtle and pressing problems of life.

The answers to ethical questions, whether momentous as the agonized query of Hamlet or trivial as the smallest matter of conformity to convention, are not to be found at the back of the book. The various means which have been devised to deal with ethical problems range from the mute acceptance of authority, through the poet's inspiration and the gambler's hunch, to the moral philosopher's direct and systematic analysis of the foundations of morality. Admittedly, the philosopher's commitment "to seek the truth, and to follow it wherever it leads" puts him under a harsh discipline. To earn the title of "rational animal," we are not obligated to think through every moral situation to its very roots; but once we go beyond immediate action to a consideration of the reasons for our actions, we are in reason's territory, and there, logic rules. In truth, we have only two alternatives, to reflect on moral matters or to remain silent. We would have to use reason even to argue for the soundness of refraining from rational discussion. The philosopher Epictetus, confronted by a sceptic, made plain the inescapability of committing ourselves to the use of logic:

When one of the company said, "Convince me that logic is necessary," Epictetus asked: "Do you wish me to demonstrate this to you?" "Yes." "Then must I use a demonstrative form of argument?" And when this was admitted: "Then how will you know whether I argue fallaciously?" And as the man was silent: "Don't you see," said Epictetus, "how even you yourself acknowledge that *logic is necessary, since without its assistance you cannot so much as know whether it is necessary or not?*"

Principles and Practices

To think about morality, deeply and honestly, is the main business of ethical theorists, and in this, we can all participate to some degree. But more often than not, it is an instructive and chastening experience to seek out the theory that lies beneath actual practice, for we can then see the inconsistencies of ordinary moral thought and practice. We condemn as lazy the man who chooses the life of a beachcomber, yet we envy and admire anyone who is sufficiently wealthy to spend his time doing nothing. We disapprove of the "climber" when he is someone we dislike, yet praise the same quality when it appears in a "go-getter" who is our friend. We say that "honesty is the best policy," yet acknowledge in our actions and words the good taste and practicality of telling white, gray, and black lies. It would be difficult to reconcile the principles underlying such judgments, and we can see why common sense morality is usually distrusted by systematic ethical theorists. On examination, it proves to be a murky and illogical collection of rules which are bound together only by the slender threads of chance and custom.

When observation and experience reveal to us how great the distance is between the high-flown ideals to which men give lip service and the down-to-earth expediency of the morality they practice, we may lose confidence in the efficacy of moral principles and theories. But moral principles cannot be escaped. Even the most cynical moral opportunist, in his recommendation that we act in each case only to promote our best interests, is setting up a principle to govern behavior. It is different *in content* but not *in kind* from the Socratic ideal of the life of reason or the Utilitarian goal of "the greatest good of the greatest number." Our moral integrity suffers when our principles are allowed to remain underground or when they are inconsistent with each other or with our actions.

We all have beliefs in accordance with which we judge actions and characters, our own and those of others, to be right or wrong, good or bad; we have aspirations which we strive to realize; and we have a conception, dim or clear, of the best way to live. When we endeavor to fill in the blank places in our moral theory, to eliminate as far as possible contradictory directives for behavior; when we endeavor to know what principles we act upon and how these are related to the principles to which we give intellectual assent; and when we endeavor to know *why* we think an ideal or moral judgment is correct, we have made a good beginning in the direction of applying reason to the moral life, of seeking an ethical theory.

Reason and Morality

Reason is applied to moral situations and problems in different ways, depending upon the purposes of the investigator. The *social scientist* undertakes to describe how men actually behave, and he may or may not draw conclusions from his inquiry as to how they ought to act. The *casuist*, drawing upon moral principles, law, religion, and related areas, attempts to decide concrete cases of morality. The *moralist*, whether a literary light or religious leader, tells men what he thinks they ought to do and exhorts them to follow the right way. Finally, the *ethical theorist* undertakes the systematic questioning and critical examination of the underlying principles of morality. These ways of dealing with morality are not mutually exclusive, and it is not uncommon for an individual to combine all four in his approach to morality.

For the social scientist, the examination of moral behavior entails the processes of definition, classification, and generalization. He observes and compares the mores, customs, traditions, morals, and laws of different societies and formulates theories about the role of morals in society; or he may study the relationship between technological and moral-cultural change; or he may report the facts, points of view, and actions taken in specific cases of moral conduct. Although his findings are relevant to conclusions reached by others interested in morality, the social scientist as such is essentially engaged in *descriptive* activity.

Casuistry — applied ethics — deals with individual moral problems, such as matters of conscience and conflicts of obligation. The casuist acts on some occasions in an *advisory* capacity, guiding individuals in their choice of actions, *e.g.*, he may attempt to resolve the conflicting duties of the father of a starving family who has no other course than to steal. He also has an *adjudicative* function, for he must bring to bear various principles which he regards as relevant to a particular case, and reach a judgment as to the guilt and responsibility of the offender by weighing the various circumstances of the case. Confronted with the problem of being both just and merciful to a hungry man who has stolen bread, a judge in a court of law would find himself engaged in casuistry in order to balance the principle of justice and the principle of mercy to meet the demands of a practical situation.

The moralist is concerned to keep alive the values he considers worthwhile and to improve the moral quality of his community. Seeking to win men over to his ethical convictions and to exhort them to act in accordance with them, he acts in a manner which is primarily *persuasive* and *prescriptive*. To him, such actions as the stealing of bread provide the impetus and occasion to warn men away from what is wrong and to guide them towards what is right.

The ethical theorist, were he to examine the case of the hungry thief, would be interested in it chiefly as an illustration of a more general problem, namely, whether or not it is possible to reconcile the principle of justice — which demands that each man be given what is due him — with the principle of mercy — which requires that extenuating circumstances be taken into account. In dealing with principles which establish standards for action, the ethical theorist has in common with the casuist and the moralist an interest in the normative, *i.e.*, the *regulative*, phase of ethics. His distinctive function, however, is a *deliberative* one, for he is interested in the examination of underlying assumptions and the critical evaluation of principles.

History and Ethical Theory

The development of ethical theory in western civilization has been by the gradual accretion of insights, rather than by a systematic evolution in a straight line of progress. Two principal influences, divergent in origin and direction, have provided most of the concepts with which ethical theorists in the western world deal. In the Greek tradition, ethics was conceived as relating to the "good life." Inquiry was directed towards discovering the nature of happiness; differences of opinion regarding the characteristics of the happiest life and the means for achieving it enliven the writings of the ancient philosophers. A quite different orientation was introduced by the Judaeo-Christian ethic. In this tradition, the ideals of righteousness before God and the love of God and neighbor, not the happy or pleasant life, constitute the substance of morality. These two influences are represented in a major cleavage between those theorists who regard duty and the right as the primary ethical concepts and those who view happiness and the good life as the fundamental concerns of ethics. If we make an effort to reconcile these diverse views, we are faced with the difficult task of defining the relationship between "doing what is right" and "being happy."

The diverse traditions of the Greek and Judaeo-Christian ethics, in combination with the many other historical and cultural factors operative in the formation of ideas, produce a multiplicity of systems in ethics. To the extent that ethical theory addresses itself to the problems current in the time of its formulation, it necessarily manifests this variety. This is the case because history itself does not follow an orderly course in which problematic situations are neatly solved and filed away before a new set of problems arises. The content of ethical theories, as a consequence, is largely a series of problems posed, solutions tendered, objections made, and replies attempted. The problems which occupy a generation may not be solved, yet fresh difficulties may demand to be treated — a German sage is reported to have observed that problems are never solved, but are merely superseded by new ones. But the very issues which have been put aside in favor of more pressing matters may reappear generations, or even centuries, later, to be considered afresh. Within any one ethical theory, there is system, rational structure, and a high degree of definiteness, but the history of ethical theory in the heterogeneous western tradition is markedly irregular, unsystematic, and unsettled. Ethics is, in consequence, all the richer and the more challenging.

The Nature of Ethical Theory

The initial problem of ethical theory is that of defining the nature of ethics. Any definition of a discipline so long in tradition and so rich in variety is made vague by the demands of inclusiveness. Broadly conceived, ethical theorizing is concerned with the construction of a rational system of moral principles, and, as we have seen, with the direct and systematic examination of the underlying assumptions of morality. More specifically we find among the enterprises attempted by ethical theorists: (1) the analysis and explanation of moral judgments and behavior; (2) the investigation and clarification of the meanings of moral terms and statements; (3) the establishment of the validity of (a) a set of norms or standards for the governing of behavior, or (b) an ideal of human character to be achieved, or (c) ultimate goals to be striven for. We may still call a man an ethical theorist, even if he does not attempt all these tasks.[1]

The more specific our statement of what ethical theory is, the more we find ourselves committed to a particular ethical theory. To define ethics as the study of the conditions for man's happiness would provide an appropriate description of ethics as it was conceived by Aristotle, but not as it was understood by Immanuel Kant. Or, conversely, if we portray ethics as the study of man's

---

[1] *A note on terminology:* The term "moral" is essentially equivalent to the term "ethical." Etymologically, these terms are identical, the former being derived from the Latin word "*mores*," the latter from the Greek word "*ethos*," both words referring to customary behavior. Both terms may be used with two different antonyms. Ordinarily, the opposite of "moral" is taken to be "immoral," so that we mean by a "moral man" one who is good and does what is right, and by an "immoral man" one who is bad and does what is wrong. However, "moral" may also be used in a wider sense to refer simultaneously to right and wrong. In this case, its antonym is "amoral." In this usage, men are "moral" in the sense that certain of their actions, *e.g.*, the way parents treat their children, the way we handle our obligations, the ideals by which we live, etc., are subject to judgments of right and wrong. By contrast, the functioning of the digestive system, like the operation of a machine or the flavor of an apple, would be considered amoral, *i.e.*, they are objects to which moral judgments are irrelevant. The same analysis may be made of the term "ethical," *i.e.*, its antonym may be either "unethical," *i.e.*, it may refer to what is wrong, or it may have as an antonym "non-ethical," in which case it would apply to objects which are not subject to moral or ethical evaluation.

irrevocable duties, we will be characterizing Kant's theory adequately, but we would have a completely misleading notion of the ethics of Aristotle. Further, although the classical ethical theorists attempt to present systems of moral principles and the reasons why they are valid, there are ethical theorists — the positivists, in particular — who deny the logical defensibility of such systems. Again, there are theorists who insist that those who attach great importance to the factual aspect of morality should be classified as social scientists and not as ethical theorists at all. And even on a point of general agreement, diversity may nevertheless persist. For example, although many ethical theorists agree that it is necessary to analyze the meaning of the language of morality, they use methods which vary so greatly as to produce strikingly different results.

In regard to the definition of ethics, as for the many other unresolved problems of ethical theory, the best appreciation of the meaning and importance of a problem comes from an examination of the various solutions which have been attempted. Each ethical theorist conceives ethics in his own way, and to obtain a truly meaningful conception of ethics, there is no substitute for acquaintance with the ethical theories themselves. From participating in the clashes of opinion, we shall discover that the challenge of ethics consists rather in the stimulation of its questions than in the finality of its answers. There is, moreover, the promise of the essential benefits of all philosophical controversy — the achievement of a measure of intellectual independence and maturity and a sense of security in dealing with abstract concepts. And, in addition, for those who enter into the spirit of the philosophic enterprise, the traditions of ethics provide an adventure into a whole new range of ideas.

CHAPTER 2

Knowledge and Virtue

PLATO

T he birth of Plato (427–347 B.C.) coincides closely with the death of Pericles, the greatest leader of democratic Athens, and with the beginning of the Peloponnesian War, which drained the strength of the Greek city-states. He lived in a period of moral degeneration and continuous political turmoil. If, as has been said, the magnificent intellect of Plato was the flower of Athenian political and moral excellence, it must be added that as the flower was unfolding, the plant was beginning to wither. Plato's reaction to the confusion of the times was an uncompromising assertion of the validity of a high and absolute morality and the disavowal of government of the many in favor of government by "philosopher kings."

An aristocrat in fact as well as in thought, Plato's ancestry may be traced on his father's side to the last king of Athens and on his mother's side to the family of Solon, the founder of Athenian law. His position and wealth enabled him to receive the best education possible for an Athenian youth and to spend most of his life in the pursuit of knowledge. The decisive point of Plato's career occurred in his twentieth year, when he was drawn into the orbit of Socrates (469–399 B.C.), probably the most forceful personality of ancient Greece. Through the skillful exchanges of questions and answers, *i.e.*, the "dialectical method," Socrates was able to stimulate to greater mental effort those with whom he came in contact. Alternately, he adopted the roles of "gadfly" and "midwife": he stung his contemporaries to mental activity through exposing their unexamined beliefs, yet patiently delivered them of their latent ideas. Plato was Socrates' devoted recorder and faithful defender. However, the true greatness of Plato arises from his construction of an enduring philosophical system in which he integrates the insights of Socrates with his own.

The teachings of Socrates were as disturbing to the Athenian populace as they were attractive to the Socratic circle. In 399 B.C., Socrates was condemned to death on the charge that he was "an evil-doer and a curious person, searching into things under the earth and above the heaven; and making the worse appear the better cause, and teaching all this to others." The trial and death of Socrates — so unforgettably described in Plato's *Apology*, *Crito*, and *Phaedo* — had the effect upon Plato of vindicating his mistrust of Athenian democracy. He left Athens and traveled for twelve years, spending time in Egypt, Greece, Italy, and Sicily. In his fortieth year, at the peak of his intellectual development, Plato returned to Athens and founded the first of the great schools of antiquity, the Academy. He taught with outstanding success and increasing fame until his death at the age of eighty.

The writings of Plato are in dialogue form, which is admirably suited to show the strength of the Socratic method. Plato himself does not appear as a character in the dialogues, but in almost all of them, he speaks through Socrates. As a result, it is not always possible to distinguish with historical accuracy the Socratic from the Platonic conceptions in the dialogues. Generally, however, in his earlier dialogues Plato seems not to go beyond the teachings of Socrates, whereas he develops his own positive doctrine in the later ones. The *Charmides*, in which the meaning of "temperance" is sought, and the *Euthyphro*, in which successive definitions of "piety" are examined and dismissed, are representative of the earlier dialogues generally classified as "Socratic." Outstanding among the dialogues of Plato's mature period are the *Gorgias*, which is particularly important for ethics, the *Thaeatetus*, in which the theory of knowledge is discussed, the *Phaedrus* and the *Symposium*, in which the Platonic doctrine of love is developed, the *Timaeus*, in which an account of the universe is given, and the master work, the *Republic*, in which Plato gives us the most comprehensive statement of his philosophy.

Plato's ethical theory, like that of the other Greek philosophers, is an attempt to provide an answer to the question, "What is the good life?" Following the Socratic dictum, "virtue is knowledge," Plato develops the thesis that the life of reason is the happiest and best. For him, this means that knowledge produces a harmonious man, in the sense that when reason governs the desires and passions, an orderly and well-balanced personality results. Indeed, *only* knowledge can lead to virtue; when a man is ignorant, his personality is disorganized, for the unruly desires and passions then control him. By contrast, when a man truly *knows* what is good, *i.e.*, when he knows what promotes harmony, he will *do* what is good. Hence, it is the virtuous man, *i.e.*, the rational man, who is truly happy. This view is sharply opposed to that of the Sophist, Callicles, who proclaims, "He who would truly live, ought to allow his desires to wax to the uttermost." At the same time, Plato's position avoids the other extreme, exemplified by the Cynic philosopher, Antisthenes, who asserts, "better madness than a pursuit of pleasure." In the history of Greek philosophy, Plato stands as a distinguished advocate of the well-rounded life, guided by reason.

In the *Dialogues*, two basic philosophical conceptions are found which are especially relevant to ethics, namely, the doctrine of *teleology* and the *theory of ideas*. According to the doctrine of teleology, everything in the universe has a purpose or proper function within a harmonious hierarchy of purposes. The ultimate explanation of things is purposive rather than mechanical. The underlying question in all of Plato's investigations is the "why" of an event rather than the "how." He makes graphic the value of the teleological type of explanation in recounting Socrates' reasons for remaining in prison in preference to escaping:

> [Suppose that the mechanist who] endeavored to explain the causes of my several actions in detail, went on to show that . . . I am sitting here in a curved posture because my . . . bones are lifted at their joints by the contraction or relaxation of the muscles . . . [He would be failing] to mention the true cause, which is that . . . I have thought it better and more right to remain here and undergo my sentence. . . . There is surely a strange confusion of causes and conditions in all this.[a]

Man, too, has his purpose or proper function. His value, like that of everything else in the universe, depends upon his effectiveness in fulfilling his function. In turn, the success of an individual in realizing his purpose is determined by the effective functioning of the basic constituents of his personality. The morally virtuous man is one who is in rational, biological, and emotional balance, or, in Platonic terms, one who is *wise, temperate, courageous*, and *just*. In the virtuous man, desires and passions function harmoniously under the governance of reason. He is the truly happy man who "sets in order his own inner life and is his own master, and his own law, and at peace with himself. . . . He is no longer many, but has become one entirely temperate and perfectly adjusted nature."

A second doctrine in the Platonic philosophy which is basic to his ethics is the *theory of Ideas*, or *Forms*. This theory involves the belief that general conceptions are not derived from experience but are logically prior to it. For example, each of us knows what a perfect circle is, even though every circle we have seen or might attempt to draw falls short of perfection. It is by means of our concept of a perfect circle that we identify circular objects. Moreover, the idea of the nature of a perfect circle is the same for everyone and never varies. But because all things in the world of space and time change, the idea of circularity which men possess cannot be an idea *of* anything in the physical world. Consequently, our concept of circularity must be *of* an unchanging object, *i.e.*, an object which is nonspatial, nontemporal, and in no way dependent upon us. It is this kind of unchanging object which Plato terms a *Form* or *Idea*. Without such permanent, fixed Forms, he maintains, there could be no general names for objects nor common discussion of them, for the world of sensory experience is constantly changing and varies from man to man.

The Forms are more *real* than the objects of the spatio-temporal world, Plato reasons, in the sense that they are presupposed in any explanation of the observable world. The search for knowledge is, accordingly, a search for the real, and the knowledge gained is *absolute*, *universal*, and *objective*. What holds for knowledge in general holds for ethical knowledge in particular. Plato insists, for example, that we must have knowledge of the Form, Justice, in order to recognize a just man or a just act, and that the basis of our ethical judgment, *i.e.*, the Form itself, is invariant. Thus, Plato is unalterably opposed to ethical irrationalism — the view that reason is impotent in ethics — and relativism — the view that "man is the measure" of moral values.

Plato's analysis of morality and reality culminates in his account of the *Form* or *Idea of the Good* — the conception through which he unites the principle of teleology and the theory of Forms with ethics. The Good is at once the final goal which all things in the universe are seeking to realize and the ultimate source of their intelligibility and meaning. Plato tells us that:

> . . . In the world of knowledge the [Idea of the Good] appears last of all, it is seen only with an effort; and, when seen, is also inferred to be the universal author of all things beautiful and right, parent of light and of the lord of light in this visible world, and the immediate source of reason and truth in the intellectual; and this is the power upon which he who would act rationally either in public or private life must have his eye fixed.[b]

Plato is not systematic in the development of his philosophy; both his criticisms of the Sophists' view that "man is the measure" of the good, and his positive doctrine of the Good as objective and immutable, must be extracted from the exchange of questions and answers in his dialogues. The substance of his philosophy is found in his solutions of two persistent ethical problems: (1) Why should any man be morally virtuous? and (2) Assuming the indispensability of knowledge for the moral life, what is the ultimate knowledge upon which moral virtue is based? These lead him to consideration of such subsidiary problems as: What are the merits of the just life in contrast to the unjust life? Is pleasure the supreme good? Is knowledge superior to pleasure? What is the precise meaning of "justice"?

· · ·

1. Plato gives an account of the manner in which his philosophical opponents, the Sophists, answer the question, "Why should men be morally virtuous?" They maintain that the weak value justice only because it restrains the strong. Every man would take advantage of his neighbors if he were certain that he would not be apprehended and punished, for he is interested only in his own welfare. Injustice is more profitable than justice, provided it is possible to escape detection. This conception of human nature is presented by Glaucon in the story of Gyges' ring.

Now that those who practise justice do so involuntarily and because they have not the power to be unjust will best appear if we imagine something of this kind: having given both to the just and the unjust power to do what they will, let us watch and see whither desire will lead them; then we shall discover in the very act the just and unjust man to be proceeding along the same road, following their interest, which all natures deem to be their good, and are only diverted into the path of justice by the force of law. The liberty which we are supposing may be most completely given to them in the form of such a power as is said to have been possessed by Gyges the ancestor of Croesus the Lydian. According to the tradition, Gyges was a shepherd in the service of the king of Lydia; there was a great storm, and an earthquake made an opening in the earth at the place where he was feeding his flock. Amazed at the sight, he descended into the opening, where, among other marvels, he beheld a hollow brazen horse, having doors, at which he stooping and looking in saw a dead body of stature, as appeared to him, more than human, and having nothing on but a gold ring; this he took from the finger of the dead and reascended. Now the shepherds met together, according to custom, that they might send their monthly report about the flocks to the king; into their assembly he came having the ring on his finger, and as he was sitting among them he chanced to turn the collet of the ring inside his hand, when instantly he became invisible to the rest of the company and they began to speak of him as if he were no longer present. He was astonished at this, and again touching the ring he turned the collet outwards and reappeared; he made several trials of the ring, and always with the same result — when he turned the collet inwards he became invisible, when outwards he reappeared. Whereupon he contrived to be chosen one of the messengers who were sent to the court; where as soon as he arrived he seduced the queen, and with her help conspired against the king and slew him, and took the kingdom. Suppose now that there were two such magic rings, and the just put on one of them and the unjust the other; no man can be imagined to be of such an iron nature that he would stand fast in justice. No man would keep his hands off what was not his own when he could safely take what he liked out of the market, or go into houses and lie with any one at his pleasure, or kill or release from prison whom he would, and in all respects be like a God among men. Then the actions of the just would be as the actions of the unjust; they would both come at last to the same point. And this we may truly affirm to be a great proof that a man is just, not willingly or because he thinks that justice is any good to him individually, but of necessity, for wherever any one thinks that he can safely be unjust, there he is unjust. For all men believe in their hearts that injustice is far more profitable to the individual than justice, and he who argues as I have been

JUSTICE ARRIVES OUT OF NECESSITY

supposing, will say that they are right. If you could imagine any one obtaining this power of becoming invisible, and never doing any wrong or touching what was another's, he would be thought by the lookers-on to be a most wretched idiot, although they would praise him to one another's faces, and keep up appearances with one another from a fear that they too might suffer injustice.[c]

2. Thrasymachus, the celebrated Sophist, elaborates the advantages of injustice in political and economic affairs. He makes it clear that injustice is rewarding particularly when it is conducted on a large scale. Happiness, he concludes, comes from injustice and not from justice.

. . . So entirely astray are you in your ideas about the just and unjust as not even to know that justice and the just are in reality another's good; that is to say, the interest of the ruler and stronger, and the loss of the subject and servant; and injustice the opposite; for the unjust is lord over the truly simple and just: he is the stronger, and his subjects do what is for his interest, and minister to his happiness, which is very far from being their own. Consider further, most foolish Socrates, that the just is always a loser in comparison with the unjust. First of all, in private contracts: wherever the unjust is the partner of the just you will find that, when the partnership is dissolved, the unjust man has always more and the just less. Secondly, in their dealings with the State: when there is an income-tax, the just man will pay more and the unjust less on the same amount of income; and when there is anything to be received the one gains nothing and the other much. Observe also what happens when they take an office; there is the just man neglecting his affairs and perhaps suffering other losses, and getting nothing out of the public, because he is just; moreover he is hated by his friends and acquaintances for refusing to serve them in unlawful ways.

But all this is reversed in the case of the unjust man. I am speaking, as before, of injustice on a large scale in which the advantage of the unjust is most apparent; and my meaning will be most clearly seen if we turn to that highest form of injustice in which the criminal is the happiest of men, and the sufferers or those who refuse to do injustice are the most miserable — that is to say tyranny, which by fraud and force takes away the property of others, not little by little but wholesale; comprehending in one, things sacred as well as profane, private and public; for which acts of wrong, if he were detected perpetrating any one of them singly, he would be punished and incur great disgrace — they who do such wrong in particular cases are called robbers of temples, and man-stealers and burglars and swindlers and thieves. But when a man besides taking away the money of the citizens has made slaves of them, then, instead of these names of reproach, he is termed happy and blessed, not only by the citizens but by all who hear of his having achieved the consummation of injustice. For mankind censure injustice, fearing that they may be the victims of it and not because they shrink from committing it. And thus, as I have shown, Socrates, injustice, when on a sufficient scale, has more strength and freedom and mastery than justice; and, as I said at first, justice is the interest of the stronger, whereas injustice is a man's own profit and interest.[d]

3. But constant discussion does not terminate the disagreement between Plato and the Sophists in regard to the value of justice. Underlying the Sophists' rejection of the just life is their contention that pleasure is the supreme good and that injustice is better than justice because it brings more pleasure. In the dialogue, Gorgias, Plato attempts to destroy this doctrine by focusing attention on the logical inadequacy of identifying pleasure with the good.

soc. Well, then, let us remember that Callicles, the Acharnian, says that pleasure and good are the same; but that knowledge and courage [as examples of virtue] are not the same, either with one another, or with the good.

cal. And what does our friend Socrates, of Foxton, say — does he assent to this, or not?

soc. He does not assent; neither will Callicles, when he sees himself truly. You will admit, I suppose, that good and evil fortune are opposed to each other?

cal. Yes.

soc. And if they are opposed to each other, then, like health and disease, they exclude one another; a man cannot have them both, or be without them both, at the same time?

cal. What do you mean?

soc. Take the case of any bodily affection: — a man may have the complaint in his eyes which is called ophthalmia?

cal. To be sure.

soc. But he surely cannot have the same eyes well and sound at the same time?

cal. Certainly not.

soc. And when he has got rid of his ophthalmia, has he got rid of the health of his eyes too? Is the final result, that he gets rid of them both together?

cal. Certainly not.

soc. That would surely be marvellous and absurd?

cal. Very.

soc. I suppose that he is affected by them, and gets rid of them in turns?

cal. Yes.

soc. And he may have strength and weakness in the same way, by fits?

cal. Yes.

soc. Or swiftness and slowness?

cal. Certainly.

soc. And does he have and not have good and happiness, and their opposites, evil and misery, in a similar alternation?

cal. Certainly he has.

soc. If then there be anything which a man has and has not at the same time, clearly that cannot be good and evil — do we agree? Please not to answer without consideration.

cal. I entirely agree.

soc. Go back now to our former admissions. — Did you say that to hunger, I mean the mere state of hunger, was pleasant or painful?

CAL. I said painful, but that to eat when you are hungry is pleasant.

SOC. I know; but still the actual hunger is painful: am I not right?

CAL. Yes.

SOC. And thirst, too, is painful?

CAL. Yes, very.

SOC. Need I adduce any more instances, or would you agree that all wants or desires are painful?

CAL. I agree, and therefore you need not adduce any more instances.

SOC. Very good. And you would admit that to drink, when you are thirsty, is pleasant?

CAL. Yes.

SOC. And in the sentence which you have just uttered, the word 'thirsty' implies pain?

CAL. Yes.

SOC. And the word 'drinking' is expressive of pleasure, and of the satisfaction of the want?

CAL. Yes.

SOC. There is pleasure in drinking?

CAL. Certainly.

SOC. When you are thirsty?

CAL. Yes.

SOC. And in pain?

CAL. Yes.[e]

4. The first phase of Socrates' argument is now completed: it is granted that good and evil are contradictories, i.e., mutually exclusive in one man at one time, whereas pleasure and pain may occur simultaneously in a man. If one may have pleasure and pain at the same time, but not good and evil, then there is a contradiction in identifying "good" with "pleasure" and "evil" with "pain."

Socrates continues in the same vein, after summarizing his argument to this point.

soc. Do you see the inference: — that pleasure and pain are simultaneous, when you say that being thirsty, you drink? For are they not simultaneous, and do they not affect at the same time the same part, whether of the soul or the body? — which of them is affected cannot be supposed to be of any consequence: Is not this true?

cal. It is.

soc. You said also, that no man could have good and evil fortune at the same time?

cal. Yes, I did.

soc. But you admitted, that when in pain a man might also have pleasure?

cal. Clearly.

soc. Then pleasure is not the same as good fortune, or pain the same as evil fortune, and therefore the good is not the same as the pleasant?

cal. I wish I knew, Socrates, what your quibbling means.

soc. You know, Callicles, but you affect not to know.

cal. Well, get on, and don't keep fooling: then you will know what a wiseacre you are in your admonition of me.

soc. Does not a man cease from his thirst and from his pleasure in drinking at the same time?

cal. I do not understand what you are saying.

gor. Nay, Callicles, answer, if only for our sakes; — we should like to hear the argument out.

cal. Yes, Gorgias, but I must complain of the habitual trifling of Socrates; he is always arguing about little and unworthy questions.

gor. What matter? Your reputation, Callicles, is not at stake. Let Socrates argue in his own fashion.

cal. Well, then, Socrates, you shall ask these little peddling questions, since Gorgias wishes to have them.

soc. I envy you, Callicles, for having been initiated into the great mysteries before you were initiated into the lesser. I thought that this was not allowable. But to return to our argument: — Does not a man cease from thirsting and from the pleasure of drinking at the same moment?

CAL. True.

SOC. And if he is hungry, or has any other desire, does he not cease from the desire and the pleasure at the same moment?

CAL. Very true.

SOC. Then he ceases from pain and pleasure at the same moment?

CAL. Yes.

SOC. But he does not cease from good and evil at the same moment, as you have admitted: — do you still adhere to what you said?

CAL. Yes, I do; but what is the inference?

SOC. Why, my friend, the inference is that the good is not the same as the pleasant, or the evil the same as the painful; there is a cessation of pleasure and pain at the same moment; but not of good and evil, for they are different. How then can pleasure be the same as good, or pain as evil? And I would have you look at the matter in another light, which could hardly, I think, have been considered by you when you identified them: Are not the good good because they have good [*i.e.*, the Idea of the Good] present with them, as the beautiful are those who have beauty present with them?*

5. While he is still concerned to show the inadequacy of hedonism (pleasure is the supreme " good "), Plato, in the Protagoras, *presents Socrates in the role of a constructive critic. He examines the issue here for the purpose of showing that knowledge is superior to pleasure, even though it appears to the average man that pleasure overcomes knowledge.*

Uncover your mind to me, Protagoras, and reveal your opinion about knowledge, that I may know whether you agree with the rest of the world. Now the rest of the world are of opinion that knowledge is a principle not of strength, or of rule, or of command:

their notion is that a man may have knowledge, and yet that the knowledge which is in him may be overmastered by anger, or pleasure, or pain, or love, or perhaps by fear, — just as if knowledge were a slave, and might be dragged about anyhow. Now is that your view? or do you think that knowledge is a noble and commanding thing, which cannot be overcome, and will not allow a man, if he only knows the difference of good and evil, to do anything which is contrary to knowledge, but that wisdom will have strength to help him?

I agree with you, Socrates, said Protagoras; and not only so, but I, above all other men, am bound to say that wisdom and knowledge are the highest of human things.

Good, I said, and true. But are you aware that the majority of the world are of another mind; and that men are commonly supposed to know the things which are best, and not to do them when they might? And most persons whom I have asked the reason of this have said that when men act contrary to knowledge they are overcome by pain, or pleasure, or some of those affections which I was just now mentioning.

Yes, Socrates, he replied; and that is not the only point about which mankind are in error.

Suppose, then, that you and I endeavour to instruct and inform them what is the nature of this affection which they call 'being overcome by pleasure,' and which they affirm to be the reason why they do not always do what is best.[g]

6. Socrates and Protagoras are agreed that the hedonist is forced to employ some other standard than the pleasure-pain principle. For, in evaluating pleasures and pains to obtain the greatest amount of pleasure, some sort of "measurement" is required. Since the art of measurement is reflective, the hedonist must admit his dependence upon knowledge. Socrates is interrogating Protagoras with a view to establishing this conclusion.

. . . Do you not pursue after pleasure as a good, and avoid pain as an evil?

He assented.

Then you think that pain is an evil and pleasure is a good: and even pleasure you deem an evil, when it robs you of greater pleasures than it gives, or causes pains greater than the pleasure. If, however, you call pleasure an evil in relation to some other end or standard, you will be able to show us that standard. But you have none to show.

I do not think that they have, said Protagoras.

And have you not a similar way of speaking about pain? You call pain a good when it takes away greater pains than those which it has, or gives pleasures greater than the pains: then if you have some standard other than pleasure and pain to which you refer when you call actual pain a good, you can show what that is. But you cannot.

True, said Protagoras.

. . . If you weigh pleasures against pleasures, you of course take the more and greater; or if you weigh pains against pains, you take the fewer and the less; or if pleasures against pains, then you choose that course of action in which the painful is exceeded by the pleasant, whether the distant by the near or the near by the distant; and you avoid that course of action in which the pleasant is exceeded by the painful. Would you not admit, my friends, that this is true? I am confident that they cannot deny this.

He agreed with me.

Well then, I shall say, if you agree so far, be so good as to answer me a question: Do not the same magnitudes appear larger to your sight when near, and smaller when at a distance? They will acknowledge that. And the same holds of thickness and number; also sounds, which are in themselves equal, are greater when near, and lesser when at a distance. They will grant that also. Now suppose happiness to consist in doing or choosing the greater, and in not doing or in avoiding the less, what would be the saving principle of human life? Would not the art of measuring be the saving principle; or would the power of appearance? Is not the latter that deceiving art which makes us wander up and down and take the things at one time of which we repent at another, both in our actions and in our choice of things great and small? But the art of measurement would do away with the effect of appearances, and, showing the truth, would fain teach the soul at last to find rest in the truth, and would thus save our life. Would not mankind generally acknowledge that the art which accomplishes this result is the art of measurement? . . . Both of us were agreeing that there was nothing mightier than knowledge, and that knowledge, in whatever existing, must have the advantage over pleasure and all other things; and then you said that pleasure often got the advantage even over a man who has knowledge; and we refused to allow this, and you rejoined: O Protagoras and Socrates, what is the meaning of being overcome by pleasure if not this? — tell us what you call such a state: — if we had immediately and at the time answered 'Ignorance,' you would have laughed at us. But now, in laughing at us, you will be laughing at yourselves: for you also admitted that men err in their choice of pleasures and pains; that is, in their choice of good and evil, from defect of knowledge; and you admitted further, that they err, not only from defect of knowledge in general, but of that particular knowledge which is called measuring. And you are also aware that the erring act which is done without knowledge is done in ignorance.[h]

7. Socrates concludes that when it is said that men are overcome by pleasure, it means that they are acting from ignorance: "No man voluntarily pursues evil or that which he thinks to be evil." Thus, the man who is governed by reason will not be led astray. The doctrine that "virtue is knowledge" is expanded by Plato in The Republic, *through integrating it with his "faculty psychology." His ethics rests upon two major points of this psychology: (1) the souls of all individuals consist of three basic elements or faculties, reason, spirit (passion), and appetite (desire); (2) an individual's character depends upon the comparative development of the three elements and the dominance of one faculty over the others.*

Each of the three elements of the soul (psyche) is involved in moral

behavior, and each, when it carries out its proper function, is char- WISDOM
acterized by an appropriate virtue: governing the soul by reason TEMPERANCE
constitutes wisdom; *rational regulation of desire constitutes* temper- COURAGE
ance; *the support of reason by the passions constitutes* courage; *the*
harmony of the three faculties constitutes justice, *which is the over-* ⇓
arching virtue. The same kind of analysis applies also to the function- JUSTICE
ing of society, because, for Plato, the state is the "individual writ
large." Socrates and Glaucon, discussing the virtues, agree that "the
same principles which exist in the state exist also in the individual,
and that they are three in number." The exposition of the several
virtues continues:

. . . He is to be deemed courageous whose spirit retains in
pleasure and in pain the commands of reason about what he
ought or ought not to fear. . . . And him we call wise who has
in him that little part which rules, and which proclaims these
commands; that part too being supposed to have a knowledge of
what is for the interest of each of the three parts and of the
whole . . .

And would you not say that he is temperate who has these same
elements in friendly harmony, in whom the one ruling principle
of reason, and the two subject ones of spirit and desire are equally
agreed that reason ought to rule, and do not rebel?

Certainly, he said, that is the true account of temperance
whether in the State or individual.

And surely, I said, we have explained again and again how and
by virtue of what quality a man will be just.

That is very certain.

And is justice dimmer in the individual, and is her form different, or is she the same which we found her to be in the State?

There is no difference in my opinion, he said.

Because, if any doubt is still lingering in our minds, a few com-
monplace instances will satisfy us of the truth of what I am saying.

What sort of instances do you mean?

If the case is put to us, must we not admit that the just State, or the man who is trained in the principles of such a State, will be less likely than the unjust to make away with a deposit of gold or silver? Would any one deny this?

No one, he replied.

Will the just man or citizen ever be guilty of sacrilege or theft, or treachery either to his friends or to his country?

Never.

Neither will he ever break faith where there have been oaths or agreements?

Impossible.

No one will be less likely to commit adultery, or to dishonour his father and mother, or to fail in his religious duties. . . . And the reason is that each part of him is doing its own business, whether in ruling or being ruled. . . . Are you satisfied then that the quality which makes such men and such states is justice, or do you hope to discover some other?

Not I, indeed.

Then our dream has been realized; and the suspicion which we entertained at the beginning of our work of construction, that some divine power must have conducted us to a primary form of justice, has now been verified. . . . And the division of labour which required the carpenter and the shoemaker and the rest of the citizens to be doing each his own business, and not another's, was a shadow of justice, and for that reason it was of use . . .

But in reality justice was such as we were describing, being concerned however, not with the outward man, but with the inward, which is the true self and concernment of man: for the just man does not permit the several elements within him to interfere with one another, or any of them to do the work of others, — he sets in order his own inner life, and is his own master and his own law, and at peace with himself; and when he has bound together the three principles within him, which may be compared to the higher, lower, and middle notes of the scale, and the intermediate intervals — when he has bound all these together, and is no longer many, but has become one entirely temperate and perfectly adjusted nature, then he proceeds to act, if he has to act, whether in a matter of property, or in the treatment of the body, or in some affair of politics or private business; always thinking and calling that which preserves and co-operates with this harmonious condition, just and good action, and the knowledge which presides over it, wisdom, and that which at any time impairs this condition, he will call unjust action, and the opinion which presides over it ignorance.

You have said the exact truth, Socrates.

Very good; and if we were to affirm that we had discovered the just man and the just State, and the nature of justice in each of them, we should not be telling a falsehood?

Most certainly not.[i]

8. The just man, then, is "integrated" — reason, emotion, and desire function harmoniously within him. On the other hand, the unjust individual is beset by inner "rebellion" — there is disorder within his soul. For injustice destroys the natural order of the personality, as disease detracts from bodily health. Accordingly, those actions which preserve a harmonious state in man will be deemed "good" and those which diminish it will be termed "bad." Plato is now in a position to answer the original question, "Why should any man be morally virtuous, or just?" Once the nature of justice is clearly understood, its practical superiority over injustice is manifest.

And now, I said, injustice has to be considered. . . . Must not injustice be a strife which arises among the three principles — a meddlesomeness, and interference, and rising up of a part of the soul against the whole, an assertion of unlawful authority, which is made by a rebellious subject against a true prince, of whom he is the natural vassal, — what is all this confusion and delusion but injustice, and intemperance and cowardice and ignorance, and every form of vice?

Exactly so.

And if the nature of justice and injustice be known, then the meaning of acting unjustly and being unjust, or, again, of acting justly, will also be perfectly clear. . . . They are like disease and health; being in the soul just what disease and health are in the body. . . . That which is healthy causes health, and that which is unhealthy causes disease. . . . And just actions cause justice, and unjust actions cause injustice. . . . And the creation of health is the institution of a natural order and government of one by another in the parts of the body; and the creation of disease is the production of a state of things at variance with this natural order . . .

And is not the creation of justice the institution of a natural order and government of one by another in the parts of the soul, and the creation of injustice the production of a state of things at variance with the natural order?

Exactly so, he said.

Then virtue is the health and beauty and well-being of the soul, and vice the disease and weakness and deformity of the same. . . . Do not good practices lead to virtue, and evil practices to vice?

Assuredly.

Still our old question of the comparative advantage of justice and injustice has not been answered: Which is the more profitable, to be just and act justly and practise virtue, whether seen or unseen of gods and men, or to be unjust and act unjustly, if only unpunished and unreformed?

In my judgment, Socrates, the question has now become ridiculous. We know that, when the bodily constitution is gone, life is no longer endurable, though pampered with all kinds of meats and drinks, and having all wealth and all power; and shall we be told that when the very essence of the vital principle is undermined and corrupted, life is still worth having to a man, if only he be allowed to do whatever he likes with the single exception that he is not to acquire justice and virtue, or to escape from injustice and vice; assuming them both to be such as we have described?

Yes, I said, the question is, as you say, ridiculous.[j]

9. Having expounded the nature of justice in detail, Socrates takes his listeners by surprise with his assertion that there is something

JUST = GOOD = HEALTH (HARMONY OF PERSONALITY)

higher than justice, viz., the Idea of the Good. Adeimantus presses Socrates for an explanation.

What, he said, is there a knowledge still higher than this — higher than justice and the other virtues?

Yes, I said, there is. And of the virtues too we must behold not the outline merely, as at present — nothing short of the most finished picture should satisfy us. When little things are elaborated with an infinity of pains, in order that they may appear in their full beauty and utmost clearness, how ridiculous that we should not think the highest truths worthy of attaining the highest accuracy!

A right noble thought; but do you suppose that we shall refrain from asking you what is this highest knowledge?

Nay, I said, ask if you will; but I am certain that you have heard the answer many times, and now you either do not understand me or, as I rather think, you are disposed to be troublesome; for you have often been told that the idea of good is the highest knowledge, and that all other things become useful and advantageous only by their use of this. You can hardly be ignorant that of this I was about to speak, concerning which, as you have often heard me say, we know so little; and, without which, any other knowledge or possession of any kind will profit us nothing. Do you think that the possession of all other things is of any value if we do not possess the good? or the knowledge of all other things if we have no knowledge of beauty and goodness?

Assuredly not.ᵏ

10. Plato, then, has answered the question, "What is the ultimate knowledge upon which moral virtue is based?" It is the knowledge of the Good. However, the ultimate and supreme Good is too exalted an idea to be grasped fully by the human mind. Since the Idea of the Good defies direct statement, Plato's presentation of it must take the form of an analogy. Thus, sight requires not only the eye and the object of sight but also the sun, which is the source of light. In the same way, understanding requires not only the mind and the objects of understanding but also the Good, which is the source of intelligibility. In short, visible objects can be seen only when the sun shines upon them, and truth can be known only when illuminated by the Good. Socrates spells out this analogy in conversation with Glaucon.

Why, you know, I said, that the eyes, when a person directs them towards objects on which the light of day is no longer shining, but the moon and stars only, see dimly, and are nearly blind; they seem to have no clearness of vision in them. . . . But when they are directed towards objects on which the sun shines, they see clearly and there is sight in them. . . . And the soul is like the eye: when resting upon that on which truth and being shine, the soul perceives and understands and is radiant with intelligence; but when turned towards the twilight of becoming and perishing, then she has opinion only, and goes blinking about, and is first of one opinion and then of another, and seems to have no intelligence. . . . Now, that which imparts truth to the known and the power of knowing to the knower is what I would have you term the idea of good, and this you will deem to be the cause of science, and of truth in so far as the latter becomes the subject of knowledge; beautiful too, as are both truth and knowledge, you will be right in esteeming this other nature as more beautiful than either; and, as in the previous instance, light and sight may be truly said to be like the sun, and yet not to be the sun, so in this other sphere, science and truth may be deemed to be like the good, but not the good; the good has a place of honour yet higher.

What a wonder of beauty that must be, he said, which is the author of science and truth, and yet surpasses them in beauty; for you surely cannot mean to say that pleasure is the good?

God forbid, I replied; but may I ask you to consider the image in another point of view? . . . You would say, would you not, that the sun is not only the author of visibility in all visible things, but of generation and nourishment and growth, though he himself is not generation?

Certainly.

In like manner the good may be said to be not only the author of knowledge to all things known, but of their being and essence, and yet the good is not essence, but far exceeds essence in dignity and power.[1]

11. Making use of the analogy between the eye's vision and the soul's vision, Plato goes on to discuss the conditions and circumstances of our knowledge of the good.

. . . My opinion is that in the world of knowledge the idea of good appears last of all, and is seen only with an effort; and, when seen, is also inferred to be the universal author of all things beautiful and right, parent of light and of the lord of light in this visible world, and the immediate source of reason and truth in the intellectual; and that this is the power upon which he who would act rationally either in public or private life must have his eye fixed. [It is my further conviction] that the power and capacity of learning exists in the soul already; and that just as the eye [is] unable to turn from darkness to light without the whole body, so too the instrument of knowledge can only by the movement of the whole soul be turned from the world of becoming [— the changing world of experience —] into that of being [— the world of permanent reality —], and learn by degrees to endure the sight of being, and of the brightest and best of being, or in other words, of the good . . .

And must there not be some art which will effect conversion in the easiest and quickest manner; not implanting the faculty of sight, for that exists already, but has been turned in the wrong direction, and is looking away from the truth?

Yes, [Glaucon] said, such an art may be presumed.

And whereas the other so-called virtues of the soul seem to be akin to bodily qualities, for even when they are not originally innate they can be implanted later by habit and exercise, the virtue of wisdom more than anything else contains a divine element which always remains, and by this conversion is rendered useful and profitable . . . [m]

12. Convinced that "the philosopher holding converse with the divine order, becomes orderly and divine, as far as the nature of man allows," Plato summarizes his case against those who believe that injustice is more profitable than justice. The philosopher, properly trained, can model his life after the ideal of perfection which his reason discloses to him.

[Glaucon asked:] From what point of view, then, and on what ground can we say that a man is profited by injustice or intemperance or other baseness, which will make him a worse man, even though he acquire money or power by his wickedness?

From no point of view at all.

What shall he profit, if his injustice be undetected and unpunished? He who is undetected only gets worse, whereas he who is detected and punished has the brutal part of his nature silenced and humanized; the gentler element in him is liberated, and his whole soul is perfected and ennobled by the acquirement of justice and temperance and wisdom, more than the body ever is by receiving gifts of beauty, strength and health, in proportion as the soul is more honourable than the body . . .

To this nobler purpose the man of understanding will devote the energies of his life. And in the first place, he will honour studies which impress these qualities on his soul, and will disregard others. . . . In the next place, he will regulate his bodily habit and training, and so far will he be from yielding to brutal and irrational pleasures, that he will regard even health as quite a secondary matter; his first object will be not that he may be fair or strong or well, unless he is likely thereby to gain temperance, but he will always desire so to attemper the body as to preserve the harmony of the soul. . . . And in the acquisition of wealth there is a principle of order and harmony which he will also observe; he will not allow himself to be dazzled by the foolish applause of the world, and heap up riches to his own infinite harm . . .

He will look at the city which is within him, and take heed that no disorder occur in it, such as might arise either from superfluity or from want; and upon this principle he will regulate his property and gain or spend according to his means. . . . And, for the same reason, he will gladly accept and enjoy such honours as he deems likely to make him a better man; but those, whether private or public, which are likely to disorder his life, he will avoid . . .

Then, if that is his motive, he will not be a statesman.

By the dog of Egypt, he will! in the city which is his own he certainly will, though in the land of his birth perhaps not, unless he have a divine call.

I understand; you mean that he will be a ruler in the city of which we are the founders, and which exists in idea only; for I do not believe that there is such an one anywhere on earth?

In heaven, I replied, there is laid up a pattern of it, methinks, which he who desires may behold, and beholding, may set his own house in order. But whether such an one exists, or ever will exist in fact, is no matter; for he will live after the manner of that city, having nothing to do with any other.[n]

Questions

1. "Everything in the universe has a purpose or proper function within a harmonious hierarchy of purposes." In Plato's ethics, what is man's proper function, and how is it related to his moral worth?
2. What is the connection between *knowledge* and *moral conduct* in Plato's moral theory? What arguments can be put forward to support his view, and what can be said against it?
3. Describe Socrates' dialectical method, and evaluate it as a technique for philosophical debate. What limitations on its effectiveness result from the Sophists' rejection of the laws of logic?
4. Reconstruct the Sophists' conception of human motivation, and develop its implications for their definition of "justice."
5. What are Plato's objections to the hedonism of the Sophists? How does he support the view that reason is indispensable even to hedonists?
6. Explain the concept of "harmony" in Plato's ethical theory, and relate it to his definition of the cardinal virtues.
7. Against the Sophists' argument that injustice is more profitable than justice, Socrates holds the belief that it is better to be done an injustice than to commit one. What arguments are offered by both

parties to the debate, in defense and in attack? Evaluate the short-term and long-run practicality of these conflicting moral theories.

8. Describe the psychological theory underlying Plato's ethics. How is it related to his conception of the state?

9. What is the place of the "Idea of the Good" in Plato's general philosophical position? In his ethical theory?

10. Using Plato's analogy between vision and understanding, describe the way in which knowledge of the good may be sought. Where can one expect to find the model of perfection which Plato recommends as the proper guide to moral excellence? Why should men seek the idea of the good?

Key to selections:

PLATO, *The Dialogues of Plato*, vols. I, II, and III, tr. B. Jowett, 3rd ed., New York, Oxford University Press, 1892.

From *Phaedo*
a 98–99.

From *Gorgias*
e 495–496.
f 496–497.

From *Protagoras*
g 352–353.
h 354–357.

From *The Republic*
b Bk. VII, 517.
c Bk. II, 359–360.
d Bk. I, 343–344.
i Bk. IV, 442–444.
j Bk. IV, 444–445.
k Bk. VI, 504–505.
l Bk. VI, 508–509.
m Bk. VII, 517–519.
n Bk. IX, 591–592.

Guide to Additional Reading

INEXPENSIVE EDITIONS:

PLATO, *Apology, Crito, Republic I–II*, Great Books Foundation (Regnery).

——, *The Republic*, Everyman's Library (Dutton).

——, ——, Living Library (McClelland).

——, ——, Modern Library (Random House).

——, *Meno*, Little Library of Liberal Arts (Liberal Arts Press).

——, *Phaedo*, Little Library of Liberal Arts (Liberal Arts Press).

——, *Republic, VI–VII*, Great Books Foundation (Regnery).

——, *Five Dialogues*, Everyman's Library (Dutton).

Plato, Selected Passages, World's Classics (Oxford University Press).

Plato, Selections, Modern Student's Library (Scribner's).

Portable Plato, Viking Portable Library (Viking).

Socratic Discourses of Plato and Xenophon, Everyman's Library (Dutton).

The Philosophy of Plato, Modern Library (Random House).

Trial and Death of Socrates, Golden Treasury Series (Macmillan).

DISCUSSION AND COMMENTARY:

Gould, J. *The Development of Plato's Ethics*, Cambridge, Cambridge University Press, 1955.

Jaeger, W. W., *Paideia, The Ideals of Greek Culture*, vol. III, Oxford, Basil Blackwell and Mott, Ltd., 1944.

Nettleship, R. L., *Lectures on the Republic of Plato*, London, Macmillan and Company, Ltd., 1937.

Pater, W., *Plato and Platonism*, London, Macmillan and Company, Ltd., 1910.

Shorey, P., *What Plato Said*, Chicago, University of Chicago Press, 1933.

Taylor, A. E., *Plato, The Man and His Works*, London, Methuen and Company, Ltd., 1926.

CHAPTER 3

Moral
Character

ARISTOTLE

Aristotle (384–322 B.C.), the philosopher with whom only Plato compares in influence upon the history of western thought, was born in the Greek colony of Stagira in Macedonia. His father, Nicomachus, a student of natural history and an eminent physician, held the post of physician to Amnytas II, King of Macedonia, father of Philip the Great, until his death in Aristotle's eighteenth year. At his father's death, Aristotle, who had been brought up in an atmosphere of science and scholarship, went to Athens to study philosophy under Plato, and he remained at the Academy until Plato's death in 347 B.C.

While Aristotle was unquestionably Plato's most talented student, he was by no means his most devoted disciple: "Dear is Plato, but dearer still is truth." It has been suggested that his refusal to defer to the master cost him the nomination to succeed Plato as the head of the Academy. In any event, Aristotle was passed over in favor of Speusippus, a man who did not approach him in intellectual stature. In 343 B.C. Aristotle was selected as tutor to Alexander, the thirteen year old son of King Philip of

Macedonia. It was Philip who planned and began the world conquest which Alexander the Great so nearly fulfilled. There is no evidence that Aristotle, in his three years as tutor, modified the influence of father upon son or in any way affected the subsequent thoughts and deeds of Alexander; neither is there evidence that Aristotle ever recognized the significance of Alexander's goal of political unity. A bond of friendship was formed between teacher and pupil, however, and it is reported that Alexander later subsidized some of Aristotle's researches in the natural sciences.

At the age of forty-nine, Aristotle returned to Athens and founded the Lyceum, the second of the four great schools of antiquity. An immediate success as a lecturer, he entered into the enormously productive period of his life: combining the roles of encyclopedist, scientist, and philosopher, he is reputed to have written over four hundred works, to have conducted and directed prodigious researches in botany and zoology, and to have amassed one of the great libraries of the Greek world. As the result of an anti-Macedonian uprising after the death of Alexander in 323 B.C., Aristotle left Athens. It is said by some authorities that he was accused of dangerous teachings and indicted by the Athenian citizens, just as Socrates had been seventy-six years earlier, but that he, in contrast to Socrates, accepted the option of exile. Aristotle died at Chalcis on the island of Euboea in the next year.

According to Aristotle's own classification, his works deal with: the *theoretical* sciences, *e.g.*, *Metaphysics*, *Physics*, *De Caelo* (astronomy), *De Generatione et Corruptione* (biology), *De Anima* (psychology); the *practical* sciences, *e.g.*, *Nicomachean Ethics*, *Eudemian Ethics*, *Politics*; the *productive* or *poetical* sciences, *e.g.*, *Rhetoric*, *Poetics*; and *logic*, *e.g.*, *Organon*. On such impressive evidence, it is not surprising that it is said of Aristotle that for his time he knew all that was to be known.

Historically, Aristotles' *Nichomachean Ethics* is the first systematic treatment of ethics in western civilization. It belongs in the tradition begun by Socrates and advanced by Plato, a tradition which stresses both the supremacy of man's rational nature and the purposive nature of the universe. Nevertheless, within this broad framework, the ethical theories of Aristotle and his teacher, Plato, stand in sharp contrast. This difference stems from conflicting conceptions of the nature of the ultimate moral principle and is a consequence of different metaphysical positions. Aristotle takes issue with Plato's thesis that individual objects are intelligible only in terms of immutable forms or ideas which exist in and of themselves. According to Aristotle's doctrine, the forms which make objects understandable cannot exist apart from particular objects. That is, individual objects, for Aristotle, are a *unity* of a universal, repeatable form and a unique content or matter: "no form without matter, no matter without form." Consequently, Aristotle rejects the Platonic view that the moral evaluations of daily life presuppose a "good" which is independent of experience, personality, and circumstances. Rather, he insists that the basic moral principle is immanent in the activities of our daily lives and can be discovered only through a study of them.

In keeping with his general position, Aristotle begins his ethical inquiry with an empirical investigation of what it is that men fundamentally desire. In his search, he finds such goals as wealth and honors inadequate. He points out that an ultimate end for man must be one which is, first, *self-sufficient* — "that which [even] when isolated makes life desirable and lacking in nothing" — second, *final* — "that which is always desirable in itself and never for the sake of something else" — and third, *attainable by man*. Men are agreed, Aristotle maintains, that happiness alone is the goal which meets these requirements. However, he recognizes that this is no more than a preliminary agreement about what it is that we should investigate in ethics. More specifically, we want to know the nature of happiness and the conditions of its attainment.

Following Plato, Aristotle tells us that happiness must be explained in terms of reason, man's distinctive function or activity. In his philosophical system, however, this view is significantly modified by the doctrine of *potentiality* and *actuality*. Just as the acorn actualizes its unique potentiality by becoming an oak, so too man actualizes his distinctive or defining potentiality by living the life of reason. To Aristotle, this means that happiness depends upon the actualization — the full realization — of man's rationality.

Consideration of the conditions requisite to the attainment of happiness leads Aristotle into a discussion of virtue. For him, as for other Greek philosophers, "virtue" refers to the excellence of a thing, *i.e.*, the disposition to perform effectively its proper function. For example, a "virtuous" knife cuts well, and a "virtuous" physician successfully restores his patients to health. By the same token, Aristotle argues, a virtuous man lives according to reason, thus realizing his distinctive potentiality. However, he subdivides human virtue into two types, the *moral* and the *intellectual*. The moral virtues concern the habitual choice of actions in accordance with rational principles. The contemplation of theoretical truths and the discovery of the rational principles which ought to control everyday actions give rise to the intellectual virtues. But while contemplation, that activity by which men may attain the highest human happiness, is limited to the divinely gifted few, the practical virtues, with their lesser degrees of happiness, are within reach of the ordinary man.

Aristotle, then, in harmony with the Greek tradition, stresses the value of contemplation, but withal, is much impressed with the fact that men live for the most part at the level of practical decision and routine behavior. The good habits necessary to moral virtue are not strictly personal matters but can best be formed in a sound social and legal structure:

... It is difficult to get from youth up a right training for virtue if one has not been brought up under right laws; for to live temperately and hardily is not pleasant to most people, especially when they are young. For this reason their nurture and occupations should be fixed by law; for they will not be painful when they have become customary. But it is surely not enough that when they are young they should get the right nurture and attention; since they must, even when they are grown up, practice and be habituated to them, we shall need laws for this as well, and generally speaking to cover the whole of life; for most people obey necessity rather than argument, and punishments rather than the sense of what is noble.[a]

• • •

1. Aristotle assumes that any investigation, practical or theoretical, has a teleological basis; that is, it aims at some end or good. By using examples from ordinary experience, he attempts to show that ends or goods form a hierarchy.

Every art and every inquiry, and similarly every action and pursuit, is thought to aim at some good; and for this reason the good has rightly been declared to be that at which all things aim. But a certain difference is found among ends; some are activities, others are products apart from the activities that produce them. Where there are ends apart from the actions, it is the nature of the products to be better than the activities. Now, as there are many actions, arts, and sciences, their ends also are many; the end of the medical art is health, that of shipbuilding a vessel, that of strategy victory, that of economics wealth. But where such arts fall under a single capacity — as bridle-making and the other arts concerned with the equipment of horses fall under the art of riding, and this and every military action under strategy, in the same way other arts fall under yet others — in all of these the ends of the master arts are to be preferred to all the subordinate ends; for it is for the sake of the former that the latter are pursued. It makes no difference whether the activities themselves are the ends of the actions, or something else apart from the activities, as in the case of the sciences just mentioned.[b]

2. Analogously, each theoretical pursuit has its appropriate end, but the science of politics — ethics and social philosophy — includes all the others, in the sense that it ascertains their importance and development. For this reason, the science of politics can have as its proper end nothing less than "the good for man."

If, then, there is some end of the things we do, which we desire for its own sake (everything else being desired for the sake of this), and if we do not choose everything for the sake of something else (for at that rate the process would go on to infinity, so that our desire would be empty and vain), clearly this must be the good and the chief good. Will not the knowledge of it, then, have a great influence on life? Shall we not, like archers who have a mark to aim at, be more likely to hit upon what is right? If so, we must try, in outline at least to determine what it is, and of which of the sciences or capacities it is the object. It would seem to belong to the most authoritative art and that which is most truly the master art. And politics appears to be of this nature; for it is this that ordains which of the sciences should be studied in a state, and which each class of citizens should learn and up to what point they should learn them; and we see even the most highly esteemed of capacities to fall under this, e.g. strategy, economics, rhetoric; now, since politics uses the rest of the sciences, and since, again, it legislates as to what we are to do and what we are to abstain from, the end of this science must include those of the others, so that this end must be the good for man. For even if the end is the same for a single man and for a state, that of the state seems at all events something greater and more complete whether to attain or to preserve; though it is worth while to attain the end merely for one man, it is finer and more godlike to attain it for a nation or for city-states.ᶜ

3. Aristotle warns us against expecting a high degree of precision in our study of political science, since it deals with the human variable. As such, it is a subject matter best handled by men of experience.

Our discussion will be adequate if it has as much clearness as the subject-matter admits of, for precision is not to be sought for alike in all discussions, any more than in all the products of the crafts. Now fine and just actions, which political science investigates, admit of much variety and fluctuation of opinion, so that they may be thought to exist only by convention, and not by nature. And goods also give rise to a similar fluctuation because they bring harm to many people; for before now men have been undone by reason of their wealth, and others by reason of their courage. We must be content, then, in speaking of such subjects and with such premisses to indicate the truth roughly and in outline, and in speaking about things which are only for the most part true and with premisses of the same kind to reach conclusions that are no better. In the same spirit, therefore, should each type of statement be *received;* for it is the mark of an educated man to look for precision in each class of things just so far as the nature of the subject admits; it is evidently equally foolish to accept probable reasoning from a mathematician and to demand from a rhetorician scientific proofs.

Now each man judges well the things he knows, and of these he is a good judge. And so the man who has been educated in a subject is a good judge of that subject, and the man who has received an all-round education is a good judge in general. Hence a young man is not a proper hearer of lectures on political science; for he is inexperienced in the actions that occur in life, but its discussions start from these and are about these; and, further, since he tends to follow his passions, his study will be vain and unprofitable, because the end aimed at is not knowledge but action. And it makes no difference whether he is young in years or youthful in character; the defect does not depend on time, but on his living, and pursuing each successive object, as passion directs. For to such persons, as to the incontinent, knowledge brings no profit; but to those who desire and act in accordance with a rational principle knowledge about such matters will be of great benefit.[d]

4. Among those who are sufficiently mature to discuss ethics, there is verbal agreement that the good for man is happiness, but opinions about its precise nature vary.

Let us resume our inquiry and state, in view of the fact that all knowledge and every pursuit aims at some good, what it is that we say political science aims at and what is the highest of all goods achievable by action. Verbally there is very general agreement; for both the general run of men and people of superior refinement say that it is happiness, and identify living well and doing well with being happy; but with regard to what happiness is they differ, and the many do not give the same account as the wise. For the former think it is some plain and obvious thing, like pleasure, wealth, or honour; they differ, however, from one another — and often even the same man identifies it with different things, with health when he is ill, with wealth when he is poor; but, conscious of their ignorance, they admire those who proclaim some great ideal that is above their comprehension. Now some thought [e.g., Plato] that apart from these many goods there is another which is self-subsistent and causes the goodness of all these as well. To examine all the opinions that have been held were perhaps somewhat fruitless; enough to examine those that are most prevalent or that seem to be arguable.[e]

5. Aristotle then proceeds to discuss the general criteria which make possible the identification of man's chief good.

Let us again return to the good we are seeking, and ask what it can be. It seems different in different actions and arts; it is different in medicine, in strategy, and in the other arts likewise. What then is the good of each? Surely that for whose sake everything else is done. In medicine this is health, in strategy victory, in architecture a house, in any other sphere something else, and in every action and pursuit the end; for it is for the sake of this that all men do whatever else they do. Therefore, if there is an end for all that we do, this will be the good achievable by action, and if there are more than one, these will be the goods achievable by action.

So the argument has by a different course reached the same point; but we must try to state this even more clearly. Since there are evidently more than one end, and we choose some of these (e.g. wealth, flutes, and in general instruments) for the sake of something else, clearly not all ends are final ends; but the chief good is evidently something final. Therefore, if there is only one final end, this will be what we are seeking, and if there are more than one, the most final of these will be what we are seeking. Now we call that which is in itself worthy of pursuit more final than that which is worthy of pursuit for the sake of something else, and that which is never desirable for the sake of something else more final than the things that are desirable both in themselves and for the sake of that other thing, and therefore we call final without qualification that which is always desirable in itself and never for the sake of something else.

Now such a thing happiness, above all else, is held to be; for this we choose always for itself and never for the sake of something else, but honour, pleasure, reason, and every virtue we choose indeed for themselves (for if nothing resulted from them we should still choose each of them), but we choose them also for the sake of happiness, judging that by means of them we shall be happy. Happiness, on the other hand, no one chooses for the sake of these, nor, in general, for anything other than itself.

From the point of view of self-sufficiency the same result seems to follow; for the final good is thought to be self-sufficient. Now by self-sufficient we do not mean that which is sufficient for a man by himself, for one who lives a solitary life, but also for parents, children, wife, and in general for his friends and fellow citizens, since man is born for citizenship. But some limit must be set to this; for if we extend our requirement to ancestors and descendants and friends' friends we are in for an infinite series. Let us examine this question, however, on another occasion; the self-sufficient we now define as that which when isolated makes life desirable and lacking in nothing; and such we think happiness to be; and further we think it most desirable of all things, without being counted as one good thing among others — if it were so counted it would clearly be made more desirable by the addition of even the least of goods; for that which is added becomes an excess of goods, and of goods the greater is always more desirable. Happiness, then, is something final and self-sufficient, and is the end of action.[f]

6. Although it is agreed that happiness meets these criteria, Aristotle recognizes that the precise nature of happiness still remains to be explained. His definition of happiness contains two vital concepts: "activity of soul," which means the exercise of reason; and "in accordance with virtue," which describes the quality of the performance.

Presumably, however, to say that happiness is the chief good seems a platitude, and a clearer account of what it is is still desired. This might perhaps be given, if we could first ascertain the function of man. For just as for a flute-player, a sculptor, or any artist, and, in general, for all things that have a function or activity, the good and the 'well' is thought to reside in the function, so would it seem to be for man, if he has a function. Have the carpenter, then, and the tanner certain functions or activities, and has man none? Is he born without a function? Or as eye, hand, foot, and in general each of the parts evidently has a function, may one lay it down that man similarly has a function apart from all these? What then can this be? Life seems to be common even to plants, but we are seeking what is peculiar to man. Let us exclude, therefore, the life of nutrition and growth. Next there would be a life of perception, but *it* also seems to be common even to the horse, the ox, and every animal. There remains, then, an active life of the element that has a rational principle; of this, one part has such a principle in the sense of being obedient to one, the other in the sense of possessing one and exercising thought. And, as 'life of the rational element' also has two meanings, we must state that life in the sense of activity is what we mean; for this seems to be the more proper sense of the term. Now if the function of man is an activity of soul which follows or implies a rational principle, and if we say 'a so-and-so' and 'a good so-and-so' have a function which is the same in kind, e.g. a lyre-player and a good lyre-player, and so without qualification in all cases, eminence in respect of goodness being added to the name of the function (for the function of a lyre-player is to play the lyre, and that of a good lyre-player is to do so well): if this is the case, [and we state the function of man to be a certain kind of life, and this to be an activity or actions of the soul implying a rational principle, and the function of a good man to be the good and noble performance of these, and if any action is well performed when it is performed in accordance with the appropriate excellence: if this is the case,] human good turns out to be activity of soul in accordance with virtue, and if there are more than one virtue, in accordance with the best and most complete.

But we must add 'in a complete life.' For one swallow does not make a summer, nor does one day; and so too one day, or a short time, does not make a man blessed and happy. . . . [Also, a happy man] needs the external goods as well; for it is impossible, or not easy, to do noble acts without the proper equipment. In many actions we use friends and riches and political power as instruments; and there are some things the lack of which takes the lustre from happiness, as good birth, goodly children, beauty; for the man who is very ugly in appearance or ill-born or solitary and childless is not very likely to be happy, and perhaps a man would be still less likely if he had thoroughly bad children or friends or had lost good children or friends by death.[g]

7. Aristotle's definition of happiness cannot be fully understood until the nature of virtue has been thoroughly examined. But the nature of virtue, in turn, depends upon the structure of the soul, which contains both rational and irrational components. Two functions fall to the rational part, the control of man's irrational propensities and the exercise of reason for its own sake.

Since happiness is an activity of soul in accordance with perfect virtue, we must consider the nature of virtue; for perhaps we shall thus see better the nature of happiness. The true student of politics, too, is thought to have studied virtue above all things; for he wishes to make his fellow citizens good and obedient to the laws. As an example of this we have the lawgivers of the Cretans and the Spartans, and any others of the kind that there may have been. And if this inquiry belongs to political science, clearly the pursuit of it will be in accordance with our original plan. But clearly the virtue we must study is human virtue; for the good we were seeking was human good and the happiness human happiness. By human virtue we mean not that of the body but that of the soul; and happiness also we call an activity of soul. But if this is so, clearly the student of politics must know somehow the facts about soul, as the man who is to heal the eyes or the body as a whole must know about the eyes or the body; and all the more since politics is more prized and better than medicine; but even among doctors the best educated spend much labour on acquiring knowledge of the body. The student of politics, then, must study the soul, and must study it with these objects in view, and do so just to the extent which is sufficient for the questions we are discussing; for further precision is perhaps something more laborious than our purposes require.

Some things are said about it, adequately enough, even in the discussions outside our school, and we must use these; e.g. that one element in the soul is irrational and one has a rational principle. Whether these are separated as the parts of the body or of anything divisible are, or are distinct by definition but by nature inseparable, like convex and concave in the circumference of a circle, does not affect the present question.

Of the irrational element one division seems to be widely distributed, and vegetative in its nature, I mean that which causes nutrition and growth; for it is this kind of power of the soul that one must assign to all nurslings and to embryos, and this same power to full-grown creatures; this is more reasonable than to assign some different power to them. Now the excellence of this seems to be common to all species and not specifically human . . . let us leave the nutritive faculty alone, since it has by its nature no share in human excellence.

There seems to be also another irrational element in the soul — one which in a sense, however, shares in a rational principle. For we praise the rational principle of the continent man and of the incontinent, and the part of their soul that has such a principle, since it urges them aright and towards the best objects; but there is found in them also another element naturally opposed to the rational principle, which fights against and resists that principle. For exactly as paralyzed limbs when we intend to move them to the right turn on the contrary to the left, so is it with the soul; the impulses of incontinent people move in contrary directions. But while in the body we see that which moves astray, in the soul we do not. No doubt, however, we must none the less suppose that in the soul too there is something contrary to the rational principle, resisting and opposing it. In what sense it is distinct from the other elements does not concern us. Now even this seems to have a share in a rational principle, as we said, at any rate in the continent man it obeys the rational principle — and presumably in the temperate and brave man it is still more obedient; for in him it speaks, on all matters, with the same voice as the rational principle.

Therefore the irrational element also appears to be twofold. For the vegetative element in no way shares in a rational principle, but the appetitive, and in general the desiring element in a sense shares in it, in so far as it listens to and obeys it; this is the sense in which we speak of 'taking account' of one's father or one's friends, not that in which we speak of 'accounting' for a mathematical property. That the irrational element is in some sense persuaded by a rational principle is indicated also by the giving of advice and by all reproof and exhortation. And if this element also must be said to have a rational principle, that which has a rational principle (as well as that which has not) will be twofold, one subdivision having it in the strict sense and in itself, and the other having a tendency to obey as one does one's father.[h]

8. The virtues corresponding to the two functions of reason are the intellectual and the moral. The wise man personifies the intellectual virtues, whereas the continent man typifies the moral virtues. The former's excellence is attained through instruction and evidenced by knowledge. The excellence of the latter is produced by habits of choice and expressed in practical actions tempered by both the circumstance and the individual.

Virtue too is distinguished into kinds in accordance with this difference; for we say that some of the virtues are intellectual and others moral, philosophic wisdom and understanding and practical wisdom being intellectual, liberality and temperance moral. For in speaking about a man's character we do not say that he is wise or has understanding but that he is good-tempered or temperate; yet we praise the wise man also with respect to his state of mind; and of states of mind we call those which merit praise virtues.

Virtue, then, being of two kinds, intellectual and moral, intellectual virtue in the main owes both its birth and its growth to teaching (for which reason it requires experience and time), while moral virtue comes about as a result of habit, whence also its name *ethike* is one that is formed by a slight variation from the word *ethos* (habit). From this it is also plain that none of the moral virtues arises in us by nature; for nothing that exists by nature can form a habit contrary to its nature. For instance the stone which by nature moves downwards cannot be habituated to move upwards, not even if one tries to train it by throwing it up ten thousand times; nor can fire be habituated to move downwards, nor can anything else that by nature behaves in one way be trained to behave in another. Neither by nature, then, nor contrary to nature do the virtues arise in us; rather we are adapted by nature to receive them, and are made perfect by habit.

Again, of all the things that come to us by nature we first acquire the potentiality and later exhibit the activity (this is plain in the case of the senses; for it was not by often seeing or often hearing that we got these senses, but on the contrary we had them before we used them, and did not come to have them by using them); but the virtues we get by first exercising them, as also happens in the case of the arts as well. For the things we have to learn before we can do them, we learn by doing them, e.g. men become builders by building and lyre-players by playing the lyre; so too we become just by doing just acts, temperate by doing temperate acts, brave by doing brave acts.[i]

9. Aristotle turns his attention to the task of explaining moral virtue. He analyzes human personality into three elements, "passions, faculties, and states of character." Since passions — e.g., anger and fear — and faculties — e.g., the ability to feel anger and fear — are not in and of themselves blameworthy or praiseworthy, virtue must be a state of character. Experience shows that the states of character which enable a man to fulfill his proper function aim at an intermediary point between the opposing extremes of excess and deficiency. The morally virtuous man, then, always chooses to act according to the "golden mean," but, Aristotle points out, the mean is not the same for all individuals.

We must . . . not only describe [moral] virtue as a state of character, but also say what sort of state it is. We may remark, then, that every virtue or excellence both brings into good condition the thing of which it is the excellence and makes the work of that thing be done well; e.g. the excellence of the eye makes both the eye and its work good; for it is by the excellence of the eye that we see well. Similarly the excellence of the horse makes a horse both good in itself and good at running and at carrying its rider and at awaiting the attack of the enemy. Therefore, if this is true in every case, the virtue of man also will be the state of character which makes a man good and which makes him do his own work well.

How this is to happen we have stated already, but it will be made plain also by the following consideration of the specific nature of virtue. In everything that is continuous and divisible it is possible to take more, less, or an equal amount, and that either in terms of the thing itself or relatively to us; and the equal is an intermediate between excess and defect. By the intermediate in the object I mean that which is equidistant from each of the extremes, which is one and the same for all men; by the intermediate relatively to us that which is neither too much nor too little — and this is not one, nor the same for all. For instance, if ten is many and two is few, six is the intermediate, taken in terms of the object; for it exceeds and is exceeded by an equal amount; this is intermediate according to arithmetical proportion. But the intermediate relatively to us is not to be taken so; if ten pounds are too much for a particular person to eat and two too little, it does not follow that the trainer will order six pounds; for this also is perhaps too much for the person who is to take it, or too little — too little for Milo, too much for the beginner in athletic exercises. The same is true of running and wrestling. Thus a master of any art avoids excess and defect, but seeks the intermediate and chooses this — the intermediate not in the object but relatively to us.ʲ

10. Aristotle is now ready to assemble the results of his investigation into a definition of moral virtue.

. . . Virtue, then, is a state of character concerned with choice, lying in a mean, i.e. the mean relative to us, this being determined by a rational principle, and by that principle by which the man of practical wisdom would determine it. Now it is a mean between two vices, that which depends on excess and that which depends on defect; and again it is a mean because the vices respectively fall short of or exceed what is right in both passions and actions, while virtue both finds and chooses that which is intermediate. Hence in respect of its substance and the definition which states its essence virtue is a mean, with regard to what is best and right an extreme.

But not every action nor every passion admits of a mean; for some have names that already imply badness, e.g. spite, shamelessness, envy, and in the case of actions adultery, theft, murder; for all of these and suchlike things imply by their names that they are themselves bad, and not the excesses or deficiencies of them. It is not possible, then, ever to be right with regard to them; one must always be wrong. Nor does goodness or badness with regard to such things depend on committing adultery with the right woman, at the right time, and in the right way, but simply to do any of them is to go wrong. It would be equally absurd, then, to expect that in unjust, cowardly, and voluptuous action there should be a mean, an excess, and a deficiency; for at that rate there would be a mean of excess and of deficiency, an excess of excess, and a deficiency of deficiency. But as there is no excess and deficiency of temperance and courage because what is intermediate is in a sense an extreme, so too of the actions we have mentioned there is no mean nor any excess and deficiency, but however they are done they are wrong; for in general there is neither a mean of excess and deficiency, nor excess and deficiency of a mean.[k]

11. His general formulation of moral virtue completed, Aristotle proceeds to a direct examination of specific moral virtues.

We must, however, not only make this general statement, but also apply it to the individual facts. For among statements about conduct those which are general apply more widely, but those which are particular are more genuine, since conduct has to do with individual cases, and our statements must harmonize with the facts in these cases. We may take these cases from our table. With regard to feelings of fear and confidence courage is the mean; of the people who exceed, he who exceeds in fearlessness has no name (many of the states have no name), while the man who exceeds in confidence is rash, and he who exceeds in fear and falls short in confidence is a coward. With regard to pleasures and pains — not all of them, and not so much with regard to the pains — the mean is temperance, the excess self-indulgence. Persons deficient with regard to the pleasures are not often found; hence such persons also have received no name. But let us call them 'insensible.'

With regard to giving and taking of money the mean is liberality, the excess and the defect prodigality and meanness. In these actions people exceed and fall short in contrary ways; the prodigal exceeds in spending and falls short in taking, while the mean man exceeds in taking and falls short in spending. . . . With regard to money there are also other dispositions — a mean, magnificence (for the magnificent man differs from the liberal man; the former deals with large sums, the latter with small ones),

an excess, tastelessness and vulgarity, and a deficiency, nig-
gardliness . . .

With regard to honour and dishonour the mean is proper pride,
the excess is known as a sort of 'empty vanity,' and the deficiency
is undue humility; and as we said liberality was related to magnificence, differing from it by dealing with small sums, so there
is a state similarly related to proper pride, being concerned with
small honours while that is concerned with great. For it is possible
to desire honour as one ought, and more than one ought, and less,
and the man who exceeds in his desires is called ambitious, the
man who falls short unambitious, while the intermediate person
has no name. The dispositions also are nameless, except that
that of the ambitious man is called ambition. Hence the people
who are at the extremes lay claim to the middle place; and we ourselves sometimes call the intermediate person ambitious and sometimes unambitious, and sometimes praise the ambitious man and
sometimes the unambitious. The reason of our doing this will be
stated in what follows; but now let us speak of the remaining
states according to the method which has been indicated.

With regard to anger also there is an excess, a deficiency, and a
mean. Although they can scarcely be said to have names, yet
since we call the intermediate person good-tempered let us call
the mean good temper; of the persons at the extremes let the one
who exceeds be called irascible, and his vice irascibility, and the
man who falls short an inirascible sort of person, and the deficiency inirascibility.[1]

*12. Next, the intellectual virtues are investigated, i.e., the virtues
which accompany the proper exercise of reason in its various functions. The primary tasks of man's intellect are first, to give us knowledge of invariable and fixed principles, and second, to provide a
rational guide for action in daily life. The pursuit and discovery
of truth is the aim of* philosophical wisdom, *while the purpose of*
practical wisdom *is intelligent conduct. The basis for intelligent conduct is the union of true knowledge of what we ought to do and the*

desire to do it. Aristotle contrasts his view with that of Socrates on this point. He holds that Socrates was correct in associating virtue with principles discovered by reason, but wrong in the assumption that knowledge of the good is necessarily accompanied by a desire to act upon this knowledge.

We divided the virtues of the soul and said that some are virtues of character and others of intellect. Now we have discussed in detail the moral virtues; with regard to the others let us express our view as follows, beginning with some remarks about the soul. We said before that there are two parts of the soul — that which grasps a rule or rational principle, and the irrational; let us now draw a similar distinction within the part which grasps a rational principle. And let it be assumed that there are two parts which grasp a rational principle — one by which we contemplate the kind of things whose originative causes are invariable, and one by which we contemplate variable things; for where objects differ in kind the part of the soul answering to each of the two is different in kind, since it is in virtue of a certain likeness and kinship with their objects that they have the knowledge they have.

... The virtue of a thing is relative to its proper work. Now there are three things in the soul which control action and truth — sensation, reason, desire.

Of these sensation originates no [moral] action; this is plain from the fact that the lower animals have sensation but no share in [such] action.[1]

What affirmation and negation are in thinking, pursuit and avoidance are in desire; so that since moral virtue is a state of character concerned with choice, and choice is deliberate desire,

[1] Aristotle's analysis in this passage is directed toward those actions of men of which it may be said, in some sense, that their "moving principle is in the agent himself, he being aware of the particular circumstances of the action," *i.e., voluntary actions.* He ascribes no moral significance to *involuntary actions, i.e.,* actions for which men are not responsible — *e.g.,* actions resulting from external forces, those arising "by reason of ignorance" of the particular circumstances, and those done because of excessive pain or the fear of excessive pain.

therefore both the reasoning must be true and the desire right, if the choice is to be good, and the latter must pursue just what the former asserts. Now this kind of intellect and of truth is practical; of the intellect which is contemplative, not practical nor productive, the good and the bad state are truth and falsity respectively (for this is the work of everything intellectual); while of the part which is practical and intellectual the good state is truth in agreement with right desire.

The origin of [moral] action — its efficient, not its final cause [2] — is choice, and that of choice is desire and reasoning with a view to an end. This is why choice cannot exist either without reason and intellect or without a moral state; for good action and its opposite cannot exist without a combination of intellect and character. Intellect itself, however, moves nothing, but only the intellect which aims at an end and is practical; for this rules the productive intellect as well, since every one who makes makes for an end, and that which is made is not an end in the unqualified sense (but only an end in a particular relation, and the end of a particular operation) — only that which is *done* is that; for good action is an end, and desire aims at this. Hence choice is either desiderative reason or ratiocinative desire, and such an origin of action is a man.

. . . This is why some say that all the virtues are forms of practical wisdom . . . Socrates in one respect was on the right track while in another he went astray; in thinking that all the virtues were forms of practical wisdom he was wrong, but in saying they implied practical wisdom he was right. This is confirmed by the fact that even now all men, when they define virtue, after naming the state of character and its objects add 'that (state) which is in accordance with the right rule'; now the right rule is that which is in accordance with practical wisdom. All men, then, seem somehow to divine that this kind of state is virtue, viz. that which is

[2] Aristotle distinguishes the *efficient cause*, the agent or force which produces an effect, from the *final cause*, the end or purpose "for the sake of which a thing is done." For example, the efficient cause of the mural on the wall of an auditorium is the painter, while its final cause is the decoration of the room.

in accordance with practical wisdom. But we must go a little further. For it is not merely the state in accordance with the right rule, but the state that implies the *presence* of the right rule, that is virtue; and practical wisdom is a right rule about such matters. Socrates, then, thought the virtues were rules or rational principles (for he thought they were, all of them, forms of scientific knowledge), while we think they *involve* a rational principle.ᵐ

13. Although Aristotle acknowledges the importance of reason as a guide to moral action, he maintains that philosophic wisdom is superior even to practical wisdom. He defends his esteem for contemplation by showing that the life of contemplation comes closest to meeting the conditions for happiness.

If happiness is activity in accordance with virtue, it is reasonable that it should be in accordance with the highest virtue; and this will be that of the best thing in us. Whether it be reason or something else that is this element which is thought to be our natural ruler and guide and to take thought of things noble and divine, whether it be itself also divine or only the most divine element in us, the activity of this in accordance with its proper virtue will be perfect happiness. That this activity is contemplative we have already said.

Now this would seem to be in agreement both with what we said before and with the truth. For, firstly, this activity is the best (since not only is reason the best thing in us, but the objects of reason are the best of knowable objects); and, secondly, it is the most continuous, since we can contemplate truth more continuously than we can *do* anything. And we think happiness has pleasure mingled with it, but the activity of philosophic wisdom is admittedly the pleasantest of virtuous activities; at all events the pursuit of it is thought to offer pleasures marvellous for their purity and their enduringness, and it is to be expected that those who know will pass their time more pleasantly than those who inquire. And the self-sufficiency that is spoken of must belong most to the contemplative activity. For while a philosopher, as well as a just man or one possessing any other virtue, needs the necessaries of life, when they are sufficiently equipped with things of that sort the just man needs people towards whom and with whom he shall act justly, and the temperate man, the brave man, and each of the others is in the same case, but the philosopher, even when by himself, can contemplate truth, and the better the wiser he is; he can perhaps do so better if he has fellow-workers, but still he is the most self-sufficient. And this activity alone would seem to be loved for its own sake; for nothing arises from it apart from the contemplating, while from practical activities we gain more or less apart from the action. And happiness is thought to depend on leisure; for we are busy that we may have leisure, and make war that we may live in peace. Now the activity of the practical virtues is exhibited in political or military affairs, but the actions concerned with these seem to be unleisurely. Warlike actions are completely so (for no one chooses to be at war, or provokes war, for the sake of being at war; any one would seem absolutely murderous if he were to make enemies of his friends in order to bring about battle and slaughter); but the action of the statesman is also unleisurely, and — apart from the political action itself — aims at despotic power and honours, or at all events happiness, for him and his fellow citizens — a happiness different from political action, and evidently sought as being different. So if among virtuous actions political and military actions are distinguished by nobility and greatness, and these are unleisurely and aim at an end and are not desirable for their sake, but the activity of reason, which is contemplative, seems both to be superior in serious worth and to aim at no end beyond itself, and to have its pleasure proper to itself (and this augments the activity), and the self-sufficiency, leisureliness, unweariedness (so far as this is possible for man), and all the other attributes ascribed to the supremely happy man are evidently those connected with this activity, it follows that this will be the complete happiness of man, if it be allowed a complete term of life (for none of the attributes of happiness is *in*complete).

But such a life would be too high for man; for it is not in so far as he is man that he will live so, but in so far as something divine is present in him; and by so much as this is superior to our composite nature is its activity superior to that which is the exercise of the other kind of virtue. If reason is divine, then, in comparison with man, the life according to it is divine in comparison with human life. But we must not follow those who advise us, being men, to think of human things, and, being mortal, of mortal things, but must, so far as we can, make ourselves immortal, and strain every nerve to live in accordance with the best thing in us; for even if it be small in bulk, much more does it in power and worth surpass everything. This would seem, too, to be each man himself, since it is the authoritative and better part of him. It would be strange, then, if he were to choose not the life of his self but that of something else. And what we said before will apply now; that which is proper to each thing is by nature best and most pleasant for each thing; for man, therefore, the life according to reason is best and pleasantest, since reason more than anything else *is* man. This life therefore is also the happiest.[n]

Questions

1. In the context of Greek philosophy, what is meant by "virtue"?
2. What are the essential features of a suitable goal for man, in Aristotle's view?
3. "Happiness is an activity of soul in accordance with virtue." Explain and expand this definition, and show how it leads to the conclusion that the contemplative life is the happiest.
4. Outline Aristotle's psychological theory. How does it bear on his ethical theory?
5. What arguments can you offer either for or against Aristotle's contention that not all studies admit of the same degree of precision?
6. What differences exist between Aristotle's "golden mean" and an "absolute mean"? Provide illustrations which make the contrast clear.
7. Distinguish between the *moral* and *intellectual* virtues, defining and illustrating each type. What are the means by which they are acquired?

8. In what respects do the ethical theories of Plato and Aristotle stand in sharp contrast? In what respects are they alike?

9. What is Aristotle's judgement of the Socratic thesis, "virtue is knowledge"? How does Aristotle conceive the relation between virtue and knowledge?

10. Do you regard the ideal of the "life of reason" as out of date? Discuss.

Key to selections:

ARISTOTLE, *Nichomachean Ethics*, tr. W. D. Ross, from *The Works of Aristotle*, vol. IX, W. D. Ross, ed., Oxford, The Clarendon Press, 1925. With the kind permission of the publishers.

a Bk. X, 1179b31–1180a4.	h Bk. I, 1102a5–1103a3.
b Bk. I, 1094a1–18.	i Bks. I & II, 1103a4–1103b2.
c Bk. I, 1094a18–1094b10.	j Bk. II, 1106a14–1106b8.
d Bk. I, 1094b12–1095a11.	k Bk. II, 1106b36–1107a26.
e Bk. I, 1095a13–29.	l Bk. II, 1107a27–1108a8.
f Bk. I, 1097a15–1097b22.	m Bk. VI, 1138b35–1139b5,
g Bk. I, 1097b23–1098a19,	1144b17–29.
1099a31–1099b6.	n Bk. X, 1177a12–1178a8.

Guide to Additional Reading

INEXPENSIVE EDITIONS:

Aristotle, *Ethics, I, Politics, I*, Great Books Foundation (Regnery).
——, *Nichomachean Ethics*, Everyman's Library (Dutton).
——, *Poetics, Ethics, II*, Great Books Foundation (Regnery).
    Aristotle Selections, Modern Student's Library (Scribner's).
    Introduction to Aristotle, Modern Library (Random House).

DISCUSSION AND COMMENTARY:

Jaeger, W. W., *Aristotle*, New York, Methuen and Company, Ltd., 1934.
Joachim, H. H., Aristotle: *The Nicomachean Ethics*, London, Oxford University Press, 1954.
Mure, G. R. G., *Aristotle*, London, Ernest Benn, Ltd., 1932.
Ross, W. D., *Aristotle*, New York, Methuen and Company, Ltd., 1923.
Stewart, J. A., *Notes in the Nichomachean Ethics*, Oxford, the Clarendon Press, 1892.

CHAPTER 4

The Pleasant Life

EPICURUS

Epicureanism was one of the philosophies which arose during the decline of ancient Greece, as a source of relief from increasing social disorganization. Of these "salvation philosophies," which flourished until the Graeco-Roman culture was superseded by the Christian, Epicureanism was distinguished for the constancy of its doctrine. In its teachings, happiness was defined as serenity, achieved through the simple pleasures which preserve bodily health and peace of mind. To realize their ideal, the members of the Epicurean community, insofar as it was possible, refrained from participation in the affairs of the troubled world, spending their time in philosophical conversation.

Epicurus (342 or 341–270 B.C.), inheriting Athenian citizenship from his parents, was born and educated on the island of Samos in the Aegean Sea, where he spent the first two decades of his life. When, following the death of Alexander the Great in 323 B.C., the Athenians were driven out of Samos, Epicurus went to Asia Minor. After teaching there for several years, he moved to Athens (306 B.C.) and until his death, taught in his famous garden. The

"Garden of Epicurus" served as a sanctuary from the turmoil of the outer world for a select group of men who applied in their daily lives the precepts of their mentor. Epicurus' Garden ranked as one of the great schools of antiquity, along with Plato's Academy, Aristotle's Lyceum, and Zeno's Stoa.

It is a prank of history that the word "epicure" is frequently used to denote a gourmet or a fastidious voluptuary. Epicurus' enemies in fact accused him of sensualism, but his philosophical teachings and the frugality and simplicity of his life effectively refuted their charge. It was the nobility of his character which accounted for his great popularity. Indeed, the biographer of ancient philosophers, Diogenes Laertius (third century, A.D.), eulogized him in the following manner:

> . . . Epicurus has witnesses enough and to spare of his unsurpassed kindness to all men. There is his country which honoured him with bronze statues, his friends so numerous they could not even be reckoned by entire cities, and his disciples who all remained bound for ever by the charm of his teaching, except Metrodorus . . . overweighted perhaps by Epicurus' excessive goodness. There is also the permanent continuance of the school after almost all the others had come to an end, and that though it had a countless succession of heads from among the disciples. There is again his grateful devotion to his parents, his generosity to his brothers, and his gentleness towards his servants. . . . In short there is his benevolence to all.

Although Epicurus was a very prolific writer, only a few letters and fragments of his writings are extant. They give little more than a summary of his theories of physics and astronomy, his theory of knowledge, and his ethics. However, a fuller view of his doctrines is provided by the works of his disciples, of whom the most distinguished is the Roman, Lucretius Carus (94–55? B.C.). Lucretius' *De Rerum Natura* (*On the Nature of Things*) is both fine poetry and an excellent statement of Epicureanism; in it, he says of Epicurus:

> When human life to view lay foully prostrate upon earth crushed down under the weight of religion . . . a man of Greece ventured first

to lift up his mortal eyes to her face and first to withstand her to her face. Him neither story of gods nor thunderbolts nor heaven with threatening roar could quell: they only chafed the more the eager courage of his soul, filling him with desire to be the first to burst the fast bars of nature's portals. (Book I.)

The ethical theory of Epicurus stems from the Cyrenaic doctrine formulated by Aristippus (*c.* 435–356 B.C.), who, even though he was a student of Socrates, advocates the hedonistic principle that pleasure is the supreme good. While Epicurus and the Cyrenaics have widely different conceptions of the pleasant life, the former stressing peace of mind and the latter sensual pleasures, they concur with respect to general principles. Both maintain that human nature is so constituted that men always seek what they believe will give them pleasure and avoid what they believe will give them pain, and that pleasure is the only intrinsic good and pain the only intrinsic evil. Again, both are agreed that "no pleasure is a bad thing in itself." Yet, they enjoin us to choose our pleasures judiciously, for "the means which produce some pleasures bring with them disturbances many times greater than the pleasures." Aristippus and Epicurus teach that the man who wishes to be happy must cultivate his ability to choose the right pleasures; and, they assert, only those actions which further an individual's enjoyment can have moral significance for him. Beyond this point, however, Epicureanism and Cyrenaicism diverge.

In opposition to Aristippus, Epicurus maintains that the *duration of pleasures is more important than their intensity* in achieving happiness. Consequently, he argues that the mental pleasures are in general superior to the physical, since they are longer-lasting, albeit less intense. Although he finds the physical pleasures unobjectionable in themselves, he contends that the pursuit of them for their own sake does not lead to happiness, but to the reverse. Experience shows us that the desire for a life filled with intense pleasures will be frustrated, because there are not enough of them in the ordinary course of events. What is more, the pleasures derived from such objectives as fame, wealth, and the like, are usually outweighed by the pains necessary to procure them; and the pains consequent upon such activities as feasting, drinking, and merrymaking either cancel the pleasures or leave a balance of pain. From these considerations, Epicurus can only conclude that Aristippus' standard of judging what is good, *i.e.*, "the most intense sensual pleasure of the moment," is entirely self-defeating.

The chief difference between Cyrenaicism and Epicureanism lies in their divergent conception of the nature of true pleasure. Fundamental to their disagreement is the distinction between *active* or *positive* pleasure, which comes from the gratification of specific wants and desires, and *passive* or *negative* pleasure, which is the absence of pain. Aristippus sets as the goal of life a constant round of active pleasures, whereas Epicurus maintains that the active pleasures are important only insofar as they terminate the pain of unfulfilled desires. For Epicurus, the passive pleasures are more fundamental than the active, since it is through them that happiness is gained. Man's ultimate goal is not a constant succession of intense sensual pleasures, but rather, it is the state of serenity, *ataraxia*, which characterizes "freedom from trouble in the mind and pain in the body."

Epicurus assures us that the calm and repose of the good life are within the reach of all. It is necessary that we keep our desires at a minimum, however, and distinguish the natural and necessary desires from those which are artificial, *e.g.*, longings for wealth, excitement, fame, and power. The latter are not merely unnecessary to health and tranquillity, but are in fact destructive of them. By contrast, the satisfaction of the natural desires — *i.e.*, of the desires which must be fulfilled to preserve bodily health and mental peace — and the freedom from pain which accompanies such satisfaction, lead to happiness.

Epicurus tells us that our good can be realized through philosophy, the quest for knowledge. It must be understood, however, that the function of philosophy is preeminently practical:

Vain is the word of a philosopher which does not heal any suffering of man. For just as there is no profit in medicine if it does not expel the diseases of the body, so there is no profit in philosophy either, if it does not expel the suffering of the mind.[a]

By nature men seek pleasure, but by knowledge they are guided to the choice of the true pleasures. Without deliberation, we cannot hope either to forestall needless and artificial desires or to secure the pleasures required for happiness. In addition, without knowledge of the nature of things, we cannot rid ourselves of the fears and superstitions which destroy tranquillity.

Epicurus undertakes to demonstrate the groundlessness of the two overwhelming fears that troubled his contemporaries, the *fear of death* and the *fear of divine retribution*. The philosophy of nature which he finds best suited to the task of destroying these terrifying chimeras is the "atomism" of Democritus (fifth century, B.C.), in which the universe is explained wholly in terms of "atoms in motion in the void." Arguing that Democritus' mechanistic account of the universe is adequate to explain all that occurs, Epicurus holds that it is superfluous to postulate the interference of the gods in human affairs.[1] Moreover, the Democritean theory of the soul supports his arguments against the fear of death: the soul is no more than a collection of small atoms within the body, and death is only the dispersal of the soul-atoms. In any case, we need not fear death, "since as long as we exist, death is not with us; but when death comes, then we do not exist."

Despite the general suitability of Democritean atomism as an account of nature, its theory of motion is said by Epicurus to be incomplete in a way which has serious consequences for ethics.

---

[1] Epicurus does not deny that there are gods. However, he argues that it does not follow logically from the existence of gods, nor does experience testify, that "the greatest misfortunes befall the wicked and the greatest blessings the good by the gift of the gods." (Principal Doctrines, I.) He also says on the subject: "If God listened to the prayers of men, all men would quickly have perished: for they are for ever praying for evil against one another." (Fragments, no. 58.)

A further argument against divine causation of human good or evil is presented in a paradox attributed to Epicurus by Lactantius, in which the logical difficulties of the conception of an all-powerful and all-good deity are treated. For a statement of this paradox, see Ch. vi, no. 1.

In dealing with the motion of atoms, he observes that if their original motion is only a uniform downward fall, it is impossible to account for the collisions of atoms necessary to form complex bodies. Hence, he assumes that atoms deviate spontaneously, or "swerve," in their course. But this kind of motion, being irregular and unpredictable, introduces an element of freedom or indeterminacy into the universe which is excluded by the absolute determinism of Democritus. The advantage of the Epicurean interpretation for ethics becomes evident when it is realized that men fear, more than the hand of the gods, the control of an inexorable fate or necessity of the kind implied by Democritus' deterministic atomism. However, because his theory of motion leaves a margin of indeterminacy, Epicurus believes it admits of the possibility that men can to some extent influence and control the course of their lives. He therefore exhorts us to realize that while "necessity is an evil . . . there is no necessity to live under the control of necessity."

Through the true philosophy, Epicurus tells us, we can see that the fear of death, of the interference of the gods, and of the hard grip of necessity are without foundation in reality. Philosophy serves us well — it is not only an indispensable tool for the good life, but it is also the most pleasant of activities: "In all other occupations the fruit comes painfully after completion, but in philosophy pleasure goes hand in hand with knowledge . . ." Wherefore, Epicurus admonishes: "Let no one when young delay to study philosophy, nor when he is old, grow weary of his study. For no one can come too early or too late to secure the health of his soul."

• • •

1. In setting forth the nature of the universe, Epicurus lays down the fundamental principles, "nothing is created out of nothing," and "nothing is destroyed into nothing." Moreover, he reaffirms the Democritean doctrine that nature consists solely of atoms in motion in empty space. Together, these tenets support his argument that only

natural causes operate in the world, and, in addition, they provide a
reassuring stability and permanence in the basic stuff of the universe.

. . . Nothing is created out of that which does not exist: for if
it were, everything would be created out of everything with no
need of seeds. And again, if that which disappears were destroyed
into that which did not exist, all things would have perished,
since that into which they were dissolved would not exist. Furthermore, the universe always was such as it is now, and always will
be the same. For there is nothing into which it changes: for outside
the universe there is nothing which could come into it and bring
about the change.

Moreover, the universe is bodies and space: for that bodies
exist, sense itself witnesses in the experience of all men . . . And
if there were not that which we term void and place and intangible
existence, bodies would have nowhere to exist and nothing through
which to move, as they are seen to move. And besides these two
nothing can even be thought of . . . Furthermore, among bodies
some are compounds, and others those of which compounds are
formed. And these latter are indivisible and unalterable if, that is,
all things are not to be destroyed into the non-existent, but something permanent is to remain behind at the dissolution of compounds: they are completely solid in nature, and can by no means
be dissolved in any part. So it must needs be that the first-begin-
nings are indivisible corporeal existences . . .

Moreover, we must suppose that the atoms do not possess any
of the qualities belonging to perceptible things, except shape,
weight, and size, and all that necessarily goes with shape. For
every quality changes; but the atoms do not change at all, since
there must needs be something which remains solid and indissoluble at the dissolution of compounds, which can cause changes;
not changes into the non-existent or from the non-existent, but
changes effected by the shifting of position of some particles, and
by the addition or departure of others. For this reason it is essential that the bodies which shift their position should be imperish-
able and should not possess the nature of what changes, but parts

and configuration of their own. For thus much must needs remain constant . . .

And the atoms move continuously for all time, some of them falling straight down, others swerving, and others recoiling from their collisions. And of the latter, some are borne on separating to a long distance from one another, while others again recoil and recoil, whenever they chance to be checked by the interlacing with others, or else shut in by atoms interlaced around them. For on the one hand the nature of the void which separates each atom by itself brings this about, as it is not able to afford resistance, and on the other hand the hardness which belongs to the atoms makes them recoil after collision to as great a distance as the interlacing permits separation after the collision. And these motions have no beginning, since the atoms and the void are the cause. . . .[b]

2. The doctrine that everything is made up of material atoms applies not only to inanimate and living bodies, but also to the soul. The atoms of the soul are exceedingly fine; enclosed within the body, they are the means by which sensations occur in us. With this theory, Epicurus is well situated to attack the fear of what comes after death. When, in death, the atoms of the soul leave the body, we become incapable of sensation, and it is therefore impossible for us to experience painful punishments after we die. Yet, we should be comforted by the knowledge that the atoms which compose our soul are in themselves indestructible. Furthermore, Epicurus attempts to prove that those who argue that the soul is immortal because it is incorporeal are reasoning from a false premise.

Next, referring always to the sensations and the feelings for in this way you will obtain the most trustworthy ground of belief, you must consider that the soul is a body of fine particles distributed throughout the whole structure, and most resembling wind with a certain admixture of heat, and in some respects like to one of these and in some to the other. There is also the part which is many degrees more advanced even than these in fineness of composition, and for this reason is more capable of feeling in harmony with the rest of the structure as well. Now all this is made manifest by the activities of the soul and the feelings and the readiness of its movements and its processes of thought and by what we lose at the moment of death. Further, you must grasp that the soul possesses the chief cause of sensation: yet it could not have acquired sensation, unless it were in some way enclosed by the rest of the structure. And this in its turn having afforded the soul this cause of sensation acquires itself too a share in this contingent capacity from the soul. Yet it does not acquire all the capacities which the soul possesses: and therefore when the soul is released from the body, the body no longer has sensation. For it never possessed this power in itself, but used to afford opportunity for it to another existence, brought into being at the same time with itself: and this existence, owing to the power now consummated within itself as a result of motion, used spontaneously to produce for itself the capacity of sensation and then to communicate it to the body as well, in virtue of its contact and correspondence of movement, as I have already said. Therefore, so long as the soul remains in the body, even though some other part of the body be lost, it will never lose sensation; nay more, whatever portions of the soul may perish too, when that which enclosed it is removed either in whole or in part, if the soul continues to exist at all, it will retain sensation. On the other hand the rest of the structure, though it continues to exist either as a whole or in part, does not retain sensation, if it has once lost that sum of atoms, however small it be, which together goes to produce the nature of the soul. Moreover, if the whole structure is dissolved, the soul is dispersed and no longer has the same powers nor performs its movements, so that it does not possess sensation either. For it is impossible to imagine it with sensation, if it is not in this organism and cannot effect these movements, when what encloses and surrounds it is no longer the same as the surroundings in which it now exists and performs these movements. Furthermore, we must clearly comprehend as well, that the incorporeal in the general acceptation of the term is applied to that which could be thought of as such as an independent existence. Now it is impossible to conceive the incorporeal as a separate existence, except the void: and the void can neither act nor be acted upon, but only provides opportunity of motion through itself to bodies. So that those who say that the soul is incorporeal are talking idly. For it would not be able to act or be acted on in any respect, if it were of this nature. But as it is, both these occurrences are clearly distinguished in respect of the soul.[c]

3. While Epicurus does not deny the existence of divine beings, he is much concerned to dispel the notion that the gods interfere in any way with the events of nature. He opposes as impious the belief of many of his contemporaries that the heavenly bodies are gods or under the control of gods. On the contrary, he maintains that the heavenly bodies are natural phenomena and that accurate knowledge of at least the general principles of their motions is requisite to happiness. Freedom from the fear of punishment or of annihilation after death and from the fear of the gods can be achieved only when we understand the true nature of things.

Furthermore, the motions of the heavenly bodies and their turnings and eclipses and risings and settings, and kindred phenomena to these, must not be thought to be due to any being who controls and ordains or has ordained them and at the same time enjoys perfect bliss together with immortality (for trouble and care and anger and kindness are not consistent with a life of blessedness, but these things come to pass where there is weakness and fear and dependence on neighbours). Nor again must we believe that they, which are but fire agglomerated in a mass, possess blessedness, and voluntarily take upon themselves these movements. But we must preserve their full majestic significance in all expressions which we apply to such conceptions, in order that there may not arise out of them opinions contrary to this notion of majesty. Otherwise this very contradiction will cause the greatest disturbance in men's souls. Therefore we must believe that it is due to the original inclusion of matter in such agglomerations during the birth-process of the world that this law of regular succession is also brought about.

Furthermore, we must believe that to discover accurately the cause of the most essential facts is the function of the science of nature, and that blessedness for us in the knowledge of celestial phenomena lies in this and in the understanding of the nature of the existences seen in these celestial phenomena, and of all else that is akin to the exact knowledge requisite for our happiness . . . nothing which suggests doubt or alarm can be included at all in that which is naturally immortal and blessed. Now this we can ascertain by our mind is absolutely the case . . .

And besides all these matters in general we must grasp this point, that the principal disturbance in the minds of men arises because they think that these celestial bodies are blessed and immortal, and yet have wills and actions and motives inconsistent with these attributes; and because they are always expecting or imagining some everlasting misery, such as is depicted in legends, or even fear the loss of feeling in death as though it would concern them themselves; and, again, because they are brought to this pass not by reasoned opinion, but rather by some irrational presentiment, and therefore, as they do not know the limits of pain, they suffer a disturbance equally great or even more extensive than if they had reached this belief by opinion. But peace of mind is being delivered from all this, and having a constant memory of the general and most essential principles.

Wherefore we must pay attention to internal feelings and to external sensations in general and in particular, according as the subject is general or particular, and to every immediate intuition in accordance with each of the standards of judgement. For if we pay attention to these, we shall rightly trace the causes whence arose our mental disturbance and fear, and, by learning the true causes of celestial phenomena and all other occurrences that come to pass from time to time, we shall free ourselves from all which produces the utmost fear in other men.[d]

4. In setting forth the principles of the good life, Epicurus recommends that we keep always before us the two fundamental beliefs for which he has provided the metaphysical basis: first, god is truly blessed — and therefore above dealing in rewards and punishments for men — and second, "death is nothing to us." Fortified with these ideas, we can hope to live a pleasant life, and a pleasant life is more to be desired than a long one.

First of all believe that god is a being immortal and blessed, even as the common idea of a god is engraved on men's minds, and do not assign to him anything alien to his immortality or ill-suited to his blessedness: but believe about him everything that can uphold his blessedness and immortality. For gods there are, since the knowledge of them is by clear vision. But they are not such as the many believe them to be: for indeed they do not consistently represent them as they believe them to be. And the impious man is not he who denies the gods of the many, but he who attaches to the gods the beliefs of the many. For the statements of the many about the gods are not conceptions derived from sensation, but false suppositions, according to which the greatest misfortunes befall the wicked and the greatest blessings the good by the gift of the gods. For men being accustomed always to their own virtues welcome those like themselves, but regard all that is not of their nature as alien . . .

The blessed and immortal nature knows no trouble itself nor causes trouble to any other, so that it is never constrained by anger or favour. For all such things exist only in the weak . . .

Become accustomed to the belief that death is nothing to us. For all good and evil consists in sensation, but death is deprivation of sensation. And therefore a right understanding that death is nothing to us makes the mortality of life enjoyable, not because it adds to it an infinite span of time, but because it takes away the craving for immortality. For there is nothing terrible in life for the man who has truly comprehended that there is nothing terrible in not living. So that the man speaks but idly who says that he fears death not because it will be painful when it comes, but because it is painful in anticipation. For that which gives no trouble when it comes, is but an empty pain in anticipation. So death, the most terrifying of ills, is nothing to us, since so long as we exist, death is not with us; but when death comes, then we do not exist. It does not then concern either the living or the dead, since for the former it is not, and the latter are no more.

But the many at one moment shun death as the greatest of evils, at another yearn for it as a respite from the evils in life. But the wise man neither seeks to escape life nor fears the cessation of life, for neither does life offend him nor does the absence of life seem to be any evil. And just as with food he does not seek simply the larger share and nothing else, but rather the most pleasant, so he seeks to enjoy not the longest period of time, but the most pleasant.[e]

5. In Epicurus' view, all our actions are directed towards bodily and mental pleasures. Although pleasure is intrinsically good, we will find that the most pleasant life sometimes requires us to undergo pain for the sake of greater pleasure.

. . . Since pleasure is the first good and natural to us, for this very reason we do not choose every pleasure, but sometimes we pass over many pleasures, when greater discomfort accrues to us as the result of them: and similarly we think many pains better than pleasures, since a greater pleasure comes to us when we have endured pains for a long time. Every pleasure then because of its natural kinship to us is good, yet not every pleasure is to be chosen: even as every pain also is an evil, yet not all are always of a nature to be avoided. Yet by a scale of comparison and by the consideration of advantages and disadvantages we must form our judgement on all these matters. For the good on certain occasions we treat as bad, and conversely the bad as good . . .

No one when he sees evil deliberately chooses it, but is enticed by it as being good in comparison with a greater evil and so pursues it.[f]

6. To understand how we should live in order to enjoy the most pleasant and serene existence, Epicurus tells us, we must know the nature of the various desires and the different pleasures which come from their satisfaction.

We must consider that of desires some are natural, others vain, and of the natural some are necessary and others merely natural; and of the necessary some are necessary for happiness, others for the repose of the body, and others for very life . . .

Unhappiness comes either through fear or through vain and unbridled desire: but if a man curbs these, he can win for himself the blessedness of understanding. . . . Of desires, all that do not lead to a sense of pain, if they are not satisfied, are not necessary, but involve a craving which is easily dispelled, when the object is hard to procure or they seem likely to produce harm. . . . Wherever in the case of desires which are physical, but do not lead to a sense of pain, if they are not fulfilled, the effort is intense, such pleasures are due to idle imagination, and it is not owing to their own nature that they fail to be dispelled, but owing to the empty imaginings of the man. . . .

The disturbance of the soul cannot be ended nor true joy created either by the possession of the greatest wealth or by honour and respect in the eyes of the mob or by anything else that is associated with causes of unlimited desires. . . . We must not violate nature, but obey her; and we shall obey her if we fulfil the necessary desires and also the physical, if they bring no harm to us, but sternly reject the harmful. . . . The man who follows nature and not vain opinions is independent in all things. For in reference to what is enough for nature every possession is riches, but in reference to unlimited desires even the greatest wealth is not riches but poverty.

In so far as you are in difficulties, it is because you forget nature; for you create for yourself unlimited fears and desires. It is better for you to be free of fear lying upon a pallet, than to have a golden couch and a rich table and be full of trouble. . . . Thanks be to blessed Nature because she has made what is necessary easy to supply, and what is not easy unnecessary. . . . The right understanding of these facts enables us to refer all choice and avoidance to the health of the body and the soul's freedom from disturbance, since this is the aim of the life of blessedness. For it is to obtain this end that we always act, namely, to avoid pain and fear. And when this is once secured for us, all the tempest of the soul is dispersed, since the living creature has not to wander as though in search of something that is missing, and to look for some other thing by which he can fulfil the good of the soul and the good of the body. For it is then that we have need of pleasure, when we feel pain owing to the absence of pleasure; but when we do not feel pain, we no longer need pleasure. And for this cause we call pleasure the beginning and end of the blessed life. For we recognize pleasure as the first good innate in us, and from pleasure we begin every act of choice and avoidance, and to pleasure we return again, using the feeling as the standard by which we judge every good.[g]

7. *Reflection on the desires will lead us to the view that frugality and simplicity are the true roads to happiness. Mere sensual enjoyment leads ultimately to unhappiness, but a good digestion keeps the body well, and philosophical contemplation keeps the soul at peace. The overall virtue which we should seek to cultivate is* prudence; *it is the most valuable of all moral attributes and the source of all the virtues by which we are enabled to live happily.*

And again independence of desire we think a great good — not that we may at all times enjoy but a few things, but that, if we do not possess many, we may enjoy the few in the genuine persuasion that those have the sweetest pleasure in luxury who least need it, and that all that is natural is easy to be obtained, but that which is superfluous is hard. And so plain savours bring us a pleasure equal to a luxurious diet, when all the pain due to want is removed; and bread and water produce the highest pleasure, when one who needs them puts them to his lips. To grow accustomed therefore to simple and not luxurious diet gives us health to the full, and makes a man alert for the needful employments of life, and when after long intervals we approach luxuries disposes us better towards them, and fits us to be fearless of fortune.

When, therefore, we maintain that pleasure is the end, we do not mean the pleasures of profligates and those that consist in sensuality, as is supposed by some who are either ignorant or disagree with us or do not understand, but freedom from pain in the body and from trouble in the mind. For it is not continuous drinkings and revellings, nor the satisfaction of lusts, nor the enjoyment of fish and other luxuries of the wealthy table, which produce a pleasant life, but sober reasoning, searching out the motives for all choice and avoidance, and banishing mere opinions, to which are due the greatest disturbance of the spirit. . . .

The pleasure in the flesh is not increased, when once the pain due to want is removed, but is only varied: and the limit as regards pleasure in the mind is begotten by the reasoned understanding of these very pleasures and of the emotions akin to them, which used to cause the greatest fear to the mind.

Infinite time contains no greater pleasure than limited time, if one measures by reason the limits of pleasure.

The flesh perceives the limits of pleasure as unlimited and unlimited time is required to supply it. But the mind, having attained a reasoned understanding of the ultimate good of the flesh and its limits and having dissipated the fears concerning the time to come, supplies us with the complete life, and we have no further need of infinite time: but neither does the mind shun pleasure, nor, when circumstances begin to bring about the departure from life, does it approach its end as though it fell short in any way of the best life.

He who has learned the limits of life knows that that which removes the pain due to want and makes the whole of life complete is easy to obtain; so that there is no need of actions which involve competition.

. . . The beginning and the greatest good is prudence. Wherefore prudence is a more precious thing even than philosophy: for from prudence are sprung all the other virtues, and it teaches us that it is not possible to live pleasantly without living prudently and honourably and justly, nor, again, to live a life of prudence, honour, and justice without living pleasantly. For the virtues are by nature bound up with the pleasant life, and the pleasant life is inseparable from them. For indeed who, think you, is a better man than he who holds reverent opinions concerning the gods, and is at all times free from fear of death, and has reasoned out the end ordained by nature? [h]

8. Epicurus describes the prudent man as one who knows that the truly good things are easy to obtain and that evils are either short-lived or slight. The prudent man also knows that he himself, not destiny, controls the factors which decide his happiness, and he has the power to turn chance occurrences to good account. Moreover, the wise decision rather than the fortunate outcome is the prudent man's choice.

[The prudent man] understands that the limit of good things is easy to fulfil and easy to attain, whereas the course of ills is either short in time or slight in pain:

Pain does not last continuously in the flesh, but the acutest pain is there for a very short time, and even that which just exceeds the pleasure in the flesh does not continue for many days at once. . . .

He laughs at destiny, whom some have introduced as the mistress of all things. He thinks that with us lies the chief power in determining events, some of which happen by necessity and some by chance, and some are within our control; for while necessity cannot be called to account, he sees that chance is inconstant, but that which is in our control is subject to no master, and to it are naturally attached praise and blame. For, indeed, it were better to follow the myths about the gods than to become a slave to the destiny of the natural philosophers: for the former suggests a hope of placating the gods by worship, whereas the latter involves a necessity which knows no placation. As to chance, he does not regard it as a god as most men do (for in a god's acts there is no disorder), nor as an uncertain cause of all things: for he does not believe that good and evil are given by chance to man for the framing of a blessed life, but that opportunities for great good and great evil are afforded by it. He therefore thinks it better to be unfortunate in reasonable action than to prosper in unreason. For it is better in a man's actions that what is well chosen should fail, rather than that what is ill chosen should be successful owing to chance.[i]

9. When he turns his attention to the nature of community life, Epicurus finds that the principle of justice is required to assure mutual help among men and to prevent them from injuring one another. To these ends, men form a social compact, with justice governing their interrelations. Epicurus points out that although justice is the same for all when it is considered as a general principle, it manifests variations when it is applied in specific situations.

The justice which arises from nature is a pledge of mutual advantage to restrain men from harming one another and save them from being harmed.

For all living things which have not been able to make compacts not to harm one another or be harmed, nothing ever is either just or unjust; and likewise too for all tribes of men which have been unable or unwilling to make compacts not to harm or be harmed.

Justice never is anything in itself, but in the dealings of men with one another in any place whatever and at any time it is a kind of compact not to harm or be harmed.

Injustice is not an evil in itself, but only in consequence of the fear which attaches to the apprehension of being unable to escape those appointed to punish such actions.

It is not possible for one who acts in secret contravention of the terms of the compact not to harm or be harmed, to be confident that he will escape detection, even if at present he escapes a thousand times. For up to the time of death it cannot be certain that he will indeed escape.

In its general aspect justice is the same for all, for it is a kind of mutual advantage in the dealings of men with one another: but with reference to the individual peculiarities of a country or any other circumstances the same thing does not turn out to be just for all.

Among actions which are sanctioned as just by law, that which is proved on examination to be of advantage in the requirements of men's dealings with one another, has the guarantee of justice, whether it is the same for all or not. But if a man makes a law and it does not turn out to lead to advantage in men's dealings with each other, then it no longer has the essential nature of justice. And even if the advantage in the matter of justice shifts from one side to the other, but for a while accords with the general concept, it is none the less just for that period in the eyes of those who do not confound themselves with empty sounds but look to the actual facts.

Where, provided the circumstances have not been altered, actions which were considered just, have been shown not to accord with the general concept in actual practice, then they are not just. But where, when circumstances have changed, the same actions which were sanctioned as just no longer lead to advantage, there they were just at the time when they were of advantage for the dealings of fellow-citizens with one another; but subsequently they are no longer just, when no longer of advantage.[j]

10. In our concern for our safety, Epicurus tells us, we are likely to be misled by seeming protections against the misdeeds of our neighbors. He recommends as the surest protection that we "release ourselves from the prison of affairs and politics" and withdraw into the company of a few select friends. In this, he is in effect referring to the ideal Epicurean community, of which the Garden of Epicurus was the actual embodiment.

To secure protection from men anything is a natural good, by which you may be able to attain this end.

Some men wished to become famous and conspicuous, thinking that they would thus win for themselves safety from other men. Wherefore if the life of such men is safe, they have obtained the good which nature craves; but if it is not safe, they do not possess that for which they strove at first by the instinct of nature. . . .

The most unalloyed source of protection from men, which is secured to some extent by a certain force of expulsion, is in fact the immunity which results from a quiet life and the retirement from the world. . . .

Of all the things which wisdom acquires to produce the blessedness of the complete life, far the greatest is the possession of friendship.

The same conviction which has given us confidence that there is nothing terrible that lasts for ever or even for long, has also seen the protection of friendship most fully completed in the limited evils of this life. . . .

As many as possess the power to procure complete immunity from their neighbours, these also live most pleasantly with one another, since they have the most certain pledge of security . . . ᵏ

11. From his own diligent application of his ethical theory, Epicurus draws confidence to assure those who follow his teachings that they may expect more than ordinary mortal blessedness.

Some men throughout their lives gather together the means of life, for they do not see that the draught swallowed by all of us at birth is a draught of death. Against all else it is possible to provide security, but as against death all of us mortals alike dwell in an unfortified city. . . .

[But] I have anticipated thee, Fortune, and entrenched myself against all thy secret attacks. And we will not give ourselves up as captives to thee or to any other circumstance; but when it is time for us to go, spitting contempt on life and on those who here vainly cling to it, we will leave life crying aloud in a glorious triumph-song that we have lived well. We must try to make the end of the journey better than the beginning, as long as we are journeying; but when we come to the end, we must be happy and content. . . .

Meditate therefore on these things and things akin to them night and day by yourself, and with a companion like to yourself, and never shall you be disturbed waking or asleep, but you shall live like a god among men. For a man who lives among immortal blessings is not like to a mortal being.[1]

Questions

1. Although Epicurus is a hedonist, he is opposed to the philosophy that teaches, "Eat, drink, and be merry, for tomorrow you die." Reconstruct Epicurus' theory of pleasure so as to account for his opposition to this view. Can you find additional arguments for or against the theory of the sensualistic hedonists?

2. Outline the view of nature which Epicurus adopted from Democritus, stating its premises and noting the changes he made in the original doctrine. How does the atomistic metaphysic fit into Epicurus' ethical theory?

3. What is *ataraxia?* What is its role in the Epicurean ethic, and how is it achieved?

4. Freedom from the fear of death and of the heavy hand of the gods is one of the chief benefits promised by Epicurus' ethics. What conception of death and of the nature of the gods does he offer in order to bring about release from these fears? Do you believe Epicurus' arguments are effective?

5. Discuss the role of the study of philosophy in Epicureanism.

6. What is the significance of Epicurus' assertion that "prudence is more precious than philosophy"?

7. What does Epicurus attempt to accomplish by calling attention to the differences between "natural" and "unnatural" desires? What are the chief differences? How is this distinction related to the contrast between the duration and intensity of pleasures, and between active and passive pleasures?

8. Discuss the role of freedom in Epicurus' ethical theory, especially as an antidote to fatalism.

9. Describe and discuss Epicurus' conception of justice. Is it satisfactory for the organization of an ordinary social group? Why is it unnecessary in the Garden of Epicurus? What activities and values distinguish the Epicurean community from ordinary communities?

10. Draw up a panel of arguments for and against hedonism as an ethical theory, utilizing the ideas of Epicurus for the affirmative, and the ideas of Plato and Aristotle for the negative.

Key to selections:

EPICURUS, *Epicurus: The Extant Remains*, tr. Cyril Bailey, Oxford, The Clarendon Press, 1926. With the kind permission of the publishers.

The following abbreviations are used:

Her. — the letter of *Epicurus to Herodotus;*
Men. — the letter of *Epicurus to Menoeceus;*
P.D. — *Principal Doctrines;*
Frag. — *Fragments.* (Roman Numerals refer to the Vatican collection, Arabic numerals to remains assigned to certain books.)

ª Frag. 54.
ᵇ Her. 39–41,
    54,
    43–44.
ᶜ Her. 63–67.
ᵈ Her. 77–78,
    81–82.
ᵉ Men. 123–124,
  P.D. I,
  Men. 125–126.
ᶠ Men. 129–130,
  Frag. XVI.
ᵍ Men. 127,
  Frag. 74,
  P.D. XXVI,
  P.D. XXX,
  Frag. LXXXI,
  Frag. XXI,

Frag. 45–46, 48,
Frag. 67,
Men. 128.
ʰ Men. 131–132,
  P.D. XVIII–XXI,
  Men. 133.
ⁱ Men. 133,
  P.D. IV,
  Men. 133–135.
ʲ P.D. XXXI–XXXVIII.
ᵏ P.D. VI–VII,
    XIV,
    XXVII–XXVIII,
    XL.
ˡ Frag. XXX–XXXI,
    XLVII–XLVIII,
  Men. 135.

Guide to Additional Reading

INEXPENSIVE EDITIONS OF RELATED WORKS:

LUCRETIUS, *Of the Nature of Things*, Everyman's Library (Dutton).
——, *On the Nature of Things* (Books I–IV), Great Books Foundation (Regnery).

DISCUSSION AND COMMENTARY:

Bailey, C., *The Greek Atomists and Epicurus*, Oxford, The Clarendon Press, 1928.

Dewitt, N. W., *Epicurus and His Philosophy*, Minneapolis, University of Minnesota Press, 1954.

Hicks, R. D., *Stoic and Epicurean*, New York, Charles Scribner's Sons, 1910.

Laertius, Diogenes, *Lives and Opinions of Eminent Philosophers*, tr. R. D. Hicks, Cambridge, Loeb Classical Library, Harvard University Press, 1925.

Murray, G., *Five Stages of Greek Religion*, Oxford, The Clarendon Press, 1925.

Zeller, E., *Stoics, Epicureans and Sceptics*, London, Longmans, Green and Company, Ltd., 1892.

CHAPTER 5

Self-Discipline

EPICTETUS

The philosophy of Epictetus, a Roman Stoic, developed from the teachings of Zeno (336–264 B.C.), who founded the *Stoa Poikile* (Painted Porch), the last of the four most famous schools of ancient Athens. Dependence upon Greek thought is typical of Roman philosophy; in the long history of the Roman Empire, no indigenous philosophies of merit were produced. Of all the Greek philosophical systems transplanted to Rome, Stoicism was probably the most successful. By the close of the second century B.C., the Stoic philosophy was firmly rooted in its new environment, and in the succeeding four centuries, it was accepted by members of both the lower and upper strata of society. It became extremely popular with the Roman soldiery as a philosophy of manly indifference to hardship, and, in addition, it appealed as a "citadel of the soul" to such outstanding intellectuals as Cicero, Seneca, Emperor Marcus Aurelius, and Epictetus. The pressing need for the prophylactic powers of the Stoic philosophy was generated by the sordidness and debauchery of the era, for which one of Epictetus' observations serves well as a description: "[Men] bite and vilify each other, and take possession of public assemblies, as wild beasts do of solitudes and mountains; and convert courts of justice into dens of robbers. [They] are intemperate, adulterers, seducers . . ."

There is but little information about the personal history of Epictetus. The precise date and location of his birth are unknown, but what little evidence there is indicates that he was born in the Greek city of Hierapolis in Phrygia about 50 A.D. It is reported that as a child he was sold into slavery by his parents, and he became part of the household of a profligate Roman soldier. An apt characterization of Epictetus, even as a young man, is given in an anecdote narrated by Origen: Upon one occasion in which his angry master was twisting his leg, Epictetus commented, "You will break my leg," whereupon the master twisted harder and broke the leg. To this, Epictetus rejoined with utter calm, "Did I not tell you so? ' In keeping with Roman practice, Epictetus was allowed to attend the lectures of a contemporary teacher of Stoic philosophy, since he showed great intellectual ability. When his master died, he gained his freedom. By this time, he had already achieved some fame as a philosopher, and elected to remain in Rome as a teacher. When, in 89 A.D., the despotic emperor Domitian forced all philosophers to leave Rome, Epictetus went to Nicopolis. There he started another school, in which he taught until his death in c. 130 A.D.

Epictetus was more distinguished as a lecturer than as a writer. Nothing has been preserved of his original writings; but Arrian, one of his disciples, transcribed his lectures on ethics and had them edited in eight volumes. The most important of these works are the *Discourses of Epictetus* and the *Enchiridion*, or *Manual*. Epictetus' aim was "to excite his hearers to virtue," and when he gave his lectures, we have it from Arrian, "his audience could not help being affected in the very manner he intended they should. '

•

The Stoics identify as the moral man one who lives in accordance with the dictates of reason, and they portray him as a self-sufficient individual, capable of disciplining his desires and of remaining supremely indifferent to life's vicissitudes. In virtue of their moral principles and their conception of the good life, the Stoics regard themselves as belonging in the Socratic tradition. They maintain, as do their forerunners, the Cynics,[1] that the lesson to be drawn from the life and teachings of Socrates is that man's virtue and happiness depend not on material success but on the formation of a character which is true to his essential nature, his *rationality*. Furthermore, the Stoics contend, it is through conduct in conformity with their rational nature that men are united with each other and with the universe. The meaning of the Socratic exhortation, "Know thyself," is then clear, for it is only through self-knowledge that a man can participate in the moral community and fulfill his function in the grand design of the universe.

The Stoic view of the universe, compounded from among a wide range of Greek theories by the founder of the Stoa, Zeno, and his brilliant successors, Cleanthes (*c.* 310–230 B.C.) and Chrysippus (280–209 B.C.), lends support to the Stoic ethic. Drawing chiefly from the doctrines of the early physical philosopher, Heraclitus (*c.* 500 B.C.),[2] they depict the universe as an organic unity in which the form and purpose of each part is determined by God, who is thought of as a rational principle

---

[1] Led by Antisthenes of Athens (*c.* 444–358 B.C.), a disciple of Socrates, the Cynic school subscribed to a doctrine which emphasized self-discipline and stressed virtue for its own sake. The Cynics were convinced of the intrinsic worthlessness of man's ordinary desires and objectives and of the lack of relevance to man's well-being of the dictates of custom and convention.

The negative aspect of the Cynic teachings has been recorded indelibly in the stories about Diogenes of Sinope (*c.* 412–323 B.C.). Diogenes is reputed to have lived in a tub, ignoring all the social amenities, and to have carried a lighted lantern day and night, looking for an honest man. Legend has it that when Alexander the Great rode up to the old Cynic while he was basking in the sun and offered to grant him any favor, Diogenes responded, "Only stand out of my light."

[2] According to Heraclitus, the underlying material of the universe is "ever-living Fire," from which everything comes and to which everything strives to return. However, notwithstanding the fact that the physical universe at any instant is basically nothing but "fire" in constant flux, the cosmic process of transformation is ordered and intelligible, because it conforms to an immutable law of necessity, the *Logos*.

immanent in the whole. The Stoics understand God as both the vital force which creates all things in this internally connected universe and as the cosmic intelligence which governs it from within. This conception of God — called "pantheism" — serves as a basis for the ethical insights of the Stoics, since man, as a rational being is a "fragment torn from God." All men possess the ability to comprehend the divine nature, and the good life consists in living in conformity with it. For, as Epictetus says, "Where the essence of God is, there too is the essence of good. What is the essence of God? . . . Right Reason? Certainly. Here, then, without more ado, seek the essence of good."

Epictetus is more interested than other Roman Stoics in metaphysics and remains more loyal than they to the original position of the Stoa. Nevertheless, his attitude towards speculation about the nature of things is more pious than probing, more religious than philosophical, more practical than theoretical. For Epictetus, man's inherent value, his kinship to God, and his duty to be worthy of his Maker, as well as the hindrances which he encounters in his attempt to live nobly, are the indisputable facts to which the philosopher should direct his attention. The conditions and limitations of the moral life are already given in human nature:

> But what says Zeus? 'Epictetus, if it were possible I would have made your body and your possessions (those trifles that you prize) free and untrammelled. But as things are — never forget this — this body is not yours, it is but a clever mixture of clay. But since I could not make it free, I gave you a portion of our divinity, this faculty of impulse to act and not to act, of will to get and will to avoid . . .' [3]

The mission of the sage is to urge men to examine themselves and to discipline their will to conform to reason.

According to Epictetus, the man who *values virtue for its own sake* is the happy man. Virtue, he tells us, is a condition of the

---

[3] *The Discourses of Epictetus with the Encheiridion and Fragments*, tr. George Long, London, George Bell and Sons, 1877, Book I, Chapter I.

will wherein it is governed by reason, with the result that the virtuous person seeks only those things which are within his power and avoids those things which are beyond it. Unhappiness is the inevitable lot of anyone who desires that which he cannot obtain. The wise man, then, resigns himself to limiting his desires to matters within his control. With respect to desires which cannot be satisfied, he is literally *apathetic, i.e.,* he has no feelings about them. In addition, he knows that *whatever is beyond an individual's control is irrelevant to ethics.* The virtuous man finds within himself all that is necessary to achieve happiness — morally, he is entirely self-sufficient.

In answering the question, "What is within our power?" Epictetus reaffirms one of the distinctive doctrines of Stoicism: it is our *attitudes* towards events, not events themselves, which we can control. Nothing is by its own nature calamitous — even death is terrible only if we fear it. Again, although one may fail to carry out the actions prescribed by divine providence — *i.e.,* in the execution of one's duties, circumstances may prevent a successful outcome — he should remain unconcerned. For example, if because of poverty a man is unable to feed his children, he should not be disturbed as long as he sincerely makes the effort to provide for them. If he *wills* to do his duty, he is fulfilling his obligation, for only this much lies within his power. Moreover, he may be sure that all that happens comes about by divine necessity, and that whatever God does is for the best.

Epictetus, as a moral adviser, counsels us to cultivate an attitude of indifference to good and bad fortune alike, since external events are beyond our control. Therefore, the prudent man does not allow himself to be enslaved by the demands of his body or to become emotionally attached to persons or objects. But we are warned that happiness requires unremitting self-discipline:

Practise yourself, for heaven's sake, in little things; and thence proceed to greater. "I have a pain in my head." Do not lament. "I have a pain in my ear." Do not lament. I do not say you may never groan; but do not groan in spirit; or, if your servant be a long while in bringing you something to bind your head, do not croak and go into hysterics, and

say, "Everybody hates me." For, who would not hate such a one? . . .
Relying for the future on these principles, walk erect and free . . .[a]

• • •

*1. Epictetus maintains that proper perspective in ethics requires
us to understand the metaphysical conception of divine* providence:
*cosmic reason, rather than chance, is the governing principle of all
things. The universe operates according to laws with which human
reason is in harmony and which we should strive to understand.*

What then, after all, is the world? Who governs it? Has it no
governor? How is it possible, when neither a city nor a house can
remain, ever so short a time, without some one to govern and
take care of it, that this vast and beautiful system should be ad-
ministered in a fortuitous and disorderly manner? . . . The philosophers say, that we are first to learn that there is a God; and
that his providence directs the whole; and that it is not merely
impossible to conceal from him our actions, but even our thoughts
and emotions. . . .

. . . He then . . . understands the administration of the universe, and has learned that the principal and greatest and most
comprehensive of all things is this vast system, extending from
men to God; and that from Him the seeds of being are descended,
not only to one's father or grandfather, but to all things that are
produced and born on earth; and especially to rational natures,
as they alone are qualified to partake of a communication with the
Deity, being connected with him by reason . . . All things serve
and obey the (laws of the) universe; the earth, the sea, the sun,
the stars, and the plants and animals of the earth. Our body
likewise obeys the same, in being sick and well, young and old,
and passing through the other changes decreed. It is therefore
reasonable that what depends on ourselves, that is, our own understanding, should not be the only rebel. For the universe is powerful
and superior, and consults the best for us by governing us in
conjunction with the whole. And further; opposition, besides that

it is unreasonable, and produces nothing except a vain struggle, throws us into pain and sorrows.[b]

2. *Since all things are in harmony under divine supervision, it is essential that man, as a "fragment of God," should recognize his proper place and status in the scheme of things.*

. . . A person asked him, how any one might be convinced that his every act is under the supervision of God? Do not you think, said Epictetus, that all things are mutually connected and united?

"I do."

Well; and do not you think, that things on earth feel the influence of the heavenly powers?

"Yes."

Else how is it that in their season, as if by express command, God bids the plants to blossom and they blossom, to bud and they bud, to bear fruit and they bear it, to ripen it and they ripen; — and when again he bids them drop their leaves and withdrawing into themselves to rest and wait, they rest and wait? Whence again are there seen, on the increase and decrease of the moon, and the approach and departure of the sun, so great changes and transformations in earthly things? Have then the very leaves, and our own bodies, this connection and sympathy with the whole; and have not our souls much more? But our souls are thus connected and intimately joined to God, as being indeed members and distinct portions of his essence; and must not he be sensible of every movement of them, as belonging and connatural to himself? Can even you think of the divine administration, and every other divine subject, and together with these of human affairs also; can you at once receive impressions on your senses and your understanding, from a thousand objects; at once assent to some things, deny or suspend your judgment concerning others, and preserve in your mind impressions from so many and various objects, by whose aid you can revert to ideas similar to those which first impressed you? Can you retain a variety of arts and the memorials of ten thousand things? And is not God capable of surveying all things, and being present with all, and in communication with all? Is the sun capable of illuminating so great a portion of the universe, and of leaving only that small part of it unilluminated, which is covered by the shadow of the earth, — and cannot He who made and moves the sun, a small part of himself, if compared with the whole, — cannot he perceive all things?

"But I cannot," say you, "attend to all things at once."

Who asserts that you have equal power with Zeus? Nevertheless he has assigned to each man a director, his own good [spirit], and committed him to that guardianship; a director sleepless and not to be deceived. To what better and more careful guardian could he have committed each one of us? So that when you have shut your doors, and darkened your room, remember, never to say that you are alone; for you are not alone; but God is within . . .

. . . You are a primary existence. You are a distinct portion of the essence of God; and contain a certain part of him in yourself. Why then are you ignorant of your noble birth? Why do not you consider whence you came? Why do not you remember, when you are eating, who you are who eat; and whom you feed? When you are in the company of women; when you are conversing; when you are exercising; when you are disputing; do not you know, that it is the Divine you feed; the Divine you exercise? You carry a God about with you, poor wretch, and know nothing of it. Do you suppose I mean some god without you of gold or silver? It is within yourself that you carry him; and you do not observe that you profane him by impure thoughts and unclean actions. If the mere external image of God were present, you would not dare to act as you do; and when God himself is within you, and hears and sees all, are not you ashamed to think and act thus; insensible of your own nature, and at enmity with God? [c]

3. Through his pantheism, Epictetus introduces into his ethical theory a strain which is cosmopolitan: he maintains that since men, as rational beings, are part of the universal city of God, or cosmic reason, each man is a part of the whole and as such should recognize his duty to all his fellow men.

We should reason in some such manner concerning ourselves. Who are you? A man. If then, indeed, you consider yourself isolatedly, it is natural that you should live to old age, should be prosperous and healthy; but if you consider yourself as a man, and as a part of the whole, it will be fit, in view of that whole, that you should at one time be sick; at another, take a voyage, and be exposed to danger; sometimes be in want; and possibly die before your time. Why, then, are you displeased? Do not you know, that otherwise . . . you are no longer a man? For what is a man? A part of a commonwealth; first and chiefly of that which includes both gods and men; and next, of that to which you immediately belong, which is a miniature of the universal city. . . . You are a citizen of the universe, and a part of it; not a subordinate, but a principal part. You are capable of comprehending the Divine economy; and of considering the connections of things. What then does the character of a citizen imply? To hold no private interest; to deliberate of nothing as a separate individual, but rather like the hand or the foot, which, if they had reason, and comprehended the constitution of nature, would never pursue, or desire, but with a reference to the whole. Hence the philosophers rightly say, that, if it were possible for a wise and good man to foresee what was to happen, he might co-operate in bringing on himself sickness, and death, and mutilation, being sensible that these things are appointed in the order of the universe; and that the whole is superior to a part, and the city to the citizen. But, since we do not foreknow what is to happen, it becomes our duty to hold to what is more agreeable to our choice, for this too is a part of our birthright.[d]

4. In order to live in a manner befitting our rational nature, we must "make the best of what is in our power, and take the rest as it occurs." For Epictetus, the faculty of will *is within man's control and constitutes the ultimate source of ethical behavior.*

Man, be not ungrateful, nor, on the other hand, unmindful of your superior advantages; but for sight, and hearing, and indeed for life itself, and the supports of it, as fruits, and wine, and oil, be thankful to God; but remember that He hath given you another thing, superior to them all, which uses them, proves them, estimates the value of each. For what is it that pronounces upon the value of each of these faculties? Is it the faculty itself? Did you ever perceive the faculty of sight or hearing, to say anything concerning itself? Or wheat, or barley, or horses, or dogs? No. These things are appointed as instruments and servants, to obey that which is capable of using things as they appear. If you inquire the value of anything; of what do you inquire? What is the faculty that answers you? How then can any faculty be superior to this, which uses all the rest as instruments, and tries and pronounces concerning each of them? For which of them knows what itself is; and what is its own value? Which of them knows, when it is to be used, and when not? Which is it, that opens and shuts the eyes, and turns them away from improper objects? Is it the faculty of sight? No; but that of Will. Which is it, that opens and shuts the ears? Which is it, by which they are made curious and inquisitive; or on the contrary deaf, and unaffected by what is said? Is it the faculty of hearing? No; but that of Will. This, then, recognizing itself to exist amidst other faculties, all blind and deaf, and unable to discern anything but those offices, in which they are appointed to minister and serve; itself alone sees clearly, and distinguishes the value of each of the rest. Will this, I say, inform us, that anything is supreme, but itself? What can the eye, when it is opened, do more than see? But whether we ought to look upon the wife of any one, and in what manner, what is it that decides us? The faculty of Will. Whether we ought to believe, or disbelieve what is said; or whether, if we do believe, we ought to be moved by it, or not, what is it that decides us? Is it not the faculty of Will? Again; the very faculty of eloquence, and that which ornaments discourse, if any such peculiar faculty there be, what does it more than merely ornament and arrange expressions, as curlers do the hair? But whether it be better to speak, or to be silent; or better to speak in this, or in that manner; whether this be decent, or indecent; and the season and use of each; what is it that decides for us, but the faculty of Will? What then, would you have it appear, and bear testimony against itself? What means this? If the case be thus, then that which serves may be superior to that to which it is subservient; the horse to the rider; the dog to the hunter; the instrument to the musician; or servants to the king. What is it that makes use of all the rest? The Will. What takes care of all? The Will. What destroys the whole man, at one time, by hunger; at another, by a rope, or a precipice? The Will. Has man, then, anything stronger than this? And how is it possible, that what is liable to restraint should be stronger than what is not? What has a natural power to restrain the faculty of sight? The Will and its workings. And it is the same with the faculties of hearing and of speech. And what has a natural power of restraining the Will? Nothing beyond itself, only its own perversion. Therefore in the Will alone is vice: in the Will alone is virtue.[e]

5. In establishing the metaphysical and moral primacy of the will, Epictetus undermines the philosophy of Epicurus. The doctrine that matter is the most excellent and real thing, he points out, can have been asserted only if its author had the will *to do so.*

Since, then, the Will is such a faculty, and placed in authority over all the rest, suppose it to come forth and say to us, that the body is, of all things, the most excellent! If even the body itself pronounced itself to be the most excellent, it could not be borne. But now, what is it, Epicurus, that pronounces all this? What was it, that composed volumes concerning "the End," "the Nature of things," "the Rule"; that assumed a philosophic beard; that, as it was dying, wrote, that it was "then spending its last and happiest day"? Was this the body, or was it the faculty of Will? And can you, then, without madness, admit anything to be superior to this? Are you in reality so deaf and blind? What, then, does any one dishonor the other faculties? Heaven forbid! Does any one assert that there is no use or excellence in the faculty of sight? Heaven forbid! It would be stupid, impious, and ungrateful to God. But we render to each its due. There is some use in an ass, though not so much as in an ox; and in a dog, though not so much as in a servant: and in a servant, though not so much as in the citizens; and in the citizens, though not so much as in the magistrates. And though some are more excellent than others, those uses, which the last afford, are not to be despised. The faculty of eloquence has thus its value, though not equal to that of the Will. When therefore I talk thus, let not any one suppose, that I would have you neglect eloquence, any more than your eyes, or ears, or hands, or feet, or clothes, or shoes. But if you ask me what is the most excellent of things, what shall I say? I cannot say, eloquence, but a right Will; for it is this which makes use of that, and of all the other faculties, whether great or small. If this be set right, a bad man becomes good; if it be wrong, a good man becomes wicked. By this we are unfortunate or fortunate; we disapprove or approve each other. In a word, it is this which, neglected, forms unhappiness; and, well cultivated, happiness.[f]

6. *The avoidance of frustration and disappointment requires both the* control of those things which are in our power — *our attitudes and reactions to things* — *and the* avoidance of those things which are beyond our control — *externals such as wealth and fame. Epictetus explains frustration as the consequence of false judgments of things, by which we are led to attempt to control what is actually uncontrollable by us.*

There are things which are within our power, and there are things which are beyond our power. Within our power are opinion, aim, desire, aversion, and, in one word, whatever affairs are our own. Beyond our power are body, property, reputation, office, and, in one word, whatever are not properly our own affairs.

Now the things within our power are by nature free, unrestricted, unhindered; but those beyond our power are weak, dependent, restricted, alien. Remember then, that, if you attribute freedom to things by nature dependent, and take what belongs to others for your own, you will be hindered, you will lament, you will be disturbed, you will find fault both with Gods and men. But if you take for your own only that which is your own, and view what belongs to others just as it really is, then no one will ever compel you, no one will restrict you, you will find fault with no one, you will accuse no one, you will do nothing against your will; no one will hurt you, you will not have an enemy, nor will you suffer any harm.

Aiming therefore at such great things, remember that you must not allow yourself any inclination, however slight, towards the attainment of the others; but that you must entirely quit some of them, and for the present postpone the rest. But if you would have these, and possess power and wealth likewise, you may miss the latter in seeking the former; and you will certainly fail of that, by which alone happiness and freedom are procured.

Seek at once, therefore, to be able to say to every unpleasing semblance, "You are but a semblance and by no means the real thing." And then examine it by those rules which you have; and first and chiefly, by this: whether it concerns the things which are within our own power, or those which are not; and if it concerns anything beyond our power, be prepared to say that it is nothing to you.

Remember that desire demands the attainment of that of which you are desirous; and aversion demands the avoidance of that to which you are averse; that he who fails of the object of his desires, is disappointed; and he who incurs the object of his aversion, is wretched. If, then, you shun only those undesirable things which you can control, you will never incur anything which you shun. But if you shun sickness, or death, or poverty, you will run the risk of wretchedness. Remove aversion, then, from all things that are not within our power, and transfer it to things undesirable, which are within our power. But for the present altogether restrain desire; for if you desire any of the things not within our own power, you must necessarily be disappointed; and you are not yet secure of those which are within our power, and so are legitimate objects of desire. Where it is practically necessary for you to pursue or avoid anything, do even this with discretion, and gentleness, and moderation.⁸

7. If the free, happy individual is one who confines his desires to those things which depend upon his own will and who is thus in harmony with God's will, then even death will appear trivial. For, the proper attitude towards such events will be one of apathy — *indifference, imperturbability. After all, Epictetus argues, every event follows from the divine nature with logical necessity, and, therefore only men's judgments of things cause distress. One should accept with equanimity what is inevitable; no event is terrible when viewed by the disciplined mind.*

[Remember] that such is, and was, and will be, the nature of the world, nor is it possible that things should be otherwise than they now are; and that not only men and other creatures upon earth partake of this change and transformation, but diviner things also. For indeed even the four elements are transformed and metamorphosed; and earth becomes water, and water air, and this again is transformed into other things. And the same manner of transformation happens from things above to those below. Whoever endeavors to turn his mind towards these points, and persuade himself to receive with willingness what cannot be avoided, will pass his life in moderation and harmony. . . . Remember that you are an actor in a drama of such sort as the author chooses. If short, then in a short one; if long, then in a long one. If it be his pleasure that you should act a poor man, see that you act it well; or a cripple, or a ruler, or a private citizen. For this is your business, to act well the given part; but to choose it, belongs to another. . . .

. . . You hear the vulgar say, "Such a one, poor soul! is dead." Well, his father died: his mother died. "Ay, but he was cut off in the flower of his age, and in a foreign land." Observe these contrary ways of speaking; and abandon such expressions. Oppose to one custom, a contrary custom; to sophistry, the art of reasoning, and the frequent use and exercise of it. Against specious appearances we must set clear convictions, bright and ready for use. When death appears as an evil, we ought immediately to remember, that evils are things to be avoided, but death is inevitable. For what can I do, or where can I fly from it? . . . Whither shall I fly from death? Show me the place, show me the people, to whom I may have recourse, whom death does not overtake. Show me the charm to avoid it. If there be none, what would you have me do? I cannot escape death; but cannot I escape the dread of it? Must I die trembling, and lamenting? For the very origin of the disease lies in wishing for something that is not obtained. Under the influence of this, if I can make outward things conform to my own inclination, I do it; if not, I feel inclined to tear out the eyes of whoever hinders me. For it is the nature of man not to endure the being deprived of good; not to endure the falling into evil. And so, at last, when I can neither control events, nor tear out the eyes of him who hinders me, I sit down, and groan, and revile him whom I can; Zeus, and the rest of the gods. For what are they to me, if they take no care of me? . . .

Men are disturbed not by things, but by the views which they take of things. Thus death is nothing terrible . . . But the terror consists in our notion of death, that it is terrible. When, therefore, we are hindered, or disturbed, or grieved, let us never impute it to others, but to ourselves; that is, to our own views. It is the action of an uninstructed person to reproach others for his own misfortunes; of one entering upon instruction, to reproach himself; and of one perfectly instructed, to reproach neither others nor himself. . . . Demand not that events should happen as you wish; but wish them to happen as they do happen, and you will go on well.[h]

8. Epictetus observes that a person who is resigned to the limitations of human power and the inevitability of all that occurs will not give way to sorrow at his own misfortunes or those of others.

The only real thing is, to study how to rid life of lamentation, and complaint, and *Alas!* and *I am undone*, and misfortune, and failure; and to learn what death, what exile, what a prison, what poison is; that he may be able to say in a prison, like Socrates, "My dear Crito, if it thus pleases the gods, thus let it be"; and not, "Wretched old man, have I kept my gray hairs for this!" [Do you ask] who speaks thus? Do you think I quote some mean and despicable person? Is it not Priam who says it? Is it not Oedipus? Nay, how many kings say it? For what else is tragedy, but the dramatized sufferings of men, bewildered by an admiration of externals? If one were to be taught by fictions, that things beyond our will are nothing to us, I should rejoice in such a fiction, by which I might live prosperous and serene. . . . When you see any one weeping for grief, either that his son has gone abroad, or that he has suffered in his affairs; take care not to be overcome by the apparent evil. But discriminate, and be ready to say, "What hurts this man is not this occurrence itself, for another man might not be hurt by it; — but the view he chooses to take of it." As far as conversation goes, however, do not disdain to accommodate yourself to him, and if need be, to groan with him. Take heed, however, not to groan inwardly too.[i]

9. Epictetus advocates the life of self-control — i.e., mastery of one's desires — and the possession of a virtuous disposition. For, "It is not poverty that causes sorrow, but covetous desires. . . . Nothing is meaner than the love of pleasure, the love of gain, and indolence. Nothing is nobler than magnanimity, meekness, and philanthropy." This is in direct opposition to the hedonistic view of the Epicureans.

[We represent] those intractable philosophers who do not think pleasure to be in itself the natural state of man; but merely an incident of those things in which his natural state consists, — justice, moderation, and freedom. Why, then, should the soul rejoice and be glad in the minor blessings of the body, as Epicurus says, and not be pleased with its own good, which is the very greatest? And yet Nature has given me likewise a sense of shame; and I am covered with blushes when I think I have uttered any indecent expression. This emotion will not suffer me to recognize pleasure as a good and the end of life. . . . If you are dazzled by the semblance of any promised pleasure, guard yourself against being bewildered by it; but let the affair wait your leisure, and procure yourself some delay. Then bring to your mind both points of time; that in which you shall enjoy the pleasure, and that in which you will repent and reproach yourself, after you have enjoyed it; and set before you, in opposition to these, how you will rejoice and applaud yourself, if you abstain. And even though it should appear to you a seasonable gratification, take heed that its enticements and allurements and seductions may not subdue you; but set in opposition to this, how much better it is to be conscious of having gained so great a victory. . . . Chastise your passions, that they may not chastise you. . . . It belongs to a wise man to resist pleasure; and to a fool to be enslaved by it.[j]

10. Having given warning that hedonism is a false doctrine, Epictetus tells us that "two rules we should have always ready — that there is nothing good or evil save in the will; and, that we are not to lead events, but to follow them." Employing these rules, the wise man will guard the virtues which are his only true possessions and the source of his serenity, and he will avoid the disappointments and disturbances which plague those who pursue externals like fame, honors, and wealth.

When you have lost anything external, have always at hand the consideration of what you have got instead of it; and if that be of more value, do not by any means call yourself a loser; whether it be a horse for an ass; an ox for a sheep; a good action for a piece of money; a due composure of mind for a dull jest; or modesty for indecent talk. By continually remembering this, you will preserve your character such as it ought to be. Otherwise, consider that you are spending your time in vain; and all that to which you are now applying your mind, you are about to spill and overturn. And there needs but little, merely a small deviation from reason, to destroy and overset all. A pilot does not need so much apparatus to overturn a ship as to save it; but if he exposes it a little too much to the wind, it is lost; even if he should not do it by design, but only for a moment be thinking of something else, it is lost. Such is the case here, too. If you do but nod a little, all that you have hitherto accomplished is gone. Take heed, then, to the appearances of things. Keep yourself watchful over them. It is no inconsiderable matter that you have to guard; but modesty, fidelity, constancy, docility, innocence, fearlessness, serenity; in short, freedom. For what will you sell these? Consider what the purchase is worth. "But shall I not get such a thing instead of it?" Consider, if you do not get it, what it is that you have instead. Suppose I have decency, and another the office of tribune; I have modesty, and he the praetorship? But I do not applaud where it is unbecoming; I will pay no undeserved honor; for I am free, and the friend of God, so as to obey him willingly; but I must not value anything else, neither body, nor possessions, nor fame; in short, nothing. For it is not His will that I should value them. For if this had been His pleasure, He would have placed in them my good, which now He hath not done; therefore I cannot transgress his commands. Seek in all things your own highest good, — and for other aims, recognize them as far as the case requires, and in accordance with reason, contented with this alone. Otherwise you will be unfortunate, disappointed, restrained, hindered." These are the established laws, these the statutes. Of these one ought to be an expositor, and to these obedient . . .[k]

11. Epictetus outlines the proper subject matter of philosophy and emphasizes the importance of the application of ethical theory to actual behavior: "It is not reasonings that are wanted now, for there are books stuffed full of stoical reasonings. 'What is wanted, then?' The man who shall apply them; whose actions may bear testimony to his doctrines."

There are three topics in philosophy, in which he who would be wise and good must be exercised. That of the *desires* and *aversions*, that he may not be disappointed of the one, nor incur the other.

That of the *pursuits* and *avoidances*, and, in general, the duties of life; that he may act with order and consideration, and not carelessly. The third includes integrity of mind and prudence, and, in general, whatever belongs to the judgment.

Of these points, the principal and most urgent is that which reaches the passions; for passion is produced no otherwise than by a disappointment of one's desires and an incurring of one's aversions. It is this which introduces perturbations, tumults, misfortunes, and calamities; this is the spring of sorrow, lamentation, and envy; this renders us envious and emulous, and incapable of hearing reason.

The next topic regards the duties of life. For I am not to be undisturbed by passions, in the same sense as a statue is; but as one who preserves the natural and acquired relations; as a pious person, as a son, as a brother, as a father, as a citizen.

The third topic belongs to those scholars who are now somewhat advanced; and is a security to the other two, that no bewildering semblance may surprise us, either in sleep, or wine, or in depression. . . .

[But] — Philosophy . . . doth not promise to procure any outward good for man; otherwise it would admit something beyond its proper theme. For as the material of a carpenter is wood; of a statuary, brass; so of the art of living, the material is each man's own life.

"What, then, is my brother's life?"

That, again, is matter for his own art, but is external to you; like property, health, or reputation. Philosophy promises none of these. . . . The beginning of philosophy, at least to such as enter upon it in a proper way, and by the door, is a consciousness of our own weakness and inability in necessary things. For we came into the world without any natural idea of a right-angled triangle; of a diesis, or a semitone, in music; but we learn each of these things by some artistic instruction. Hence, they who do not understand them, do not assume to understand them. But who ever came into the world without an innate idea of good and evil; fair and base; becoming and unbecoming; happiness and misery; proper and improper; what ought to be done, and what not to be done? Hence we all make use of the terms, and endeavor to apply our impressions to particular cases. "Such a one hath acted well, not well; right, not right; is unhappy, is happy; is just, is unjust." Which of us refrains from these terms? Who defers the use of them, till he has learnt it; as those do, who are ignorant of lines and sounds? The reason of this is, that we come instructed, in some degree, by nature, upon these subjects; and from this beginning, we go on to add self-conceit. "For why," say you, "should I not know what fair or base is? Have I not the idea of it?" You have. "Do I not apply this idea to the particular instance?" You do. "Do I not apply it rightly then?" Here lies the whole question; and here arises the self-conceit. Beginning from these acknowledged points, men proceed, by applying them improperly, to reach the very position most questionable. For, if they knew how to apply them also, they would be all but perfect. . . . What seems to each man, is not sufficient to determine the reality of a thing. For even in weights and measures we are not satisfied with the bare appearance; but for everything we find some rule. And is there then, in the present case, no rule preferable to what seems? Is it possible, that what is of the greatest necessity in human life, should be left incapable of determination and discovery?

There must be some rule. And why do we not seek and discover it, and, when we have discovered, ever after make use of it, without fail, so as not even to move a finger without it. For this, I conceive, is what, when found, will cure those of their madness, who make use of no other measure, but their own perverted way of thinking. Afterwards, beginning from certain known and determinate points, we may make use of general principles, properly applied to particulars.

Thus, what is the subject that falls under our inquiry? Pleasure. Bring it to the rule. Throw it into the scale. Must good be something in which it is fit to confide, and to which we may trust? Yes. Is it fit to trust to anything unstable? No. Is pleasure, then, a stable thing? No. Take it, then, and throw it out of the scale, and drive it far distant from the place of good things.

But, if you are not quick-sighted, and one balance is insufficient, bring another. Is it fit to be elated by good? Yes. Is it fit, then, to be elated by a present pleasure? See that you do not say it is; otherwise I shall not think you so much as worthy to use a scale Thus are things judged, and weighed, when we have the rules ready. This is the part of philosophy, to examine, and fix the rules; and to make use of them, when they are known, is the business of a wise and good man.[1]

Questions

1. Outline the most important features of the Stoic ethic. Do these factors account for the fact that a slave and an emperor could both be Stoics?

2. What is the relationship between Stoic metaphysics and Stoic ethics? Do you think that rationalism and pantheism necessarily result in an ethical theory that values "virtue for its own sake"?

3. Explain and discuss the Stoic doctrine that virtue consists in living "according to nature." Can you define "nature" in such a way that this doctrine would no longer be acceptable?

4. Discuss critically Epictetus' recommendation that we "make the best of what is in our power, and take the rest as it occurs." What things are within our control, according to the Stoics?

5. Describe in detail what the Stoics mean by "apathy." Do you believe this is the most satisfactory state men can achieve?

6. If a debate between Epictetus and Epicurus could be arranged, what arguments would each put forward against the moral philosophy of the other? Could they agree on any major issues of theory? Could they agree on any major principles of conduct?

7. How does Epictetus conceive of the proper subject matter of philosophy? Which is more important to him, the activity of reasoning or acting according to reason? Would he, accordingly, agree or disagree with Plato's tenet, "virtue is knowledge"?

8. How true to the original doctrines of the Stoics is the term "stoic" as it is commonly used today?

9. The Stoics are credited with influencing considerably the development of international law. Examine their ethical doctrines for the principles which account for this contribution. Can you find further political implications of the Stoic ethic?

10. (a) Do you think the Stoics influenced the thinking of the early
        Christians?
    (b) Do you think that a revival of stoicism in our times is a reason-
        able possibility? Justify your answers by referring to specific
        Stoic doctrines.

Key to selections:

EPICTETUS, *The Works of Epictetus*, tr. Thomas Wentworth Higginson,
Boston, Little, Brown, and Co., 1866.

The following abbreviations are used:
Dis. — *The Discourses;*
Ench. — *The Enchiridion;*
Frag. — *Fragments.*

^a Dis.   Bk. I, Ch. XVIII.   Ench. XVII,
^b Dis.   Bk. II, Ch. XIV,   Dis.   Bk. I, Ch. XXVII,
              Bk. I, Ch. IX,   Ench. V, VIII.
      Frag. CXXXI.   ⁱ Dis.   Bk. I, Ch. IV,
^c Dis.   Bk. I, Ch. XIV,   Ench. XVI.
              Bk. II, Ch. VIII.   ^j Frag. XLVII,
^d Dis.   Bk. II, Ch. V,   Ench. XXXIV,
              Bk. II, Ch. X.   Frag. IV, CVI.
^e Dis.   Bk. II, Ch. XXIII.   ^k Dis.   Bk. IV, Ch. III.
^f Dis.   Bk. II, Ch. XXIII.   ^l Dis.   Bk. III, Ch. II,
^g Ench. I, II.   Bk. I, Ch. XV,
^h Frag. CXXIX,   Bk. II, Ch. XI.

Guide to Additional Reading

INEXPENSIVE EDITIONS:

EPICTETUS, *Enchiridion*, Little Library of Liberal Arts (Liberal Arts
        Press).
——, *Moral Discourses*, Everyman's Library (Dutton).

INEXPENSIVE EDITIONS OF RELATED WORKS:

Marcus Aurelius, *Meditations*, Everyman's Library (Dutton).
        ——,   ——, Great Books Foundation (Regnery).

Marcus Aurelius, *Meditations*, Masterpieces of Literature (Collins).
———,   ———, World's   Classics   (Oxford   University
    Press).

DISCUSSION AND COMMENTARY:

Arnold, E. V., *Roman Stoicism*, Cambridge, Cambridge University Press,
    1911.
Bevan, E., *Stoics and Sceptics*, Oxford, The Clarendon Press, 1913.
Hicks, R. D., *Stoic and Epicurean*, New York, Charles Scribner's Sons,
    1910.
Laertius, Diogenes, *Lives and Opinions of Eminent Philosophers*, tr. R. D.
    Hicks, Cambridge, Loeb Classical Library, Harvard University Press,
    1925.
Zeller, E., *Stoics, Epicureans and Sceptics*, London, Longmans, Green
    and Company, Ltd., 1892.

CHAPTER **6**

The Love of God

SAINT
AUGUSTINE

Saint Augustine (354–430) lived in a crucial period in the history of Christianity: in 313, the emperor Constantine granted liberty of worship to Christians, and in 325 the Council of Nicaea defined basic Christian doctrine, declaring all other interpretations heretical. In the attempt to put down heresies, Saint Augustine was a powerful influence. He was born in Tagaste, a small town in North Africa. His mother, though not his father, was a Christian, and until Saint Augustine's conversion to Christianity in his thirty-second year, his life followed the pattern typical of the young Roman provincial of the times. However, his boyhood pranks, his pride in his proficiency in the schools of the Roman rhetoricians, and his indulgence in sensual pleasure became a source of self-reproach when he viewed them in retrospect as a mature man and pious Christian.

Before his conversion, Saint Augustine was a highly successful teacher of rhetoric. During this phase of his career, his philosophical position shifted several times in his search for a satisfactory set of beliefs. He joined for a time the sect of Manichaeans, who explained the universe through the dualistic doctrine of God and

Satan engaged in a struggle to dominate the world. Dissatisfied with their answers to the questions which troubled him, he turned to Greek philosophy and in particular to Neo-Platonism. Here, he met with no better success, although the Neo-Platonic teachings later stood him in good stead. He rejected the pantheistic conception that man's soul is part of the World-Soul, but incorporated in his own theory of knowledge the Neo-Platonic doctrine that the ultimate in knowledge is a mystical intuition of the Supreme Reality, which only a few can experience. Saint Augustine came at last under the influence of Saint Ambrose, Bishop of Milan, who reinforced the efforts of the young man's mother, Monica, to turn him to Christianity. A decisive inner experience resulted in his conversion in 386, and he was baptized by Saint Ambrose the following year.

Saint Augustine entered the priesthood in 391, rising in the course of time to become Bishop of Hippo. He applied his great talent as a thinker and writer and his knowledge of philosophy to the study of the Holy Scriptures and other teachings of his new religion, producing numerous works on Christian doctrine. His *Confessions*, while they contain abundant autobiographical detail, are primarily a eulogy of God and a declaration of devotion and love for Him. *The City of God*, on the other hand, is an extensive philosophy of history in the framework of the Christian religion, and it functions as an elaborate theodicy — a justification of the ways of God to man. The *Enchiridion*, a work of his later years, is a manual in which he sets forth the meaning of the virtues of faith, hope, and love. The clearest expression of Saint Augustine's theory of knowledge is to be found in the work, *De Musica*. His other contributions to Christian philosophy and theology include the treatises, *On the Nature of God*, *On Free Will*, *On the Immortality of the Soul*, *On Nature and Grace*, and *On the Trinity*.

The teachings of Saint Augustine dominated Christian belief almost exclusively for more than nine centuries, after which the scholastic philosophy of Saint Thomas Aquinas (1225–1274) shared dominion with it.

Saint Augustine is the first Christian philosopher to formulate the doctrines of his religion in a comprehensive and enduring world-view. In elaborating the Christian revelation, he dedicates himself to the task of showing the way to the spiritual safety and happiness of salvation. Consequently, he carries on an unrelenting campaign to root out the heretical beliefs which mislead men in their search for the true religion. In addition, Saint Augustine undertakes the construction of a reasoned defense against charges of paradoxes, contradictions, and absurdities in Christian doctrine. The accomplishment of his task is facilitated by an effective assimilation of Greek philosophy to Christian belief.[1]

The Christian creed which is the basis of Saint Augustine's writings is contained in God's revelation as set forth in the Old and New Testaments of the Bible. Its metaphysical and ethical focus is God, the omnipotent, omniscient, and benevolent Creator of man and the universe. Man, created only "a little lower than the angels," was endowed with free will and was therefore able to choose between good and evil. Adam, the first man, chose evil, thus falling from God's favor, and his original sin is inherited by all mankind. The punishment for sin is eternal death, but God in His mercy provides the possibility of redemption through union with His Son, Jesus Christ, man's Saviour. Jesus assumes the burden of the original sin of those who have faith in Him, but men must also follow His example of humility, respect, and obedience to God's commandments. The reward of those who are infused with the Holy Spirit of God is eternal life.

The works of Saint Augustine are permeated by the gospel of love which unifies and illuminates the Christian religion. The personal, passional aspect of his love of God finds frequent expression in the *Confessions:* "Thou hast stricken my heart with Thy word, and I loved Thee. And also the heaven and earth, and

---

[1] Three important examples of Saint Augustine's adaptation of concepts from Greek philosophy are: (1) the incorporation of Plato's conception of the "Good" in the characterization of God, (2) the use of the Neo-Platonic idea of the mediating function of the *Logos* (the Cosmic Reason or Divine Word), in interpreting the role of Jesus Christ in the Holy Trinity, and (3) the use of the Neo-Platonic definition of evil as the absence of good in the resolution of the "problem of evil."

all that is therein, behold, on every side, they say that I should love Thee . . . " And, as an article of faith, the love of God and the related love of our neighbor is treated by Saint Augustine as an indispensable constituent of Christian doctrine:

All the commandments of God, then, are embraced in love, of which the apostle says: "Now the end of the commandment is charity, out of a pure heart, and of a good conscience, and of faith unfeigned." Thus the end of every commandment is charity, that is, every commandment has love for its aim. . . . This love embraces both the love of God and the love of our neighbor, and "on these two commandments hang all the law and the prophets," we may add the Gospel and the apostles. For it is from these that we hear this voice: The end of the commandment is charity, and God is love.[a]

In loving God, Saint Augustine tells us, we love truth. On the attainment of true knowledge, men will discover as he did that, "where I found truth, there I found my God, who is truth itself . . ." Men come to know truth through inner experience and conviction. Moreover, they must make an effort of will to prepare the mind to receive truth. Saint Augustine maintains that one cannot obtain true knowledge without faith: one should first believe in order to understand. The intellectual knowledge of God, however, does not by itself suffice for the perfect and ultimate comprehension of Him which is man's happiness. For this, one must go beyond reason to mystical vision, the spiritual seeing of God which transcends reason. Faith, knowledge, and mystical vision may be conceived as progressive steps on the way to the transcendental understanding of God, who is the essence of all truth.

Knowledge of God is indispensable to man's blessedness, but, Saint Augustine holds, it is false pride for anyone to believe that he can know God by his own efforts. Only when God by His grace illuminates the mind can it grasp the truth. Similarly, salvation can be achieved only through God's grace. In the Augustinian theology, each man is predestined by God either to salvation or to damnation. Since all men are stained with original sin, they deserve only punishment. Consequently, salvation is a free gift of God bestowed upon the chosen few. Without divine grace, neither faith nor good works can assure salvation. No human mind can penetrate the mystery of God's wisdom in electing some but not others to be saved. Trusting in God's goodness, and despite the fact that we cannot judge whether we will be saved or not, we are obligated to seek God and to live according to His commandments.[2]

The struggle of man to turn away from evil and seek the good is described by Saint Augustine in *The City of God*. The whole history of mankind from the fall of man to the Last Judgment is depicted as a conflict between the "City of God" and the "City of Man." Those who live in the earthly city pursue material interests and carnal pleasures. They suffer not only the frustrations brought about by their false beliefs while on earth, but also endure the everlasting alienation from God which is the punishment of the sinful. By contrast, the citizens of the City of God form a "mystical and unanimous society of saints in Heaven and believers on Earth." Through the redemptive mission of Jesus Christ, God's True Word, they enjoy both spiritual peace on earth and the eternal blessedness of the vision of God which is man's true happiness.

. . .

1. In the support and defense of Christian doctrine, Saint Augustine is obliged to resolve some of the most troublesome metaphysical problems of ethics. Among these, perhaps the most crucial challenge to the effectiveness of his ethical theory and a natural point of entry into his entire moral philosophy is the so-called "problem of evil," viz., how to reconcile the existence of evil in the world with the omnipotence and benevolence of God. The paradoxical nature of this problem is clearly evident from the formulation of it attributed to the Greek philosopher, Epicurus:

[2] There is an unreconciled conflict between Saint Augustine's theological doctrine of divine predestination, with its implication of human impotency, and his philosophical defense of human freedom of will, with its implication of moral responsibility.

Either God would remove evil out of this world, and cannot: or He can, and will not; or, He has not the power nor will; or, lastly, He has both the power and will. If He has the will, and not the power, this shows weakness, which is contrary to the nature of God. If He has the power, and not the will, it is malignity, and this is no less contrary to His nature. If He is neither able nor willing, He is both impotent and malignant, and consequently cannot be God. If He be both willing and able (which alone is consonant to the nature of God), whence comes evil, or why does He not prevent it? [3]

As a starting point for his treatment of the problem of evil, Saint Augustine insists that God is perfectly good and all things come from Him. Since God in His goodness cannot create anything evil, it follows that evil cannot be a positive characteristic of things. However, the things which God creates are less than wholly good, and they are evil only insofar as they lack goodness.

What is called evil in the universe is but the absence of good: . . . In the bodies of animals, disease and wounds mean nothing but the absence of health; for when a cure is effected, that does not mean that the evils which were present — namely, the diseases and wounds — go away from the body and dwell elsewhere: they altogether cease to exist; for the wound or disease is not a substance, but a defect in the fleshly substance — the flesh itself being a substance, and therefore something good, of which those evils — that is, privations of the good which we call health — are accidents. Just in the same way, what are called vices in the soul are nothing but privations of natural good. And when they are cured, they are not transferred elsewhere: when they cease to exist in the healthy soul, they cannot exist anywhere else.

[3] Various answers to the paradoxical problem of evil have been given in its long and controversial history: (1) if the reality of evil is denied, it follows that there is no paradox — as, for example, when it is argued that what appears evil to man is really good in the overall view of the universe; (2) if it is conceded that God's power is finite, then the existence of evil is not paradoxical; (3) if it is held that man's limited intellect cannot grasp the mystery, then he must trust in God's goodness and accept the paradox unresolved; (4) if as Saint Augustine asserts, God is both supremely good and all-powerful, and yet evil is not illusory, the paradox can be attacked by defining evil as nothing more than the absence of good.

*All beings were made good, but not being made perfectly good, are
liable to corruption:* All things that exist, therefore, seeing that the
Creator of them all is supremely good, are themselves good. But
because they are not, like their Creator, supremely and unchange-
ably good, their good may be diminished and increased. But for
good to be diminished is an evil, although, however much it may
be diminished, it is necessary, if the being is to continue, that some
good should remain to constitute the being. For however small
or of whatever kind the being may be, the good which makes it a
being cannot be destroyed without destroying the being itself.
An uncorrupted nature is justly held in esteem. But if, still
further, it be incorruptible, it is undoubtedly considered of still
higher value. When it is corrupted, however, its corruption is an
evil, because it is deprived of some sort of good. For if it be deprived of no good, it receives no injury; but it does receive
injury, therefore it is deprived of good. Therefore, so long as a
being is in process of corruption, there is in it some good of which
it is being deprived; and if a part of the being should remain
which cannot be corrupted, this will certainly be an incorruptible
being, and accordingly the process of corruption will result in
the manifestation of this great good. But if it do not cease to be
corrupted, neither can it cease to possess good of which corruption
may deprive it. But if it should be thoroughly and completely
consumed by corruption, there will then be no good left, because
there will be no being. Wherefore corruption can consume the
good only by consuming the being. Every being, therefore, is a
good; a great good, if it cannot be corrupted; a little good, if it
can: but in any case, only the foolish or ignorant will deny that
it is a good. And if it be wholly consumed by corruption, then the
corruption itself must cease to exist, as there is no being left in
which it can dwell.[b]

2. *Nevertheless, it still remains to resolve another part of the problem of evil. If God is able to do all things, why does He permit man
to choose evil? Or, if God is free to do whatsoever He will, why should
He will evil? Saint Augustine argues that since God is all-powerful,*

He can prevent evil if He so wills, so that His permitting evil must reflect His goodness in some way. He explains that God's mercy and justice are served by presenting man with a choice *between good and evil. Whichever man chooses, God's will is fulfilled, and even evil choices are turned to good account by Him. In his present imperfect state, man cannot always perceive the wisdom of God's ways, but Saint Augustine is confident that in the fullness of faith, all will become clear.*

The omnipotent God does well even in the permission of evil: Nor can we doubt that God does well even in the permission of what is evil. For He permits it only in the justice of His judgment. And surely all that is just is good. Although, therefore, evil, in so far as it is evil, is not a good; yet the fact that evil as well as good exists, is a good. For if it were not a good that evil should exist, its existence would not be permitted by the omnipotent God, who without doubt can as easily refuse to permit what He does not wish, as bring about what He does wish. And if we do not believe this, the very first sentence of our creed is endangered, wherein we profess to believe in God the Father Almighty. For He is not truly called Almighty if He cannot do whatsoever He pleases, or if the power of His almighty will is hindered by the will of any creature whatsoever . . .

The will of God is never defeated, though much is done that is contrary to His will: These are the great works of the Lord, sought out according to all His pleasure, and so wisely sought out, that when the intelligent creation, both angelic and human, sinned, doing not His will but their own, He used the very will of the creature which was working in opposition to the Creator's will as an instrument for carrying out His will, the supremely Good thus turning to good account even what is evil, to the condemnation of those whom in His justice He has predestined to punishment, and to the salvation of those whom in His mercy He has predestined to grace. For, as far as relates to their own consciousness, these creatures did what God wished not to be done: but in view of

God's omnipotence, they could in no wise effect their purpose. For in the very fact that they acted in opposition to His will, His will concerning them was fulfilled. And hence it is that "the works of the Lord are great, sought out according to all His pleasure," because in a way unspeakably strange and wonderful, even what is done in opposition to His will does not defeat His will. For it would not be done did He not permit it (and of course His permission is not unwilling, but willing); nor would a Good Being permit evil to be done only that in His omnipotence He can turn evil into good.

The will of God, which is always good, is sometimes fulfilled through the evil will of man: Sometimes, however, a man in the goodness of his will desires something that God does not desire, even though God's will is also good, nay, much more fully and more surely good (for His will never can be evil): for example, if a good son is anxious that his father should live, when it is God's good will that he should die. Again, it is possible for a man with evil will to desire what God wills in His goodness: for example, if a bad son wishes his father to die, when this is also the will of God. It is plain that the former wishes what God does not wish, and that the latter wishes what God does wish; and yet the filial love of the former is more in harmony with the good will of God, though its desire is different from God's, than the want of filial affection of the latter, though its desire is the same as God's. So necessary is it, in determining whether a man's desire is one to be approved or disapproved, to consider what it is proper for man, and what it is proper for God, to desire, and what is in each case the real motive of the will. For God accomplishes some of His purposes, which of course are all good, through the evil desires of wicked men.[c]

3. Although Saint Augustine has resolved the problem of evil to his satisfaction, another traditional paradox arises when it is considered that God knows in advance what choices men will make. Divine foreknowledge must be reconciled with man's freedom to choose good or evil. Because all things have causes, it would appear that if

God knows in advance what is to happen, all that happens is determined, and men cannot have free will. Then, if men are not free, punishment and reward are both unjust and ineffective. On the other hand, if man is free to choose his own course of action, God cannot have foreknowledge of human behavior, and consequently cannot be omniscient.

Saint Augustine sets about the task of showing how it is possible to retain the belief in both divine prescience and human free will. Granting that every event has a cause, he points out that man's will is one of the causes of his actions. Hence, the causal power of the will is part of the overall causal order of events foreknown by God. The paradox is effectively resolved by the distinction between the knowledge of a cause *and the* cause itself: *God's knowing in advance that an event will necessarily occur is not the same as His causing it to occur.*

But it does not follow that, though there is for God a certain order of all causes, there must therefore be nothing depending on the free exercise of our own wills, for our wills themselves are included in that order of causes which is certain to God, and is embraced by His foreknowledge, for human wills are also causes of human actions; and He who foreknew all the causes of things would certainly among those causes not have been ignorant of our wills. . . .

. . . If that is to be called *our necessity* which is not in our power, but even though we be unwilling, effects what it can effect, — as, for instance, the necessity of death, — it is manifest that our wills by which we live uprightly or wickedly are not under such a necessity; for we do many things which, if we were not willing, we should certainly not do. This is primarily true of the act of willing itself, — for if we will, it *is;* if we will not, it *is* not, — for we should not will if we were unwilling. But if we define necessity to be that according to which we say that it is necessary that anything be of such or such a nature, or be done in such and such a manner, I know not why we should have any dread of that necessity taking away the freedom of our will..For we do not put the life of God or the foreknowledge of God under necessity if we should say that it is necessary that God should live for ever, and foreknow all things; as neither is His power diminished when we say that He cannot die or fall into error, — for this is in such a way impossible to Him, that if it were possible for Him, He would be of less power. But assuredly He is rightly called omnipotent, though He can neither die nor fall into error. For He is called omnipotent on account of His doing what He wills, not on account of His suffering what He wills not; for if that should befall Him, He would by no means be omnipotent. Wherefore, He cannot do some things for the very reason that He is omnipotent.[d]

4. It follows, then, that men are themselves responsible for their misfortunes; they are free to choose, and they choose evil. For Saint Augustine, however, an evil will is a defective one. Just as he defines evil as the absence of good, so too he characterizes an evil will as one which fails to choose the good.

Let no one, therefore, look for an efficient cause of the evil will; for it is not efficient, but deficient, as the will itself is not an effecting of something, but a defect. For defection from that which supremely is, to that which has less of being, — this is to begin to have an evil will. Now, to seek to discover the causes of these defections, — causes, as I have said, not efficient, but deficient, — is as if some one sought to see darkness, or hear silence. Yet both of these are known by us, and the former by means only of the eye, the latter only by the ear; but not by their positive actuality, but by their want of it. Let no one, then, seek to know from me what I know that I do not know; unless he perhaps wishes to learn to be ignorant of that of which all we know is, that it cannot be known. . . . For when the eyesight surveys objects that strike the sense, it nowhere sees darkness but where it begins not to see. And so no other sense but the ear can perceive silence, and yet it is only perceived by not hearing. Thus, too, our mind perceives intelligible forms by understanding them; but when they are deficient, it knows them by not knowing them; for who can understand defects?

... And I know likewise, that the will could not become evil, were it unwilling to become so; and therefore its failings are justly punished, being not necessary, but voluntary. For its defections are not to evil things, but are themselves evil; that is to say, are not towards things that are naturally and in themselves evil, but the defection of the will is evil, because it is contrary to the order of nature, and an abandonment of that which has supreme being for that which has less. For avarice is not a fault inherent in gold, but in the man who inordinately loves gold, to the detriment of justice, which ought to be held in incomparably higher regard than gold. Neither is luxury the fault of lovely and charming objects, but of the heart that inordinately loves sensual pleasures, to the neglect of temperance, which attaches us to objects more lovely in their spirituality, and more delectable by their incorruptibility. Nor yet is boasting the fault of human praise, but of the soul that is inordinately fond of the applause of men, and that makes light of the voice of conscience. Pride, too, is not the fault of him who delegates power, nor of power itself, but of the soul that is inordinately enamoured of its own power, and despises the more just dominion of a higher authority. Consequently he who inordinately loves the good which any nature possesses, even though he obtain it, himself becomes evil in the good, and wretched because deprived of a greater good.[e]

5. Saint Augustine's rational justification of the Christian belief in man's moral responsibility and the presence of moral evil in the world constitutes a philosophical background for his description of the City of God and the City of Man. Those who choose good he calls citizens of the City of God, and those who choose evil are called citizens of the City of Man. To live in the heavenly city, one must follow the spirit as well as the letter of the teachings of Jesus; those who pursue the pleasures of the body or accept idolatrous or heretical beliefs must be said to "live after the flesh" in the earthly city.

. . . Though there are very many and great nations all over the earth, whose rites and customs, speech, arms, and dress, are distinguished by marked differences, yet there are no more than two kinds of human society, which we may justly call two cities, according to the language of our Scriptures. The one consists of those who wish to live after the flesh, the other of those who wish to live after the spirit; and when they severally achieve what they wish, they live in peace, each after their kind . . .

. . . If we are to ascertain what it is to live after the flesh (which is certainly evil, though the nature of flesh is not itself evil), we must carefully examine that passage of the epistle which the Apostle Paul wrote to the Galatians, in which he says, "Now the works of the flesh are manifest, which are these: adultery, fornication, uncleanness, lasciviousness, idolatry, witchcraft, hatred, variance, emulations, wrath, strife, seditions, heresies, envyings, murders, drunkenness, revellings, and such like: of the which I tell you before, as I have also told you in time past, that they which do such things shall not inherit the kingdom of God." This whole passage of the apostolic epistle being considered, so far as it bears on the matter in hand, will be sufficient to answer the question, what it is to live after the flesh. For among the works of the flesh which he said were manifest, and which he cited for condemnation, we find not only those which concern the pleasure of the flesh, as fornications, uncleanness, lasciviousness, drunkenness, revellings, but also those which, though they be remote from fleshly pleasure, reveal the vices of the soul. For who does not see that idolatries, witchcrafts, hatreds, variance, emulations, wrath, strife, heresies, envyings, are vices rather of the soul than of the flesh? For it is quite possible for a man to abstain from fleshly pleasures for the sake of idolatry or some heretical error; and yet, even when he does so, he is proved by this apostolic authority to be living after the flesh; and in abstaining from fleshly pleasure, he is proved to be practising damnable works of the flesh. Who that has enmity has it not in his soul? or who would say to his enemy, or to the man he thinks his enemy, You have a bad flesh towards me, and not rather, You have a bad spirit towards me? In fine, if any one heard of what I may call "carnalities," he would not fail to attribute them to the carnal part of man; so no one doubts that animosities [4] belong to the soul of man.[f]

6. *It must be realized, Saint Augustine points out, that supreme good and evil refer to eternity, not to the brief moment of this life. Those who seek happiness in this world and through their own efforts cannot be either truly happy or truly moral. Not only those who pursue the carnal pleasures, but also those who rely upon reason as the foundation of morality, are in error. Unaided by divine guidance, reason cannot provide a cure for the evils of life.*

What the Christians believe regarding the supreme good and evil, in opposition to the philosophers, who have maintained that the supreme good is in themselves: If, then, we be asked what the city of God has to say upon these points, and, in the first place, what its opinion regarding the supreme good and evil is, it will reply that life eternal is the supreme good, death eternal the supreme evil, and that to obtain the one and escape the other we must live rightly. And thus it is written, "The just lives by faith," for we do not as yet see our good, and must therefore live by faith; neither have we in ourselves power to live rightly, but can do so only if He who has given us faith to believe in His help do help us when we believe and pray. As for those who have supposed that the sovereign good and evil are to be found in this life . . . all these have, with a marvellous shallowness, sought to find their blessedness in this life and in themselves. Contempt has been poured upon such ideas by the Truth, saying by the prophet, "The Lord knoweth the thoughts of men" (or, as the Apostle Paul cites the passage, "The Lord knoweth the thoughts of the *wise*") "that they are vain."

For what flood of eloquence can suffice to detail the miseries of this life? . . . For when, where, how, in this life can these primary objects of nature be possessed so that they may not be assailed by unforeseen accidents? Is the body of the wise man

---

[4] *Anima* is the Latin word for "soul."

exempt from any pain which may dispel pleasure, from any disquietude which may banish repose? The amputation or decay of the members of the body puts an end to its integrity, deformity blights its beauty, weakness its health, lassitude its vigour, sleepiness or sluggishness its activity, — and which of these is it that may not assail the flesh of the wise man? Comely and fitting attitudes and movements of the body are numbered among the prime natural blessings; but what if some sickness makes the members tremble? what if a man suffers from curvature of the spine to such an extent that his hands reach the ground, and he goes upon all-fours like a quadruped? Does not this destroy all beauty and grace in the body, whether at rest or in motion? What shall I say of the fundamental blessings of the soul, sense and intellect, of which the one is given for the perception, and the other for the comprehension of truth? But what kind of sense is it that remains when a man becomes deaf and blind? where are reason and intellect when disease makes a man delirious? We can scarcely, or not at all, refrain from tears, when we think of or see the actions and words of such frantic persons, and consider how different from and even opposed to their own sober judgment and ordinary conduct their present demeanour is. And what shall I say of those who suffer from demoniacal possession? Where is their own intelligence hidden and buried while the malignant spirit is using their body and soul according to his own will? And who is quite sure that no such thing can happen to the wise man in this life? Then, as to the perception of truth, what can we hope for even in this way while in the body, as we read in the true book of Wisdom, "The corruptible body weigheth down the soul, and the earthly tabernacle presseth down the mind that museth upon many things?" And eagerness or desire of action ... is also reckoned among the primary advantages of nature; and yet is it not this which produces those pitiable movements of the insane, and those actions which we shudder to see, when sense is deceived and reason deranged? [g]

7. *When we appreciate the feebleness of unaided human reason, we see that faith, hope, and love are the fundamental virtues of the*

true Christian, who seeks peace and happiness through God. The virtues of prudence, temperance, justice, and fortitude which the rationalistic Greek philosophers value so highly are nothing more than prideful vices unless they are used in the service of the true religion.

What shall I say of that virtue which is called *prudence?* Is not all its vigilance spent in the discernment of good from evil things, so that no mistake may be admitted about what we should desire and what avoid? And thus it is itself a proof that we are in the midst of evils, or that evils are in us; for it teaches us that it is an evil to consent to sin, and a good to refuse this consent. And yet this evil, to which prudence teaches and *temperance* enables us not to consent, is removed from this life neither by prudence nor by temperance. And *justice*, whose office it is to render to every man his due, whereby there is in man himself a certain just order of nature, so that the soul is subjected to God, and the flesh to the soul, and consequently both soul and flesh to God, — does not this virtue demonstrate that it is as yet rather labouring towards its end than resting in its finished work? For the soul is so much the less subjected to God as it is less occupied with the thought of God; and the flesh is so much the less subjected to the spirit as it lusts more vehemently against the spirit. So long, therefore, as we are beset by this weakness, this plague, this disease, how shall we dare to say that we are safe? and if not safe, then how can we be already enjoying our final beatitude? Then that virtue which goes by the name of *fortitude* is the plainest proof of the ills of life, for it is these ills which it is compelled to bear patiently. And this holds good, no matter though the ripest wisdom co-exists with it. . . .

Therefore the Apostle Paul, speaking not of men without prudence, temperance, fortitude, and justice, but of those whose lives were regulated by true piety, and whose virtues were therefore true, says, "For we are saved by hope: now hope which is seen is not hope; for what a man seeth, why doth he yet hope for?

But if we hope for that we see not, then do we with patience wait for it." As, therefore, we are saved, so we are made happy by hope. And as we do not as yet possess a present, but look for a future salvation, so is it with our happiness, and this "with patience"; for we are encompassed with evils, which we ought patiently to endure, until we come to the ineffable enjoyment of unmixed good; for there shall be no longer anything to endure. Salvation, such as it shall be in the world to come, shall itself be our final happiness. And this happiness these philosophers refuse to believe in, because they do not see it, and attempt to fabricate for themselves a happiness in this life, based upon a virtue which is as deceitful as it is proud . . .

That where there is no true religion there are no true virtues: For though the soul may seem to rule the body admirably, and the reason the vices, if the soul and reason do not themselves obey God, as God has commanded them to serve Him, they have no proper authority over the body and the vices. For what kind of mistress of the body and the vices can that mind be which is ignorant of the true God, and which, instead of being subject to His authority, is prostituted to the corrupting influences of the most vicious demons? It is for this reason that the virtues which it seems to itself to possess, and by which it restrains the body and the vices that it may obtain and keep what it desires, are rather vices than virtues so long as there is no reference to God in the matter. For although some suppose that virtues which have a reference only to themselves, and are desired only on their own account, are yet true and genuine virtues, the fact is that even then they are inflated with pride, and are therefore to be reckoned vices rather than virtues. For as that which gives life to the flesh is not derived from flesh, but is above it, so that which gives blessed life to man is not derived from man, but is something above him; and what I say of man is true of every celestial power and virtue whatsoever.[h]

8. *All men earnestly desire peace, but the misdirected methods of the City of Man fail to achieve it. Those who dwell in God's city*

know that peace is not achieved by war, but by love. Hence, all men should obey and teach the precepts of Jesus, "Love God" and "Love thy neighbor as thyself."

The whole use, then, of things temporal has a reference to this result of earthly peace in the earthly community, while in the city of God it is connected with eternal peace. And therefore, if we were irrational animals, we should desire nothing beyond the proper arrangement of the parts of the body and the satisfaction of the appetites — nothing, therefore, but bodily comfort and abundance of pleasures, that the peace of the body might contribute to the peace of the soul. For if bodily peace be awanting, a bar is put to the peace even of the irrational soul, since it cannot obtain the gratification of its appetites. And these two together help out the mutual peace of soul and body, the peace of harmonious life and health. For as animals, by shunning pain, show that they love bodily peace, and, by pursuing pleasure to gratify their appetites, show that they love peace of soul, so their shrinking from death is a sufficient indication of their intense love of that peace which binds soul and body in close alliance. But, as man has a rational soul, he subordinates all this which he has in common with the beasts to the peace of his rational soul, that his intellect may have free play and may regulate his actions, and that he may thus enjoy the well-ordered harmony of knowledge and action which constitutes, as we have said, the peace of the rational soul. And for this purpose he must desire to be neither molested by pain, nor disturbed by desire, nor extinguished by death, that he may arrive at some useful knowledge by which he may regulate his life and manners. But, owing to the liability of the human mind to fall into mistakes, this very pursuit of knowledge may be a snare to him unless he has a divine Master, whom he may obey without misgiving, and who may at the same time give him such help as to preserve his own freedom. And because so long as he is in this mortal body, he is a stranger to God, he walks by faith, not by sight; and he therefore refers all peace, bodily or spiritual or both, to that peace which mortal man has with the immortal God, so that he exhibits the well-ordered obedience of faith to eternal law. But as this divine Master inculcates two precepts, — the love of God and the love of our neighbour, — and as in these precepts a man finds three things he has to love, — God, himself, and his neighbour, — and that he who loves God loves himself thereby, it follows that he must endeavour to get his neighbour to love God, since he is ordered to love his neighbour as himself. He ought to make this endeavour in behalf of his wife, his children, his household, all within his reach, even as he would wish his neighbour to do the same for him if he needed it; and consequently he will be at peace, or in well-ordered concord, with all men as far as in him lies. And this is the order of this concord, that a man, in the first place, injure no one, and, in the second, do good to every one he can reach.[i]

9. It is not possible to judge from a man's earthly history whether he is blessed or not, for " in the mingled web of human affairs, God's judgment is present, though it cannot be discerned." We must accept without complaint the knowledge that good men may suffer earthly misfortunes, while wicked men may enjoy life.

In this present time we learn to bear with equanimity the ills to which even good men are subject, and to hold cheap the blessings which even the wicked enjoy. And consequently, even in those conditions of life in which the justice of God is not apparent, His teaching is salutary. For we do not know by what judgment of God this good man is poor and that bad man rich; why he who, in our opinion, ought to suffer acutely for his abandoned life enjoys himself, while sorrow pursues him whose praiseworthy life leads us to suppose he should be happy; why the innocent man is dismissed from the bar not only unavenged, but even condemned, being either wronged by the iniquity of the judge, or overwhelmed by false evidence, while his guilty adversary, on the other hand, is not only discharged with impunity, but even has his claims admitted; why the ungodly enjoys good health, while the godly pines in sickness; why ruffians are of the soundest constitution, while they who could not hurt any one even with a word are from infancy afflicted with complicated disorders; why he who is useful to society is cut off by premature death, while those who, as it might seem, ought never to have been so much as born have lives of unusual length; why he who is full of crimes is crowned with honours, while the blameless man is buried in the darkness of neglect. But who can collect or enumerate all the contrasts of this kind? But if this anomalous state of things were uniform in this life, in which, as the sacred Psalmist says, "Man is like to vanity, his days as a shadow that passeth away," — so uniform that none but wicked men won the transitory prosperity of earth, while only the good suffered its ills, — this could be referred to the just and even benign judgment of God. We might suppose that they who were not destined to obtain those ever-lasting benefits which constitute human blessedness were either deluded by transitory blessings as the just reward of their wicked-ness, or were, in God's mercy, consoled by them, and that they who were not destined to suffer eternal torments were afflicted with temporal chastisement for their sins, or were stimulated to greater attainment in virtue. But now, as it is, since we not only see good men involved in the ills of life, and bad men enjoying the good of it, which seems unjust, but also that evil often over-takes evil men, and good surprises the good, the rather on this account are God's judgments unsearchable, and His ways past finding out. Although, therefore, we do not know by what judg-ment these things are done or permitted to be done by God, with whom is the highest virtue, the highest wisdom, the highest justice, no infirmity, no rashness, no unrighteousness, yet it is salutary for us to learn to hold cheap such things, be they good or evil, as attach indifferently to good men and bad, and to covet those good things which belong only to good men, and flee those evils which belong only to evil men. But when we shall have come to that judgment, the date of which is called peculiarly the day of judgment, and sometimes the day of the Lord, we shall then recognize the justice of all God's judgments, not only of such as shall then be pronounced, but of all which take effect from the beginning, or may take effect before that time. And in that day we shall also recognise with what justice so many, or almost all, the just judgments of God in the present life defy the scrutiny of human sense or insight, though in this matter it is not concealed from pious minds that what is concealed is just.[j]

10. The Last Judgment will be a day of reckoning where virtue and vice will be clearly seen and just reward and punishment meted out. The City of Man will be dissolved and its citizens condemned to eternal death. This is not the ordinary death in which the soul leaves the body, but a "second death," in which God abandons the soul. While eternal punishment is a harsh judgment, the enormity of man's sin merits it. But God in His goodness is not only just, but also merciful, for He sent to man His only Son through whom the citizens of the City of God are saved.

Of the greatness of the first transgression, on account of which eternal punishment is due to all who are not within the pale of the Saviour's grace: But eternal punishment seems hard and unjust to human perceptions, because in the weakness of our mortal condition there is wanting that highest and purest wisdom by which it can be perceived how great a wickedness was committed in that first transgression. The more enjoyment man found in God, the greater was his wickedness in abandoning Him; and he who destroyed in himself a good which might have been eternal, became worthy of eternal evil. Hence the whole mass of the human race is condemned; for he who at first gave entrance to sin has been punished with all his posterity who were in him as in a root, so that no one is exempt from this just and due punishment, unless delivered by mercy and undeserved grace; and the human race is so apportioned that in some is displayed the efficacy of merciful grace, in the rest the efficacy of just retribution. . . .

That everything which the grace of God does in the way of rescuing us from the inveterate evils in which we are sunk, pertains to the future world, in which all things are made new: Nevertheless, in the "heavy yoke that is laid upon the sons of Adam, from the day that they go out of their mother's womb to the day that they return to the mother of all things," there is found an admirable though painful monitor teaching us to be sober-minded, and convincing us that this life has become penal in consequence of that outrageous wickedness which was perpetrated in Paradise, and that all to which the New Testament invites belongs to that future inheritance which awaits us in the world to come, and is offered for our acceptance, as the earnest that we may, in its own due time, obtain that of which it is the pledge. Now, therefore, let us walk in hope, and let us by the spirit mortify the deeds of the flesh, and so make progress from day to day. For "the Lord knoweth them that are His"; and "as many as are led by the Spirit of God, they are sons of God," but by grace, not by nature. For there is but one Son of God by nature, who in His compassion became Son of man for our sakes, that we, by nature sons of men, might by grace become through Him sons of God. For He, abiding unchangeable, took upon Him our nature, that thereby He might take us to Himself; and, holding fast His own divinity, He became partaker of our infirmity, that we, being changed into some better thing, might, by participating in His righteousness and immortality, lose our own properties of sin and mortality, and preserve whatever good quality He had implanted in our nature, perfected now by sharing in the goodness of His nature. For as by the sin of one man we have fallen into a misery so deplorable, so by the righteousness of one Man, who also is God, shall we come to a blessedness inconceivably exalted. Nor ought any one to trust that he has passed from the one man to the other until he shall have reached that place where there is no temptation, and have entered into the peace which he seeks in the many and various conflicts of this war, in which "the flesh lusteth against the spirit, and the spirit against the flesh." [k]

11. The final vision of God, permitted to those who have lived in righteousness and been blessed with God's grace, is "the reward of our faith."

Of the beatific vision: And now let us consider, with such ability as God may vouchsafe, how the saints shall be employed when they are clothed in immortal and spiritual bodies, and when the flesh shall live no longer in a fleshly but a spiritual fashion. And indeed, to tell the truth, I am at a loss to understand the nature of that employment, or, shall I rather say, repose and ease, for it has never come within the range of my bodily senses. And if I should speak of my mind or understanding, what is our understanding in comparison of its excellence? For then shall be that "peace of God which," as the apostle says, "passeth all understanding," — that is to say, all human, and perhaps all angelic understanding, but certainly not the divine. That it passeth ours there is no doubt; but if it passeth that of the angels, — and he who says "*all* understanding" seems to make no exception in their favour, — then we must understand him to mean that neither we nor the angels can understand, as God understands, the peace which God Himself enjoys. Doubtless this passeth all understanding but His own. But as we shall one day be made to participate, according to our slender capacity, in His peace, both in ourselves, and with our neighbour, and with God our chief good, in this respect the angels understand the peace of God in their own measure, and men too, though now far behind them, whatever spiritual advance they have made. For we must remember how great a man he [Saint Paul] was who said, "We know in part, and we prophesy in part, until that which is perfect is come"; and "Now we see through a glass, darkly; but then face to face."

Of the eternal felicity of the city of God, and of the perpetual Sabbath: How great shall be that felicity, which shall be tainted with no evil, which shall lack no good, and which shall afford leisure for the praises of God, who shall be all in all! For I know not what other employment there can be where no lassitude shall slacken activity, nor any want stimulate to labour. I am admonished also by the sacred song, in which I read or hear the words, "Blessed are they that dwell in Thy house, O Lord; they will be still praising Thee." All the members and organs of the incorruptible body, which now we see to be suited to various necessary uses, shall contribute to the praises of God; for in that life necessity shall have no place, but full, certain, secure, everlasting felicity. For all those parts of the bodily harmony, which are distributed through the whole body, within and without, and of which I have just been saying that they at present elude our observation, shall then be discerned; and, along with the other great and marvellous discoveries which shall then kindle rational minds in praise of the great Artificer, there shall be the enjoyment of a beauty which appeals to the reason. What power of movement such bodies shall possess, I have not the audacity rashly to define, as I have not the ability to conceive. Nevertheless I will say that in any case, both in motion and at rest, they shall be, as in their appearance, seemly; for into that state nothing which is unseemly shall be admitted. One thing is certain, the body shall forthwith be wherever the spirit wills, and the spirit shall will nothing which is unbecoming either to the spirit or to the body. True honour shall be there, for it shall be denied to none who is worthy, nor yielded to any unworthy; neither shall any unworthy person so much as sue for it, for none but the worthy shall be there. True peace shall be there, where no one shall suffer opposition either from himself or any other. God Himself, who is the Author of virtue, shall there be its reward; for, as there is nothing greater or better, He has promised Himself. What else was meant by His word through the prophet, "I will be your God, and ye shall be my people," than, I shall be their satisfaction, I shall be all that men honourably desire, — life, and health, and nourishment, and plenty, and glory, and honour, and peace, and all good things? This, too, is the right interpretation of the saying of the apostle, "That God may be all in all." He shall be the end of our desires who shall be seen without end, loved without cloy, praised without weariness. This outgoing of affection, this employment, shall certainly be, like eternal life itself, common to all.

But who can conceive, not to say describe, what degrees of honour and glory shall be awarded to the various degrees of merit? Yet it cannot be doubted that there shall be degrees. And in that blessed city there shall be this great blessing, that no inferior shall envy any superior, as now the archangels are not envied by the angels, because no one will wish to be what he has not received, though bound in strictest concord with him who has received; as in the body the finger does not seek to be the eye, though both members are harmoniously included in the complete structure of the body. And thus, along with his gift, greater or less, each shall receive this further gift of contentment to desire no more than he has.[1]

12. His vast description of the cities of God and of Man completed, Saint Augustine expresses the hope that he has communicated the meaning of the love of God through giving a true account of the true religion.

Since, then, the supreme good of the city of God is perfect and eternal peace, not such as mortals pass into and out of by birth and death, but the peace of freedom from all evil, in which the immortals ever abide, who can deny that that future life is most blessed, or that, in comparison with it, this life which now we live is most wretched, be it filled with all blessings of body and soul and external things? And yet, if any man uses this life with a reference to that other which he ardently loves and confidently hopes for, he may well be called even now blessed, though not in reality so much as in hope. But the actual possession of the happiness of this life, without the hope of what is beyond, is but a false happiness and profound misery. For the true blessings of the soul are not now enjoyed; for that is no true wisdom which does not direct all its prudent observations, manly actions, virtuous self-restraint, and just arrangements, to that end in which God shall be all and all in a secure eternity and perfect peace. . . .

There we shall rest and see, see and love, love and praise. This is what shall be in the end without end. For what other end do we propose to ourselves than to attain to the kingdom of which there is no end?

I think I have now, by God's help, discharged my obligation in writing this large work. Let those who think I have said too little, or those who think I have said too much, forgive me; and let those who think I have said just enough join me in giving thanks to God. Amen.ᵐ

Questions

1. Describe the Christian conception of God's nature and the nature of man. In Saint Augustine's ethical theory, what can be done by God and what by man himself to realize the Christian ideal?

2. What does Saint Augustine mean when he speaks of "the love of God"? What place does it occupy in his ethical theory?

3. What is the "problem of evil," and to what extent do Saint Augustine's definitions of good and evil resolve the paradox?

4. Discuss the principal differences between citizens of the "City of God" and citizens of the "City of Man." What place, if any, may be assigned to time and space in distinguishing the two cities?

5. How can knowledge assist a man to pass from the City of Man to the City of God? Is there any clear sign, in a man's personal history, of his future reward or punishment?

6. Why does Saint Augustine reject the philosophic enterprise as an end in itself? What does he regard as the correct use of reason?

7. Compare the Christian virtues with the Greek virtues, and discuss Saint Augustine's attitude towards the latter.

8. Explain the concept of "Judgment Day." How do God's grace and Jesus' role as man's Savior affect the outcome of the Last Judgment?

9. Discuss Saint Augustine's conception of the "vision of God" as the ultimate reward of faith. Explain the significance, in this connection, of Saint Paul's phrase, "Now we see through a glass darkly, but then face to face."

10. From a review of the principal elements of Saint Augustine's ethical theory, reconstruct his theory of the relative roles of faith and knowledge in the achievement of the good life.

Key to selections:

SAINT AUGUSTINE, *Enchiridion*, tr. J. F. Shaw, from *The Works of Aurelius Augustine*, vol. 9, Rev. Marcus Dods, ed., Edinburgh, T. & T. Clark, 1892.

ᵃ Ch. CXXI.   ᵇ Chs. XI–XII.   ᶜ Chs. XCVI, C–CI.

SAINT AUGUSTINE, *City of God*, vols. 1 and 2, tr. Rev. Marcus Dods, Edinburgh, T. & T. Clark, 1881.

d Bk. V:9–10.   h Bk. XIX:4, 25.   l Bk. XXII:29–30.
e Bk. XII:7–8.   i Bk. XIX:14.   m Bk. XIX:20,
f Bk. XIV:1–2.   j Bk. XX:2.   XXII:30.
g Bk. XIX:4.   k Bk. XXI:12, 15.

Guide to Additional Reading

INEXPENSIVE EDITIONS:

SAINT AUGUSTINE, *Confessions*, Black and Gold Library (Liveright).
——,   ——, Everyman's Library (Dutton).
——,   —— (Books I–VIII), Great Books Foundation (Regnery).
——,   —— (Books IX–XIII), Great Books Foundation (Regnery).
——,   ——, Modern Library (Random House).
——, *The City of God*, Everyman's Library (Dutton), 2 vols.
——,   ——, Hafner Library of Classics (Hafner), 2 vols.
——,   ——, Modern Library (Random House).

DISCUSSION AND COMMENTARY:

Bourke, V. J., *Augustine's Quest of Wisdom*, Milwaukee, Bruce Publishing Company, 1945.

Cochrane, C. N., *Christianity and Classical Culture*, Oxford, The Clarendon Press, 1940.

Tolley, W. P., *The Idea of God in the Philosophy of St. Augustine*, New York, R. R. Smith, Inc., 1930.

Warfield, B., *Studies in Tertullian and Augustine*, New York, Oxford University Press, 1931.

CHAPTER 7

Self-Interest

THOMAS
HOBBES

Thomas Hobbes (1588–1679) was born in Malmesbury, England, of poor and uneducated parents. Because he was precocious, however, his uncle provided the financial assistance needed to send him to Oxford University. There, finding the curriculum of scholastic logic boring and Aristotelian physics confusing and irksome, he devoted much of his time to independent reading of literary classics. Upon graduation in 1608, Hobbes was selected as a tutor for the young son of the Cavendish family, a family to which he was attached for almost the whole of his life. In this capacity, he had sufficient time to reflect, travel, and to become acquainted with such outstanding contemporary philosophers and scientists as Galileo, Bacon, Kepler, and Descartes.

It is reported that at the age of forty, quite by chance, Hobbes became enamored of the deductive certainty of mathematics. "Being in a gentleman's library, Euclid's *Elements* lay open, and 'twas the forty-seventh [theorem of Book I]. He read the proposition. 'By God,' he said, 'this is impossible.' So he reads the demonstration of it which referred him back to such a proposition: which proposition he read. That referred him back to another, which he also read. [And so back to the self-evident axioms, when] at last he was demonstratively convinced of that truth. This made him in love with geometry." Presumably, at about the same time, he read Galileo's *Dialogues* and became firmly convinced that a systematic philosophy must be based upon the physical principle that every change is a change in motion. The deductive form of geometry and the materialism of physics became essential features of his philosophy, which was then in its formative stage.

During the period of Hobbes' intellectual development, the English political scene was one of constant crisis and turbulence. While the tension between Parliament and King Charles I was at its peak, Hobbes wrote a political treatise defending the doctrine of absolute sovereignty. He believed that absolute sovereignty was the necessary condition of a secure and peaceful society, arguing that if supreme authority were to be divided and limited, as, for example, between the King and Parliament, only chaos could result. Though he made no explicit reference to the current situation, Hobbes imagined that he was in danger of reprisal from Parliament and fled to France. During this self-imposed and unnecessary exile (1640–1651), he engaged in philosophical inquiry, tutored the future Charles II, and wrote his important political treatise, *De Cive* (*On the State*) in 1642, and his major philosophical work, *Leviathan*, in 1651.

Upon his return to England, Hobbes remained aloof from the political scene, but continued to write. The most significant work of this period was *De Homine* (*On Man*), published in 1658. Although Hobbes' writings exhibit fine scholarship, they are particularly distinguished by their penetration and originality. It has been said of Hobbes, "He has read much, if one considers his long life; but his contemplation was much more than his reading. He was wont to say that if he had read as much as other men he would have known no more than other men."

Historically, Thomas Hobbes is the first philosopher to apply systematically the basic assumptions of seventeenth-century science to human behavior. Impressed with the advance in "natural philosophy" achieved by Copernicus in astronomy, Galileo in physics, and Harvey in physiology, Hobbes attempts to obtain comparable results in the other divisions of philosophy.[1] He envisions a unification of all the branches of philosophy, the study of physical bodies, the study of living bodies, and the study of political bodies. Convinced that the key to the success of physics resided in its underlying assumption of *mechanistic materialism* — the view that everything is ultimately reducible to material bodies in motion — Hobbes extends this doctrine to psychology and to political and moral philosophy. He insists that although the several sciences investigate different subject matters, the basic laws of each describe the motions of bodies.

Hobbes' moral philosophy is directly related to his psychological theory, in which he constructs his mechanistic conception of motivation. He opposes the prevailing notion of his time that the mind and body are different substances, maintaining that *mental phenomena are nothing but physiological motions*. The thoroughgoing nature of his psychology comes out most forcibly in his mechanistic analysis of voluntary actions. These he traces to a variety of "animal motions," which he calls *endeavors, i.e.,* predispositions to act in a certain direction. Endeavors are mechanically initiated by sensory stimuli, augmented by the action of imagination and memory, and guided by a calculated appraisal of the situation. The most important kinds of endeavors are *desires* and *aversions*. Desires move one to pursue objects, and aversions move one to avoid objects. Endeavors are not only the chief determinants of behavior, but they are also the basis of evaluations.

Evaluating objects or actions as good or evil depends, Hobbes insists, upon no other basis than desires and aversions. No objects

---

[1] "Philosophy" was for some time used interchangeably with "knowledge" or "science." For example, physics was referred to as one of the branches of *natural philosophy*, and psychology and ethics were included under *moral philosophy*.

or actions are intrinsically good, *i.e.*, good by their very nature. Rather, men call "good" the objects of their desires, whereas they call "evil" the objects of their aversions. Therefore, evaluations are *transient* and *relative to the individual*. Values are transient, because the desire for an object may change to indifference or even to aversion: what is good on one occasion may on another be ethically neutral or even evil. Values are relative to the individual, because one person may love an object to which a second is indifferent and which a third may hate: the same object is then simultaneously good, neutral, and evil.

Another feature of Hobbes' psychological theory which reflects his mechanistic materialism is his conception of human nature as completely and exclusively egoistic. He depicts men as being by nature entirely selfish and devoid of any genuine feelings of sympathy, benevolence, or sociability. Each individual is preoccupied exclusively with the gratification of his own desires, and his success in maintaining a continuous flow of gratifications is the measure of his happiness. The means for attaining the objects of desire Hobbes calls "power." He maintains that in a natural state, men are approximately equal in their mental and physical powers. Under these conditions, intense competition eliminates virtually all chances for an individual to achieve happiness and, what is more serious, threatens his very survival.

Hobbes believes that reason points to voluntary collective organization as the most effective way for individuals to utilize their powers. When a person's right to do whatever will satisfy his desires is deputed to a central governing authority, the conditions requisite to his survival and happiness are provided. Each individual asserts in effect: "I authorize, and give up my right of governing myself, to this man or to this assembly of men, on this condition, that thou give up thy right and authorize all his actions in like manner." It is through a "social contract" that the state of nature is transformed into a civil society:

A *commonwealth* is said to be *instituted* when a *multitude* of men do agree, and *covenant, every one, with everyone*, that to whatsoever *man*, or *as-*

sembly of men, shall be given by the major part, the *right* to *present* the person of them all, that is to say, to be their *representative;* everyone, as well he that *voted for it*, as he that *voted against it*, shall *authorize* all the actions and judgments, of that man, or assembly of men, in the same manner, as if they were his own, to the end, to live peaceably amongst themselves, and be protected against other men.[a]

With the establishment of the commonwealth through the social contract, Hobbes tells us, the necessary and sufficient condition for moral obligation is present. Whatever is in accordance with the law of the sovereign is *right*, whereas that which deviates from it is *wrong*. Hobbes thus establishes *civil authority and law as the foundation of morality*. He is arguing that morality requires social authority, which must be in the hands of the sovereign. The will of a sovereign power whose authority is absolute and indivisible constitutes the only law by which man's behavior can be properly regulated. Morality, then, is based upon law — the law of the absolute sovereign. Only with the institution of a government which can reward right action and punish wrongdoing is moral conduct possible. For, without a civil authority, it would be foolish and dangerous to follow the precepts of morality, whereas with it, morality turns out to be the "dictate of reason." In the last analysis, men are moral only because it is conducive to individual security, and the prime condition of security is absolute civil power.

• • •

1. The elements of Hobbes' psychological theory are presented in a set of principles which govern the various "motions" of the human mind.

There be in animals, two sorts of *motions* peculiar to them: one called *vital;* begun in generation, and continued without interruption through their whole life; such as are the *course* of the *blood*, the *pulse*, the *breathing*, the *concoction, nutrition, excretion*, etc to which motions there needs no help of imagination: the other is *animal motion*, otherwise called *voluntary motion;* as to *go*, to *speak*, to *move* any of our limbs, in such manner as is first fancied in our minds. That sense is motion in the organs and interior parts of man's body, caused by the action of the things we see, hear, etc.; and that fancy is but the relics of the same motion, remaining after sense, has been already said in the first and second chapters. And because *going, speaking,* and the like voluntary motions, depend always upon a precedent thought of *whither, which way,* and *what;* it is evident, that the imagination is the first internal beginning of all voluntary motion. And although un-studied men do not conceive any motion at all to be there, where the thing moved is invisible; or the space it is moved in is, for the shortness of it, insensible; yet that doth not hinder, but that such motions are. For let a space be never so little, that which is moved over a greater space, whereof that little one is part, must first be moved over that. These small beginnings of motion, within the body of man, before they appear in walking, speaking, strik-ing, and other visible actions, are commonly called ENDEAV-OUR.

This endeavour, when it is toward something which causes it, is called APPETITE, or DESIRE; the latter, being the general name; and the other oftentimes restrained to signify the desire of food, namely *hunger* and *thirst*. And when the endeavour is fromward something, it is generally called AVERSION. These words, *appetite* and *aversion*, we have from the Latins; and they both of them signify the motions, one of approaching, the other of retiring . . . For nature itself does often press upon men those truths, which afterwards, when they look for somewhat beyond nature, they stumble at. For the Schools find in mere appetite to go, or move, no actual motion at all: but because some motion they must acknowledge, they call it metaphorical motion; which is but an absurd speech: for though words may be called meta-phorical; bodies and motions can not.

That which men desire, they are also said to LOVE: and to HATE those things for which they have aversion. So that desire and love are the same thing; save that by desire, we always signify the absence of the object; by love, most commonly the presence of the same. So also by aversion, we signify the absence; and by hate, the presence of the object.

Of appetites and aversions, some are born with men; as appetite of food, appetite of excretion, and exoneration, which may also and more properly be called aversions, from somewhat they feel in their bodies; and some other appetites, not many. The rest, which are appetites of particular things, proceed from experience, and trial of their effects upon themselves or other men. For of things we know not at all, or believe not to be, we can have no further desire, than to taste and try. But aversion we have for things, not only which we know have hurt us, but also that we do not know whether they will hurt us, or not.

Those things which we neither desire, nor hate, we are said to *contemn;* CONTEMPT being nothing else but an immobility, or contumacy of the heart, in resisting the action of certain things; and proceeding from that the heart is already moved otherwise, by other more potent objects; or from want of experience of them.

And because the constitution of a man's body is in continual mutation, it is impossible that all the same things should always cause in him the same appetites, and aversions: much less can all men consent, in the desire of almost any one and the same object.[b]

2. Hobbes interprets the traditional ethical concepts, "good" and "evil," in terms of this mechanistic psychological theory.

But whatsoever is the object of any man's appetite or desire, that is it which he for his part calleth *good:* and the object of his hate and aversion, *evil;* and of his contempt, *vile* and *inconsiderable.* For these words of good, evil, and contemptible, are ever used with relation to the person that useth them: there being nothing simply and absolutely so; nor any common rule of good and evil, to be taken from the nature of the objects themselves.[c]

3. For man in a pre-social state, the desires and aversions which underlie his judgments of good and evil are directed towards his primary objective, self-preservation. Continual success in preserving oneself, Hobbes terms "felicity" or "happiness." Various objects of desire, i.e., goods such as friendship, riches, and intelligence, promote this felicity. Friends are good because they come to our defense when we are in difficulties; riches are good because they buy the allies we need for our security; intelligence is good because it alerts us to danger.

When the objects of desire are examined from the point of view of effectiveness in promoting felicity, they are termed "powers." Hobbes ascribes to men in their natural state a general tendency to "a perpetual and restless desire of power after power that ceaseth only in death." When several men desire the same object, enmity arises; and because nature endows men equally with the various mental and physical powers, the confidence which each one feels in his ability intensifies the likelihood of conflict.

Nature hath made men so equal, in the faculties of the body, and mind; as that though there be found one man sometimes manifestly stronger in body, or of quicker mind than another; yet when all is reckoned together, the difference between man, and man, is not so considerable, as that one man can thereupon claim to himself any benefit, to which another may not pretend, as well as he. For as to the strength of body, the weakest has strength enough to kill the strongest, either by secret machination, or by confederacy with others, that are in the same danger with himself.

And as to the faculties of the mind, setting aside the arts grounded upon words, and especially that skill of proceeding upon general, and infallible rules, called science; which very few have, and but in few things; as being not a native faculty, born with us; nor attained, as prudence, while we look after somewhat else, I find yet a greater equality amongst men, than that of strength. For prudence, is but experience; which equal time, equally bestows on all men, in those things they equally apply themselves unto. That which may perhaps make such equality incredible, is but a vain conceit of one's own wisdom, which almost all men think they have in a greater degree, than the vulgar; that is, than all men but themselves, and a few others, whom by fame, or for concurring with themselves, they approve. For such is the nature of men, that howsoever they may acknowledge many others to be more witty, or more eloquent, or more learned; yet they will hardly believe there be many so wise as themselves; for they see their own wit at hand, and other men's at a distance. But this proveth rather that men are in that point equal, than unequal. For there is not ordinarily a greater sign of the equal distribution of any thing, than that every man is contented with his share.

From this equality of ability, ariseth equality of hope in the attaining of our ends. And therefore if any two men desire the same thing, which nevertheless they cannot both enjoy, they become enemies; and in the way to their end, which is principally their own conservation, and sometimes their delectation only, endeavour to destroy, or subdue one another. And from hence it comes to pass, that where an invader hath no more to fear, than another man's single power; if one plant, sow, build, or possess a convenient seat, others may probably be expected to come prepared with forces united, to dispossess, and deprive him, not only of the fruit of his labour, but also of his life, or liberty. And the invader again is in the like danger of another.

And from this diffidence of one another, there is no way for any man to secure himself, so reasonable, as anticipation; that is, by force, or wiles, to master the persons of all men he can, so long, till he see no other power great enough to endanger him: and this is no more than his own conservation requireth, and is generally allowed. Also because there be some, that taking pleasure in contemplating their own power in the acts of conquest, which they pursue farther than their security requires; if others, that otherwise would be glad to be at ease within modest bounds, should not by invasion increase their power, they would not be able, long time, by standing only on their defence, to subsist. And by consequence, such augmentation of dominion over men being necessary to a man's conservation, it ought to be allowed him.

Again, men have no pleasure, but on the contrary a great deal of grief, in keeping company, where there is no power able to over-awe them all. For every man looketh that his companion should value him, at the same rate he sets upon himself: and upon all signs of contempt, or undervaluing, naturally endeavours, as far as he dares, (which amongst them that have no common power to keep them in quiet, is far enough to make them destroy each other), to extort a greater value from his contemners, by damage; and from others, by the example.[d]

4. From his examination of the contentiousness of men in the absence of political organization, Hobbes discovers three sources of controversy in human nature. The natural condition of man, he says, is universal war. He does not claim that the "state of nature" actually existed historically; rather, it exists in any time or place where civil society is not functioning.

So that in the nature of man, we find three principal causes of quarrel. First, competition; secondly, diffidence; thirdly, glory.

The first, maketh men invade for gain; the second, for safety; and the third, for reputation. The first use violence, to make themselves masters of other men's persons, wives, children, and cattle; the second, to defend them; the third, for trifles, as a word, a smile, a different opinion, and any other sign of undervalue, either direct in their persons, or by reflection in their kindred, their friends, their nation, their profession, or their name.

Hereby it is manifest, that during the time men live without a common power to keep them all in awe, they are in that condition which is called war; and such a war, as is of every man, against every man. For WAR, consisteth not in battle only, or the act of fighting; but in a tract of time, wherein the will to contend by battle is sufficiently known: and therefore the notion of *time*, is to be considered in the nature of war; as it is in the nature of weather. For as the nature of foul weather, lieth not in a shower or two of rain; but in an inclination thereto of many days together: so the nature of war, consisteth not in actual fighting; but in the known disposition thereto, during all the time there is no assurance to the contrary. All other time is PEACE.

Whatsoever therefore is consequent to a time of war, where every man is enemy to every man; the same is consequent to the time, wherein men live without other security, than what their own strength, and their own invention shall furnish them withal. In such condition, there is no place for industry; because the fruit thereof is uncertain: and consequently no culture of the earth; no navigation, nor use of the commodities that may be imported by sea; no commodious building; no instruments of moving, and removing, such things as require much force; no knowledge of the face of the earth; no account of time; no arts; no letters; no society; and which is worst of all, continual fear, and danger of violent death; and the life of man, solitary, poor, nasty, brutish, and short. . . .

It may peradventure be thought, there was never such a time, nor condition of war as this; and I believe it was never generally so, over all the world: but there are many places, where they live so now. For the savage people in many places of America, except the government of small families, the concord whereof dependeth on natural lust, have no government at all; and live at this day in that brutish manner, as I said before. Howsoever, it may be perceived what manner of life there would be, where there were no common power to fear, by the manner of life, which men that have formerly lived under a peaceful government, use to degenerate into, in a civil war.

But though there had never been any time, wherein particular men were in a condition of war one against another; yet in all times, kings, and persons of sovereign authority, because of their independency, are in continual jealousies, and in the state and posture of gladiators; having their weapons pointing, and their eyes fixed on one another; that is, their forts, garrisons, and guns upon the frontiers of their kingdoms; and continual spies upon their neighbours; which is a posture of war. But because they uphold thereby, the industry of their subjects; there does not follow from it, that misery, which accompanies the liberty of particular men.[e]

5. Hobbes argues that society originates out of self-interest and fear, not out of natural feeling for one's fellow man. He defends as natural and reasonable the interest each man takes in his own welfare and happiness. In a state of nature, the first and only rule of life is self-protection, and men have a natural right to do anything which serves this end.

. . . All society therefore is either for gain, or for glory; that is, not so much for love of our fellows, as for the love of ourselves. But no society can be great or lasting, which begins from vain glory. Because that glory is like honour; if all men have it no man hath it, for they consist in comparison and precellence. Neither doth the society of others advance any whit the cause of my glorying in myself; for every man must account himself, such as he can make himself without the help of others. But though the benefits of this life may be much furthered by mutual help; since yet those may be better attained to by dominion than by the society of others, I hope no body will doubt, but that men would much more greedily be carried by nature, if all fear were removed, to obtain dominion, than to gain society. We must therefore resolve, that the original of all great and lasting societies consisted not in the mutual good will men had towards each other, but in the mutual fear they had of each other.

The cause of mutual fear consists partly in the natural equality of men, partly in their mutual will of hurting: whence it comes to pass, that we can neither expect from others, nor promise to ourselves the least security. For if we look on men full-grown, and consider how brittle the frame of our human body is, which perishing, all its strength, vigour, and wisdom itself perisheth with it; and how easy a matter it is, even for the weakest man to kill the strongest: there is no reason why any man, trusting to his own strength, should conceive himself made by nature above others. They are equals, who can do equal things one against the other; but they who can do the greatest things, namely, kill, can do equal things. All men therefore among themselves are by nature equal; the inequality we now discern, hath its spring from the civil law. . . .

Among so many dangers therefore, as the natural lusts of men do daily threaten each other withal, to have a care of one's self is so far from being a matter scornfully to be looked upon, that one has neither the power nor wish to have done otherwise. For every man is desirous of what is good for him, and shuns what is evil, but chiefly the chiefest of natural evils, which is death; and this he doth by a certain impulsion of nature, no less than that whereby a stone moves downward. It is therefore neither absurd nor reprehensible, neither against the dictates of true reason, for a man to use all his endeavours to preserve and defend his body and the members thereof from death and sorrows. But that which is not contrary to right reason, that all men account to be done justly, and with right. Neither by the word *right* is anything else signified, than that liberty which every man hath to make use of his natural faculties according to right reason. Therefore the first foundation of natural right is this, that *every man as much as in him lies endeavour to protect his life and members.*

But because it is in vain for a man to have a right to the end, if the right to the necessary means be denied him, it follows, that since every man hath a right to preserve himself, he must also be allowed a right *to use all the means, and do all the actions, without which he cannot preserve himself.*

Now whether the means which he is about to use, and the action he is performing, be necessary to the preservation of his life and members or not, he himself, by the right of nature, must be judge. For if it be contrary to right reason that I should judge of mine own peril, say, that another man is judge. Why now, because he judgeth of what concerns me, by the same reason, because we are equal by nature, will I judge also of things which do belong to him. Therefore it agrees with right reason, that is, it is the right of nature that I judge of his opinion, that is, whether it conduce to my preservation or not.

Nature hath given to *every one a right to all;* that is, it was lawful for every man, in the bare state of nature, or before such time as men had engaged themselves by any covenants or bonds, to do what he would, and against whom he thought fit, and to possess, use, and enjoy all what he would, or could get. Now because whatsoever a man would, it therefore seems good to him because he wills it, and either it really doth, or at least seems to him to contribute towards his preservation, (but we have already allowed him to be judge, in the foregoing article, whether it doth or not, insomuch as we are to hold all for necessary whatsoever he shall esteem so), and . . . it appears that by the right of nature those things may be done, and must be had, which necessarily conduce to the protection of life and members, it follows, that in the state of nature, to have all, and do all, is lawful for all. And this is that which is meant by that common saying, *nature hath given all to all.* From whence we understand likewise, that in the state of nature profit is the measure of right.

But it was the least benefit for men thus to have a common right to all things. For the effects of this right are the same, almost, as if there had been no right at all. For although any man might say of every thing, *this is mine,* yet could he not enjoy it, by reason of his neighbour, who having equal right and equal power, would pretend the same thing to be his.

If now to this natural proclivity of men, to hurt each other, which they derive from their passions, but chiefly from a vain esteem of themselves, you add, the right of all to all, wherewith one by right invades, the other by right resists, and whence arise perpetual jealousies and suspicions on all hands, and how hard a thing it is to provide against an enemy invading us with an intention to oppress and ruin, though he come with a small number, and no great provision; it cannot be denied but that the natural state of men, before they entered into society, was a mere war, and that not simply, but a war of all men against all men. For what is WAR, but that same time in which the will of contesting by force is fully declared, either by words or deeds? [f]

6. Defending himself against the possible charge of cynicism, Hobbes shows that there are no grounds for objections against self-interested action in the natural state. Social relations are not derived from the original nature of man, but are artificially created. In point of fact, society is only a means to the furthering of each individual's interests and happiness. Moreover, Hobbes maintains, the concept of moral obligation has neither meaning nor application in the state of nature. Rather, the basic moral concepts, right and wrong, just and unjust, arise concomitantly with the establishment of a civil society.

It may seem strange to some man, that has not well weighed these things; that nature should thus dissociate, and render men apt to invade, and destroy one another: and he may therefore, not trusting to this inference, made from the passions, desire perhaps to have the same confirmed by experience. Let him therefore consider with himself, when taking a journey, he arms himself, and seeks to go well accompanied; when going to sleep, he locks his doors; when even in his house he locks his chests; and this when he knows there be laws, and public officers, armed, to revenge all injuries shall be done him; what opinion he has of his fellow-subjects, when he rides armed; of his fellow citizens, when he locks his doors; and of his children, and servants, when he locks his chests. Does he not there as much accuse mankind by his actions, as I do by my words? But neither of us accuse man's nature in it. The desires, and other passions of man, are in themselves no sin. No more are the actions, that proceed from those passions, till they know a law that forbids them: which till laws be made they cannot know: nor can any law be made, till they have agreed upon the person that shall make it. . . .

To this war of every man, against every man, this also is consequent; that nothing can be unjust. The notions of right and wrong, justice and injustice have there no place. Where there is no common power, there is no law: where no law, no injustice. Force, and fraud, are in war the two cardinal virtues. Justice, and injustice are none of the faculties neither of the body, nor mind. If they were, they might be in a man that were alone in the world, as well as his senses, and passions. They are qualities, that relate to men in society, not in solitude. It is consequent also to the same condition, that there be no propriety, no dominion, no *mine* and *thine* distinct; but only that to be every man's, that he can get; and for so long, as he can keep it. And thus much for the ill condition, which man by mere nature is actually placed in; though with a possibility to come out of it, consisting partly in the passions, partly in his reason.

The passions that incline men to peace, are fear of death; desire of such things as are necessary to commodious living; and a hope by their industry to obtain them. And reason suggesteth convenient articles of peace, upon which men may be drawn to agreement. These articles, are they, which otherwise are called the Laws of Nature.[g]

7. *The termination of the perpetual warfare of the state of nature is brought about through the instrumentality of reason. First, an individual becomes aware, through rational deliberation, of his need for security. Second, reason discovers those precepts or "laws of nature" by which peace may be realized.*

A LAW OF NATURE, *lex naturalis*, is a precept or general rule, found out by reason, by which a man is forbidden to do that, which is destructive of his life, or taketh away the means of preserving the same; and to omit that, by which he thinketh it may be best preserved. For though they that speak of this subject, use to confound *jus*, and *lex, right* and *law:* yet they ought to be distinguished; because RIGHT, consisteth in liberty to do, or to forbear; whereas LAW, determineth, and bindeth to one of them: so that law, and right, differ as much, as obligation, and liberty; which in one and the same matter are inconsistent.

And because the condition of man, as hath been declared in the precedent chapter, is a condition of war of every one against every one: in which case every one is governed by his own reason; and there is nothing he can make use of, that may not be a help unto him, in preserving his life against his enemies; it followeth, that in such a condition, every man has a right to every thing; even to one another's body. And therefore, as long as this natural right of every man to every thing endureth, there can be no security to any man, how strong or wise soever he be, of living out the time, which nature ordinarily alloweth men to live. And consequently it is a precept, or general rule of reason, *that every man, ought to endeavour peace, as far as he has hope of obtaining it; and when he cannot obtain it, that he may seek, and use, all helps, and advantages of war.* The first branch of which rule, containeth the first, and fundamental law of nature; which is, *to seek peace, and follow it.* The second, the sum of the right of nature; which is, *by all means we can, to defend ourselves.*

From this fundamental law of nature, by which men are commanded to endeavour peace, is derived this second law; that *a man be willing, when others are so too, as far-forth, as for peace, and defence of himself he shall think it necessary, to lay down this right to all things; and be contented with so much liberty against other men, as he would allow other men against himself.* For as long as every man holdeth this right, of doing any thing he liketh; so long are all men in the condition of war. But if other men will not lay down their right, as well as he; then there is no reason for any one, to divest himself of his: for that were to expose himself to prey, which no man is bound to, rather than to dispose himself to peace . . .

Right is laid aside, either by simply renouncing it; or by transferring it to another. By *simply* RENOUNCING; when he cares not to whom the benefit thereof redoundeth. By TRANSFERRING; when he intendeth the benefit thereof to some certain person, or persons. And when a man hath in either manner abandoned, or granted away his right; then is he said to be OBLIGED, or BOUND, not to hinder those, to whom such right is granted, or abandoned, from the benefit of it: and that he *ought*, and it is his DUTY, not to make void that voluntary act of his own: and that such hindrance is INJUSTICE, and INJURY, as being *sine jure;* the right being before renounced, or transferred. So that *injury,* or *injustice,* in the controversies of the world, is somewhat like to that, which in the disputations of scholars is called *absurdity.* For as it is there called an absurdity, to contradict what one maintained in the beginning: so in the world, it is called injustice, and injury, voluntarily to undo that, which from the beginning he had voluntarily done . . .

Whensoever a man transferreth his right, or renounceth it; it is either in consideration of some right reciprocally transferred to himself; or for some other good he hopeth for thereby. For it is a voluntary act: and of the voluntary acts of every man, the object is some *good to himself.* And therefore there be some rights, which no man can be understood by any words, or other signs, to have abandoned, or transferred. As first a man cannot lay down the right of resisting them, that assault him by force, to take away his life; because he cannot be understood to aim thereby, at any good to himself. The same may be said of wounds, and chains, and imprisonment; both because there is no benefit consequent to such patience; as there is to the patience of suffering another to be wounded, or imprisoned: as also because a man cannot tell, when he seeth men proceed against him by violence, whether they intend his death or not. And lastly the motive, and end for which this renouncing, and transferring of right is introduced, is nothing else but the security of a man's person, in his life, and in the means of so preserving life, as not to be weary of it. And therefore if a man by words, or other signs, seem to despoil himself of the end, for which those signs were intended; he is not to be understood as if he meant it, or that it was his will; but that he was ignorant of how such words and actions were to be interpreted.[h]

8. When the egoistic nature of man is taken into account, it is manifest that the first two laws of nature in and of themselves are not binding upon the individual. Consequently, another law is necessary to make the first two effective.

From that law of nature, by which we are obliged to transfer to another, such rights, as being retained, hinder the peace of mankind, there followeth a third; which is this, *that men perform their covenants made:* without which, covenants are in vain, and but empty words; and the right of all men to all things remaining, we are still in the condition of war.

And in this law of nature, consisteth the fountain and original of JUSTICE. For where no covenant hath preceded, there hath no right been transferred, and every man has right to every thing; and consequently, no action can be unjust. But when a covenant is made, then to break it is *unjust:* and the definition of INJUS–TICE, is no other than *the not performance of covenant.* And whatsoever is not unjust, is *just.*

But because covenants of mutual trust, where there is a fear of not performance on either part . . . are invalid; though the original of justice be the making of covenants; yet injustice actually there can be none, till the cause of such fear be taken away; which while men are in the natural condition of war, cannot be done. Therefore before the names of just, and unjust can have place, there must be some coercive power, to compel men equally to the performance of their covenants, by the terror of some punishment, greater than the benefit they expect by the breach of their covenant; and to make good that propriety, which by mutual contract men acquire, in recompense of the universal right they abandon: and such power there is none before the erection of a commonwealth. And this is also to be gathered out of the ordinary definition of justice in the Schools: for they say, that *justice is the constant will of giving to every man his own.* And therefore where there is no *own,* that is no propriety, there is no injustice; and where there is no coercive power erected, that is, where there is no commonwealth, there is no propriety; all men having right to all things: therefore where there is no commonwealth, there nothing is unjust. So that the nature of justice, consisteth in keeping of valid covenants: but the validity of convenants begins not but with the constitution of a civil power, sufficient to compel men to keep them: and then it is also that propriety begins.[i]

9. Hobbes concludes that the laws of nature may be summed up in a rule which everyone accepts, the Golden Rule.

These are the laws of nature, dictating peace, for a means of the conservation of men in multitudes; and which only concern the doctrine of civil society. There be other things tending to the destruction of particular men; as drunkenness, and all other parts of intemperance; which may therefore also be reckoned amongst those things which the law of nature hath forbidden; but are not necessary to be mentioned, nor are pertinent enough to this place.

And though this may seem too subtle a deduction of the laws of nature, to be taken notice of by all men; whereof the most part are too busy in getting food, and the rest too negligent to understand; yet to leave all men inexcusable, they have been contracted into one easy sum, intelligible even to the meanest capacity; and that is, *Do not that to another, which thou wouldest not have done to thyself;* which sheweth him, that he has no more to do in learning the laws of nature, but, when weighing the actions of other men with his own, they seem too heavy, to put them into the other part of the balance, and his own into their place, that his own passions, and self-love, may add nothing to the weight; and then there is none of these laws of nature that will not appear unto him very reasonable.[j]

10. Reason not only dictates peace and security in society, but it also prescribes the means by which they can be insured. It was apparent to Hobbes that there must be some civil power to determine and interpret what is right, wrong, good, and bad in society. Such authority must be vested in a single sovereign power — either an individual or an assembly — to prevent the occurrence of jurisdictional disputes between one authority and another. Hobbes believes that matters of conscience, for example, must be controlled entirely by the sovereign. Thus, even church affairs should be dominated by the secular ruler, "God's lieutenant on earth."

. . . I observe the *diseases* of a commonwealth, that proceed from the poison of seditious doctrines, whereof one is, *That every private man is judge of good and evil actions.* This is true in the condition of mere nature, where there are no civil laws; and also under civil government, in such cases as are not determined by the law. But otherwise, it is manifest, that the measure of good and evil actions, is the civil law; and the judge the legislator, who is always representative of the commonwealth. From this false doctrine, men are disposed to debate with themselves, and dispute the commands of the commonwealth; and afterwards to obey, or disobey them, as in their private judgments they shall think fit; whereby the commonwealth is distracted and *weakened.*

Another doctrine repugnant to civil society, is, that *whatsoever a man does against his conscience, is sin;* and it dependeth on the presumption of making himself judge of good and evil. For a man's conscience, and his judgment is the same thing, and as the judgment, so also the conscience may be erroneous. Therefore, though he that is subject to no civil law, sinneth in all he does against his conscience, because he has no other rule to follow but his own reason; yet it is not so with him that lives in a commonwealth; because the law is the public conscience, by which he hath already undertaken to be guided. Otherwise in such diversity, as there is of private consciences, which are but private opinions, the commonwealth must needs be distracted, and no man dare to obey the sovereign power, further than it shall seem good in his own eyes. . . . There is [another] doctrine, plainly, and directly against the essence of a commonwealth; and it is this, *that the sovereign power may be divided.* For what is it to divide the power of a commonwealth, but to dissólve it; for powers divided mutually destroy each other. And for these doctrines, men are chiefly beholding to some of those, that making profession of the laws, endeavour to make them depend upon their own learning, and not upon the legislative power.[k]

11. In its ultimate consequences, then, Hobbes' ethical theory leads to the political doctrine of absolute sovereignty, designed to end the natural war of every man with every other man.

To the care of the sovereign, belongeth the making of good laws. But what is a good law? By a good law, I mean not a just law: for no law can be unjust. The law is made by the sovereign power, and all that is done by such power, is warranted, and owned by every one of the people; and that which every man will have so, no man can say is unjust. It is in the laws of a commonwealth, as in the laws of gaming: whatsoever the gamesters all agree on, is injustice to none of them. A good law is that, which is *needful*, for the *good of the people*, and withal *perspicuous*.

For the use of laws, which are but rules authorized, is not to bind the people from all voluntary actions; but to direct and keep them in such a motion, as not to hurt themselves by their own impetuous desires, rashness or indiscretion; as hedges are set, not to stop travellers, but to keep them in their way. And therefore a law that is not needful, having not the true end of a law, is not good. A law may be conceived to be good, when it is for the benefit of the sovereign; though it be not necessary for the people; but it is not so. For the good of the sovereign and people, cannot be separated. It is a weak sovereign, that has weak subjects; and a weak people, whose sovereign wanteth power to rule them at his will. Unnecessary laws are not good laws; but traps for money: which where the right of sovereign power is acknowledged, are superfluous; and where it is not acknowledged, insufficient to defend the people. . . .

The office of the sovereign, be it a monarch or an assembly, consisteth in the end, for which he was trusted with the sovereign power, namely the procuration of *the safety of the people;* to which he is obliged by the law of nature, and to render an account thereof to God, the author of that law, and to none but him. But by safety here, is not meant a bare preservation, but also all other contentments of life, which every man by lawful industry, without danger, or hurt to the commonwealth, shall acquire to himself.

And this is intended should be done, not by care applied to individuals, further than their protection from injuries, when they shall complain; but by a general providence, contained in public instruction, both of doctrine, and example; and in the making and executing of good laws, to which individual persons may apply their own cases.

And because, if the essential rights of sovereignty . . . be taken away, the commonwealth is thereby dissolved, and every man returneth into the condition, and calamity of a war with every other man, which is the greatest evil that can happen in this life; it is the office of the sovereign, to maintain those rights entire . . .[1]

Questions

1. Outline Hobbes' psychological theory. What effect does it have on his definitions of "good" and "evil"? On his moral philosophy in general?

2. In Hobbes' view, what is the "natural state" of man? To what political theory does this lead him?

3. How does Hobbes define "happiness"? Why can it not be achieved in a state of nature?

4. Discuss Hobbes' theory of the formation of society. How would he deal with the thesis that "man is by nature a social animal"?

5. What arguments does Hobbes offer in defense of his egoistic theory of human relations? Can you find arguments or evidence against his view?

6. What does Hobbes mean by "laws of nature"? Where do they originate? Do you agree that they are really laws of nature?

7. What use does Hobbes make of the doctrines of materialism and mechanism? Are these doctrines essential to his ethical theory?

8. In Hobbes' ethical theory, what is the basis of morality? Do the same moral principles apply in a state of war and in a civil society?

9. Compare and contrast the status of the term "good" with the status of the term "right" in Hobbes' moral philosophy.

10. Do you believe that there are some situations in which you would not prefer peace and security? Relate your answer to Hobbes' ethical theory.

Key to selections:

THOMAS HOBBES, *Leviathan* and *Philosophical Rudiments*, from *The English Works of Thomas Hobbes*, vols. II and III, Sir William Molesworth, ed., London, John Bohn, 1839.

From *Leviathan*
[a] Ch. XVIII, p. 159.
[b] Ch. VI, pp. 38–41.
[c] Ch. VI, p. 41.
[d] Ch. XIII, pp. 110–112.
[e] Ch. XIII, pp. 112–113,
      pp. 114–115.
[g] Ch. XIII, pp. 113–114,
      pp. 114–116.
[h] Ch. XIV, pp. 116–118,
      pp. 118–119,
      pp. 119–120.
[i] Ch. XV, pp. 130–131.

[j] Ch. XV, pp. 144–145.
[k] Ch. XXIX, pp. 310–311,
      p. 313.
[l] Ch. XXX, pp. 335–336,
      pp. 322–323.
From *Philosophical Rudiments*
[f] Ch. I, pp. 5–7,
      pp. 8–11.

Guide to Additional Reading

INEXPENSIVE EDITIONS:

HOBBES, T., *Leviathan*, Everyman's Library (Dutton).
——,   —— (Selections), Great Books Foundation (Regnery).
        English Philosophers from Bacon to Mill, Modern Library
        (Random House).
        Hobbes Selections, Modern Student's Library (Scribner's).

DISCUSSION AND COMMENTARY:

Catlin, G. E. G., *Thomas Hobbes as Philosopher, Publicist and Man of Letters*, Oxford, Basil Blackwell and Mott, Ltd., 1922.
Gooch, G. P., *Hobbes*, London, Humphrey Milford, 1940.
Stephen, L., *Hobbes*, London, Macmillan and Company, Ltd., 1904.
Taylor, A. E., *Thomas Hobbes*, London, Constable and Company, Ltd. 1908.
Warrender, H., *The Political Philosophy of Hobbes*, Oxford, Clarendon Press, 1957.

CHAPTER 8

Nature and Reason

**BENEDICT
DE SPINOZA**

An uncommon devotion to intellectual independence and integrity is exemplified in the personal history of Spinoza (1632–1677). He was born of Jewish parents who had sought refuge in Amsterdam, Holland, from Spanish persecution. From the scholars of the Synagogue, Spinoza acquired a thorough knowledge of the Old Testament, such Hebrew religious classics as the *Talmud* and the mystical *Kabbala*, and the teachings of noted Jewish theologians. In addition, he mastered the works of Christian philosophers and the secular writings which marked the beginnings of the modern scientific era.

An early tendency to rebel against the narrow formalism and orthodoxy of his religion reached a critical point when Spinoza was twenty-four years old. His disregard of entreaties, bribes, and threats to his life intended to force him to at least outward conformity to Judaism resulted in his excommunication, in 1656, from the Jewish community. Changing his Hebrew name, Baruch, to its Latin equivalent, Benedict, he pursued his nonconformist

157

views as a philosopher in the Christian world, but he did not become a Christian. In fact, his position in regard to religious matters has, since his lifetime, been a subject of debate. While there is virtual unanimity in placing him in the first ranks of the philosophers, there has never been agreement as to whether he was a "God-intoxicated man" or an atheist who made frequent use of the word "God" when he meant nothing more than "Nature."

Following his excommunication, Spinoza withdrew from Amsterdam, living in several remote Dutch villages until he settled in The Hague, where he spent the last seven years of his life. Supporting himself by the humble occupation of lens-grinding, he devoted his evenings to philosophical composition. He enjoyed the loyalty of a few friends and disciples and maintained a learned correspondence with such distinguished men of the times as Henry Oldenburg, of the Royal Society of England, Christian Huyghens, the physicist, and Gottfried Leibniz, the philosopher.

Through his commentary on the writings of the philosopher Descartes, Spinoza proved himself a competent scholar. His *Tractatus Theologico-Politicus* (1670) raised a storm of protest by its strong plea for freedom of thought and criticism, a radical idea in the seventeenth century. Moreover, the criticisms of traditional religion contained in the work alienated religious leaders and some of his own friends. For the sake of peace, Spinoza kept his subsequent writings from public view, and they were not published until the year of his death. These comprised chiefly a political treatise, an incomplete essay, "On the Improvement of the Understanding," and his main work, *Ethics, Demonstrated in Geometrical Order*. The latter, composed mainly of definitions, axioms, and propositions with their proofs, testifies to Spinoza's conviction that the rigorous method of mathematics is the appropriate method for philosophy.

Spinoza's reputation among the scholars of the day as a learned and profound thinker brought him, in 1673, an offer of a professorship in philosophy at the great University of Heidelberg. His explanation for refusing this honorable post bespeaks his dedication to the contemplative way of life: he did not wish to take time away from philosophical reflection for the training of disciples, nor did he wish to teach in public, where he would almost certainly suffer from the disturbance of religious quarrels through his persistence in his own way of understanding God.

•

Spinoza's ethical theory is the culmination of a complex philosophical system which involves not only the nature of man, but also the nature of God and man's relation to God. For Spinoza, the key to ethics lies in the proposition, "All things . . . are in God, and all things which come to pass, come to pass solely through the laws of the infinite nature of God, and follow . . . from the necessity of his essence." He thus equates God with Nature, or Reality, or the Universe, and characterizes the complex totality as a rational unity in which everything follows with logical necessity from the nature of the whole.[1] Because it shares in the rationality of the divine order, the mind of man is able to know God, or Nature. The wise man, aware that moral excellence and the happiness it brings are proportionate to his knowledge of God, devotes himself to the cultivation of his reason.

Although man is essentially a rational being in a rational universe, his intellect is imperfect and limited. He has a natural tendency to view events in relation to himself, and therefore can form only confused and inadequate ideas of reality. In such a state, the mind projects upon the external world its judgments of what is good or evil to man, thus fostering the illusion that good and evil exist as objective realities in the universe. But in the Spinozistic view, the distinction between good and evil is not applicable to the universe as such, for the universe is God, and

[1] From Spinoza's pantheism — his identification of God with Nature — and his characterization of God as a fixed rational order, it is evident that his conception of the divine being is markedly different from that of the Judaeo-Christian religious tradition. Spinoza dismisses as superstition the belief that God transcends nature and is a merciful and just Person who acts with free will. Moreover, miracles, acts of divine providence, prayer, and the working of divine purpose are rejected as inconsistent with the logical necessity of events.

God is necessarily perfect. Hence, the uneducated man is mentally and morally weak. In his ignorance of the order of Nature he is subject to what appears to him to be the whim of events. In these circumstances, he is beset by the uncontrolled and conflicting emotions which cause his unhappiness. In contrast,

. . . the strong man has ever first in his thoughts, that all things follow from the necessity of the divine nature; so that whatsoever he deems to be hurtful and evil, and whatsoever, accordingly, seems to him impious, horrible, unjust, and base, assumes that appearance owing to his own disordered, fragmentary, and confused view of the universe. Wherefore he strives before all things to conceive things as they really are, and to remove the hindrances to true knowledge, such as are hatred, anger, envy, derision, pride, and similar emotions . . .[a]

The removal of the ills which destroy happiness, therefore, can be accomplished only by freeing the mind from its bondage to the emotions which becloud it: how to do this is the basic ethical problem for man.

To free himself from bondage, the rational man attacks the difficulty at its source. He seeks knowledge of the causes of things, accepting without protest the unchangeable order of events. At the zenith of his intellectual power, he rises far above the limited perspective of his personal interests to the view of all things "under the aspect of eternity." The pursuit and possession of objective knowledge free his mind from error; and emotional conflict, which Spinoza always correlates with intellectual confusion, gives way to emotional stability. When he understands that each object and each event has a fixed place in the rational order of Nature, the reflective man is well on his way to felicity.

In Spinoza's ethical theory, human effort to acquire knowledge and virtue is accounted for by a striving for self-preservation (*conatus*). In man, whose essential nature is rational, this striving is directed towards the perfection of the intellect. The happiness enjoyed by the rational man accompanies his "knowledge of the union existing between the mind and the whole of nature." The contemplation of reality under the aspect of eternity leads man to his highest good, the "intellectual love of God," which is the understanding of God as the eternal Being in whose rational order each of us has his proper place. In this way, man proceeds from the state of human bondage to the state of human freedom — from the wretchedness of an unstable emotional existence to the happiness of the tranquil life of reason.

• • •

1. In his essay "On the Improvement of the Understanding," Spinoza examines the false values which arise out of misunderstandings of the nature of the true good for man. He concludes that it is necessary to surrender the pursuit of such goals as riches, fame, and pleasure, since they consume mental energy and time which should be given to meditation.

After experience had taught me that all the usual surroundings of social life are vain and futile; seeing that none of the objects of my fears contained in themselves anything either good or bad, except in so far as the mind is affected by them, I finally resolved to inquire whether there might be some real good having power to communicate itself, which would affect the mind singly, to the exclusion of all else: whether, in fact, there might be anything of which the discovery and attainment would enable me to enjoy continuous, supreme, and unending happiness. I say "I *finally* resolved," for at first sight it seemed unwise willingly to lose hold on what was sure for the sake of something then uncertain. I could see the benefits which are acquired through fame and riches, and that I should be obliged to abandon the quest of such objects, if I seriously devoted myself to the search for something different and new. I perceived that if true happiness chanced to be placed in the former I should necessarily miss it; while if, on the other hand, it were not so placed, and I gave them my whole attention, I should equally fail.

I therefore debated whether it would not be possible to arrive at the new principle, or at any rate at a certainty concerning its existence, without changing the conduct and usual plan of my life; with this end in view I made many efforts, but in vain. For the ordinary surroundings of life which are esteemed by men (as their actions testify) to be the highest good, may be classed under the three heads — Riches, Fame, and the Pleasures of Sense: with these three the mind is so absorbed that it has little power to reflect on any different good. By sensual pleasure the mind is enthralled to the extent of quiescence, as if the supreme good were actually attained, so that it is quite incapable of thinking of any other object; when such pleasure has been gratified it is followed by extreme melancholy, whereby the mind, though not enthralled, is disturbed and dulled.

The pursuit of honours and riches is likewise very absorbing, especially if such objects be sought simply for their own sake, inasmuch as they are then supposed to constitute the highest good. In the case of fame the mind is still more absorbed, for fame is conceived as always good for its own sake, and as the ultimate end to which all actions are directed. Further, the attainment cf riches and fame is not followed as in the case of sensual pleasures by repentance, but, the more we acquire, the greater is our delight, and, consequently, the more are we incited to increase both the one and the other; on the other hand, if our hopes happen to be frustrated we are plunged into the deepest sadness. Fame has the further drawback that it compels its votaries to order their lives according to the opinions of their fellow-men, shunning what they usually shun, and seeking what they usually seek.[b]

2. Spinoza argues that the things most men value are evil, rather than good, and only unhappiness can follow from "the love of what is perishable." He is in quest of a good which cannot be destroyed by external causes. Since the process of inquiry itself allays the anxieties which usually accompany the pursuit of material objectives, he has an indication of the direction in which he must look for true happiness.

When I saw that all these ordinary objects of desire would be obstacles in the way of a search for something different and new

— nay, that they were so opposed thereto, that either they or it would have to be abandoned, I was forced to inquire which would prove the most useful to me: for, as I say, I seemed to be willingly losing hold on a sure good for the sake of something uncertain. However, after I had reflected on the matter, I came in the first place to the conclusion that by abandoning the ordinary objects of pursuit, and betaking myself to a new quest, I should be leaving a good, uncertain by reason of its own nature, as may be gathered from what has been said, for the sake of a good not uncertain in its nature (for I sought for a fixed good), but only in the possibility of its attainment.

Further reflection convinced me, that if I could really get to the root of the matter I should be leaving certain evils for a certain good. I thus perceived that I was in a state of great peril, and I compelled myself to seek with all my strength for a remedy, however uncertain it might be; as a sick man struggling with a deadly disease, when he sees that death will surely be upon him unless a remedy be found, is compelled to seek such a remedy with all his strength, inasmuch as his whole hope lies therein. All the objects pursued by the multitude not only bring no remedy that tends to preserve our being, but even act as hindrances, causing the death not seldom of those who possess them, and always of those who are possessed by them. There are many examples of men who have suffered persecution even to death for the sake of their riches, and of men who in pursuit of wealth have exposed themselves to so many dangers, that they have paid away their life as a penalty for their folly. Examples are no less numerous of men, who have endured the utmost wretchedness for the sake of gaining or preserving their reputation. Lastly, there are innumerable cases of men, who have hastened their death through over-indulgence in sensual pleasure. All these evils seem to have arisen from the fact, that happiness or unhappiness is made wholly to depend on the quality of the object which we love. When a thing is not loved, no quarrels will arise concerning it — no sadness will be felt if it perishes — no envy if it is possessed by another — no fear, no hatred, in short no disturbances of the mind. All these arise from the love of what is perishable, such as the objects already mentioned. But love towards a thing eternal and infinite feeds the mind wholly with joy, and is itself unmingled with any sadness, wherefore it is greatly to be desired and sought for with all our strength. Yet it was not at random that I used the words, "If I could go to the root of the matter," for, though what I have urged was perfectly clear to my mind, I could not forthwith lay aside all love of riches, sensual enjoyment, and fame. One thing was evident, namely, that while my mind was employed with these thoughts it turned away from its former objects of desire, and seriously considered the search for a new principle; this state of things was a great comfort to me, for I perceived that the evils were not such as to resist all remedies. Although these intervals were at first rare, and of very short duration, yet afterwards, as the true good became more and more discernible to me, they became more frequent and more lasting; especially after I had recognized that the acquisition of wealth, sensual pleasure, or fame, is only a hindrance, so long as they are sought as ends not as means; if they be sought as means, they will be under restraint, and, far from being hindrances, will further not a little the end for which they are sought, as I will show in due time.[c]

3. Spinoza concludes from this inquiry that although man's capabilities are limited, he can aspire to a greater perfection both for himself and for his fellow men.

. . . Man conceives a human character much more stable than his own, and sees that there is no reason why he should not himself acquire such a character. Thus he is led to seek for means which will bring him to this pitch of perfection, and calls everything which will serve as such means a true good. The chief good is that he should arrive, together with other individuals if possible, at the possession of the aforesaid character. What that character is we shall show in due time, namely, that it is the knowledge of the union existing between the mind and the whole of nature.

This, then, is the end for which I strive, to attain to such a character myself, and to endeavour that many should attain to it with me. In other words, it is part of my happiness to lend a helping hand, that many others may understand even as I do, so that their understanding and desire may entirely agree with my own. In order to bring this about, it is necessary to understand as much of nature as will enable us to attain to the aforesaid character, and also to form a social order such as is most conducive to the attainment of this character by the greatest number with the least difficulty and danger.[d]

4. In the essay "On the Improvement of the Understanding," Spinoza cautions us that "before all things, a means must be devised for improving the understanding and purifying it, as far as may be at the outset, so that it may apprehend things without error, and in the best possible way." Therefore, in his detailed and systematic work, the Ethics, *he both presents his positive theory and exposes the conceptual errors which mislead men in their search for happiness. One of the common misconceptions results from viewing the world as God's purposive scheme. Because of this mistake, men are misled into believing that objects and events in nature are either inherently good or inherently bad.*

. . . There remain misconceptions not a few, which might and may prove very grave hindrances to the understanding of the concatenation of things. . . . I have therefore thought it worth while to bring these misconceptions before the bar of reason.

All such opinions spring from the notion commonly entertained, that all things in nature act as men themselves act, namely, with an end in view. It is accepted as certain, that God himself directs all things to a definite goal (for it is said that God made all things for man, and man that he might worship him). I will, therefore, consider this opinion, asking first, why it obtains general credence, and why all men are naturally so prone to adopt it? Secondly, I will point out its falsity; and, lastly, I will show how it has given rise to prejudices about good and bad, right and wrong, praise and blame, order and confusion, beauty and ugliness, and the like. However, this is not the place to deduce these misconceptions from the nature of the human mind. It will be sufficient here, if I assume as a starting point, what ought to be universally admitted, namely, that all men are born ignorant of the causes of things, that all have the desire to seek what is useful to them, and that they are conscious of such desire. Herefrom it follows, first, that men think themselves free inasmuch as they are conscious of their volitions and desires, and never even dream, in their ignorance, of the causes which have disposed them so to wish and desire. Secondly, that men do all things for an end, namely, for that which is useful to them, and which they seek. Thus it comes to pass that they only look for a knowledge of the final causes of events, and when these are learned, they are content, as having no cause for further doubt. If they cannot learn such causes from external sources, they are compelled to turn to considering themselves, and reflecting what end would have induced them personally to bring about the given event, and thus they necessarily judge other natures by their own. Further, as they find in themselves and outside themselves many means which assist them not a little in their search for what is useful, for instance, eyes for seeing, teeth for chewing, herbs and animals for yielding food, the sun for giving light, the sea for breeding fish, &c., they come to look on the whole of nature as a means for obtaining such conveniences. Now as they are aware, that they found these conveniences and did not make them, they think they have cause for believing, that some other being has made them for their use. . . .

Consider, I pray you, the result: among the many helps of nature they were bound to find some hindrances, such as storms, earthquakes, diseases, &c.: so they declared that such things happen, because the gods are angry at some wrong done them by men, or at some fault committed in their worship. Experience day by day protested and showed by infinite examples, that good and evil fortunes fall to the lot of pious and impious alike; still they would not abandon their inveterate prejudice, for it was more easy for them to class such contradictions among other unknown things of whose use they were ignorant, and thus to retain their actual and innate condition of ignorance, than to destroy the whole fabric of their reasoning and start afresh. . . .

We must not omit to notice that the followers of this doctrine, anxious to display their talent in assigning final causes, have imported a new method of argument in proof of their theory – namely, a reduction, not to the impossible, but to ignorance; thus showing that they have no other method of exhibiting their doctrine. For example, if a stone falls from a roof on to someone's head, and kills him, they will demonstrate by their new method, that the stone fell in order to kill the man; for, if it had not by God's will fallen with that object, how could so many circumstances (and there are often many concurrent circumstances) have all happened together by chance? Perhaps you will answer that the event is due to the facts that the wind was blowing, and the man was walking that way. "But why," they will insist, "was the wind blowing and why was the man at that very time walking that way?" If you again answer, that the wind had then sprung up because the sea had begun to be agitated the day before, the weather being previously calm, and that the man had been invited by a friend, they will again insist: "But why was the sea agitated, and why was the man invited at that time?" So they will pursue their questions from cause to cause, till at last you take refuge in the will of God – in other words, the sanctuary of ignorance. . . .

After men persuaded themselves, that everything which is created is created for their sake, they are bound to consider as the chief quality in everything that which is most useful to themselves, and to account those things the best of all which have the most beneficial effect on mankind. Further, they were bound to form abstract notions for the explanation of the nature of things, such as *goodness, badness, order, confusion, warmth, cold, beauty, deformity,* and so on. . . .

Everything which conduces to health and the worship of God they have called *good,* everything which hinders these objects they have styled *bad;* and inasmuch as those who do not understand the nature of things do not verify phenomena in any way, but merely imagine them after a fashion, and mistake their imagination for understanding, such persons firmly believe that there is an *order* in things, being really ignorant both of things and their own nature. . . .ᶜ

5. *Spinoza finds the doctrine of free will to be particularly pernicious. In his*

judgment, it is from ignorance of the true causes of our actions that we come to believe that anything we do can possibly be otherwise than it actually is. The will is nothing but a form of the intellect, he argues, and as such can act only according to the fixed laws which govern all thought.

. . . Thus an infant believes that of its own free will it desires milk, an angry child believes that it freely desires vengeance, a timid child believes that it freely desires to run away; further, a drunken man believes that he utters from the free decision of his mind words which, when he is sober, he would willingly have withheld: thus, too, a delirious man, a garrulous woman, a child, and others of like complexion, believe that they speak from the free decision of their mind, when they are in reality unable to restrain their impulse to talk. Experience teaches us no less clearly than reason, that men believe themselves to be free, simply because they are conscious of their actions, and unconscious of the causes whereby those actions are determined; and, further, it is plain that the dictates of the mind are but another name for the appetites, and therefore vary according to the varying state of the body. Every one shapes his actions according to his emotion, those who are assailed by conflicting emotions know not what they wish; those who are not attacked by any emotion are readily swayed this way or that. All these considerations clearly show that a mental decision and a bodily appetite, or determined state, are simultaneous, or rather are one and the same thing, which we call decision, when it is regarded under and explained through the attribute of thought, and a conditioned state, when it is regarded under the attribute of extension, and deduced from the laws of motion and rest. . . . I wish to call attention to another point, namely, that we cannot act by the decision of the mind, unless we have a remembrance of having done so. For instance, we cannot say a word without remembering that we have done so. Again, it is not within the free power of the mind to remember or forget a thing at will. Therefore the freedom of the mind must in any case be limited to the power of uttering or not uttering something which it remembers. But when we dream that we speak, we believe that we speak from a free decision of the mind, yet we do not speak, or, if we do, it is by a spontaneous motion of the body. Again, we dream that we are concealing something, and we seem to act from the same decision of the mind as that, whereby we keep silence when awake concerning something we know. Lastly, we dream that from the free decision of our mind we do something, which we should not dare to do when awake.

Now I should like to know whether there be in the mind two sorts of decisions, one sort illusive, and the other sort free? If our folly does not carry us so far as this, we must necessarily admit, that the decision of the mind, which is believed to be free, is not distinguishable from the imagination or memory, and is nothing more than the affirmation, which an idea, by virtue of being an idea, necessarily involves. Wherefore these decisions of the mind arise in the mind by the same necessity, as the ideas of things actually existing. Therefore those who believe, that they speak or keep silence or act in any way from the free decision of their mind, do but dream with their eyes open.[e]

5. Belief in the freedom of the will is pernicious, Spinoza maintains, because it introduces an element of uncertainty into life. Furthermore, the delusion that we have the power and freedom to do whatever we wish raises false hopes. True freedom, he says, is action in accordance with the laws of our reason. In support of his position, Spinoza enumerates its beneficial effects on human conduct. His doctrine is good, he says:

1. Inasmuch as it teaches us to act solely according to the decree of God, and to be partakers in the Divine nature, and so much the more, as we perform more perfect actions and more and more understand God. Such a doctrine not only completely tranquillizes our spirit, but also shows us where our highest happiness and blessedness is, namely, solely in the knowledge of God, whereby we are led to act only as love and piety shall bid us.

We may thus clearly understand, how far astray from a true estimate of virtue are those who expect to be decorated by God with high rewards for their virtue, and their best actions, as for having endured the direst slavery; as if virtue and the service of God were not in itself happiness and perfect freedom.

2. Inasmuch as it teaches us, how we ought to conduct ourselves with respect to the gifts of fortune, or matters which are not in our own power, and do not follow from our nature. For it shows us, that we should await and endure fortune's smiles or frowns with an equal mind, seeing that all things follow from the eternal decree of God by the same necessity, as it follows from the essence of a triangle, that the three angles are equal to two right angles.

3. This doctrine raises social life, inasmuch as it teaches us to hate no man, neither to despise, to deride, to envy, or to be angry with any. Further, as it tells us that each should be content with his own, and helpful to his neighbor, not from any womanish pity, favour, or superstition, but solely by the guidance of reason, according as the time and occasion demand . . .

4. Lastly, this doctrine confers no small advantage on the commonwealth; for it teaches how citizens should be governed and led, not so as to become slaves, but so that they may freely do whatsoever things are best.[f]

6. Spinoza's approach to psychology reflects his deterministic view of human behavior. He asserts that the emotions are natural phenomena, subject to definite laws, and should therefore be studied according to the same geometrical method as the rest of nature.

Most writers on the emotions and on human conduct seem to be treating rather of matters outside nature than of natural phenomena following nature's general laws. They appear to conceive man to be situated in nature as a kingdom within a kingdom: for they believe that he disturbs rather than follows nature's order, that he has absolute control over his actions, and that he is determined solely by himself. They attribute human infirmities and fickleness, not to the power of nature in general, but to some mysterious flaw in the nature of man, which accordingly they bemoan, deride, despise, or, as usually happens, abuse: he, who succeeds in hitting off the weakness of the human mind more eloquently or more acutely than his fellows, is looked upon as a seer. Still there has been no lack of very excellent men (to whose toil and industry I confess myself much indebted), who have written many noteworthy things concerning the right way of life, and have given much sage advice to mankind. But no one, so far as I know, has defined the nature and strength of the emotions, and the power of the mind against them for their restraint.

. . . Such persons will doubtless think it strange that I should attempt to treat of human vice and folly geometrically, and should wish to set forth with rigid reasoning those matters which they cry out against as repugnant to reason, frivolous, absurd, and dreadful. However, such is my plan. Nothing comes to pass in nature, which can be set down to a flaw therein; for nature is always the same, and everywhere one and the same in her efficacy and power of action; that is, nature's laws and ordinances, whereby all things come to pass and change from one form to another, are everywhere and always the same; so that there should be one and the same method of understanding the nature of all things whatsoever, namely, through nature's universal laws and rules. Thus the passions of hatred, anger, envy, and so on, considered in themselves, follow from this same necessity and efficacy of nature; they answer to certain definite causes, through which they are understood, and possess certain properties as worthy of being known as the properties of anything else, whereof the contemplation in itself affords us delight. I shall, therefore, treat of the nature and strength of the emotions according to the same method, as I employed heretofore in my investigations concerning God and the mind. I shall consider human actions and desires in exactly the same manner, as though I were concerned with lines, planes, and solids.[g]

7. The focal point of Spinoza's complex psychological theory is the concept of conatus, *the striving for self-preservation and self-perfection which characterizes all things. Man's drive to preserve his existence and perfect his essential nature is not only the basis of all behavior, but it is also the foundation of virtue. Because man's essential nature is rational, the preservation of his being prescribes obedience to reason, and this constitutes virtue.*

PROP. XX. The more every man endeavours, and is able to seek what is useful to him — in other words, to preserve his own being — the more is he endowed with virtue; on the contrary, in proportion as a man neglects to seek what is useful to him, that is, to preserve his own being, he is wanting in power . . .

PROP. XXI. No one can desire to be blessed, to act rightly, and to live rightly, without at the same time wishing to be, to act, and to live — in other words, to actually exist . . .

PROP. XXII. No virtue can be conceived as prior to this endeavour to preserve one's own being . . .

Corollary. — The effort for self-preservation is the first and only foundation of virtue. For prior to this principle, nothing can be conceived, and without it no virtue can be conceived . . .

PROP. XXIV. To act absolutely in obedience to virtue is in us the same thing as to act, to live, or to preserve one's being (these three terms are identical in meaning) in accordance with the dictates of reason on the basis of seeking what is useful to one's self . . .

PROP. XXVI. Whatsoever we endeavour in obedience to reason is nothing further than to understand; neither does the mind, in so far as it makes use of reason, judge anything to be useful to it, save such things as are conducive to understanding.

Proof. — The effort for self-preservation is nothing else but the essence of the thing in question, which, in so far as it exists such as it is, is conceived to have force for continuing in existence and doing such things as necessarily follow from its given nature. But the essence of reason is nought else but our mind, in so far as it clearly and distinctly understands; therefore whatsoever we endeavour in obedience to reason is nothing else but to understand.

Again, since this effort of the mind wherewith the mind endeavours, in so far as it reasons, to preserve its own being is nothing else but understanding; this effort at understanding is the first and single basis of virtue, nor shall we endeavour to understand things for the sake of any ulterior object; on the other hand, the mind, in so far as it reasons, will not be able to conceive any good for itself, save such things as are conducive to understanding.[h]

8. The same striving for self-preservation which dictates conformity to reason generates the powerful emotions, desire, pleasure, *and* pain, *from which all other emotions are derived. Even judgments of good and evil are decided by the emotions: each man terms "good" those things which give pleasure, i.e., whatever he believes increases his perfection; he terms "evil" those things which are painful, i.e., whatever he believes diminishes his perfection.[2] That is to say:*

. . . We in no case desire a thing because we deem it good, but, contrariwise, we deem a thing good because we desire it: consequently we deem evil that which we shrink from; every one, therefore, according to his particular emotions, judges or estimates what is good, what is bad, what is better, what is worse, lastly, what is best, and what is worst. Thus a miser thinks that abundance of money is the best, and want of money the worst; an ambitious man desires nothing so much as glory, and fears nothing so much as shame. To an envious man nothing is more delightful than another's misfortune, and nothing more painful than another's success. So every man, according to his emotions, judges a thing to be good or bad, useful or useless.[i]

Spinoza defines the knowledge of good and evil in terms of the emotions of pleasure and pain. Then, on the ground that " an emotion

---

[2] It follows from Spinoza's theory that judgments of good and evil are subject to three kinds of error: (1) men may judge as pleasant, *i.e.*, as good, things which do not actually conserve their rational nature, *e.g.*, fame, wealth, and sensual pleasures; (2) it may not be realized that good and evil do not belong to objects considered in themselves, but are only relative to the emotions of pleasure and pain; and (3) pleasure, the *criterion* of human good, may be mistaken for the *source* of the true good for man, which is the knowledge of God.

can only be controlled or destroyed by another emotion," not by a mere idea, he asserts that the effectiveness of the knowledge of good and evil is proportionate to its own emotive force, not to its truth. The emotions vary in their power, and the emotive strength of ordinary moral knowledge may easily be overwhelmed by baser emotions.

PROP. VIII. The knowledge of good and evil is nothing else but the emotions of pleasure or pain, in so far as we are conscious thereof.

Proof. — We call a thing good or evil, when it is of service or the reverse in preserving our being, that is, when it increases or diminishes, helps or hinders, our power of activity. Thus, in so far as we perceive that a thing affects us with pleasure or pain, we call it good or evil; wherefore the knowledge of good and evil is nothing else but the idea of the pleasure or pain, which necessarily follows from that pleasurable or painful emotion . . . .

PROP. XIV. A true knowledge of good and evil cannot check any emotion by virtue of being true, but only in so far as it is considered as an emotion.

Proof. — An emotion is an idea, whereby the mind affirms of its body a greater or less force of existing than before; therefore it has no positive quality, which can be destroyed by the presence of what is true; consequently the knowledge of good and evil cannot, by virtue of being true, restrain any emotion. But, in so far as such knowledge is an emotion if it have more strength for restraining emotion, it will to that extent be able to restrain the given emotion. Q.E.D.

PROP. XV. Desire arising from the knowledge of good and bad can be quenched or checked by many of the other desires arising from the emotions whereby we are assailed.

Proof. — From the true knowledge of good and evil, in so far as it is an emotion, necessarily arises desire, the strength of which is proportioned to the strength of the emotion wherefrom it arises. But, inasmuch as this desire arises (by hypothesis) from the fact of our truly understanding anything, it follows that it is also present with us, in so far as we are active, and must therefore be understood through our essence only; consequently its force and increase can be defined solely by human power. Again, the desires arising from the emotions whereby we are assailed are stronger, in proportion as the said emotions are more vehement; wherefore their force and increase must be defined solely by the power of external causes, which, when compared with our own power, indefinitely surpass it; hence the desires arising from like emotions may be more vehement, than the desire which arises from a true knowledge of good and evil, and may, consequently, control or quench it. Q.E.D.

PROP. XVI. Desire arising from the knowledge of good and evil, in so far as such knowledge regards what is future, may be more easily controlled or quenched, than the desire for what is agreeable at the present moment.

Proof. — Emotion towards a thing, which we conceive as future, is fainter than emotion towards a thing that is present. But desire, which arises from the true knowledge of good and evil, though it be concerned with things which are good at the moment, can be quenched or controlled by any headstrong desire (by the last Prop., the proof whereof is of universal application). Wherefore desire arising from such knowledge, when concerned with the future, can be more easily controlled or quenched, etc. Q.E.D.

PROP. XVII. Desire arising from the true knowledge of good and evil, in so far as such knowledge is concerned with what is contingent, can be controlled far more easily still, than desire for things that are present.

Note. — I think I have now shown the reason, why men are moved by opinion more readily than by true reason, why it is that the true knowledge of good and evil stirs up conflicts in the soul, and often yields to every kind of passion. This state of things gave rise to the exclamation of the poet: —

> "The better path I gaze at and approve,
> The worse — I follow."

Ecclesiastes seems to have had the same thought in his mind, when he says, "He who increaseth knowledge increaseth sorrow." I have not written the above with the object of drawing the conclusion, that ignorance is more excellent than knowledge, or that a wise man is on a par with a fool in controlling his emotions, but because it is necessary to know the power and the infirmity of our nature, before we can determine what reason can do in restraining the emotions, and what is beyond her power . . .ʲ

9. "Human infirmity in moderating and checking the emotions" Spinoza calls bondage, "for, when a man is a prey to his emotions he is not his own master, but lies at the mercy of fortune." By contrast, a man is free when his actions are determined solely by the laws of his reason. The power of the mind to understand the emotions determines the extent to which freedom can be achieved. But it is particularly difficult to control the emotions, or passions, which arise when the mind is passive, i.e., responsive to external causes rather than expressive of the inner activity of the mind. When human actions and judgments are dominated by such "passive" emotions as love and hate, hope and fear, envy and anger, the moral influence of the emotions associated with the active intellect *is necessarily feeble by comparison. But, reaffirming his confidence in the power of reason, Spinoza assures us that with a sober appreciation of the strength of the emotions, we are able to pass from bondage to freedom.*

PROP. III. An emotion, which is a passion, ceases to be a passion, as soon as we form a clear and distinct idea thereof.

Proof. — An emotion, which is a passion, is a confused idea. If, therefore, we form a clear and distinct idea of a given emotion, that idea will only be distinguished from the emotion, in so far as it is referred to the mind only, by reason; therefore, the emotion will cease to be a passion. Q.E.D.

Corollary. — An emotion therefore becomes more under our control, and the mind is less passive in respect to it, in proportion as it is more known to us.

. . . Everyone has the power of clearly and distinctly under-standing himself and his emotions, if not absolutely, at any rate in part, and consequently of bringing it about, that he should be-come less subject to them. To attain this result, therefore, we must chiefly direct our efforts to acquiring, as far as possible, a clear and distinct knowledge of every emotion, in order that the mind may thus, through emotion, be determined to think of those things which it clearly and distinctly perceives, and wherein it fully acquiesces: and thus that the emotion itself may be separated from the thought of an external cause, and may be associated with true thoughts; whence it will come to pass, not only that love, hatred, etc., will be destroyed, but also that the appetites or desires, which are wont to arise from such emotion, will become incapable of being excessive.[k]

10. The contrast between those things which are known to occur necessarily and those things which it is believed may possibly have been otherwise is also relevant to the achievement of freedom. When Reason governs, men understand that in this determinate universe, all things are as they must be and cannot be otherwise. As a conse-quence, they are better able to control the passions.

PROP. VI. The mind has greater power over the emotions and is less subject thereto, in so far as it understands all things as necessary.

Proof. — The mind understands all things to be necessary and to be determined to existence and operation by an infinite chain of causes; therefore, it thus far brings it about, that it is less subject to the emotions arising therefrom, and feels less emotion toward the things themselves. Q.E.D.

Note. — The more this knowledge, that things are necessary, is applied to particular things, which we conceive more distinctly and vividly, the greater is the power of the mind over the emo-tions, as experience also testifies. For we see, that the pain arising from the loss of any good is mitigated, as soon as the man who has lost it perceives, that it could not by any means have been preserved. So also we see that no one pities an infant, because it cannot speak, walk, or reason, or lastly, because it passes so many years, as it were, in unconsciousness. Whereas, if most people were born full-grown and only one here and there as an infant, every one would pity the infants; because infancy would not then be looked on as a state natural and necessary, but as a fault or delinquency in Nature; and we may note several other instances of the same sort.[1]

11. It has now been made clear that the passage from the state of bondage to the state of freedom requires the assiduous application of reason. Not only the emotions, but also the whole order of Nature must be studied, and the continuous study of the causal order of Nature leads ultimately to the highest or "third" kind of knowledge.[3] At this level, the mind no longer views things merely as finite and temporal, but rather, it grasps their essential characteristics under the aspect of eternity. Men come to understand themselves as part of God, or Nature, both bodily and mentally. By this means, it is possible to achieve the greatest good, viz., the intellectual love of God.

PROP. XXV. The highest endeavour of the mind, and the highest virtue is to understand things by the third kind of knowledge.

Proof. — The third kind of knowledge proceeds from an adequate idea of certain attributes of God to an adequate knowledge of the essence of things; and, in proportion as we understand things more in this way, we better understand God; therefore the highest virtue of the mind, that is the power, or nature, or highest endeavour of the mind, is to understand things by the third kind of knowledge. Q.E.D.

PROP. XXIX. Whatsoever the mind understands under the

---

[3] Knowledge of the first kind is mere belief or imagination; knowledge of the second kind is scientific knowledge or knowledge of causes and effects; and knowledge of the third kind is "intuition," in which individual things are understood through a comprehension of God.

form of eternity, it does not understand by virtue of conceiving the present actual existence of the body, but by virtue of conceiving the essence of the body under the form of eternity.

PROP. XXX. Our mind, in so far as it knows itself and the body under the form of eternity, has to that extent necessarily a knowledge of God, and knows that it is in God, and is conceived through God.

Proof. — Eternity is the very essence of God, in so far as this involves necessary existence. Therefore to conceive things under the form of eternity, is to conceive things in so far as they are conceived through the essence of God as real entities, or in so far as they involve existence through the essence of God; wherefore our mind, in so far as it conceives itself and the body under the form of eternity, has to that extent necessarily a knowledge of God, and knows etc. Q.E.D.

PROP. XXXII. Whatsoever we understand by the third kind of knowledge, we take delight in, and our delight is accompanied by the idea of God as cause.

Proof. — From this kind of knowledge arises the highest possible mental acquiescence, that is, pleasure, and this acquiescence is accompanied by the idea of the mind itself, and consequently the idea also of God as cause. Q.E.D.

Corollary. — From the third kind of knowledge necessarily arises the intellectual love of God. From this kind of knowledge arises pleasure accompanied by the idea of God as cause, that is, the love of God; not in so far as we imagine him as present, but in so far as we understand him to be eternal; this is what I call the intellectual love of God.

PROP. XXXIII. The intellectual love of God, which arises from the third kind of knowledge, is eternal.[m]

12. Spinoza reviews the findings of his ethical theory:

. . . In order that this power of the mind over the emotions may be better understood, it should be specially observed that the emotions are called by us strong, when we compare the emotion of one man with the emotion of another, and see that one man is more troubled than another by the same emotion; or when we are comparing the various emotions of the same man one with another, and find that he is more affected or stirred by one emotion than by another. For the strength of every emotion is defined by a comparison of our own power with the power of an external cause. Now the power of the mind is defined by knowledge only, and its infirmity or passion is defined by the privation of knowledge only: it therefore follows, that that mind is most passive, whose greatest part is made up of inadequate ideas, so that it may be characterized more readily by its passive states than by its activities: on the other hand, that mind is most active, whose greatest part is made up of adequate ideas, so that, although it may contain as many inadequate ideas as the former mind, it may yet be more easily characterized by ideas attributable to human virtue, than by ideas which tell of human infirmity. Again, it must be observed, that spiritual unhealthiness and misfortunes can generally be traced to excessive love for something which is subject to many variations, and which we can never become masters of. For no one is solicitous or anxious about anything, unless he loves it; neither do wrongs, suspicions, enmities, etc., arise, except in regard to things whereof no one can be really master.

We may thus readily conceive the power which clear and distinct knowledge, and especially that third kind of knowledge, founded on the actual knowledge of God, possesses over the emotions: if it does not absolutely destroy them, in so far as they are passions; at any rate, it causes them to occupy a very small part of the mind. Further, it begets a love towards a thing immutable and eternal, whereof we may really enter into possession; neither can it be defiled with those faults which are inherent in ordinary love; but it may grow from strength to strength, and may engross the greater part of the mind, and deeply penetrate it.[n]

13. The closing note of the Ethics *is a final eulogy to the rational life.*

Note. — I have thus completed all I wished to set forth touching the mind's power over the emotions and the mind's freedom. Whence it appears, how potent is the wise man, and how much he surpasses the ignorant man, who is driven only by his lusts. For the ignorant man is not only distracted in various ways by external causes without ever gaining the true acquiescence of his spirit, but moreover lives, as it were unwitting of himself, and of God, and of things, and as soon as he ceases to suffer, ceases also to be.

Whereas the wise man, in so far as he is regarded as such, is scarcely at all disturbed in spirit, but, being conscious of himself, and of God, and of things, by a certain eternal necessity, never ceases to be, but always possesses true acquiescence of his spirit.

If the way which I have pointed out as leading to this result seems exceedingly hard, it may nevertheless be discovered. Needs must it be hard, since it is so seldom found. How would it be possible, if salvation were ready to our hand, and could without great labour be found, that it should be by almost all men neglected? But all things excellent are as difficult as they are rare.°

Questions

1. Discuss the significance for Spinoza's ethical theory of his statement, "Whatever is, is in God . . ."
2. Explain Spinoza's belief that "the love of what is perishable" is incompatible with true happiness. Do you agree with his position?
3. Why does Spinoza attach great importance to "the improvement of the understanding"?
4. What difference to ethical theory does it make when one denies that the universe is a purposive scheme?
5. What reasons does Spinoza give for his belief that it is morally wrong to believe that men have free will? In what sense does he say man is "free"?

6. Discuss the ethical significance of Spinoza's doctrine of *conatus*, the striving for self-preservation and self-perfection.

7. How does Spinoza estimate the relative strength of emotion and reason? What method does he recommend for the study of the emotions?

8. What are the means by which men can escape from human bondage? Are there any external forces which can aid man to pass from bondage to freedom?

9. Why does Spinoza devote himself to a detailed discussion of the emotions? What connection does he establish between emotion and error? What moral significance does he attach to intellectual error?

10. Explain what is meant by "the intellectual love of God." How does this enter into the moral life?

Key to selections:

BENEDICT DE SPINOZA, *On the Improvement of the Understanding* and *The Ethics*, tr. R. H. M. Elwes, from *The Chief Works of Benedict Spinoza*, vol. II, London, George Bell and Sons, 1898. Proofs, corollaries, notes, and references to prior proofs have been omitted from selections from *The Ethics*, except where otherwise indicated.

From *On the Improvement of the Understanding*

   b pp. 3–4.   c pp. 4–6.   d pp. 6–7.

From *The Ethics*
a Part IV, Prop. LXXIII, Note.   i Part IV.
e Part I, Appendix.   j Part III, Prop. XXXIX, Note.
f Part III, Prop. II, Note.   k Part IV.
g Part II, Prop. XLIX, Note.   l–p Part V.
h Part III, Introduction.

Guide to Additional Reading

INEXPENSIVE EDITIONS:

SPINOZA, B., *Ethics*, Hafner Library of Classics (Hafner).
——, *Ethics, On the Correction of the Understanding*, Everyman's Library (Dutton).

Spinoza Selections, Modern Student's Library (Scribners').
The Philosophy of Spinoza, Modern Library (Random House).

DISCUSSION AND COMMENTARY:

Broad, C. D., *Five Types of Ethical Theory*, New York, Harcourt, Brace and Company, 1928, Chapter II.
Hampshire, S., *Spinoza*, Harmondworth, Penguin Books Ltd., 1954.
Joachim, H. H., *A Study of the Ethics of Spinoza*, Oxford, The Clarendon Press, 1901.
McKeon, R., *The Philosophy of Spinoza*, New York, Longmans, Green and Company, 1928.
Wolfson, H. A., *The Philosophy of Spinoza*, Cambridge, Harvard University Press, 1948.

CHAPTER 9

Conscience in Morality

JOSEPH BUTLER

Joseph Butler (1692–1752), it has been said, "was more than a good writer, he was a good man; and what is an addition even to this eulogy, he was a sincere Christian." The youngest of eight children, Joseph was born at Wantage, England, just three years after the passage of the Toleration Act which allowed all religious sects to worship freely. His father, a middle-class shopkeeper and a God-fearing member of the Protestant Dissenters (a Presbyterian group), recognized early that his son was intellectually gifted and determined that he should be trained for the ministry. Accordingly, Joseph was sent to a grammar school and then to Tewkesbury Academy where he distinguished himself by his originality in theology. While he was at the Academy, however, he became convinced that the relatively liberal doctrine of the Dissenters was inferior to the conservative theology of the Church of England. In view of this change of allegiance, in 1714 he entered Oriel College, Oxford, where, despite his disappointment at finding the lectures "frivolous" and the disputations "unintelligible," he completed his theological training. Butler's ecclesiastical career, in which he made his reputation at once, began in 1719 when he was appointed preacher to the Rolls Chapel in London.

Butler's first published work was *Fifteen Sermons Preached at the Rolls Chapel* (1726). Although it has been said that these were wonderful sermons to sleep through, they contain his chief statement of ethical theory. He was assigned to the obscure parsonage of Stanhope the same year that his book appeared. When, in the year 1736, Queen Caroline asked if the brilliant Butler were dead, she was told, "No, madam, he is not *dead*, but he is *buried*." Thereupon Butler was recalled to London to serve as a Court Chaplain. Almost immediately upon his arrival, *The Analogy of Religion, Natural and Revealed, to the Constitution and Course of Nature* (1736) was published. This became one of the most influential books of the century, despite the uncompromising difficulty of its argument. In it, Butler comes to the defense of *Theism* — the traditional view that God, while a transcendent Being, is immanent in the universe and concerned with the affairs of men — against the doctrine of *Deism* — the view that since God is a transcendent Being, he can have no concern with or influence upon human affairs.

His fame secure, Butler was elevated to the Deanery of St. Paul in 1740. King George II, however, was still not satisfied with the recognition accorded to him and opened the way to additional promotions and honors. At the time of his death, Butler occupied the important Bishopric of Durham. He remains the most capable defender of his faith against religious scepticism and the free-thinking of the Age of Reason.

•

Bishop Joseph Butler is the most distinguished in a line of English and Scottish philosophers for whom the ground of morality is "conscience." In his ethical theory, conscience is conceived as a *reflective or rational faculty which discerns the moral characteristic of actions*. Consequently, he is not a defender of the popular, unsophisticated view that the conscience is like an additional eye which can perceive directly the rightness or wrongness of conduct.

Nevertheless, his conception of it is closer to this view than to the one in which "conscience" is understood as a name for mere feelings of approval and disapproval due to psychological and social conditioning. For him, the judgements of conscience are not based on moral sense or feelings, but on moral reason.

Although Butler was a devoutly religious clergyman, he studiously avoids basing his arguments upon supernatural authority. The general goal of his philosophical inquiry is the substantiation of revealed Christianity by means of a reasoned study of human nature. For his purpose, it would be begging the question to argue from the same revelations which he intends to reinforce. Accordingly, he resolves to confirm the Christian principles through data which each man can find within himself. Against the contention of his educated contemporaries that reasoning conflicts with revealed religion and discredits it, Butler holds that the results of his rational method of introspection will be evidence for rather than against Christianity:

It is come, I know not how, to be taken for granted by many persons that Christianity is not so much a subject of inquiry; but that it is, now at length, discovered to be fictitious. And accordingly they treat it as if, in the present age, this were an agreed point among all people of discernment; and nothing remained, but to set it up as a principal subject of mirth and ridicule, as it were by way of reprisals, for its having so long interrupted the pleasures of the world. On the contrary, thus much at least will be here found, not taken for granted, but proved, that any reasonable man, who will thoroughly consider the matter may be as much assured as he is of his own being, that it is not, however, so clear a case, that there is 'nothing in it. There is, I think, strong evidence of its truth; but it is certain no one can, upon principles of reason, be satisfied of the contrary.[1]

The intellectual basis for irreligion in the England of Butler's day was constituted by a fusion of two assumptions; first, that

[1] Joseph Butler, "Advertisement" prefixed to *The Analogy of Religion, Natural and Revealed, to the Constitution and Course of Nature*, New York, Robert Carter and Brothers, 1849.

men are exclusively egoistic, *i.e.*, they are committed to the satisfaction of their immediate desires, and second, that no moral obligation is valid if it runs counter to the way men are by nature capable of acting. Butler rejects the first of these as bad psychology in general; and in particular, he criticizes Thomas Hobbes, the most influential exponent of the egoistic theory. According to Butler, Hobbes failed to detect the difference between the *immediate gratification of desire* and the *achievement of self-preservation*. The former, being merely a momentary satisfaction of a particular drive, may or may not serve a man's genuine self-interest. On the other hand, self-preservation, which is a form of self-love, represents a selection of desires which culminates in the individual's well-being. At the same time, Butler gives a classic refutation of psychological hedonism (the theory that pleasure is the motive of all conduct) by pointing out that although pleasure *accompanies* the satisfaction of desire, the desire is for a particular object, not for the pleasure which accompanies it. Otherwise, desires would be "objectless" and undirected to *specific* situations.

Butler accepts with reservations the second of the assumptions made by the anti-religious thinkers of his day; *i.e.*, he grants that rules governing what men ought to do must be confined to what men can do within the limits of human nature. However, he insists that a clear understanding of what is meant by "human nature" is necessary. To begin with, the springs of all human actions are specific passions and appetites, but introspection reveals that we also have the means by which these impulses can be regulated, *viz.*, self-love, benevolence, and conscience. In and of themselves, the basic drives and the desire to satisfy them are ethically neutral. For example, when a man is driven by thirst, his only object is to find water. However, the moral element appears when the problem of *regulation* is considered. Private and public well-being depend upon the proper choice and limitation of the desires to be satisfied.

Self-love is the effective regulative principle which operates when an individual organizes his desires so as to promote his own best interests. When he controls his appetites so as to further the public good, the operative principle is that of *benevolence*. Yet, Butler tells us, there is no guarantee that these regulative principles of self-love and benevolence will always reinforce and complement one another. Under these circumstances, conflicts between personal and social interests are resolved by a regulative principle of a higher order, namely, the *conscience*. The conscience is reason functioning as the arbiter of conflicting interests of self-love and benevolence; it is the author of and authority for our moral obligations; it prompts us to the performance of our duties. Thus, the conscience is the "knowledge of right" within each man which makes him a "moral agent." We are unconditionally obligated to follow the dictates of conscience, Butler explains, because the conscience carries with it the "light of self-attestment." In other words, the authority of conscience is self-evident, and there can be no appeal from it to any higher principle.

Butler concludes that the results of his rational investigation of human nature and morality strengthen faith in Christian ethics through confirming its underlying principle. This he draws from *Romans* (ii:14–15): "For when the Gentiles, which have not the law, do by nature the things contained in the law, these, having not the law, are a law unto themselves: Which shew the work of the law written in their hearts, their conscience also bearing witness . . ." For Butler, this means that "everyone may find within himself the rule of right, and obligations to follow it."

• • •

1. Butler's ethical theory rests upon a teleological conception of man. He is convinced that in order to understand the ethical concepts, "virtue" and "vice," one must first study the appropriate design and intent of human nature.

There are two ways in which the subject of morals may be treated. One begins from inquiring into the abstract relations of things: the other from a matter of fact, namely, what the particular nature of man is, its several parts, their economy or constitution; from whence it proceeds to determine what course of life it is, which is correspondent to this whole nature. In the former method the conclusion is expressed thus, that vice is contrary to the nature and reason of things: in the latter, that it is a violation or breaking in upon our own nature. Thus they both lead us to the same thing, our obligations to the practice of virtue; and thus they exceedingly strengthen and enforce each other. The first seems the most direct formal proof, and in some respects the least liable to cavil and dispute: the latter is in a peculiar manner adapted to satisfy a fair mind; and is more easily applicable to the several particular relations and circumstances in life.

The following Discourses proceed chiefly in this latter method ... They were intended to explain what is meant by the nature of man, when it is said that virtue consists in following, and vice in deviating from it; and by explaining to show that the assertion is true. . . .

Whoever thinks it worth while to consider this matter thoroughly, should begin with stating to himself exactly the idea of a system, economy, or constitution of any particular nature, or particular anything: and he will, I suppose, find, that it is a one or a whole, made up of several parts; but yet, that the several parts even considered as a whole do not complete the idea, unless in the notion of a whole you include the relations and respects which those parts have to each other. Every work both of nature and of art is a system: and as every particular thing, both natural and artificial, is for some use or purpose out of and beyond itself, one may add, to what has been already brought into the idea of a system, its conduciveness to this one or more ends. Let us instance in a watch — Suppose the several parts of it taken to pieces, and placed apart from each other; let a man have ever so exact a notion of these several parts, unless he considers the respects and relations which they have to each other, he will not have anything like the idea of a watch. Suppose these several parts brought together and any how united: neither will he yet, be the union ever so close, have an idea which will bear any resemblance to that of a watch. But let him view those several parts put together, or consider them as to be put together in the manner of a watch; let him form a notion of the relations which those several parts have to each other — all conducive in their respective ways to this purpose, showing the hour of the day; and then he has the idea of a watch. Thus it is with regard to the inward frame of man.[a]

2. For Butler, then, human nature is a system whose constituent elements are harmoniously ordered. He examines several other meanings of the term "nature" and concludes that if they are employed, no ethical distinctions can be made.

. . . If by following nature were meant only acting as we please, it would indeed be ridiculous to speak of nature as any guide in morals: nay the very mention of deviating from nature would be absurd; and the mention of following it, when spoken by way of distinction, would absolutely have no meaning. For did ever any one act otherwise than as he pleased? And yet the ancients speak of deviating from nature as vice; and of following nature so much as a distinction, that according to them the perfection of virtue consists therein. So that language itself should teach people another sense to the words *following nature*, than barely acting as we please.

. . . By nature is often meant no more than some principle in man, without regard either to the kind or degree of it. Thus the passion of anger, and the affection of parents to their children, would be called equally *natural*. And as the same person hath often contrary principles, which at the same time draw contrary ways, he may by the same action both follow and contradict his nature in this sense of the word; he may follow one passion and contradict another.

. . . *Nature* is frequently spoken of as consisting in those passions which are strongest, and most influence the actions; which being vicious ones, mankind is in this sense naturally vicious, or vicious by nature. Thus St. Paul says of the Gentiles, *who were dead in trespasses and sins, and walked according to the spirit of disobedience, that they were by nature the children of wrath.* They could be no otherwise *children of wrath* by nature, than they were vicious by nature.[b]

3. Butler proceeds to a careful analysis of human nature as he understands it, to establish "that there are as real and the same kind of indications in human nature, that we were made for society and to do good to our fellow-creatures, as that we were intended to take care of our own life and health and private good . . ." *He presents a detailed discussion of the appetites and passions and of two of the principles which regulate behavior, benevolence and self-love. Butler cautions against supposing that these principles are in natural opposition.*

First, there is a natural principle of *benevolence* in man; which is in some degree to *society*, what *self-love* is to the *individual*. And if there be in mankind any disposition to friendship; if there be any such thing as compassion, for compassion is momentary love; if there be any such thing as the paternal or filial affections; if there be any affection in human nature, the object and end of which is the good of another, this is itself benevolence, or the love of another. Be it ever so short, be it in ever so low a degree, or ever so unhappily confined; it proves the assertion, and points out what we were designed for, as really as though it were in a higher degree and more extensive. I must, however, remind you that though benevolence and self-love are different; though the former tends most directly to public good, and the latter to private: yet they are so perfectly coincident that the greatest satisfactions to ourselves depend upon our having benevolence in a due degree; and that self-love is one chief security of our right behaviour towards society. It may be added, that their mutual coinciding, so that we can scarce promote one without the other, is equally a proof that we were made for both.

Secondly, this will further appear, from observing that the *several passions* and *affections*, which are distinct, both from benevolence and self-love, do in general contribute and lead us to *public* good as really as to *private*. It might be thought too minute and particular, and would carry us too great a length, to distinguish between and compare together the several passions or appetites distinct from benevolence, whose primary use and intention is the security and good of society; and the passions distinct from self-love, whose primary intention and design is the security and good of the individual. It is enough to the present argument, that desire of esteem from others, contempt and esteem of them, love of society as distinct from affection to the good of it, indignation against successful vice, that these are public affections or passions; have an immediate respect to others, naturally lead us to regulate our behaviour in such a manner as will be of service to our fellow-creatures. If any or all of these may be considered likewise as private affections, as tending to private good; this does not hinder them from being public affections too, or destroy the good influence of them upon society, and their tendency to public good. It may be added, that as persons without any conviction from reason of the desirableness of life, would yet of course preserve it merely from the appetite of hunger; so by acting merely from regard (suppose) to reputation, without any consideration of the good of others, men often contribute to public good. In both these instances they are plainly instruments in the hands of another, in the hands of Providence, to carry on ends, the preservation of the individual and good of society, which they themselves have not in their view or intention. The sum is, men have various appetites, passions, and particular affections, quite distinct both from self-love and from benevolence: all of these have a tendency to promote both public and private good, and may be considered as respecting others and ourselves equally and in common: but some of them seem most immediately to respect others, or tend to public good; others of them most immediately to respect self, or tend to private good: as the former are not benevolence, so the latter are not self-love: neither sort are instances of our love either to ourselves or others; but only instances of our Maker's care and love both of the individual and the species, and proofs that he intended we should be instruments of good to each other, as well as that we should be so to ourselves.[c]

4. Butler criticizes further the erroneous but popular notion that there is a natural opposition between self-love and benevolence.

There seems no other reason to suspect that there is any such peculiar contrariety, but only that the courses of action which benevolence leads to, has a more direct tendency to promote the good of others, than that course of action, which love of reputation suppose, or any other particular affection leads to. But that any affection tends to the happiness of another, does not hinder its tending to one's own happiness too. That others enjoy the benefit of the air and the light of the sun, does not hinder but that these are as much one's own private advantage now, as they would be if we had the property of them exclusive of all others. So a pursuit which tends to promote the good of another, yet may have as great tendency to promote private interest, as a pursuit which does not tend to the good of another at all, or which is mischievous to him. All particular affections whatever, resentment, benevolence, love of arts, equally lead to a course of action for their own gratification, *i.e.*, the gratification of ourselves; and the gratification of each gives delight: so far then it is manifest they have all the same respect to private interest. Now take into consideration further, concerning these three pursuits, that the end of the first is the harm, of the second, the good of another, of the last, somewhat indifferent; and is there any necessity, that these additional considerations should alter the respect, which we before saw these three pursuits, had to private interest; or render any one of them less conducive to it, than any other? Thus one man's affection is to honour as his end; in order to obtain which he thinks no pains too great. Suppose another, with such a singularity of mind, as to have the same affection to public good as his end, which he endeavours with the same labour to obtain. In case of success, surely the man of benevolence hath as great enjoyment as the man of ambition; they both equally having the end of their affections, in the same degree, tended to: but in case of disappointment, the benevolent man has clearly the advantage; since endeavouring to do good considered as a virtuous pursuit, is gratified by its own consciousness, *i.e.*, is in a degree its own reward.[d]

5. After differentiating between self-love and benevolence, Butler turns to the task of refuting the belief popularized by Thomas Hobbes that self-love is reducible to the unrestrained gratifications of impulses. He points out that any such reduction fails to take into account an important distinction: the object of self-love is general and internal, i.e., the individual is concerned to achieve a lifetime of happiness, but the object of an impulse is particular and external, e.g., the object of hunger is food, not the pleasure which arises from eating, and the object of revenge is to inflict pain, not the satisfaction of being avenged. Clearly, then, since impulses are specific and external, they can be in conflict with the long-term objective of self-love.

Every man hath a general desire of his own happiness; and likewise a variety of particular affections, passions, and appetites to particular external objects. The former proceeds from, or is self-love; and seems inseparable from all sensible creatures, who can reflect upon themselves and their own interest or happiness, so as to have that interest an object to their minds: what is to be said of the latter is, that they proceed from, or together make up that particular nature, according to which man is made. The object the former pursues is somewhat internal, our own happiness, enjoyment, satisfaction; whether we have, or have not, a distinct particular perception what it is, or wherein it consists: the objects of the latter are this or that particular external thing, which the affections tend towards, and of which it hath always a particular idea or perception. The principle we call self-love never seeks any thing external for the sake of the thing, but only as a means of happiness or good: particular affections rest in the external things themselves. One belongs to man as a reasonable creature reflecting upon his own interest or happiness. The other, though quite distinct from reason, are as much a part of human nature.

That all particular appetites and passions are towards *external things themselves*, distinct from the *pleasure arising from them*, is manifested from hence; that there could not be this pleasure, were it not for that prior suitableness between the object and the passion: there could be no enjoyment or delight from one thing more than another, from eating food more than from swallowing a stone, if there were not an affection or appetite to one thing more than another.

Every particular affection, even the love of our neighbour, is as really our own affection, as self-love; and the pleasure arising from its gratification is as much my own pleasure, as the pleasure self-love would have, from knowing I myself should be happy some time hence, would be my own pleasure. And if, because every particular affection is a man's own, and the pleasure arising from its gratification his own pleasure, or pleasure to himself, such particular affection must be called self-love; according to this way of speaking, no creature whatever can possibly act but merely from self-love; and every action and every affection whatever is to be resolved up into this one principle. But then this is not the language of mankind: or if it were, we should want words to express the difference, between the principle of an action, proceeding from cool consideration that it will be to my own advantage; and an action, suppose of revenge, or of friendship, by which a man runs upon certain ruin, to do evil or good to another. It is manifest the principles of these actions are totally different, and so want different words to be distinguished by: all that they agree in is, that they both proceed from, and are done to gratify an inclination in a man's self. But the principle or inclination in one case is self-love: in the other, hatred or love of another. There is then a distinction between the cool principle of self-love, or general desire of our own happiness, as one part of our nature, and one principle of action; and the particular affections towards particular external objects, as another part of our nature, and another principle of action. How much soever therefore is to be allowed to self-love, yet it cannot be allowed to be the whole of our inward constitution; because, you see, there are other parts or principles which come into it.[e]

6. Through illustration, Butler strengthens the distinction between a governing principle and a particular impulse. He makes manifest the natural *superiority of the one over the other.*

Man may act according to that principle or inclination which for the present happens to be strongest, and yet act in a way disproportionate to, and violate his real proper nature. Suppose a brute creature by any bait to be allured into a snare, by which he is destroyed. He plainly followed the bent of his nature, leading him to gratify his appetite: there is an entire correspondence between his whole nature and such an action: such action therefore is natural. But suppose a man, foreseeing the same danger of certain ruin, should rush into it for the sake of a present gratification; he in this instance would follow his strongest desire, as did the brute creature: but there would be as manifest a disproportion, between the nature of a man and such an action, as between the meanest work of art and the skill of the greatest master in that art: which disproportion arises, not from considering the action singly in *itself*, or in its *consequences;* but from *comparison* of it with the nature of the agent. And since such an action is utterly disproportionate to the nature of man, it is in the strictest and most proper sense unnatural; this word expressing that disproportion. Therefore instead of the word *disproportionate to his nature*, the word *unnatural* may now be put; this being more familiar to us: but let it be observed, that it stands for the same thing precisely.

Now what is it which renders such a rash action unnatural? Is it that he went against the principle of reasonable and cool self-love, considered *merely* as a part of his nature? No: for if he had acted the contrary way, he would equally have gone against a principle, or part of his nature, namely, passion or appetite. But to deny a present appetite, from foresight that the gratification of it would end in immediate ruin or extreme misery, is by no means an unnatural action; whereas to contradict or go against cool self-love for the sake of such gratification, is so in the instance before us. Such an action then being unnatural; and its being so not arising from a man's going against a principle or desire barely, nor in going against that principle or desire which happens for the present to be strongest; it necessarily follows, that there must be some other difference or distinction to be made between these two principles, passion and cool self-love, than what I have yet taken notice of. And this difference, not being a difference in strength or degree, I call a difference in *nature* and in *kind*. And since, in the instance still before us, if passion prevails over self-love, the consequent action is unnatural; but if self-love prevails over passion, the action is natural: it is manifest that self-love is in human nature a superior principle to passion. This may be contradicted without violating that nature; but the former cannot. So that, if we will act conformably to the economy of man's nature, reasonable self-love must govern. Thus, without particular consideration of conscience, we may have a clear conception of the *superior nature* of one inward principle to another; and see that there really is this natural superiority, quite distinct from degrees of strength and prevalency.[f]

7. *The highest of the governing principles is the reflective principle of conscience. It both influences and evaluates behavior by means of approval and disapproval.*

There is a principle of reflection in men, by which they distinguish between, approve and disapprove their own actions. We are plainly constituted such sort of creatures as to reflect upon our own nature. The mind can take a view of what passes within itself, its propensions, aversions, passions, affections, as respecting such objects, and in such degrees; and of the several actions consequent thereupon. In this survey it approves of one, disapproves of another, and towards a third is affected in neither of these ways, but is quite indifferent. This principle in man, by which he approves or disapproves his heart, temper, and actions, is conscience; for this is the strict sense of the word, though sometimes it is used so as to take in more. And that this faculty tends to restrain men from doing mischief to each other, and leads them to do good, is too manifest to need being insisted upon. Thus a parent has the affection of love to his children: this leads him to take care of, to educate, to make due provision for them; the natural affection leads to this: but the reflection that it is his proper business, what belongs to him, that it is right and commendable so to do; this added to the affection becomes a much more settled principle, and carries him on through more labour and difficulties for the sake of his children, than he would undergo from that affection alone, if he thought it, and the course of action it led to, either indifferent or criminal. This indeed is impossible, to do that which is good and not to approve of it; for which reason they are frequently not considered as distinct, though they really are: for men often approve of the actions of others, which they will not imitate, and likewise do that which they approve not. It cannot possibly be denied that there is this principle of reflection or conscience in human nature. Suppose a man to relieve an innocent person in great distress; suppose the same man afterwards, in the fury of anger, to do the greatest mischief to a person who had given no just cause of offense; to aggravate the injury, add the circumstances of former friendship, and obligation from the injured person; let the man who is supposed to have done these two different actions, coolly reflect upon them afterwards, without regard to their consequences to himself: to assert that any common man would be affected in the same way towards these different actions, that he would make no distinction between them, but approve or disapprove them equally, is too glaring a falsity to need being confuted. There is therefore this principle of reflection or conscience in mankind. It is needless to compare the respect it has to private good, with the respect it has to public; since it plainly tends as much to the latter as to the former, and is commonly thought to tend chiefly to the latter.[g]

8. It has already been pointed out that although benevolence and self-love may not always prevail over desire, their lack of power does not reduce their proper authority. The same contrast between actual power and natural authority is seen to apply to conscience. Even if conscience should fail to control conduct, it possesses its natural authority undiminished.

Let us now take a view of the nature of man, as consisting partly of various appetites, passions, affections, and partly of the principle of reflection or conscience; leaving quite out all consideration of the different degrees of strength, in which either of them prevail, and it will further appear that there is this natural superiority of one inward principle to another, and that it is even part of the idea of reflection or conscience.

Passion or appetite implies a direct simple tendency towards such and such objects, without distinction of the means by which they are to be obtained. Consequently it will often happen there will be a desire of particular objects, in cases where they cannot be obtained without manifest injury to others. Reflection or conscience comes in, and disapproves the pursuit of them in these circumstances; but the desire remains. Which is to be obeyed, appetite or reflection? Cannot this question be answered, from the economy and constitution of human nature merely, without saying which is strongest? Or need this at all come into consideration? Would not the question be *intelligibly* and fully answered by saying, that the principle of reflection or conscience being compared with the various appetites, passions, and affections in men, the former is manifestly superior and chief, without regard to strength? And how often soever the latter happens to prevail, it is mere *usurpation:* the former remains in nature and in kind its superior; and every instance of such prevalence of the latter is an instance of breaking in upon and violation of the constitution of man.

All this is no more than the distinction, which everybody is acquainted with, between *mere power* and *authority:* only instead of being intended to express the difference between what is possible, and what is lawful in civil government; here it has been shown applicable to the several principles in the mind of man. Thus that principle, by which we survey, and either approve or disapprove our own heart, temper, and actions, is not only to be considered as what is in its turn to have some influence; which may be said of every passion, of the lowest appetites: but likewise as being superior; as from its very nature manifestly claiming superiority over all others; insomuch that you cannot form a notion of this faculty, conscience, without taking in judgment, direction, superintendency. This is a constituent part of the idea, that is, of the faculty itself: and, to preside and govern, from the very economy and constitution of man, belongs to it. Had it strength, as it had right; had it power, as it had manifest authority, it would absolutely govern the world.

This gives us a further view of the nature of man; shows us what course of life we were made for: not only that our real nature leads us to be influenced in some degree by reflection and conscience; but likewise in what degree we are to be influenced by it, if we will fall in with, and act agreeably to the constitution of our nature: that this faculty was placed within to be our proper governor; to direct and regulate all under principles, passions, and motives of action. This is its right and office: thus sacred is its authority. And how often soever men violate and rebelliously refuse to submit to it, for supposed interest which they cannot otherwise obtain, or for the sake of passion which they cannot otherwise gratify; this makes no alteration as to the *natural right* and *office* of conscience.[h]

9. The basis for the authority of conscience does not arise from any external source. Rather, the very existence of conscience is its own sufficient justification.

The inquiries which have been made by men of leisure after some general rule, the conformity to, or disagreement from which, should denominate our actions good or evil, are in many respects of great service. Yet let any plain honest man, before he engages in any course of action, ask himself, Is this I am going about right, or is it wrong? Is it good, or is it evil? I do not in the least doubt, but that this question would be answered agreeably to truth and virtue, by almost any fair man in almost any circumstance. Neither do there appear any cases which look like exceptions to this; but those of superstition, and of partiality to ourselves. Superstition may perhaps be somewhat of an exception: but partiality to ourselves is not; this being itself dishonesty. For a man to judge that to be the equitable, the moderate, the right part for him to act, which he would see to be hard, unjust, oppressive in another; this is plain vice, and can proceed only from great unfairness of mind.

But allowing that mankind hath the rule of right within himself, yet it may be asked, "What obligations are we under to attend to and follow it?" I answer: it has been proved that man by his nature is a law to himself, without the particular distinct consideration of the positive sanctions of that law; the rewards and punishments which we feel, and those which from the light of reason we have ground to believe, are annexed to it. The question then carries its own answer along with it. Your obligation to obey this law, is its being the law of your nature. That your conscience approves of and attests to such a course of action, is itself alone an obligation. Conscience does not only offer itself to show us the way we should walk in, but it likewise carries its own authority with it, that it is our natural guide; the guide assigned us by the Author of our nature: it therefore belongs to our condition of being, it is our duty to walk in that path, and follow this guide, without looking about to see whether we may not possibly forsake them with impunity.[i]

10. Butler summarizes the basic points of his ethical theory in the following manner:

. . . We may from it form a distinct notion of what is meant by *human nature*, when virtue is said to consist in following it, and vice in deviating from it.

As the idea of a civil constitution implies in it united strength, various subordinations, under one direction, that of the supreme authority; the different strength of each particular member of the society not coming into the idea; whereas, if you leave out the subordination, the union, and the one direction, you destroy and lose it: so reason, several appetites, passions, and affections, prevailing in different degrees of strength, is not *that* idea or notion of *human nature*; but *that nature* consists in these several principles considered as having a natural respect to each other, in the several passions being naturally subordinate to the one superior principle of reflection or conscience. Every bias, instinct, propension within, is a natural part of our nature, but not the whole: add to these the superior faculty, whose office it is to adjust, manage, and preside over them, and take in this its natural superiority, and you complete the idea of human nature. And as in civil government the constitution is broken in upon, and violated by power and strength prevailing over authority; so the constitution of man is broken in upon and violated by the lower faculties or principles within prevailing over that which is in its nature supreme over them all. Thus, when it is said by ancient writers, that tortures and death are not so contrary to human nature as injustice; by this to be sure is not meant, that the aversion to the former in mankind is less strong and prevalent than their aversion to the latter: but that the former is only contrary to our nature considered in a partial view, and which takes in only the lowest part of it, that which we have in common with the brutes; whereas the latter is contrary to our nature, considered in a higher sense, as a system and constitution contrary to the whole economy of man.

Every man, in his physical nature is one individual single agent. He has likewise properties and principles, each of which may be considered separately, and without regard to the respects which they have to each other. Neither of these are the nature we are taking a view of. But it is the inward frame of man considered as a *system* or *constitution:* whose several parts are united, not by a physical principle of individuation, but by the respects they have to each other; the chief of which is the subjection which the appetites, passions, and particular affections have to the one supreme principle of reflection or conscience. The system or constitution is formed by and consists in these respects and this subjection. Thus, the body is a *system or constitution:* so is a tree: so is every machine. Consider all the several parts of a tree, without the natural respects they have to each other, and you have not at all the idea of a tree; but add these respects, and this gives you the idea. The body may be impaired by sickness, a tree may decay, a machine be out of order, and yet the system and constitution of them not totally dissolved. There is plainly somewhat which answers to all this in the moral constitution of man. Whoever will consider his own nature, will see that the several appetites, passions, and particular affections, have different respects amongst themselves. They are restraints upon, and are in proportion to each other. This proportion is just and perfect, when all those under principles are perfectly coincident with conscience, so far as their nature permits, and in all cases, under its absolute and entire direction. The least excess or defect, the least alteration of the due proportions amongst themselves, or of their coincidence with conscience, though not proceeding into action, is some degree of disorder in the moral constitution. But perfection, though plainly intelligible and unsupposable, was never attained by any man. If the higher principle of reflection maintains its place, and as much as it can corrects that disorder, and hinders it from breaking out into action, this is all that can be expected from such a creature as man. And though the appetites and passions have not their exact due proportion to each other; though they often strive for mastery with judgment or reflection: yet, since the superiority of this principle to all others is the chief respect which forms the constitution, so far as this superiority is maintained, the character, the man, is good, worthy, virtuous.ʲ

Questions

1. What does Butler mean when he says that virtue consists in "acting according to nature" and vice consists in "acting contrary to nature"?

2. Discuss Butler's conception of "nature" and "human nature." To what difficulties do the popular misconceptions of human nature lead?

3. Reconstruct Butler's argument against the belief that self-love and benevolence are naturally opposed. Do you regard his position a sound one?

4. How does Butler refute the Hobbesian doctrine that self-love is nothing but the unlimited gratification of impulses?

5. List Butler's "governing principles" in human nature. How is "conscience" related to the other principles?

6. Discuss Butler's contention that the authority of conscience does not arise from any external source.

7. Explain what Butler means when he asserts that "every man is naturally a law unto himself."

8. In what respects is Butler's conception of "conscience" different from popular conceptions? In what respects is it similar?

9. How do you think Butler would respond to the objection that the consciences of men are not all the same?

10. What attitude does Butler take to the anti-religious sentiments of his contemporaries? To what extent, if any, does he employ theological arguments to support his ethical theory?

Key to selections:

JOSEPH BUTLER, *Sermons*, New York, Robert Carter & Brothers, 1873.

a Preface, pp. vi–viii,
b Sermon II, pp. 40–41.
c Sermon I, pp. 27–30.
d Sermon XI, pp. 132–133.
e Sermon XI, pp. 126–128.
f Sermon II, pp. 43–44.

g Sermon I, pp. 30–32.
h Sermon II, pp. 44–46
i Sermon II, pp. 48–49.
j Sermon III, pp. 47–48,
    fn. p. 48.

Guide to Additional Reading

INEXPENSIVE EDITIONS:

BUTLER, J., *Five Sermons*, Little Library of Liberal Arts (Liberal Arts Press).

DISCUSSION AND COMMENTARY:

Broad, C. D., *Five Types of Ethical Theory*, New York, Harcourt Brace and Company, 1930, Chapter III.

Duncan-Jones, A., *Butler's Moral Philosophy*, Harmondsworth, Penguin Books, Inc., 1952.

Mossner, E. C., *Bishop Butler and the Age of Reason*, New York, The Macmillan Company, 1936.

Raphael, D. D., *The Moral Sense*, London, Oxford University Press, 1947.

CHAPTER **10**

Morality and Sentiment

DAVID HUME

Davidavid Hume (1711–1776) is undoubtedly one the most influential figures in the history of thought. In the year 1737, however, when Hume's *Treatise of Human Nature* was published, there was little prospect that such a statement would ever be made. The first and most decisive of his philosophical publications—involving a devastating attack on speculative metaphysics—appeared in that year, but it received virtually no notice from his contemporaries. A revised and somewhat popularized version of much of the *Treatise, An Inquiry concerning the Human Understanding* (1748), marked the beginning of the modest philosophical reputation which Hume enjoyed during his lifetime. In 1751 Hume published *An Inquiry concerning the Principles of Morals* as an amplification of the theory of morality which he had suggested in the *Treatise.* Hume says of this latter *Inquiry* that "of all my writings, historical, philosophical, or literary, [it is] incomparably the best." Another of his philosophical works, *The Dialogues concerning Natural Religion,* written in 1752 but published posthumously, deserves special mention. It is here that Hume sets forth his sceptical views about the proofs of God's existence and the determinations of His nature. It is ironic that even after Hume's death, people did not fully appreciate him

205

as a first-rate philosopher. They readily dismissed him as an annoying atheist of the period instead of addressing themselves to his subtle arguments.

Oddly enough, however, Hume did become a famous figure in the latter part of his life as a result of his general literary excellence and in particular for his historical writings. His *History of England* (1754–1762) became and remained for a long time a classic in the field. This work influenced subsequent historians to include social and literary developments as well as political ones in their accounts. The illustrious historian, Edward Gibbon (1737–1794), acknowledged his debt to Hume.

As might be expected from someone born of an aristocratic family in Edinburgh, Scotland, Hume attended Edinburgh University. As might not be expected, however, he spent much of his working life serving as a librarian to the Edinburgh Faculty of Law. His efforts at obtaining a Chair of Philosophy at this and another institution were unsuccessful.

A brilliant but nonetheless modest man, Hume commented about himself shortly before his death as follows: "I was, I say, a man of mild disposition, of command of temper, of an open, social, and cheerful humor, capable of attachment, but little susceptible of enmity, and of great moderation in all my passions."

•

Attributing the successes of natural philosophy (physical science) to the empirical, experimental method of inquiry, Hume is convinced that it can and must be employed in other domains of philosophical investigation. It is a central thesis of Hume's understanding of this method that factual knowledge arises solely from the data supplied by the senses (and memories of such data) and that it is extended in usefulness by means of cause and effect inferences. Regarded very loosely, this thesis would have been acceptable to most of the scientists and many of the philosophers of the Newtonian era; but, regarded strictly, it constituted a radical departure from their thinking and from the thinking of their predecessors. Hume's most striking and consequential deviation concerns the "traditional" view of causality. According to this view, there is a force or necessary connection between a cause A and its effect B. Factual knowledge of this relationship involves not only the constant sequential and spatial conjunction of A-like and B-like events provided by the senses but also the natural, necessary connection between such events supplied by reason. Hume attacks this latter feature as groundless and argues that the traditionalist mistakenly equates a psychologically determined expectation of B to follow A—a mental habit derived from his past observations of constantly conjoined A-like and B-like events—with a distinct or *a priori* contribution from reason.

Certain results of Hume's investigation of moral philosophy under his strict empirical method of inquiry are sufficiently foreshadowed by the account of causality embedded in that method to allow instruction by resemblance, contrast and comparability. Thus, a generic similarity: Moral assertions, *e.g.,* "Helping the injured is good" or "Wilful murder is bad," no less than scientific assertions, *e.g.,* "Acid causes litmus paper to turn red," are highly confirmed generalizations from experience, and, as such, are only contingently true; they are not laws of nature known with *a priori* certainty. Next, a differentiation: The basis of a causal statement is the experienced constant conjunction of two sets of similar events where all of the events in both sets may be regarded as *external*. But the basis of a moral assertion is the experienced constant conjunction of two sets of similar events where the events of the first set may be regarded as *external* while those of the second set may only be regarded as *internal;* more specifically, where the events of the first set are *voluntary actions* while those of the second set are either *feelings of approval* or *feelings of disapproval*. And finally, a rough comparability: Just as we are constituted to attribute causal necessity to two sorts of constantly conjoined external events, so too we are psychologically constituted to attribute a moral quality or property to an external action constantly conjoined with our feelings of approval or disapproval.

A great deal of the foregoing is captured in Hume's summary of his discussion of moral theory in the *Treatise:*

Take any action allowed to be vicious: wilful murder, for instance. Examine it in all its lights, and see if you can find that matter of fact, or real existence, which you call *vice.* . . . You never can find it, till you turn your affection into your own breast, and find a sentiment of disapprobation, which arises in you, towards this action. Here is a matter of fact; but it is the object of feeling, not of reason. It lies in your self, not in the object. So that when you pronounce any action or character to be vicious, you mean nothing, but that from the constitution of your nature you have a feeling or sentiment of blame from the contemplation of it.[1]

One cannot reflect on this quotation without asking whether Hume reduces ethics to something personal, to, as we say, a mere matter of taste. Indeed, some philosophers who have been much influenced by Hume insist on an interpretation of this sort.[2] Hume himself recognizes that if he fails to establish that our feelings of approval and disapproval are more than idiosyncratic responses, there cannot be a morality which is in any sense objective and public. He feels, however, that in turning from reason to sentiment, he has eased the problem of avoiding radical relativism and subjectivism. According to Hume, since men have the same psychological make-up, their moral responses will be, for the most part, comparable. He is, of course, not saying that they will agree about the moral worth of every particular action. Rather, he is underscoring the fact that if we are provided with the same data, we *tend* to respond similarly. Thus, for example, in ordinary circumstances, we all believe that the sun rises in the east and sets in the west because our common natures are exposed to the same matters of fact. Human features, including both man's cognitive and passional aspects, it would seem, are similar. If two men come to a full understanding of the same set of facts and their consequences, they tend to make the same moral judgment.

In brief, Hume relies heavily on the observation that ethical disagreements generally stem from misunderstandings about the actual circumstances which surround a given act and from incomplete analyses of the consequences accruing from that act rather than from differences in our passional natures.[3]

---

[1] David Hume, *A Treatise of Human Nature,* Everyman's Library, New York, E. P. Dutton & Co., 1956, Vol. 2, p. 177.

[2] See our Chapter.

[3] Moreover, in his later writing, *The Standard of Taste,* Hume further combats the easy conclusion that morality is relativistic by reminding us that we are usually willing to assimilate, as our very own, judgments of the fully informed, impartial observer.

Hume further insists that the study of men's moral assessments reveals that socially useful acts are approved while those which are socially detrimental are disapproved. And from this he argues that since we judge acts generally by their conformity to social utility, rather than immediate, personal preferences, there is strong indication that impartiality prevails when we make moral judgments.

It would seem that Hume's empirical claim about social utility cannot provide an adequate basis for our moral obligations. One line of criticism, for example, begins with the observation that the concept of justice must be an integral part of any moral theory: The basic feature of that concept consists of an obligation to act in conformity with an inflexible set of rules; it does not appear to include the idea of promoting social utility however. Hume's rebuttal takes this into account. It is, indeed, obligatory to be just, but the reason we adopt the concept and guide our actions in conformity with it is precisely because it is socially useful to do so. It may be that a specific instance of injustice could be more beneficial to society than its corresponding instance of justice (Hume's view does not deny this). But, upon reflection, we see that such cases are not really exceptions. In becoming aware of the complications of circumstances and the unending consequences of our actions, we discover that only by strictly conforming to the rule of justice can mankind be served.

.

1. Hume raises the question of whether or not the source of morality resides solely in man's rational nature or solely in his passional nature. Initially he finds convincing features on each side.

There has been a controversy started of late, much better worth examination, concerning the general foundation of Morals; whether they be derived from Reason, or from Sentiment; whether we attain the knowledge of them by a chain of argument and induction, or by an immediate feeling and finer internal sense; whether, like all sound judgement of truth and falsehood, they should be the same to every rational intelligent being; or whether, like the perception of beauty and deformity, they be founded entirely on the particular fabric and constitution of the human species.

The ancient philosophers, though they often affirm, that virtue is nothing but conformity to reason, yet, in general, seem to consider morals as deriving their existence from taste and sentiment. On the other hand, our modern enquirers, though they also talk much of the beauty of virtue, and deformity of vice, yet have commonly endeavoured to account for these distinctions by metaphysical reasonings, and by deductions from the most abstract principles of the understanding. Such confusion reigned in these subjects, that an opposition of the greatest consequence could prevail between one system and another, and even in the parts of almost each individual system . . .

It must be acknowledged, that both sides of the question are susceptible of specious arguments. Moral distinctions, it may be said, are discernible by pure *reason:* else, whence the many disputes that reign in common life, as well as in philosophy, with regard to this subject: the long chain of proofs often produced on both sides; the examples cited, the authorities appealed to, the analogies employed, the fallacies detected, the inferences drawn, and the several conclusions adjusted to their proper principles. Truth is disputable; not taste: what exists in the nature of things is the standard of our judgement; what each man feels within himself is the standard of sentiment. Propositions in geometry may be proved, systems in physics may be controverted; but the harmony of verse, the tenderness of passion, the brilliancy of wit, must give immediate pleasure. No man reasons concerning another's beauty; but frequently concerning the justice or injustice of his actions. In every criminal trial the first object of the prisoner is to disprove the facts alleged, and deny the actions imputed to him: the second to prove, that, even if these actions were real, they might be justified, as innocent and lawful. It is confessedly by deductions of the understanding, that the first point is ascertained: how can we suppose that a different faculty of the mind is employed in fixing the other?

On the other hand, those who would resolve all moral determinations into *sentiment,* may endeavour to show, that it is impossible for reason ever to draw conclusions of this nature. To virtue, say they, it belongs to be *amiable,* and vice *odious.* This forms their very nature or essence. But can reason or argumentation distribute these different epithets to any subjects, and pronounce beforehand, that this must produce love, and that hatred? Or what other reason can we ever assign for these affections, but the original fabric and formation of the human mind, which is naturally adapted to receive them?[a]

2. *Hume suggests that finding a way of blending both positions would be attractive.*

These arguments on each side (and many more might be produced) are so plausible, that I am apt to suspect, they may, the one as well as the other, be solid and satisfactory, and that *reason* and *sentiment* concur in almost all moral determinations and conclusions. The final sentence, it is probable, which pronounces characters and actions amiable or odious, praise-worthy or blameable; that which stamps on them the mark of honour or infamy, approbation or censure; that which renders morality an active principle and constitutes virtue our happiness, and vice our misery; it is probable, I say, that this final sentence depends on some internal sense or feeling, which nature has made universal in the whole species. For what else can have an influence of this nature? But in order to pave the way for such a sentiment, and give a proper discernment of its object, it is often necessary, we find, that much reasoning should precede, that nice distinctions be made, just conclusions drawn, distant comparisons formed, complicated relations examined, and general facts fixed and ascertained. Some species of beauty, especially the natural kinds, on their first appearance, command our affection and approbation; and where they fail of this effect, it is impossible for any reasoning to redress their influence, or adapt them better to our taste and sentiment. But in many orders of beauty, particularly those of the finer arts, it is requisite to employ much reasoning, in order to feel the proper sentiment; and a false relish may frequently be corrected by argument and reflection. There are just grounds to conclude, that moral beauty partakes much of this latter species, and demands the assistance of our intellectual faculties, in order to give it a suitable influence on the human mind.[b]

3. *According to Hume, however, there can be no compromise about which of the two, reason or sentiment, is the ultimate source of morality. Two decisive arguments against reason are offered. The first is simply that morality is*

practical, ie., it influences or regulates our conduct. But the fact that reason in itself does not provide a spring of action forces us to conclude that it cannot be the source of moral conduct.

The end of all moral speculations is to teach us our duty; and, by proper representations of the deformity of vice and beauty of virtue, beget correspondent habits, and engage us to avoid the one, and embrace the other. But is this ever to be expected from inferences and conclusions of the understanding, which of themselves have no hold of the affections or set in motion the active powers of men? They discover truths: but where the truths which they discover are indifferent, and beget no desire or aversion, they can have no influence on conduct and behaviour. What is honourable, what is fair, what is becoming, what is noble, what is generous, takes possession of the heart, and animates us to embrace and maintain it. What is intelligible, what is evident, what is probable, what is true, procures only the cool assent of the understanding; and gratifying a speculative curiosity, puts an end to our researches.

Extinguish all the warm feelings and prepossessions in favour of virtue, and all disgust or aversion to vice: render men totally indifferent towards these distinctions; and morality is no longer a practical study, nor has any tendency to regulate our lives and actions.ᶜ

4. *The second argument against reason is subtle and distinctively Humean. Although we are aware of all the objective facts in a given immoral situation—such as, A promised to repay a debt to B on a certain day, A has sufficient funds to repay his or her debt on that day, A refuses to do so, etc.—the wrongness of A's action cannot be found as an item in a complex list of facts upon which we reflect in arriving at a moral judgment. Hume argues further that the rightness or wrongness is not to be discerned in relationships between any of these facts nor even between A's action and a rule about one's being expected to pay his debts.*

Reason judges either of *matter of fact* or of *relations.* Enquire then, *first,* where is that matter of fact which we here call *crime;* point it out; determine the time of its existence; describe its essence or nature; explain the sense or faculty to which it discovers itself. It resides in the mind of the person who is ungrateful. He must, therefore, feel it, and be conscious of it. But nothing is there, except the passion of ill-will or absolute indifference. You cannot say that these, of themselves, always, and in all circumstances, are crimes. No, they are only crimes when directed towards persons who have before expressed and displayed good-will towards us. Consequently, we may infer, that the crime of ingratitude is not any particular individual *fact;* but arises from a complication of circumstances, which, being presented to the spectator, excites the *sentiment* of blame, by the particular structure and fabric of his mind.

This representation, you say, is false. Crime, indeed, consists not in a particular *fact,* of whose reality we are assured by *reason;* but it consists in certain *moral relations,* discovered by reason, in the same manner as we discover by reason the truths of geometry or algebra. But what are the relations, I ask, of which you here talk? In the case stated above, I see first consist in that relation? But suppose a person bore me ill-will or did me ill-offices; and I, in return, were indifferent towards him, or did him good offices. Here is the same relation of *contrariety;* and yet my conduct is often highly laudable. Twist and turn this matter as much as you will, you can never rest the morality on relation; but must have recourse to the decisions of sentiment.

When it is affirmed that two and three are equal to the half of ten, this relation of equality I understand perfectly. I conceive, that if ten be divided into two parts, of which one has as many units as the other; and if any of these parts be compared to two added to three, it will contain as many units as that compound number. But when you draw thence a comparison to moral relations, I own that I am altogether at a loss to understand you. A moral action, a crime, such as ingratitude, is a complicated object. Does the morality consist in the relation of its parts to each other? How? After what manner? Specify the relation: be more particular and explicit in your propositions, and you will easily see their falsehood.

No, say you, the morality consists in the relation of actions to the rule of right; and they are denominated good or ill, according as they agree or disagree with it. What then is this rule of right? In what does it consist? How is it determined? By reason, you say, which examines the moral relations of actions. So that moral relations are determined by the comparison of action to a rule. And that rule is determined by considering the moral relations of objects. Is not this fine reasoning? [d]

5. Having examined the overwhelming case against reason, Hume comes down squarely on the side of sentiment as the source of morality.

. . . The hypothesis which we embrace is plain. It maintains that morality is determined by sentiment. It defines virtue to be *whatever mental action or quality gives to a spectator the pleasing sentiment of approbation;* and vice the contrary. We then proceed to examine a plain matter of fact, to wit, what actions have this influence. We consider all the circumstances in which these actions agree, and thence endeavour to extract some general observations with regard to these sentiments.ᶜ

6. Even though reason is incapable of being the source of morality, it plays an essential role in rendering moral decisions.

When a man, at any time, deliberates concerning his own conduct (as, whether he had better, in a particular emergence, assist a brother or a benenefactor), he must consider these separate relations, with all the circumstances and situations of the persons, in order to determine the superior duty and obligation; and in order to determine the proportion of lines in any triangle, it is necessary to examine the nature of that figure, and the relation which its several parts bear to each other. But notwithstanding this appearing similarity in the two cases, there is, at bottom, an extreme difference between them. A speculative reasoner concerning triangles or circles considers the several known and given relations of the parts of these figures; and thence infers some unknown relation, which is dependent on the former. But in moral deliberations we must be acquainted beforehand with all the objects, and all their relations to each other and from a comparison of the whole, fix our choice or approbation. No new fact to be ascertained; no new relation to be discovered. All the circumstances of the case are supposed to be laid before us, ere we can fix any sentence of blame or approbation. If any material circumstance be yet unknown or doubtful, we must first employ our inquiry or intellectual faculties to assure us of it; and must suspend for a time all moral decision or sentiment. While we are ignorant whether a man were aggressor or not, how can we determine whether the person who killed him be criminal or innocent? But after every circumstance, every relation is known, the understanding has no further room to operate, nor any object on which it could employ itself. The approbation or blame which then ensues, cannot be the work of the judgement, but of the heart; and is not a speculative proposition or affirmation, but an active feeling or sentiment. In the disquisitions of the understanding, from known circumstances and relations, we infer some new and unknown. In moral decisions, all the circumstances and relations must be previously known; and the mind, from the contemplation of the whole, feels some new impression of affection or disgust, esteem or contempt, approbation or blame.

Hence the great difference between a mistake of *fact* and one of *right;* and hence the reason why the one is commonly criminal and not the other. When Oedipus killed Laius, he was ignorant of the relation, and from circumstances, innocent and involuntary, formed erroneous opinions concerning the action which he committed. But when Nero killed Agrippina, all the relations between himself and the person, and all the circumstances of the fact, were previously known to him; but the motive of revenge, or fear, or interest, prevailed in his savage heart over the sentiments of duty and humanity. And when we express that detestation against him to which he himself, in a little time, became insensible, it is not that we see any relations, of which he was ignorant; but that, for the rectitude of our disposition, we feel sentiments against which he was hardened from flattery and a long perseverance in the most enormous crimes. In these sentiments then, not in a discovery of relations of any kind, do all moral determinations consist. Before we can pretend to form any decision of this kind, everything must be known and acertained on the side of the object or action. Nothing remains but to feel, on our part, some sentiment of blame or approbation; whence we pronounce the action criminal or virtuous.[f]

7. *Hume discusses the two great social virtues, benevolence and justice, extensively. He observes that the first of these is universally esteemed.*

It may be esteemed, perhaps, a superfluous task to prove, that the benevolent or softer affections are estimable; and wherever they appear, engage the approbation and good-will of mankind. The epithets *sociable,*

good-natured, humane, merciful, grateful, friendly, generous, beneficent, or
their equivalents, are known in all languages, and universally express the
highest merit, which *human nature* is capable of attaining. Where these
amiable qualities are attended with birth and power and eminent
abilities, and display themselves in the good government or useful
instruction of mankind, they seem even to raise the possessors of them
above the rank of *human nature,* and make them approach in some
measure to the divine. Exalted capacity, undaunted courage, prosperous
success; these may only expose a hero or politician to the envy and ill-will
of the public: but as soon as the praises are added of humane and
beneficent; when instances are displayed of lenity, tenderness or
friendship; envy itself is silent, or joins the general voice of approbation
and applause. . . .No qualities are more intitled to the general good-will
and approbation of mankind than beneficence and humanity, friendship
and gratitude, natural affection and public spirit, or whatever proceeds
from a tender sympathy with others, and a generous concern for our kind
and species. These wherever they appear seem to transfuse themselves, in
a manner, into each beholder, and to call forth, in their own behalf, the
same favourable and affectionate sentiments, which they exert on all
around.

We may observe that, in displaying the praises of any humane,
beneficent man, there is one circumstance which never fails to be amply
insisted on, namely, the happiness and satisfaction, derived to society
from his intercourse and good offices.[g]

8. *With respect to the virtue justice, Hume argues that its sole source is utility.
He arrives at this conclusion by asking us to imagine several sets of social and
human circumstances and to note that in these circumstances, the virtue would
be idle, in the sense that it would either be superfluous or unworkable.*

That Justice is useful to society, and consequently that *part* of its merit,
at least, must arise from that consideration, it would be a superfluous
undertaking to prove. That public utility is the *sole* origin of justice, and
that reflections on the beneficial consequences of this virtue are the *sole*
foundation of its merit; this proposition, being more curious and
important, will better deserve our examination and enquiry.

Let us suppose that nature has bestowed on the human race such profuse *abundance* of all *external* conveniencies, that, without any uncertainty in the event, without any care or industry on our part, every individual finds himself fully provided with whatever his most voracious appetites can want, or luxurious imagination wish or desire. His natural beauty, we shall suppose, surpasses all acquired ornaments: the perpetual clemency of the seasons renders useless all clothes or covering: the raw herbage affords him the most delicious fare; the clear fountain, the richest beverage. No laborious occupation required: no tillage: no navigation. Music, poetry, and contemplation form his sole business: conversation, mirth, and friendship his sole amusement.

It seems evident that, in such a happy state, every other social virtue would flourish and receive tenfold increase; but the cautious, jealous virtue of justice would never once have been dreamed of. For what purpose make a partition of goods, where every one has already more than enough? Why give rise to property, where there cannot possibly be any injury? Why call this object *mine,* when upon the seizing of it by another, I need but stretch out my hand to possess myself to what is equally valuable? Justice, in that case, being totally useless, would be an idle ceremonial, and could never possibly have place in the catalogue of virtues. . . .

Again; suppose, that, though the necessities of human race continue the same as at present, yet the mind is so enlarged, and so replete with friendship and generosity, that every man has the utmost tenderness for every man, and feels no more concern for his own interest than for that of his fellows; it seems evident, that the use of justice would, in this case, be suspended by such an extensive benevolence, nor would the divisions and barriers of property and obligation have ever been thought of. Why should I bind another, by a deed or promise, to do me any good office, when I know that he is already prompted, by the strongest inclination, to seek my happiness, and would, of himself, perform the desired service; except the hurt, he thereby receives, be greater than the benefit accruing to me? in which case, he knows that, from my innate humanity and friendship, I should be the first to oppose myself to his imprudent generosity. Why raise land marks between my neighbour's field and mine, when my heart has made no division between our interests; but shares all his joys and sorrows with the same force and vivacity as if originally my own? Every man, upon this supposition, being a second self to another, would trust all his interests to the discretion of every man; without jealousy, without partition, without distinction. And the whole human race would form only one family; where all would lie in common, and be used freely, without regard to property; but cautiously too, with as entire regard to the necessities of each individual, as if our own interests were most intimately concerned. . . .

To make this truth more evident, let us reverse the foregoing suppositions; and carrying everything to the opposite extreme, consider what would be the effect of these new situations. Suppose a society to fall into such want of all common necessaries, that the utmost frugality and industry cannot preserve the greater number from perishing, and the whole from extreme misery; it will readily, I believe, be admitted, that the strict laws of justice are suspended, in such a pressing emergence, and give place to the stronger motives of necessity and self-preservation. Is it any crime, after a shipwreck, to seize whatever means or instrument of safety one can lay hold of, without regard to former limitations of property? Or if a city besieged were perishing with hunger; can we imagine, that men will see any means of preservation before them, and lose their lives, from a scrupulous regard to what, in other situations, would be the rules of equity and justice? The use and tendency of that virtue is to procure happiness and security, by preserving order in society: but where the society is ready to perish from extreme necessity, no greater evil can be dreaded from violence and injustice; and every man may now provide for himself by all the means, which prudence can dictate, or humanity permit. The public, even in less urgent necessities, opens granaries, without the consent of proprietors, as justly supposing, that the authority of magistracy may, consistent with equity, extend so far: but were any number of men to assemble, without the tie of laws or civil jurisdiction; would an equal partition of bread in a famine, though effected by power and even violence, be regarded as criminal or injurious?

Suppose likewise, that it should be a virtuous man's fate to fall into the society of ruffians, remote from the protection of laws and government; what conduct must he embrace in that melancholy situation? He sees such a desperate rapaciousness prevail; such a disregard to equity, such contempt of order, such stupid blindness to future consequences, as must immediately have the most tragical conclusion, and must terminate in destruction to the greater number, and in a total dissolution of society to the rest. He, meanwhile, can have no other expedient than to arm himself, to whomever the sword he seizes, or the buckler, may belong: To make provision of all means of defence and security: And his particular regard to justice being no longer of use to his own safety or that of others, he must consult the dictates of self-preservation alone, without concern for those who no longer merit his care and attention.[h]

9. *Hume summarizes the foregoing argument.*

Thus, the rules of equity or justice depend entirely on the particular state and condition in which men are placed, and owe their origin and existence to that utility, which results to the public from their strict and regular observance. Reverse, in any considerable circumstance, the condition of men: Produce extreme abundance or extreme necessity: Implant in the human breast perfect moderation and humanity, or perfect rapaciousness and malice: By rendering justice totally *useless,* you thereby totally destroy its essence, and suspend its obligation upon mankind.

The common situation of society is a medium amidst all these extremes. We are naturally partial to ourselves, and to our friends; but are capable of learning the advantage resulting from a more equitable conduct. Few enjoyments are given us from the open and liberal hand of nature; but by art, labour, and industry, we can extract them in great abundance. Hence the ideas of property become necessary in all civil society: Hence justice derives its usefulness to the public: And hence alone arises its merits and moral obligation.[i]

10. *In final analysis, Hume's moral theory presumes that some, at least, of any man's passions do not have their origin in concern for himself. Thus, he insists that an individual's morality is based upon sentiments having their origin in his concern for others. Such sentiments are universally shared, since they are not affected by the relativism of any personal considerations.*

It seems a happiness in the present theory; that it enters not into that vulgar dispute concerning the *degrees* of benevolence or self-love, which prevail in human nature; a dispute which is never likely to have any issue, both because men, who have taken part, are not easily convinced, and because the phenomena, which can be produced on either side, are so dispersed, so uncertain, and subject to so many interpretations, that it is scarcely possible accurately to compare them, or draw from them any determinate inference or conclusion. It is sufficient for our present purpose, if it be allowed, what surely, without the greatest absurdity cannot be disputed, that there is some benevolence, however small, infused into our bosom; some spark of friendship for human kind; some particle of the dove kneaded into our frame, along with the elements of the wolf and serpent. Let these generous sentiments be supposed ever so weak; let them be insufficient to move even a hand or finger of our body, they must still direct the determinations of our mind, and where everything else is equal, produce a cool preference of what is useful and serviceable to mankind, above what is pernicious and dangerous. A *moral distinction,* therefore, immediately arises. . . .

. . . The notion of morals implies some sentiment common to all mankind, which recommends the same object to general approbation, and makes every man, or most men, agree in the same opinion or decision concerning it. It also implies some sentiment, so universal and comprehensive as to extend to all mankind, and render the actions and conduct, even of the persons the most remote, an object of applause or censure, according as they agree or disagree with that rule of right which is established. These two requisite circumstances belong alone to the sentiment of humanity here insisted on. The other passions produce in every breast, many strong sentiments of desire and aversion, affection and hatred; but these neither are felt so much in common, nor are so comprehensive, as to be the foundation of any general system and established theory of blame or approbation.

When a man denominates another his *enemy,* his *rival,* his *antagonist,* his *adversary,* he is understood to speak the language of self-love, and to express sentiments, peculiar to himself, and arising from his particular circumstances and situation. But when he bestows on any man the epithets of *vicious* or *odious* or *depraved,* he then speaks another language, and expresses sentiments, in which he expects all his audience are to concur with him. He must here, therefore, depart from his private and particular situation, and must choose a point of view, common to him with others; he must move some universal principle of the human frame, and touch a string to which all mankind have an accord and symphony. If he mean, therefore, to express that this man possesses qualities, whose tendency is pernicious to society, he has chosen this common point of view, and has touched the principle of humanity, in which every man, in some degree, concurs. While the human heart is compounded of the same elements as at present, it will never be wholly indifferent to public good, nor entirely unaffected with the tendency of characters and manners. And though this affection of humanity may not generally be esteemed so strong as vanity or ambition, yet, being common to all men, it can alone be the foundation of morals, or of any general system of blame or praise. One man's ambition is not another's ambition, nor will the same event or object satisfy both; but the humanity of one man is the humanity of every one, and the same object touches this passion in all human creatures.

. . . Whatever conduct gains my approbation, by touching my humanity, procures also the applause of all mankind, by affecting the same principle in them; but what serves my avarice or ambition pleases these passions in me alone, and affects not the avarice and ambition of the rest of mankind. There is no circumstance of conduct in any man provided it have a beneficial tendency, that is not agreeable to my humanity, however remote the person . . .¹

Questions

1. Do you agree with Hume's observation that if men did not experience feelings of approval or disapproval, they would not render moral judgments about actions?
2. Discuss Hume's arguments against reason as the basis of morality.
3. What is the role of reason in moral deliberation?
4. It has been pointed out that at the theoretical level, Hume's view of morality resembles his account of causality. In what ways are they similar and in what ways are they different?

5. Can Hume be defended against the charge of moral relativism, if he bases morality on sentiment?

6. How does Hume's discussion of justice show that it is based on social utility?

7. To what extent is Hume a precursor of utilitarianism, the view that moral actions are ones which promote the greatest happiness for the greatest number? Discuss.

8. Adopting Hume's view, provide arguments against an ethical intuitionist who claims we know that certain actions, by their very nature are right, and others, wrong.

9. Isolate some of the features of the psychological theory which underlie Hume's ethics.

10. Hume believes that people who are not directly involved in a moral situation can nevertheless make moral judgments about it. Do you agree with him? Discuss.

Key to selections:

DAVID HUME, *An Enquiry Concerning the Principles of Morals,* Reprinted from the edition of 1777, La Salle, Open Court, 1938.

[a]pp. 2–4.	[f]pp. 130–132.
[b]pp. 5–6.	[g]pp. 8–10.
[c]pp. 4–5.	[h]pp. 15–20.
[d]pp. 127–129.	[i]pp. 20–21.
[e]pp. 129–130.	[j]pp. 109–113.

Guide to Additional Reading

INEXPENSIVE EDITIONS:

HUME, DAVID., *An Inquiry concerning the Principles of Morals,* New York, The Liberal Arts Press, 1957.

_____, *Treatise of Human Nature,* (Everyman ed.), New York, Dutton and Co., 1950.

WOLFF, R. P. (ed.), *The Essential David Hume,* New York, The New American Library, 1969.

DISCUSSION AND COMMENTARY:

Broad, C.D., *Five Types of Ethical Theory,* New York, Harcourt, Brace and Co., 1930, Chapter IV.

Broiles, R.D., *The Moral Philosophy of David Hume,* The Hague, Martinus Nijhoff, 1964.

Kemp Smith, N. *The Philosophy of David Hume,* London, Macmillan & Co., 1941.

Macnabb, D. G. C., *David Hume: His Theory of Knowledge and Morality,* New York, Hutchinson House, 1951.

Stewart, J. B. *The Moral and Political Philosophy of David Hume,* New York, Columbia University Press, 1968.

CHAPTER 11

Duty and Reason

IMMANUEL KANT

It is said of Immanuel Kant (1724–1804) that "his failures are more important than most men's successes." This man, whose writings are prerequisite reading for all who desire to understand nineteenth and twentieth-century thought, lived a life singularly without incident. Kant lived by routine, and, although he had many friends, he never married and never ventured more than forty miles from Königsberg, East Prussia, the city of his birth and death. The German writer Heine, although without doubt exercising some poetic license, has immortalized Kant as an automaton: "Rising, coffee-drinking, writing, lecturing, dining, walking each had its set time. And when Immanuel Kant, in his gray coat, cane in hand, appeared at the door of his house, and strolled towards the small avenue of linden trees which is still called 'The Philosopher's Walk,' the neighbors knew it was exactly half-past-three by the clock."

The Kant family belonged to the lower middle class and was devoutly religious. In recognition of his son's academic ability and because of the family's religious persuasion, Immanuel's father sent him to the local Pietistic College to prepare for the ministry. Immanuel continued his studies at the University of Königsberg, and became increasingly interested in natural science and philosophy. Between the years of 1746 and 1755 he supported himself as a private teacher for various landed families in and around his native city. He was then appointed to an instructorship at his University and finally, in the year 1770, was promoted to a full Professorship. Kant was a popular and successful teacher. Perhaps surprisingly for one who was so rigorous in his own thinking, he is reputed to have given the following advice in practical pedagogy: "Attend most to the student of middle ability, the dunces are beyond help, and the geniuses help themselves."

Kant's inner life was as dramatic as his outer life was drab: he renounced the external and emotional side of religion; he evolved from a man-of-letters philosopher with a free and flowing style of writing and thinking into a "critical" philosopher with a labored style of presenting uncompromisingly profound thoughts; he transformed a spontaneous scientific curiosity into an impulse to explore the foundations of science; at first a passive follower of an accepted school of philosophy, he became the innovator of an important school of thought. What is more, he took a passionate interest in the American and French revolutions. The conservative outer mien of Kant was a deceptive facade for the inner Kant.

The most important of Kant's scientific writings is his *General Natural History and Theory of the Heavens* (1755), in which he accounts for the origin of the solar system by formulating the nebular hypothesis. His revolutionary philosophical work is *Critique of Pure Reason* (1781), in which he is concerned to demonstrate that it is possible to have certain knowledge in the natural sciences and mathematics. In his *Critique of Judgment* (1790) he analyzes aesthetics and biology. Kant endeavors to show the foundations of genuine morality in *The Fundamental Principles of the Metaphysics of Morals* (1785) and the *Critique of Practical Reason* (1788); in the latter he investigates the implications of morality for religion.

The direction of Kant's philosophical interests is revealed in his reflection that "two things fill the mind with ever new and increasing admiration and awe... *the starry heavens above and the moral law within.*" His concern is with nature and morality. Against the background of eighteenth-century scepticism, which called into question the foundations of scientific knowledge and morality, he proposes a comprehensive system of the universe in which their certainty is guaranteed. According to Kant, scepticism results from the error of seeking a basis for certainty where it cannot be found, in the *content* of experience. The grounds of certainty, he asserts, are located in the *form* of reason itself. Accordingly, he undertakes an intensive examination of the nature of thought to show how we can have certain knowledge of both scientific facts and moral duties.

Kant demonstrates by an analysis of the nature of the mental processes and of knowledge that the necessity and universality of scientific knowledge are guaranteed by the laws of the mind.[1] He calls these laws the "categories of the understanding." They are the forms of all possible knowledge and are not limited to some specific content. For example, it is the nature of the mind to think in accordance with the principle that every event must have a cause. The principle of causality is one of the categories of the understanding. Thus, despite our ignorance of the cause of a given disease, we are nevertheless certain that it has a cause, and this certainty is a product of mind, not of observation. Although it is generally held that nature itself provides the causal order of our experience, Kant reverses this position, insisting that it is the mind which orders our experience causally. Otherwise, we could not be certain, as we are, of the causal interconnection of events; for, while experience teaches us what actually happens, it does not teach us what *necessarily* happens. The categories are *a priori* — that is, they are not derived from experience; they are universally applicable to experience; and they are the necessary

---

[1] It must be added that what Kant opposes in scepticism is its theory that knowledge of experience or appearances (*phenomena*) cannot be certain. According to his theory, it is knowledge of ultimate reality or "things-in-themselves" (*noumena*) which is impossible.

preconditions of empirical knowledge. Furthermore, although all knowledge necessarily begins with experience, the *a priori* structure of it cannot be gotten by induction from experience, but can be understood only through examining the presuppositions of our orderly experience of nature.

In his search for the grounds of the validity of ethics, Kant employs the same method by which he establishes the grounds of the certainty of science. A valid moral principle, he tells us, must be independent of the empirical data of morality if it is to be binding upon all men. In short, a genuine morality, *i.e.*, a morality which is objectively and universally binding, requires an *a priori* foundation. Kant believes that ordinary moral consciousness, or conscience, reveals to every man that moral precepts are universal and necessary — they are valid for all rational beings.

Universal obligation, according to Kant, cannot be discovered by studying such empirical data as human desires or inclinations, for these vary from one person to another. The universal basis of morality in man must lie in his rational nature, since this alone is the same in everyone. No so-called moral law is valid if it is not rational, that is to say, if it cannot be applied to all rational beings without contradiction. Or, putting it another way, a moral principle must be such that a man can will that all men, including himself, should act upon it. Kant uses the test of consistency as the core of the fundamental moral law, which he calls the *categorical imperative:* those actions are right which conform to principles one can consistently will to be principles for all men, and those actions are wrong which are based upon maxims that a rational creature could not will that all men should follow.

Through the categorical imperative, then, we are enabled to distinguish right from wrong actions. However, Kant tells us, it is not only the test but it is also the unconditional directive for behavior. It is binding upon everyone because each rational man acknowledges his obligation to follow reason. The categorical imperative is, in fact, the only basis for determining our duties. Kant argues that the validity of the basic moral law is not affected by the fact that it is probably not employed in actual conduct.

Reason prescribes duty, and the moral law holds whether or not men actually follow it.

. . .

1. As a preliminary to his construction of a pure moral philosophy, Kant makes a critical analysis of the commonly accepted "good" things, like health, wealth, and friendship. Asking under what conditions these may be considered good, he concludes that they are not good under all circumstances, but only insofar as they are conjoined with something that is unqualifiedly good — a good will. To Kant, a good will represents the effort of a rational being to do what he ought to do, rather than to act from inclination or self-interest.

Nothing can possibly be conceived in the world, or even out of it, which can be called good without qualification, except a Good Will. Intelligence, wit, judgment, and the other *talents* of the mind, however they may be named, or courage, resolution, perseverance, as qualities of temperament, are undoubtedly good and desirable in many respects; but these gifts of nature may also become extremely bad and mischievous if the will which is to make use of them, and which, therefore, constitutes what is called *character*, is not good. It is the same with the *gifts of fortune*. Power, riches, honour, even health, and the general well-being and contentment with one's condition which is called *happiness*, inspire pride, and often presumption, if there is not a good will to correct the influence of these on the mind, and with this also to rectify the whole principle of acting, and adapt it to its end. The sight of a being who is not adorned with a single feature of a pure and good will, enjoying unbroken prosperity, can never give pleasure to an impartial rational spectator. Thus a good will appears to constitute the indispensable condition even of being worthy of happiness.

There are even some qualities which are of service to this good will itself, and may facilitate its action, yet which have no intrinsic unconditional value, but always presuppose a good will, and this qualifies the esteem that we justly have for them, and does not permit us to regard them as absolutely good. Moderation in the affections and passions, self-control and calm deliberation are not only good in many respects, but even seem to constitute part of the intrinsic worth of the person; but they are far from deserving to be called good without qualification, although they have been so unconditionally praised by the ancients. For without the principles of a good will, they may become extremely bad, and the coolness of a villain not only makes him far more danger-ous, but also directly makes him more abominable in our eyes than he would have been without it.[a]

2. The good will is not good because it achieves good results. Even if it were unable to attain the ends it seeks, it would still be good in itself and have a higher worth than the superficial things gained by immoral actions.

A good will is good not because of what it performs or effects, not by its aptness for the attainment of some proposed end, but simply by virtue of the volition, that is, it is good in itself, and considered by itself is to be esteemed much higher than all that can be brought about by it in favour of any inclination, nay, even of the sum total of all inclinations. Even if it should happen that, owing to special disfavour of fortune, or the niggardly pro-vision of a step-motherly nature, this will should wholly lack power to accomplish its purpose, if with its greatest efforts it should yet achieve nothing, and there should remain only the good will (not, to be sure, a mere wish, but the summoning of all means in our power), then, like a jewel, it would still shine by its own light, as a thing which has its whole value in itself. Its usefulness or fruitlessness can neither add to nor take away anything from this value. It would be, as it were, only the setting to enable us to handle it the more conveniently in common commerce, or to at-tract to it the attention of those who are not yet connoisseurs, but not to recommend it to true connoisseurs, or to determine its value.[b]

3. Experience shows that reason is a very inefficient instrument for the achievement of happiness. If nature intended man for happiness, it would have provided an instinct to this end. What we observe is that the more a man cultivates his reason, the less likely he is to find happiness. Kant concludes that reason is not intended to produce happiness, but to produce a good will.[2]

There is, however, something so strange in this idea of the absolute value of the mere will, in which no account is taken of its utility, that notwithstanding the thorough assent of even common reason to the idea, yet a suspicion must arise that it may perhaps really be the product of mere high-flown fancy, and that we may have misunderstood the purpose of nature in assigning reason as the governor of our will. Therefore we will examine this idea from this point of view.

In the physical constitution of an organized being, that is, a being adapted suitably to the purposes of life, we assume it as a fundamental principle that no organ for any purpose will be found but what is also the fittest and best adapted for that purpose. Now in a being which has reason and a will, if the proper object of nature were its *conservation*, its *welfare*, in a word, its *happiness*, then nature would have hit upon a very bad arrangement in selecting the reason of the creature to carry out this purpose. For all the actions which the creature has to perform with a view to this purpose, and the whole rule of its conduct, would be far more surely prescribed to it by instinct, and that end would have been attained thereby much more certainly than it ever can be by reason. Should reason have been communicated to this favoured creature over and above, it must only have served it to contemplate the happy constitution of its nature, to admire it,

---

[2] It is to be noted that in emphasizing duty rather than happiness in his ethical theory, Kant does not deny that happiness is desirable for man. While he holds that the immediate object of reason is the production of a good will, which is the supreme good (*supremum bonum*), he acknowledges that a man of good will *deserves* happiness. The supreme good — *i.e.*, virtue — when conjoined with happiness in proportion to it, constitutes the greatest good (*summum bonum*).

to congratulate itself thereon, and to feel thankful for it to the beneficent cause, but not that it should subject its desires to that weak and delusive guidance, and meddle bunglingly with the purpose of nature. In a word, nature would have taken care that reason should not break forth into *practical exercise*, nor have the presumption, with its weak insight, to think out for itself the plan of happiness, and of the means of attaining it. Nature would not only have taken on herself the choice of the ends, but also of the means, and with wise foresight would have entrusted both to instinct.

And, in fact, we find that the more a cultivated reason applies itself with deliberate purpose to the enjoyment of life and happiness, so much the more does the man fail of true satisfaction. And from this circumstance there arises in many, if they are candid enough to confess it, a certain degree of *misology*, that is, hatred of reason, especially in the case of those who are most experienced in the use of it, because after calculating all the advantages they derive, I do not say from the invention of all the arts of common luxury, but even from the sciences (which seem to them to be after all only a luxury of the understanding), they find that they have, in fact, only brought more trouble on their shoulders, rather than gained in happiness; and they end by envying, rather than despising, the more common stamp of men who keep closer to the guidance of mere instinct, and do not allow their reason much influence on their conduct. And this we must admit, that the judgment of those who would very much lower the lofty eulogies of the advantages which reason gives us in regard to the happiness and satisfaction of life, or who would even reduce them below zero, is by no means morose or ungrateful to the goodness with which the world is governed, but that there lies at the root of these judgments the idea that our existence has a different and far nobler end, for which, and not for happiness, reason is properly intended, and which must, therefore, be regarded as the supreme condition to which the private ends of man must, for the most part, be postponed.

For as reason is not competent to guide the will with certainty in regard to its objects and the satisfaction of all our wants (which it to some extent even multiplies), this being an end to which an implanted instinct would have led with much greater certainty; and since, nevertheless, reason is imparted to us as a practical faculty, *i.e.*, as one which is to have influence on the *will*, therefore, admitting that nature generally in the distribution of her capacities has adapted the means to the end, its true destination must be to produce a *will*, not merely good as a *means* to something else, but *good in itself*, for which reason was absolutely necessary. This will then, though not indeed the sole and complete good, must be the supreme good and the condition of every other, even of the desire of happiness. Under these circumstances, there is nothing inconsistent with the wisdom of nature in the fact that the cultivation of the reason, which is requisite for the first and unconditional purpose, does in many ways interfere, at least in this life, with the attainment of the second, which is always conditional, namely, happiness. Nay, it may even reduce it to nothing, without nature thereby failing of her purpose. For reason recognizes the establishment of a good will as its highest practical destination, and in attaining this purpose is capable only of a satisfaction of its own proper kind, namely, that from the attainment of an end, which end again is determined by reason only, notwithstanding that this may involve many a disappointment to the ends of inclination.[c]

4. Kant then proceeds to explain the relationship between good will and duty: a good will is one which acts for the sake of duty. Indeed, human actions have moral worth only if they are performed from duty. Actions that result from inclination or self-interest may be praiseworthy if they happen, for whatever reason, to accord with duty, but they are not "moral." For example, a man who preserves his life in routine conformity to duty is acting from an inclination which is according to duty, but not from duty. On the other hand, to preserve life when it has become a burden, only because duty requires it, is morally correct.

Kant does not mean that doing one's duty is always, or even generally, unpleasant. However, when our desires lead to actions which happen to conform to duty, we cannot be sure that the consciousness of duty, rather than inclination, was our motive. We can better discern the efficacy of dutifulness where it stands alone or in opposition to other motives. This, not disapproval of ordinary human motives, is what leads Kant to choose examples which are rather cold and unpleasant.

Kant warns that those who fail to understand properly the concept of duty may be tempted to act from motives which may be in accordance with duty or may be contrary to it. But even action in accordance with duty is not enough; only respect for duty makes an action moral.

We have then to develop the notion of a will which deserves to be highly esteemed for itself, and is good without a view to anything further, a notion which exists already in the sound natural understanding, requiring rather to be cleared up than to be taught, and which in estimating the value of our actions always takes the first place, and constitutes the condition of all the rest. In order to do this we will take the notion of duty, which includes that of a good will, although implying certain subjective restrictions and hindrances. These, however, far from concealing it, or rendering it unrecognisable, rather bring it out by contrast, and make it shine forth so much the brighter.

I omit here all actions which are already recognised as inconsistent with duty, although they may be useful for this or that purpose, for with these the question whether they are done *from duty* cannot arise at all, since they even conflict with it. I also set aside those actions which really conform to duty, but to which men have *no* direct *inclination*, performing them because they are impelled thereto by some other inclination. For in this case we can readily distinguish whether the action which agrees with duty is done *from duty*, or from a selfish view. It is much harder to make this distinction when the action accords with duty, and the subject has besides a *direct* inclination to it. For example, it is always a matter of duty that a dealer should not overcharge an inexperienced purchaser, and wherever there is much commerce the prudent tradesman does not overcharge, but keeps a fixed price for everyone, so that a child buys of him as well as any other. Men are thus *honestly* served; but this is not enough to make us believe that the tradesman has so acted from duty and from principles of honesty: his own advantage required it; it is out of the question in this case to suppose that he might besides have a direct inclination in favour of the buyers, so that as it were, from love he should give no advantage to one over another. Accordingly the action was done neither from duty nor from direct inclination, but merely with a selfish view.

On the other hand, it is a duty to maintain one's life; and, in addition, everyone has also a direct inclination to do so. But on this account the often anxious care which most men take for it has no intrinsic worth, and their maxim has no moral import. They preserve their life *as duty requires*, no doubt, but not *because duty requires*. On the other hand, if adversity and hopeless sorrow have completely taken away the relish for life; if the unfortunate one, strong in mind, indignant at his fate rather than desponding or dejected, wishes for death, and yet preserves his life without loving it — not from inclination or fear, but from duty — then his maxim has a moral worth.[d]

5. By the use of an illustration, Kant differentiates merely praiseworthy behavior from moral action. Altruistic actions which result from feelings of sociability deserve praise and encouragement, but they cannot be classified as possessing strictly moral value.

To be beneficent when we can is a duty; and besides this, there are many minds so sympathetically constituted that, without any other motive of vanity or self-interest, they find a pleasure in spreading joy around them, and can take delight in the satisfaction of others so far as it is their own work. But I maintain that in such a case an action of this kind, however proper, however amiable it may be, has nevertheless no true moral worth, but is on a level with other inclinations, *e.g.*, the inclination to honour, which, if it is happily directed to that which is in fact of public utility and accordant with duty, and consequently honourable, deserves praise and encouragement, but not esteem. For the maxim lacks the moral import, namely, that such actions be done *from duty*, not from inclination. Put the case that the mind of that philanthropist were clouded by sorrow of his own, extinguishing all sympathy with the lot of others, and that while he still has the power to benefit others in distress, he is not touched by their trouble because he is absorbed with his own; and now suppose that he tears himself out of this dead insensibility, and performs the action without any inclination to it, but simply from duty, then first has his action its genuine moral worth. Further still; if nature has put little sympathy in the heart of this or that man; if he, supposed to be an upright man, is by temperament cold and indifferent to the sufferings of others, perhaps because in respect of his own he is provided with the special gift of patience and fortitude, and supposes, or even requires, that others should have the same — and such a man would certainly not be the meanest product of nature — but if nature had not specially framed him for a philanthropist, would he not still find in himself a source from whence to give himself a far higher worth than that of a good-natured temperament could be? Unquestionably. It is just in this that the moral worth of the character is brought out which is incomparably the highest of all, namely, that he is beneficent, not from inclination, but from duty.[e]

6. Kant's first ethical proposition, then, is that an act must be done from duty in order to have moral worth. His second proposition is a development from the first: an act done from duty derives its moral value, not from the results it produces, but from the principle by which it is determined.

The second proposition is: That an action done from duty derives its moral worth, *not from the purpose* which is to be attained by it, but from the maxim by which it is determined, and therefore does not depend on the realization of the object of the action, but merely on the *principle of volition* by which the action has taken place, without regard to any object of desire. It is clear from what precedes that the purposes which we may have in view in our actions, or their effects regarded as ends and springs of the will, cannot give to actions any unconditional or moral worth. In what, then, can their worth lie, if it is not to consist in the will and in reference to its expected effect? It cannot lie anywhere but in the *principle of the will* without regard to the ends which can be attained by the action.[f]

7. *The first two propositions lead Kant to a definition of duty. The morally right action is one done solely out of reverence for the law, and its unique and unconditioned worth is derived from this source.*

The third proposition, which is a consequence of the two preceding, I would express thus: *Duty is the necessity of acting from respect for the law.* I may have *inclination* for an object as the effect of my proposed action, but I cannot have *respect* for it, just for this reason, that it is an effect and not an energy of will. Similarly, I cannot have respect for inclination, whether my own or another's; I can at most, if my own, approve it; if another's, sometimes even love it; *i.e.*, look on it as favourable to my own interest. It is only what is connected with my will as a principle, by no means as an effect — what does not subserve my inclination, but overpowers it, or at least in case of choice excludes it from its calculation — in other words, simply the law of itself, which can be an object of respect, and hence a command. Now an action done from duty must wholly exclude the influence of inclination, and with it every object of the will, so that nothing remains which can determine the will except objectively the *law*, and subjectively *pure respect* for this practical law, and consequently the maxim that I should follow this law even to the thwarting of all my inclinations.

Thus the moral worth of an action does not lie in the effect expected from it, nor in any principle of action which requires to borrow its motive from this expected effect. For all these effects —

agreeableness of one's condition, and even the promotion of the happiness of others — could have been also brought about by other causes, so that for this there would have been no need of the will of a rational being; whereas it is in this alone that the supreme and unconditional good can be found. The pre-eminent good which we call moral can therefore consist in nothing else than *the conception of law* in itself, *which certainly is only possible in a rational being*, in so far as this conception, and not the expected effect, determines the will. This is a good which is already present in the person who acts accordingly, and we have not to wait for it to appear first in the result.[g]

8. The supreme principle or law of morality which the good man must follow is the "categorical imperative." Rational beings, to the extent that they act rationally, will always be guided by ethical principles or maxims which can be adopted by everyone else without generating any contradiction.

But what sort of law can that be, the conception of which must determine the will, even without paying any regard to the effect expected from it, in order that this will may be called good absolutely and without qualification? As I have deprived the will of every impulse which could arise to it from obedience to any law, there remains nothing but the universal conformity of its actions to law in general, which alone is to serve the will as a principle, *i.e.*, I am never to act otherwise than so *that I could also will that my maxim should become a universal law*. Here now, it is the simple conformity to law in general, without assuming any particular law applicable to certain actions, that serves the will as its principle, and must so serve it, if duty is not to be a vain delusion and a chimerical notion. The common reason of men in its practical judgments perfectly coincides with this, and always has in view the principle here suggested. Let the question be, for example: May I when in distress make a promise with the intention not to keep it? I readily distinguish here between the two significations which the question may have: Whether it is prudent, or whether it is right, to make a false promise. The former may undoubtedly often be the case. I see clearly indeed that it is not enough to extricate myself from a present difficulty by means of this subterfuge, but it must be well considered whether there may not hereafter spring from this lie much greater inconvenience than that from which I now free myself, and as, with all my supposed *cunning*, the consequences cannot be so easily foreseen but that credit once lost may be much more injurious to me than any mischief which I seek to avoid at present, it should be considered whether it would not be more *prudent* to act herein according to a universal maxim, and to make it a habit to promise nothing except with the intention of keeping it. But it is soon clear to me that such a maxim will still only be based on the fear of consequences. Now it is a wholly different thing to be truthful from duty, and to be so from apprehension of injurious consequences. In the first case, the very notion of the action already implies a law for me; in the second case, I must first look about elsewhere to see what results may be combined with it which would affect myself. For to deviate from the principle of duty is beyond all doubt wicked; but to be unfaithful to my maxim of prudence may often be very advantageous to me, although to abide by it is certainly safer. The shortest way, however, and an unerring one, to discover the answer to this question whether a lying promise is consistent with duty, is to ask myself, Should I be content that my maxim (to extricate myself from difficulty by a false promise) should hold good as a universal law, for myself as well as for others? and should I be able to say to myself, "Every one may make a deceitful promise when he finds himself in a difficulty from which he cannot otherwise extricate himself"? Then I presently become aware that while I can will the lie, I can by no means will that lying should be a universal law. For with such a law there would be no promises at all, since it would be in vain to allege my intention in regard to my future actions to those who would not believe this allegation, or if they over-hastily did so, would pay me back in my own coin. Hence my maxim, as soon as it should be made a universal law, would necessarily destroy itself.[h]

9. Kant distinguishes the categorical *imperative from* hypothetical *imperatives. The former, an unconditional directive, prescribes
actions to be done because of the moral worth of the maxim, and not
for the sake of some consequence that may result. By contrast, a
hypothetical imperative is a conditional directive which advises us
what ought to be done if a desired goal is to be achieved. For example,
"One ought to tell the truth as a matter of principle" is a categorical
imperative, whereas "if you want to avoid punishment, you ought to
tell the truth" is a hypothetical imperative.*

The conception of an objective principle, in so far as it is
obligatory for a will, is called a command (of reason), and the
formula of the command is called an Imperative.

All imperatives are expressed by the word *ought* (or *shall*), and
thereby indicate the relation of an objective law of reason to a
will, which from its subjective constitution is not necessarily determined by it (an obligation). They say that something would
be good to do or to forbear, but they say it to a will which does
not always do a thing because it is conceived to be good to do it.
That is practically *good*, however, which determines the will by
means of the conceptions of reason, and consequently not from
subjective causes, but objectively, that is on principles which are
valid for every rational being as such. It is distinguished from the
pleasant, as that which influences the will only by means of sensation from merely subjective causes, valid only for the sense of
this or that one, and not as a principle of reason, which holds for
every one . . .

Now all *imperatives* command either *hypothetically* or *cate-
gorically*. The former represent the practical necessity of a possible
action as means to something else that is willed (or at least which
one might possibly will). The categorical imperative would be
that which represented an action as necessary of itself without
reference to another end, *i.e.,* as objectively necessary.

Since every practical law represents a possible action as good,
and on this account, for a subject who is practically determinable

by reason, necessary, all imperatives are formulae determining an action which is necessary according to the principle of a will good in some respects. If now the action is good only as a means *to something else*, then the imperative is *hypothetical;* if it is conceived as good *in itself* and consequently as being necessarily the principle of a will which of itself conforms to reason, then it is *categorical.*[i]

10. His first explicit formulation of the categorical imperative requires an individual to obey a maxim which can, without contradiction, be willed to be a rule for everyone. This means that the essence of morality lies in acting on the basis of an impersonal principle which is valid for everyone, including oneself.

When I conceive a hypothetical imperative in general I do not know beforehand what it will contain until I am given the condition [under which it is imperative, *viz.,* the desire which makes this imperative suitable to my purposes]. But when I conceive a categorical imperative I know at once what it contains. For as the imperative contains besides the law only the necessity that the maxims shall conform to this law, while the law contains no conditions restricting it, there remains nothing but the general statement that the maxim of the action should conform to a universal law, and it is this conformity alone that the imperative properly represents as necessary.

There is therefore but one categorical imperative, namely this: *Act only on that maxim whereby thou canst at the same time will that it should become a universal law.*

Now if all imperatives of duty can be deduced from this one imperative as from their principle, then, although it should remain undecided whether what is called duty is not merely a vain notion, yet at least we shall be able to show what we understand by it and what this notion means.

Since the universality of the law according to which effects are produced constitutes what is properly called *nature* in the most general sense (as to form), that is the existence of things as far as it is determined by general laws, the imperative of duty may be expressed thus: *Act as if the maxim of thy action were to become by thy will a Universal Law of Nature.*[j]

11. Kant conceives the categorical imperative to be a two-fold test. It requires first, that maxims for moral action be universalized without logical contradiction, and second, that they be universal directives for action which do not bring the will into disharmony with itself by requiring it to will one thing for itself and another thing for others. Kant illustrates failure at the former level with the first two examples which follow, and failure at the latter level with the second two examples.

1. A man reduced to despair by a series of misfortunes feels wearied of life, but is still so far in possession of his reason that he can ask himself whether it would not be contrary to his duty to himself to take his own life. Now he inquires whether the maxim of his action could become a universal law of nature. His maxim is: From self-love I adopt it as a principle to shorten my life when its longer duration is likely to bring more evil than satisfaction. It is asked then simply whether this principle founded on self-love can become a universal law of nature. Now we see at once that a system of nature of which it should be a law to destroy life by means of the very feeling whose special nature it is to impel to the improvement of life would contradict itself, and therefore could not exist as a system of nature; hence that maxim cannot possibly exist as a universal law of nature, and consequently would be wholly inconsistent with the supreme principle of all duty.

2. Another finds himself forced by necessity to borrow money. He knows that he will not be able to repay it, but sees also that nothing will be lent to him, unless he promises stoutly to repay it in a definite time. He desires to make this promise, but he has still so much conscience as to ask himself: Is it not unlawful and inconsistent with duty to get out of a difficulty in this way? Suppose, however, that he resolves to do so, then the maxim of his action would be expressed thus: When I think myself in want of money, I will borrow money and promise to repay it, although

I know that I never can do so. Now this principle of self-love or of one's own advantage may perhaps be consistent with my whole future welfare; but the question now is, Is it right? I change then the suggestion of self-love into a universal law, and state the ques- tion thus: How would it be if my maxim were a universal law? Then I see at once that it could never hold as a universal law of nature, but would necessarily contradict itself. For supposing it to be a universal law that everyone when he thinks himself in a difficulty should be able to promise whatever he pleases, with the purpose of not keeping his promise, the promise itself would be- come impossible, as well as the end that one might have in view in it, since no one would consider that anything was promised to him, but would ridicule all such statements as vain pretences.

3. A third finds in himself a talent which with the help of some culture might make him a useful man in many respects. But he finds himself in comfortable circumstances, and prefers to indulge in pleasure rather than to take pains in enlarging and improving his happy natural capacities. He asks, however, whether his maxim of neglect of his natural gifts, besides agreeing with his inclination to indulgence, agrees also with what is called duty. He sees then that a system of nature could indeed subsist with such a universal law although men (like the South Sea islanders) should let their talents rust, and resolve to devote their lives merely to idleness, amusement, and propagation of their species — in a word, to enjoyment; but he cannot possibly *will* that this should be a universal law of nature, or be implanted in us as such by a natural instinct. For, as a rational being, he necessarily wills that his faculties be developed, since they serve him, and have been given him, for all sorts of possible purposes.

4. A fourth, who is in prosperity, while he sees that others have to contend with great wretchedness and that he could help them, thinks: What concern is it of mine? Let everyone be as happy as heaven pleases, or as he can make himself; I will take nothing from him nor even envy him, only I do not wish to contribute anything to his welfare or to his assistance in distress! Now no doubt if such a mode of thinking were a universal law, the human

race might very well subsist, and doubtless even better than in a state in which everyone talks of sympathy and good-will, or even takes care occasionally to put it into practice, but on the other side, also cheats when he can, betrays the rights of men, or otherwise violates them. But although it is possible that a universal law of nature might exist in accordance with that maxim, it is impossible to *will* that such a principle should have the universal validity of a law of nature. For a will which resolved this would contradict itself, inasmuch as many cases might occur in which one would have need of the love and sympathy of others, and in which, by such a law of nature, sprung from his own will, he would deprive himself of all hope of the aid he desires.

These are a few of the many actual duties, or at least what we regard as such, which obviously fall into two classes on the one principle that we have laid down. We must be *able to will* that a maxim of our action should be a universal law. This is the canon of the moral appreciation of the action generally. Some actions are of such a character that their maxim cannot without contradiction be even *conceived* as a universal law of nature, far from it being possible that we should *will* that it *should* be so. In others this intrinsic impossibility is not found, but still it is impossible to *will* that their maxim should be raised to the universality of a law of nature, since such a will would contradict itself. It is easily seen that the former violate strict or rigorous (inflexible) duty; the latter only laxer (meritorious) duty. Thus it has been completely shown by these examples how all duties depend as regards the nature of the obligation (not the object of the action) on the same principle.[k]

12. In one of Kant's formulations of the categorical imperative, we see more clearly its social implications. It requires us to treat every human being as an end in himself and never as merely a means to an end. *In brief, we should respect all human beings impartially and avoid exploiting anyone. Ends that are ends only because they are desired give us hypothetical imperatives; but if there is an* end in itself, *the imperative to seek it is independent of desire and is therefore a categorical imperative.*

Supposing . . . that there were something *whose existence* has *in itself* an absolute worth, something which, being *an end in itself*, could be a source of definite laws, then in this and this alone would lie the source of a possible categorical imperative, *i.e.*, a practical law.

Now I say: man and generally any rational being *exists* as an end in himself, *not merely as a means* to be arbitrarily used by this or that will, but in all his actions, whether they concern himself or other rational beings, must be always regarded at the same time as an end. All objects of the inclinations have only a conditional worth, for if the inclinations and the wants founded on them did not exist, then their object would be without value. But the inclinations themselves being sources of want, are so far from having an absolute worth for which they should be desired, that on the contrary it must be the universal wish of every rational being to be wholly free from them. Thus the worth of any object which is *to be acquired* by our action is always conditional. Beings whose existence depends not on our will but on nature's, have nevertheless, if they are irrational beings, only a relative value as means, and are therefore called *things;* rational beings, on the contrary, are called *persons,* because their very nature points them out as ends in themselves, that is as something which must not be used merely as means, and so far therefore restricts freedom of action (and is an object of respect). These, therefore, are not merely subjective ends whose existence has a worth *for us* as an effect of our action, but *objective ends,* that is things whose existence is an end in itself: an end moreover for which no other can be substituted, which they should subserve *merely* as means, for otherwise nothing whatever would possess *absolute worth;* but if all worth were conditioned and therefore contingent, then there would be no supreme practical principle of reason whatever.

If then there is a supreme practical principle or, in respect of the human will, a categorical imperative, it must be one which, being drawn from the conception of that which is necessarily an end for every one because it is *an end in itself*, constitutes an *objective* principle of will, and can therefore serve as a universal practical law. The foundation of this principle is: *rational nature exists as an end in itself*. Man necessarily conceives his own existence as being so: so far then this is a *subjective* principle of human actions. But every other rational being regards its existence similarly, just on the same rational principle that holds for me: so that it is at the same time an objective principle, from which as a supreme practical law all laws of the will must be capable of being deduced. Accordingly the practical imperative will be as follows: *So act as to treat humanity, whether in thine own person or in that of any other, in every case as an end withal, never as means only.*[1]

13. Kant shows the basic identity of the first and second formulations of the categorical imperative. Those actions which, on the first formulation, cannot be universalized without contradiction, e.g., committing suicide or refusing to help the needy, will be seen on the second formulation to be inconsistent with the idea of humanity as an end in itself.

. . . The principle: So act in regard to every rational being (thyself and others), that he may always have place in thy maxim as an end in himself, is accordingly essentially identical with this other: Act upon a maxim which, at the same time, involves its own universal validity for every rational being. For that in using means for every end I should limit my maxim by the condition of its holding good as a law for every subject, this comes to the same thing as that the fundamental principle of all maxims of action must be that the subject of all ends, *i.e.*, the rational being himself, be never employed merely as means, but as the supreme condition restricting the use of all means, that is in every case as an end likewise.[m]

14. Having brought to light with logical rigor the implicit presuppositions of the common man's awareness of duty and shown it

to be a universal categorical imperative, Kant gives eloquent praise
to "pure moral philosophy" and a word of caution to those moralists
who would allow reason to be corrupted by empirical considera-
tions.

. . . We see philosophy brought to a critical position, since it has to be firmly fixed, notwithstanding that it has nothing to support it either in heaven or earth. Here it must show its purity as absolute dictator of its own laws, not the herald of those which are whispered to it by an implanted sense or who knows what tutelary nature. Although these may be better than nothing, yet they can never afford principles dictated by reason, which must have their source wholly *a priori* and thence their commanding authority, expecting everything from the supremacy of the law and the due respect for it, nothing from inclination, or else condemning the man to self-contempt and inward abhorrence.

Thus every empirical element is not only quite incapable of being an aid to the principle of morality, but is even highly prejudicial to the purity of morals, for the proper and inestimable worth of an absolutely good will consists just in this, that the principle of action is free from all influence of contingent grounds, which alone experience can furnish. We cannot too much or too often repeat our warning against this lax and even mean habit of thought which seeks for its principle amongst empirical motives and laws; for human reason in its weariness is glad to rest on this pillow, and in a dream of sweet illusions (in which, instead of Juno, it embraces a cloud) it substitutes for morality a bastard patched up from limbs of various derivation, which looks like anything one chooses to see in it; only not like virtue to one who has once beheld her in her true form.

To behold virtue in her proper form is nothing else but to contemplate morality stripped of all admixture of sensible things and of every spurious ornament of reward or self-love. How much she then eclipses everything else that appears charming to the affections, every one may readily perceive with the least exertion of his reason, if it be not wholly spoiled for abstraction.[n]

Questions

1. How does Kant's ethical theory fit into his general philosophy? What similarities does he find between the problems of scientific knowledge and of morality?
2. Account for Kant's denial of the unqualified goodness of such commonly valued assets as friendship, health, wealth, and the like, in terms of his interest in that which is good in itself. What does he regard as the only moral quality which is unqualifiedly good in itself?
3. What is the moral function of *reason* in Kant's philosophy? What is the relationship between reason and happiness?
4. Explain the relationship between *good will* and *duty* in Kant's ethics. Can you think of any alternative ways of relating them?
5. Why does Kant object to using "inclinations" or "feelings" as the basis of morality?
6. What criteria of the morality of actions does Kant establish? How would he evaluate an act of charity performed out of a natural sympathy for the sufferings of the poor?
7. State the "categorical imperative" in any of the forms Kant gives it, and use examples of moral acts to clarify its meaning. What is the basis of the moral law in Kant's system of ethics?
8. What is the role of "motives" in Kant's ethical theory?
9. What would Kant's position be as to moral values in the following situations: (a) A man who remains loyal to his wife because he loves her, and (b) A man who recognizes loyalty to his wife as an obligation, although he finds it decidedly unpleasant.
10. It has been argued against Kant that he introduces "consequences" in his categorical imperative. Examine this argument against him. What points of strength and weakness do you find in his ethical theory?

Key to selections:

IMMANUEL KANT, *Fundamental Principles of the Metaphysic of Morals*, tr. Thomas K. Abbott, from *Kant's Critique of Practical Reason and Other Works on the Theory of Ethics*, London, Longmans, Green, and Co., 1898.

[a] 1st. Sec., pp. 9–10.

[b] 1st. Sec., p. 10.

[c] 1st. Sec., pp. 10–12.

[d] 1st. Sec., pp. 12–14.

[e] 1st. Sec., pp. 14–15.

[f] 1st. Sec., p. 16.

[g] 1st. Sec., pp. 16–17.

[h] 1st. Sec., pp. 17–19.

[i] 2nd. Sec., pp. 30–31.

[j] 2nd. Sec., pp. 38–39.

[k] 2nd. Sec., pp. 39–42.

[l] 2nd. Sec., pp. 46–47.

[m] 2nd. Sec., p. 56.

[n] 2nd. Sec., pp. 43–44.
fn. p. 44.

Guide to Additional Reading

INEXPENSIVE EDITIONS:

KANT, I., *Foundations of the Metaphysic of Morals* (University of Chicago Press).

——, *Fundamental Principles of the Metaphysics of Morals*, Appleton-Century Philosophy Source Books (Appleton-Century-Crofts).

——, *Fundamental Principles of the Metaphysics of Morals*, Little Library of Liberal Arts (Liberal Arts Press).

——, *Fundamental Principles of the Metaphysics of Morals*, Great Books Foundation (Regnery).

——, *Fundamenta Principles of the Metaphysics of Morals* (Longmans, Green).

——, *Groundwork of the Metaphysics of Moral*, Hutchinson's University Library (Hutchinson).

Kant Selections, Modern Student's Library (Scribner's).

The Philosophy of Kant, Modern Library (Random House).

DISCUSSION AND COMMENTARY:

Beck, L. W., *A Commentary on Kant's Critique of Practical Reason*, Chicago, University of Chicago, 1960.

Broad, C. D., *Five Types of Ethical Theory*, New York, Harcourt, Brace and Company, 1930, Chapter V.

Lindsay, A. D., *Kant*, London, Oxford University Press, 1934.

Paton, H. J., *The Categorical Imperative*, Chicago, University of Chicago Press, 1948.

Ross, W. D., *Kant's Ethical Theory*, Oxford, Oxford University Press, 1954.

CHAPTER *12*

The Greatest Happiness Principle

JOHN STUART MILL

I t has been said of John Stuart Mill (1806–1873) that "He held as high as any man the lamp of reason, and it burned the more brightly because he lived." The intellectual heir of the utilitarian movement in England, Mill dedicated himself to clarifying the teachings of his father, James Mill, and those of Jeremy Bentham, who championed the utilitarian doctrine. In his *Autobiography*, a history of his "intellectual and moral development," John Stuart Mill describes the exacting "educational experiment" imposed upon him from age three to fourteen by his father. At the age of three, he studied Greek and arithmetic; at eight, he added Latin to his curriculum and by the time he was twelve, Mill was reading extensively in logic, philosophy, and economic theory. His training, moreover, was never a mere exercise in memorization but was designed to produce an original thinker.

At the age of twenty-one, he reached an emotional crisis which he characterized as the result of a sudden loss of enthusiasm for the original goals of his life, but which, in current parlance, would be called a "nervous breakdown." However, after several years, with fresh stimulation of his emotions and feelings as well as his intellect, he resumed his career, fulfilling his early promise. When he was twenty-five, Mill met Mrs. Taylor, whom he later married. He believed that her character and ability wielded one of the great influences in his life and helped to shape his thought. In 1823, after a brief period of legal study, Mill, upon the advice of his father, accepted a position with the East India Company. For thirty years, he held this responsible post, while devoting his spare time to writing his books. Upon retirement, when he intended to devote himself exclusively to writing, Mill was proposed as a candidate for Parliament. Despite his refusal to campaign, he was elected to office. Of his political conduct, William Gladstone, British Prime Minister, said: "He had the good sense and practical tact of politics, together with the high independent thought of a recluse. He did us all good."

Mill's major works cover a variety of subjects, but his *System of Logic* (1843) is regarded as his most important philosophical contribution. In it, he defends the inductive method of logic, showing that general laws or universal principles must be derived from empirical facts. Other outstanding works are his *Principles of Political Economy* (1848), which relates the application of Utilitarian principles to economics, his essays *On Liberty* (1859) and *Considerations on Representative Government* (1861), which are classical statements of his social and political philosophy; and the essay *Utilitarianism* (1861), his only explicit contribution to ethics. During the last few years of his life, he wrote the very distinctive *Autobiography* and *Three Essays on Religion*, both of which works were published after his death.

Unlike most philosophers, John Stuart Mill did not attempt to originate an ethical theory, but rather to defend the ethical

theory to which he was born. In his defense, however, his intellectual depth and his intense desire to find an ethics which fits the
facts of life, led him to modify and go beyond the utilitarian
doctrine as it was propounded by his father and Jeremy Bentham.
Bentham based his utilitarian philosophy on the principle that the
object of morality is the promotion of the greatest happiness of
the maximum number of members of society. He proceeded on
the premise that the happiness of any individual consists in a
favorable balance of pleasures over pains. Consequently, those
actions which tend to increase pleasure are called good and those
which tend to increase pain are called bad. For Bentham, however, utilitarianism was less important as an ethical system than
as a philosophical support for much-needed social legislation.

Bentham was motivated by the idea that "the *Public Good*
ought to be the object of the legislator: *General Utility* ought to
be the foundation of his reasonings. To know the true good of the
community is what constitutes the science of legislation; the art
consists in finding the means to realize that good." To implement
this social and political ideal, he constructed a "hedonistic calculus" by means of which pleasures and pains could be measured.
In this way, good and bad acts and, consequently, good and bad
legislation, can be evaluated in terms of such factors as intensity,
duration, and extent.[1]

In his essay, Mill is concerned less with the political implications of Bentham's doctrine than with the provision of a defensible
statement of its underlying ethical principles. In addition to answering objections put forward by opponents of utilitarianism and

---

[1] Bentham composed the following verse to aid the student in remembering the criteria
of hedonistic measurement:

> *Intense, long, certain, speedy, fruitful, pure —*
> Such marks in *pleasures* and *pains* endure.
> Such pleasures seek, if *private* be thy end:
> If it be *public*, wide let them *extend*.
> Such *pains* avoid, whichever be thy view:
> If pains *must* come, let them extend to few.

(John Bowring, ed., *The Works of Jeremy Bentham*, London, Simpkin,
Marshall and Co., 1838, vol. I, p. 16, note.)

correcting misrepresentations of it, he also restates the doctrine. In his restatement, he goes beyond Bentham's contention that the essential differences among pleasures and pains are quantitative, maintaining that they are also subject to significant qualitative differentiation. For example, anyone who has experienced the pleasure attendant upon the resolution of an intellectual problem will, Mill believes, attest to the fact that it is superior in kind to the pleasure of eating a meal.

Although Mill departs from Bentham's conception that all the significant differences among pleasures are quantitative, he accepts in principle his doctrines regarding the basic role of pleasures and pains in morality, *viz.*, *individual psychological hedonism* and *universal ethical hedonism*. According to the former, the sole motive of an action *is* an individual's desire for happiness, *i.e.*, for a balance of pleasure over pain. According to the latter, the "greatest happiness of the greatest number" *ought* to be the individual's goal and standard of conduct. Psychological hedonism is primarily a *descriptive* doctrine, since it purports to be an account of the actual motive of behavior. By contrast, universal ethical hedonism is a *normative* theory, in that it stipulates what *ought* to be done. It is a principle by which actions are evaluated in terms of their *consequences*, irrespective of the nature of the motive.

However, there are two gaps between individual psychological hedonism and universal ethical hedonism: (1) if each individual is motivated solely by the desire for his own happiness, there is no reason to assume that his actions will at the same time always promote the interests of society; and (2) the descriptive fact that men do desire their own happiness does not imply the normative principle that men *ought* to act in accordance with this desire. Mill recognizes that an adequate defense of utilitarianism must show how the transition can be made from an interest in one's own happiness to that of others, and from a psychological theory to a moral theory. He endeavors to harmonize the two varieties of hedonism by recourse to the concept of *sanctions*, the inducements to action which give binding force to moral rules.

In Mill's system of ethics, sanctions are rooted in the hedonistic motive, *i.e.*, moral rules are acknowledged and obeyed by virtue of anticipated pleasures or pains. There are both "external" and "internal" sanctions. External sanctions are those forces of punishment and reward in the universe about us which control men's actions through their fear of pain and propensity for pleasure. For example, in our society, fear of social disapproval and imprisonment are both deterrents to crime. But, Mill cautions, conformity to the letter of the law in the presence of such external sanctions is not to be taken as a sign of a true sense of moral obligation: *the ultimate moral sanction must come from within.*

The force of an internal sanction derives from the feeling of pleasure which is experienced when a moral law is obeyed and the feeling of pain which accompanies a violation of it. That the "greatest happiness principle" can be sanctioned from within is attested to by observation. In some men at least, Mill holds, the feeling of sympathy for others is so well developed that the individual's happiness depends upon the well-being of his fellow men. Thus, by means of the doctrine of internal sanctions, Mill is enabled to reconcile the psychological theory that everyone desires his own happiness with the moral theory that one ought so to act as to serve the public good. However, he acknowledges that his argument in support of sanctions does not constitute a logical demonstration of the greatest happiness principle.

Mill argues that *no direct proof of any first principle or ultimate end is possible,* and the problem of proof is in reality reduced to the problem of *rational assent:*

. . . To be incapable of proof by reasoning is common to all first principles; to the first premises of our knowledge as well as to those of our conduct. But the former, being matters of fact, may be the subject of a direct appeal to the faculties which judge of fact — namely, our senses, and our internal consciousness. . . .

The only proof capable of being given that an object is visible, is that people actually see it. The only proof that a sound is audible, is that people hear it; and so of the other sources of our experience. In like manner, I apprehend, the sole evidence it is possible to produce that anything is desirable, is that people do actually desire it. If the end which the utilitarian doctrine proposes to itself were not, in theory and in practice, acknowledged to be an end, nothing could ever convince any person that it was so. No reason can be given why the general happiness is desirable except that each person, so far as he believes it to be attainable, desires his own happiness.[a,2]

· · ·

1. Mill's first objective in defending utilitarianism is to clarify the doctrine. He attempts this both by exposing misrepresentations and by straightforward exposition of the principle. He begins by opposing those who fail to associate "utility" with pleasure and pain.

A passing remark is all that needs to be given to the ignorant blunder of supposing that those who stand up for utility as the test of right and wrong, use the term in that restricted and merely colloquial sense in which utility is opposed to pleasure. An apology is due to the philosophical opponents of utilitarianism, for even the momentary appearance of confounding them with anyone capable of so absurd a misconception; which is the more extraordinary, inasmuch as the contrary accusation of referring everything to pleasure, and that too in its grossest form, is another of the common charges against utilitarianism: and, as has been pointedly remarked by an able writer, the same sort of persons, and often the very same persons, denounce the theory "as impracticably dry when the word utility precedes the word pleasure, and as too practicably voluptuous when the word pleasure precedes the word utility." Those who know anything about the matter are aware that every writer, from Epicurus to Bentham, who maintained the theory of utility, meant by it, not something to be contradistinguished from pleasure, but pleasure itself, to-

[2] As a formal proof, this would be fallacious: "visible" is used in the sense of "*can* be seen," whereas "desirable" is used in the sense of "*ought* to be desired"; thus, the analogy is not a legitimate one. In addition, it does not follow from an admission that *each* man desires *his own* happiness that *all* men desire the happiness of *all* men. Nevertheless, the argument, such as it is, bespeaks Mill's conviction that the evidence for an ethical theory is to be sought in the facts of human experience.

gether with exemption from pain; and instead of opposing the useful to the agreeable or the ornamental, have always declared that
the useful means these, among other things. Yet the common herd,
including the herd of writers, not only in newspapers and peri-
odicals, but in books of weight and pretension, are perpetually
falling into this shallow mistake. Having caught up the word
'utilitarian,' while knowing nothing whatever about it but its
sound, they habitually express by it the rejection, or the neglect,
of pleasure in some of its forms; of beauty, of ornament, or of
amusement. Nor is the term thus ignorantly misapplied solely in
disparagement, but occasionally in compliment; as though it implied superiority to frivolity and the mere pleasures of the moment. And this perverted use is the only one in which the word is
popularly known, and the one from which the new generation
are acquiring their sole notion of its meaning. Those who introduced the word, but who had for many years discontinued it as a
distinctive appellation, may well feel themselves called upon to
resume it, if by doing so they can hope to contribute anything
towards rescuing it from this utter degradation.[b]

2. Mill then states concisely the doctrine of utility.

The creed which accepts as the foundation of morals Utility, or
the Greatest Happiness Principle, holds that actions are right in
proportion as they tend to promote happiness, wrong as they tend
to produce the reverse of happiness. By 'happiness' is intended
pleasure, and the absence of pain; by 'unhappiness,' pain, and
the privation of pleasure. To give a clear view of the moral
standard set up by the theory, much more requires to be said;
in particular, what things it includes in the ideas of pain and
pleasure; and to what extent this is left an open question. But these
supplementary explanations do not affect the theory of life on
which this theory of morality is grounded — namely, that pleasure, and freedom from pain, are the only things desirable as ends;
and that all desirable things (which are as numerous in the utilitarian as in any other scheme) are desirable either for the pleasure

inherent in themselves, or as means to the promotion of pleasure and the prevention of pain.[c]

3. Even when the principle of utility is clearly understood to be directed to pleasures and pains, however, there remains the charge that it is a "swinish" doctrine. This misconception is due to the failure to recognize that pleasures vary in kind *as well as degree.*

Now, such a theory of life excites in many minds, and among them in some of the most estimable in feeling and purpose, inveterate dislike. To suppose that life has (as they express it) no higher end than pleasure — no better and nobler object of desire and pursuit — they designate as utterly mean and groveling; as a doctrine worthy only of swine, to whom the followers of Epicurus were, at a very early period, contemptuously likened; and modern holders of the doctrine are occasionally made the subject of equally polite comparisons by its German, French, and English assailants.

When thus attacked, the Epicureans have always answered that it is not they, but their accusers, who represent human nature in a degrading light; since the accusation supposes human beings to be capable of no pleasures except those of which swine are capable. If this supposition were true, the charge could not be gainsaid, but would then be no longer an imputation: for if the sources of pleasure were precisely the same to human beings and to swine, the rule of life which is good enough for the one would be good enough for the other. The comparison of the Epicurean life to that of beasts is felt as degrading, precisely because a beast's pleasures do not satisfy a human being's conceptions of happiness. Human beings have faculties more elevated than the animal appetites, and when once made conscious of them, do not regard anything as happiness which does not include their gratification. I do not, indeed, consider the Epicureans to have been by any means faultless in drawing out their scheme of consequences from the utilitarian principle. To do this in any sufficient manner, many Stoic, as well as Christian elements require to be included. But there is no known Epicurean theory of life which does not assign to the pleasures of the intellect, of the feelings and imagination, and of the moral sentiments, a much higher value as pleasures than to those of mere sensation. It must be admitted, however, that utilitarian writers in general have placed the superiority of mental over bodily pleasures chiefly in the greater permanency, safety, uncostliness, etc., of the former — that is, in their circumstantial advantages rather than in their intrinsic nature. And on all these points utilitarians have fully proved their case; but they might have taken the other, and, as it may be called, higher ground, with entire consistency. It is quite compatible with the principle of utility to recognize the fact, that some *kinds* of pleasure are more desirable and more valuable than others. It would be absurd that while, in estimating all other things, quality is considered as well as quantity, the estimation of pleasures should be supposed to depend on quantity alone.[d]

4. The superiority of one kind of pleasure over another is properly determined by those who have experienced both kinds. Such competent judges, Mill argues, do, in fact, prefer the pleasures of the higher faculties to those of the lower.

If I am asked what I mean by difference of quality in pleasures, or what makes one pleasure more valuable than another, merely as a pleasure, except its being greater in amount, there is but one possible answer. Of two pleasures, if there be one to which all or almost all who have experience of both give a decided preference, irrespective of any feeling of moral obligation to prefer it, that is the more desirable pleasure. If one of the two is, by those who are competently acquainted with both, placed so far above the other that they prefer it, even though knowing it to be attended with a greater amount of discontent, and would not resign it for any quantity of the other pleasure which their nature is capable of, we are justified in ascribing to the preferred enjoyment a superiority in quality, so far outweighing quantity as to render it, in comparison, of small account.

Now it is an unquestionable fact that those who are equally acquainted with, and equally capable of appreciating and enjoying, both, do give a most marked preference to the manner of existence which employs their higher faculties. Few human creatures would consent to be changed into any of the lower animals, for a promise of the fullest allowance of a beast's pleasures; no intelligent human being would consent to be a fool, no instructed person would be an ignoramus, no person of feeling and conscience would be selfish and base, even though they should be persuaded that the fool, the dunce, or the rascal is better satisfied with his lot than they are with theirs. They would not resign what they possess more than he, for the most complete satisfaction of all the desires which they have in common with him. If they ever fancy they would, it is only in cases of unhappiness so extreme, that to escape from it they would exchange their lot for almost any other, however ur.desirable in their own eyes. A being of higher faculties requires more to make him happy, is capable probably of more acute suffering, and certainly accessible to it at more points, than one of an inferior type; but in spite of these liabilities, he can never really wish to sink into what he feels to be a lower grade of existence. We may give what explanation we please of this unwillingness; we may attribute it to pride, a name which is given indiscriminately to some of the most and to some of the least estimable feelings of which mankind are capable; we may refer it to the love of liberty and personal independence, an appeal to which was with the Stoics one of the most effective means for the inculcation of it; to the love of power, or to the love of excitement, both of which do really enter into and contribute to it: but its most appropriate appellation is a sense of dignity, which all human beings possess in one form or other, and in some, though by no means in exact, proportion to their higher faculties, and which is so essential a part of the happiness of those in whom it is strong, that nothing which conflicts with it could be, otherwise than momentarily, an object of desire to them. Whoever supposes that this preference takes place at a sacrifice of happiness — that the superior being, in anything like equal circumstances, is not happier than the inferior — confounds the two very different ideas, of happiness and content. It is indisputable that the being whose capacities of enjoyment are low, has the greatest chance of having them fully satisfied; and a highly-endowed being will always feel that any happiness which he can look for, as the world is constituted, is imperfect. But he can learn to bear its imperfections, if they are at all bearable; and they will not make him envy the being who is indeed unconscious of the imperfections, but only because he feels not at all the good which those imperfections qualify. It is better to be a human being dissatisfied than a pig satisfied; better to be Socrates dissatisfied than a fool satisfied. And if the fool, or the pig, is of a different opinion, it is because they only know their own side of the question. The other party to the comparison knows both sides.[e]

5. Mill moves to discount the judgments of those who abandon the higher pleasures for the lower by explaining that they are incapable, either inherently or by lack of opportunity, of enjoying the higher kind. The only competent and final judges are those who have tested the entire spectrum of pleasures.

It may be objected, that many who are capable of the higher pleasures, occasionally, under the influence of temptation, postpone them to the lower. But this is quite compatible with a full appreciation of the intrinsic superiority of the higher. Men often, from infirmity of character, make their election for the nearer good, though they know it to be the less valuable; and this no less when the choice is between two bodily pleasures, than when it is between bodily and mental. They pursue sensual indulgences to the injury of health, though perfectly aware that health is the greater good. It may be further objected, that many who begin with youthful enthusiasm for everything noble, as they advance in years sink into indolence and selfishness. But I do not believe that those who undergo this very common change, voluntarily choose the lower description of pleasures in preference to the higher. I believe that before they devote themselves exclusively to the one, they have already become incapable of the other. Capacity for the nobler feelings is in most natures a very tender plant, easily killed, not only by hostile influences, but by mere want of sustenance; and in the majority of young persons it speedily dies away if the occupations to which their position in life has devoted them, and the society into which it has thrown them, are not favorable to keeping that higher capacity in exercise. Men lose their high aspirations as they lose their intellectual tastes, because they have not time or opportunity for indulging them; and they addict themselves to inferior pleasures, not because they deliberately prefer them, but because they are either the only ones to which they have access, or the only ones which they are any longer capable of enjoying. It may be questioned whether anyone who has remained equally susceptible to both classes of pleasures, ever knowingly and calmly preferred the lower; though many, in all ages, have broken down in an ineffectual attempt to combine both.

From this verdict of the only competent judges, I apprehend there can be no appeal. On a question which is the best worth having of two pleasures, or which of two modes of existence is the most grateful to the feelings, apart from its moral attributes and from its consequences, the judgment of those who are qualified by knowledge of both, or, if they differ, that of the majority among them, must be admitted as final. And there needs be the less hesitation to accept this judgment respecting the quality of pleasures, since there is no other tribunal to be referred to even on the question of quantity. What means are there of determining which is the acutest of two pains, or the intensest of two pleasurable sensations, except the general suffrage of those who are familiar with both? Neither pains nor pleasures are homogeneous, and pain is always heterogeneous with pleasure. What is there to decide whether a particular pleasure is worth purchasing at the cost of a particular pain, except the feelings and judgment of the experienced? When, therefore, those feelings and judgment declare the pleasures derived from the higher faculties to be preferable *in kind*, apart from the question of intensity, to those of which the animal nature, disjoined from the higher faculties, is suspectible, they are entitled on this subject to the same regard.[f]

6. *The "greatest happiness principle" is restated to include the distinction drawn between the quantitative and qualitative aspects of pleasure.*

I have dwelt on this point, as being a necessary part of a perfectly just conception of Utility, or Happiness, considered as the directive rule of human conduct. But it is by no means an indispensable condition to the acceptance of the utilitarian standard; for that standard is not the agent's own greatest happiness, but the greatest amount of happiness altogether; and if it may possibly be doubted whether a noble character is always the happier for its nobleness, there can be no doubt that it makes other people happier, and that the world in general is immensely a gainer by it. Utilitarianism, therefore, could only attain its end by the general cultivation of nobleness of character, even if each individual were only benefited by the nobleness of others, and his own, so far as happiness is concerned, were a sheer deduction from the benefit. But the bare enunciation of such an absurdity as this last, renders refutation superfluous.

According to the Greatest Happiness Principle, as above explained, the ultimate end, with reference to and for the sake of which all other things are desirable (whether we are considering our own good or that of other people), is an existence exempt as far as possible from pain, and as rich as possible in enjoyments, both in point of quantity and quality; the test of quality, and the rule for measuring it against quantity, being the preference felt by those who, in their opportunities of experience, to which must be added their habits of self-consciousness and self-observation, are best furnished with the means of comparison. This, being, according to the utilitarian opinion, the end of human action is necessarily also the standard of morality; which may accordingly be defined, the rules and precepts for human conduct, by the observance of which an existence such as has been described might be, to the greatest extent possible, secured to all mankind; and not to them only, but, so far as the nature of things admits, to the whole sentient creation.[g]

7. *The process of clarification is continued through stating various objections to the doctrine and answering them. For example, the argument that utilitarianism is invalid because happiness cannot be attained is answered by Mill with a realistic description of happiness and a suggestion for the social means of achieving it.*

... When, however, it is thus positively asserted to be impossible that human life should be happy, the assertion, if not something like a verbal quibble, is at least an exaggeration. If by happiness be meant a continuity of highly pleasurable excitement, it is evident enough that this is impossible. A state of exalted pleasure lasts only moments, or in some cases, and with some intermissions, hours or days, and is the occasional brilliant flash of enjoyment, not its permanent and steady flame. Of this the philosophers who have taught that happiness is the end of life were as fully aware as those who taunt them. The happiness which they meant was not a life of rapture; but moments of such, in an existence made up of few and transitory pains, many and various pleasures, with a decided predominance of the active over the passive, and having as the foundation of the whole, not to expect more from life than it is capable of bestowing. A life thus composed, to those who have been fortunate enough to obtain it, has always appeared worthy of the name of happiness. And such an existence is even now the lot of many, during some considerable portion of their lives. The present wretched education, and wretched social arrangements, are the only real hindrance to its being attainable by almost all.

The objectors perhaps may doubt whether human beings, if taught to consider happiness as the end of life, would be satisfied with such a moderate share of it. But great numbers of mankind have been satisfied with much less. The main constituents of a satisfied life appear to be two, either of which by itself is often found sufficient for the purpose: tranquillity and excitement. With much tranquillity, many find that they can be content with very little pleasure: with much excitement, many can reconcile themselves to a considerable quantity of pain. There is assuredly no inherent impossibility in enabling even the mass of mankind to unite both; since the two are so far from being incompatible that they are in natural alliance, the prolongation of either being a preparation for, and exciting a wish for, the other. . . . When people who are tolerably fortunate in their outward lot do not find in life sufficient enjoyment to make it valuable to them, the cause generally is, caring for nobody but themselves. To those who have neither public nor private affections, the excitements of life are much curtailed, and in any case dwindle in value as the time approaches when all selfish interests must be terminated by death: while those who leave after them objects of personal affection, and especially those who have also cultivated a fellow-feeling with the collective interests of mankind, retain as lively an interest in life on the eve of death as in the vigor of youth and health. Next to selfishness, the principal cause which makes life unsatisfactory is want of mental cultivation. A cultivated mind — I do not mean that of a philosopher, but any mind to which the fountains of knowledge have been opened, and which has been taught, in any tolerable degree, to exercise its faculties — finds sources of inexhaustible interest in all that surrounds it; in the objects of nature, the achievements of art, the imaginations of poetry, the incidents of history, the ways of mankind past and present, and their prospects in the future.[h]

8. Another objection which Mill discounts is the claim that utilitarian morality is incompatible with the acts of personal sacrifice which are so revered in our Christian culture. On closer analysis, those actions of self-sacrifice which we acknowledge to be good derive their value from their promotion of the general happiness, although they may deny individual happiness. Furthermore, this is not to be misinterpreted to mean that the happiness of one individual is less important than that of another. On the contrary, each individual's happiness is equal to that of any other.

. . . Let utilitarians never cease to claim the morality of self-devotion as a possession which belongs by as good a right to them, as either to the Stoic or to the Transcendentalist. The utilitarian morality does recognize in human beings the power of sacrificing their own greatest good for the good of others. It only refuses to admit that the sacrifice is itself a good. A sacrifice which does not increase, or tend to increase, the sum total of happiness, it considers as wasted. The only self-renunciation which it applauds, is devotion to the happiness, or to some of the means of happiness, of others; either of mankind collectively, or of individuals within the limits imposed by the collective interests of mankind.

I must again repeat, what the assailants of utilitarianism seldom have the justice to acknowledge, that the happiness which forms the utilitarian standard of what is right in conduct, is not the agent's own happiness, but that of all concerned. As between his own happiness and that of others, utilitarianism requires him to be as strictly impartial as a disinterested and benevolent spectator. In the golden rule of Jesus of Nazareth, we read the complete spirit of the ethics of utility. To do as one would be done by, and to love one's neighbor as oneself, constitute the ideal perfection of utilitarian morality. As the means of making the nearest approach to this ideal, utility would enjoin, first, that laws and social arrangements should place the happiness, or (as speaking practically it may be called) the interest, of every individual, as nearly as possible in harmony with the interest of the whole; and secondly, that education and opinion, which have so vast a power over human character, should so use that power as to establish in the mind of every individual an indissoluble association between his own happiness and the good of the whole; especially between his own happiness and the practice of such modes of conduct, negative and positive, as regard for the universal happiness prescribes: so that not only he may be unable to conceive the possibility of happiness to himself, consistently with conduct opposed to the general good, but also that a direct impulse to promote the general good may be in every individual one of the habitual motives of action, and the sentiments connected therewith may fill a large and prominent place in every human being's sentient existence. If the impugners of the utilitarian morality represented it to their own minds in this its true character, I know not what recommendation possessed by any other morality they could possibly affirm to be wanting to it: what more beautiful or more exalted developments of human nature any other ethical system can be supposed to foster, or what springs of action, not accessible to the utilitarian, such systems rely on for giving effect to their mandates.[i]

9. *To the objection that men are not so constituted as always to be motivated by social concern, Mill rejoins that this is indeed true, but in no way invalidates his thesis. The greatest happiness principle is* not essential as a motive for conduct, but it is essential as the rule by which conduct is judged and sanctioned. *The psychological question of motivation is distinct from the ethical questions of obligation and evaluation. Moral evaluation is directed to actions and to the manner in which they affect the general happiness.*

They say it is exacting too much to require that people shall always act from the inducement of promoting the general interests of society. But this is to mistake the very meaning of a standard of morals, and confound the rule of action with the motive of it. It is the business of ethics to tell us what are our duties, or by what test we may know them; but no system of ethics requires that the sole motive of all we do shall be a feeling of duty; on the contrary, ninety-nine hundredths of all our actions are done from other motives, and rightly so done, if the rule of duty does not condemn them. It is the more unjust to utilitarianism that this particular misapprehension should be made a ground of objection to it, inasmuch as utilitarian moralists have gone beyond almost all others in affirming that the motive has nothing to do with the morality of the action, though much with the worth of the agent. He who saves a fellow creature from drowning does what is morally right, whether his motive be duty, or the hope of being paid for his trouble; he who betrays the friend that trusts him, is guilty of a crime, even if his object be to serve another friend to whom he is under greater obligations. But to speak only of actions done from the motive of duty, and in direct obedience to principle: it is a misapprehension of the utilitarian mode of thought, to conceive it as implying that people should fix their minds upon so wide a generality as the world, or society at large. The great majority of good actions are intended not for the benefit of the world, but for that of individuals, of which the good of the world is made up; and the thoughts of the most virtuous man need not on these occasions travel beyond the particular persons concerned, except so far as is necessary to assure himself that in benefiting them he is not violating the rights — that is, the legitimate and authorized expectations — of anyone else. The multiplication of happiness is, according to the utilitarian ethics, the object of virtue: the occasions on which any person (except one in a thousand) has it in his power to do this on an extended scale, in other words to be a public benefactor, are but exceptional; and on these occasions alone is he called on to consider public utility; in every other case, private utility, the interest or happiness of some few persons, is all he has to attend to. Those alone the influence of whose actions extends to society in general, need concern themselves habitually about so large an object. In the case of abstinences indeed — of things which people forbear to do from moral considerations, though the consequences in the particular case might be beneficial — it would be unworthy of an intelligent agent not to be consciously aware that the action is of a class which, if practiced generally, would be generally injurious, and that this is the ground of the obligation to abstain from it. The amount of regard for the public interest implied in this recognition, is no greater than is demanded by every system of morals; for they all enjoin to abstain from whatever is manifestly pernicious to society.ʲ

10. Having removed the major misconceptions about the principle of utility, Mill next proposes to investigate its ultimate sanction.

The question is often asked, and properly so, in regard to any supposed moral standard — What is its sanction? what are the motives to obey it? or more specifically, what is the source of its obligation? whence does it derive its binding force? It is a necessary part of moral philosophy to provide the answer to this question; which, though frequently assuming the shape of an objection to the utilitarian morality, as if it had some special applicability to that above others, really arises in regard to all standards. It arises, in fact, whenever a person is called on to *adopt* a standard or refer morality to any basis on which he has not been accustomed to rest it. For the customary morality, that which education and opinion have consecrated, is the only one which presents itself to the mind with the feeling of being *in itself* obligatory; and when a person is asked to believe that this morality *derives* its obligation from some general principle round which custom has not thrown the same halo, the assertion is to him a paradox; the supposed corollaries seem to have a more binding force than the original theorem; the superstructure seems to stand better without, than with, what is represented as its foundation. He says to himself, I feel that I am bound not to rob or murder, betray or deceive; but why am I bound to promote the general happiness? If my own happiness lies in something else, why may I not give that the preference? k

11. Mill argues that although the external sanctions, social and supernatural, enforce the utilitarian principle, they do not obligate us to follow it. In and of themselves, they cannot bind us satisfactorily to any moral principle, since men are truly bound only when they feel inwardly that the principle is binding upon them. It is our "feeling for humanity" which provides the ultimate sanction of the principle of utility, and this Mill calls the internal sanction.

The principle of utility either has, or there is no reason why it might not have, all the sanctions which belong to any other system of morals. Those sanctions are either external or internal. Of the external sanctions it is not necessary to speak at any length. They are, the hope of favor and the fear of displeasure from our fellow creatures or from the Ruler of the Universe, along with whatever we may have of sympathy or affection for them, or of love and awe of Him, inclining us to do His will independently of selfish consequences. There is evidently no reason why all these motives for observance should not attach themselves to the utilitarian morality, as completely and as powerfully as to any other. Indeed, those of them which refer to our fellow creatures are sure to do so, in proportion to the amount of general intelligence; for whether there be any other ground of moral obligation than the general happiness or not, men do desire happiness; and however imperfect may be their own practice, they desire and commend all conduct in others towards themselves, by which they think their happiness is promoted. With regard to the religious motive, if men believe, as most profess to do, in the goodness of God, those who think that conduciveness to the general happiness is the essence, or even only the criterion of good, must necessarily believe that it is also that which God approves. The whole force therefore of external reward and punishment, whether physical or moral, and whether proceeding from God or from our fellow men, together with all that the capacities of human nature admit, of disinterested devotion to either, become available to enforce the utilitarian morality, in proportion as that morality is recognized; and the more powerfully, the more the appliances of education and general cultivation are bent to the purpose.

So far as to external sanctions. The internal sanction of duty, whatever our standard of duty may be, is one and the same — a feeling in our own mind; a pain, more or less intense, attendant on violation of duty, which in properly cultivated moral natures rises, in the more serious cases, into shrinking from it as an impossibility. This feeling, when disinterested, and connecting itself with the pure idea of duty, and not with some particular form of it, or with any of the merely accessory circumstances, is the essence of Conscience; though in that complex phenomenon as it actually exists, the simple fact is in general all encrusted over with collateral associations, derived from sympathy, from love, and still more from fear; from all the forms of religious feeling; from the recollections of childhood and of all our past life; from self-esteem, desire of the esteem of others, and occasionally even self-abasement. This extreme complication is, I apprehend, the origin of the sort of mystical character which, by a tendency of the human mind of which there are many other examples, is apt to be attributed to the idea of moral obligation, and which leads people to believe that the idea cannot possibly attach itself to any other objects than those which, by a supposed mysterious law, are found in our present experience to excite it. Its binding force, however, consists in the existence of a mass of feeling which must be broken through in order to do what violates our standard of right, and which, if we do nevertheless violate that standard, will probably have to be encountered afterwards in the form of remorse. Whatever theory we have of the nature or origin of conscience, this is what essentially constitutes it.

The ultimate sanction, therefore, of all morality (external motives apart) being a subjective feeling in our own minds, I see nothing embarrassing to those whose standard is utility, in the question, what is the sanction of that particular standard? We may answer, the same as of all other moral standards — the conscientious feelings of mankind. Undoubtedly this sanction has no binding efficacy on those who do not possess the feelings it appeals to; but neither will these persons be more obedient to any other moral principle than to the utilitarian one. On them morality of any kind has no hold but through the external sanctions. Meanwhile the feelings exist, a fact in human nature, the reality of which, and the great power with which they are capable of acting on those in whom they have been duly cultivated, are proved by experience. No reason has ever been shown why they may not be cultivated to as great intensity in connection with the utilitarian, as with any other rule of morals.[1]

12. Regardless of whether this inner feeling for mankind is inborn or acquired, Mill contends that it can be a powerful force and a sound basis for utilitarian morality.

It is not necessary, for the present purpose, to decide whether the feeling of duty is innate or implanted. Assuming it to be innate, it is an open question to what objects it naturally attaches itself; for the philosophic supporters of that theory are now agreed that the intuitive perception is of principles of morality, and not of the details. If there be anything innate in the matter, I see no reason why the feeling which is innate should not be that of regard to the pleasures and pains of others. If there is any principle of morals which is intuitively obligatory, I should say it must be that. If so, the intuitive ethics would coincide with the utilitarian, and there would be no further quarrel between them. Even as it is, the intuitive moralists, though they believe that there are other intuitive moral obligations, do already believe this to be one; for they unanimously hold that a large *portion* of morality turns upon the consideration due to the interests of our fellow creatures. Therefore, if the belief in the transcendental origin of moral obligation gives any additional efficacy to the internal sanction, it appears to me that the utilitarian principle has already the benefit of it.

On the other hand, if, as is my own belief, the moral feelings are not innate, but acquired, they are not for that reason the less natural. It is natural to man to speak, to reason, to build cities, to cultivate the ground, though these are acquired faculties. The moral feelings are not indeed a part of our nature, in the sense of being in any perceptible degree present in all of us; but this, unhappily, is a fact admitted by those who believe the most strenuously in their transcendental origin. Like the other acquired capacities above referred to, the moral faculty, if not a part of our nature, is a natural outgrowth from it; capable, like them, in a certain small degree, of springing up spontaneously; and susceptible of being brought by cultivation to a high degree of development. Unhappily it is also susceptible, by a sufficient use of the external sanctions and of the force of early impressions, of being cultivated in almost any direction: so that there is hardly anything so absurd or so mischievous that it may not, by means of these influences, be made to act on the human mind with all the authority of conscience. To doubt that the same potency might be given by the same means to the principle of utility, even if it had no foundation in human nature, would be flying in the face of all experience.

But moral associations which are wholly of artificial creation, when intellectual culture goes on, yield by degrees to the dissolving force of analysis: and if the feeling of duty, when associated with utility, would appear equally arbitrary; if there were no leading department of our nature, no powerful class of sentiments, with which that association would harmonize, which would make us feel it congenial, and incline us not only to foster it in others (for which we have abundant interested motives), but also to cherish it in ourselves; if there were not, in short, a natural basis of sentiment for utilitarian morality, it might well happen that this association also, even after it had been implanted by education, might be analyzed away.

But there *is* this basis of powerful natural sentiment; and this it is which, when once the general happiness is recognized as the ethical standard, will constitute the strength of the utilitarian morality. This firm foundation is that of the social feelings of mankind; the desire to be in unity with our fellow creatures, which is already a powerful principle in human nature, and happily one of those which tend to become stronger, even without express inculcation, from the influences of advancing civilisation.[m]

13. Mill's moving description of the origin and nature of the feeling for humanity may serve as a fitting conclusion to his exposition of the greatest happiness principle.

The deeply-rooted conception which every individual even now has of himself as a social being, tends to make him feel it one of his natural wants that there should be harmony between his feeling and aims and those of his fellow creatures. If differences of opinion and of mental culture make it impossible for him to share many of their actual feelings — perhaps make him denounce and defy those feelings — he still needs to be conscious that his real aim and theirs do not conflict; that he is not opposing himself to what they really wish for, namely, their own good, but is, on the contrary, promoting it. This feeling in most individuals is much inferior in strength to their selfish feelings, and is often wanting altogether. But to those who have it, it possesses all the characters of a natural feeling. It does not present itself to their minds as a superstition of education, or a law despotically imposed by the power of society, but as an attribute which it would not be well for them to be without. This conviction is the ultimate sanction of the greatest-happiness morality. This it is which makes any mind, of well-developed feelings, work with, and not against, the outward motives to care for others, afforded by what I have called the external sanctions; and when those sanctions are wanting, or act in an opposite direction, constitutes in itself a powerful internal binding force, in proportion to the sensitiveness and thoughtfulness of the character; since few but those whose mind is a moral blank, could bear to lay out their course of life on the plan of paying no regard to others except so far as their own private interest compels.[n]

Questions

1. What is the "principle of utility"? Why does Mill feel called upon to defend the doctrine in such detail?
2. In what respects is Mill's conception of utilitarianism different from Bentham's?
3. What is Mill's reply to the objection that the greatest happiness principle is a "swinish doctrine"?
4. Distinguish between "psychological hedonism" and "ethical hedonism." Is it necessary to maintain both if you subscribe to either? Is it necessary to reject one if you subscribe to the other?
5. Why does Mill distinguish different kinds of pleasure? What criterion does he set up to judge differences in the quality of pleasures?
6. Discuss the role of sanctions in Mill's ethical theory, with special attention to the "feeling for humanity."
7. Elaborate on Mill's distinction between a *motive for conduct* and a *rule of conduct*. What does he mean by his assertion that the motive has nothing to do with the morality of an action?
8. Discuss Mill's statement that it is not possible to prove first prin-

ciples or ultimate goals. Do you agree with him? Can you name at least two moral philosophers who would disagree with this position?
9. Reconstruct Mill's replies to (a) the accusation that the utilitarian doctrine is incompatible with the Christian ideal of self-sacrifice, and (b) the argument that the doctrine is invalid because it is not possible for man to achieve happiness.
10. Do you believe that the utilitarian doctrine, as Mill presents it, has value for our times?

Key to selections:

JOHN STUART MILL, *Utilitarianism*, London, Longmans, Green and Co., 1897.

a Ch. IV, pp. 52–53.	h Ch. II, pp. 18–20.
b Ch. II, pp. 8–9.	i Ch. II, pp. 24–25.
c Ch. II, pp. 9–10.	j Ch. II, pp. 26–28.
d Ch. II, pp. 10–12.	k Ch. III, pp. 39–40.
e Ch. II, pp. 12–14.	l Ch. III, pp. 40–43.
f Ch. II, pp. 14–16.	m Ch. III, pp. 44–46.
g Ch. II, pp. 16–17.	n Ch. III, pp. 50–51.

Guide to Additional Reading

INEXPENSIVE EDITIONS:

MILL, J. S., *Autobiography*, World's Classics (Oxford University Press).
——, *Two Letters on the Measures of Value* (Johns Hopkins Press).
——, *Utilitarianism, Liberty and Representative Government*, Everyman's Library (Dutton).
——, *Utilitarianism*, Great Books Foundation (Regnery).
——, *Utilitarianism*, Little Library of Liberal Arts (Liberal Arts).
——, "Utilitarianism" and "On Liberty," *English Philosophers from Bacon to Mill*, Modern Library (Random House).

INEXPENSIVE EDITIONS OF RELATED WORKS:

Bentham, J., *An Introduction to the Principle of Morals and Legislation*, Hafner Library of Classics (Hafner).

DISCUSSION AND COMMENTARY:

Broad, C. D., *Five Types of Ethical Theory*, New York, Harcourt, Brace and Co., 1930, Ch. VI.

Moore, G. E., *Ethics*, New York, Home University Library, Henry Holt and Company, 1912, Chs. I and II.

Plamenatz, J., *The English Utilitarians*, Oxford, Basil Blackwell and Mott, Ltd., 1944.

Sidgwick, H., *The Methods of Ethics*, New York, The Macmillan Company, 1925, Bks. II and IV.

Stephen, L., *The English Utilitarians*, New York, G. P. Putman's Sons, 1900, vol. III.

CHAPTER 13

The Trans-valuation of Values

FRIEDRICH NIETZSCHE

Although he was descended through both his parents from theologians, Friedrich Nietzsche (1844–1900) made his reputation in philosophy through a "campaign against morality." No hint of his widespread influence on European thought is given by the facts of his history. He was born in the Prussian city of Röcken, and his father's premature death left Friedrich to be petted and spoiled as the only male in a household consisting of his mother, a younger sister, and other female relatives. His home life and early education were entirely in keeping with the family tradition of piety, but as a student at the universities of Bonn and Leipzig, Nietzsche's thinking underwent a radical transformation. He was much impressed by the vitality of the ancient Graeco-Roman civilization and by the grim realism of the contemporary principle of the "survival of the fittest." These influences, together with the pessimistic, anti-rationalistic philosophy of Arthur Schopenhauer, were the chief external sources of Nietzsche's extreme revulsion against the ideals of his time; to him, European civilization appeared despicably weak and decadent.

Throughout his life, Nietzsche was plagued by physical disability. An injury suffered in military training in 1867 made active duty impossible, but he later interrupted his academic career to seek the stimulation of the military scene as a volunteer in the Hospital Corps during the Franco-Prussian War (1870). Illness contracted while he was in service — the beginning of a lifetime of increasing physical suffering — forced him to leave the army, and he returned to the academic world. On the strength of his exceptional academic ability, he had been appointed professor of classical philology at the University of Basel in Switzerland at the age of twenty-four. By the time he was thirty-five, poor health obliged him to resign, and for nearly a decade, he travelled through Europe in a vain search for an environment in which he might recover his health.

Despite the wretchedness of protracted sickness and loneliness, Nietzsche produced a succession of brilliant books. His first important work, *The Birth of Tragedy from the Spirit of Music* (1872), was probably influenced by his brief attachment to the famous composer, Richard Wagner. Of his major philosophical works, many express in their titles his protest against the accepted ideals of his time: *Thoughts Out of Season* (1876), *Human All-Too-Human* (1880), *Beyond Good and Evil* (1886), *The Genealogy of Morals* (1887), and *The Antichrist* (1889). Nietzsche's more positive and constructive writings include *The Dawn of Day* (1881), *The Joyful Wisdom* (1882), and the dramatic *Thus Spake Zarathustra* (1884). His final work was *The Will to Power* (1889). A violent seizure, early in 1889, followed by insanity, terminated Nietzsche's career; his sister, Elizabeth Foerster-Nietzsche, edited his unfinished works and saw to their publication.

Perhaps more than any other philosopher, Nietzsche stands in need of defense against the tendency to evaluate ideas in terms of the man rather than by their own merits. Against the view sometimes expressed that Nietzsche's extremist theories and emotional style were the expression of a diseased mind, there stands the fact that his works are distinguished for brilliance of insight, shrewdness of argument, and soundness of scholarship. Moreover, his radical ideas have been welcomed by many conscientious thinkers in literature, art, pedagogy, politics, religion, and ethics, who, with him, have been alarmed by the decline of individuality and free expression in the "machine age."

•

Fortified with the conviction that philosophers must serve as "the bad conscience of their age," Nietzsche attacks relentlessly what he sees as the decadence and hypocrisy of traditional European morality — a morality which, he predicts, will inevitably lead to the eclipse of western civilization. To avert this disaster, Nietzsche proposes a moral counter-movement:

> After thousands of years of error and confusion, it is my good fortune to have rediscovered the road which leads to a Yea and to a Nay.
>
> I teach people to say Nay in the face of all that makes for weakness and exhaustion.
>
> I teach people to say Yea in the face of all that makes for strength, that preserves strength, and justifies the feeling of strength.[a]

Nietzsche holds up to ridicule the accepted ideals of the Judaeo-Christian religion and Greek rationalism, describing them as *reversals* of the true values. To implement the needed moral revolution, he presents a corrected table of virtues: in place of humility, pride; in place of sympathy and pity, contempt and aloofness; in place of love of one's neighbor, ruthless exploitation. However, Nietzsche does not intend this doctrine of the *transvaluation of values* for the "common herd," but for the few "free spirits" of the day who are intellectually fit to receive it.[1]

---

[1] Nietzsche's works are frequently, but erroneously, regarded as philosophical support for the recent National Socialist (Nazi) movement in Germany. While a few themes from his philosophy may support the Nazi doctrines, there are fundamental differences, *e.g.*, in the opposition of Nietzsche's principle of radical creative individualism to the Nazi principle of the priority of the state over the individual.

In a series of pungent aphorisms, replete with invective and wit, Nietzsche addresses himself to the aristocracy of free spirits. He exhorts them to prepare the way for the next stage in human evolution, the Superman. For Nietzsche, the Superman symbolizes the unfettered spirit, revelling in his magnificent strength and his own worth. Although man in his present condition may be regarded as the highest form of existence, his dominance over nature is still precarious. Indeed, "Man is something to be surpassed." The Superman represents a higher level of mastery over nature.

While the conception of evolution is fundamental in Nietzsche's ethical system, his interpretation of it departs from the widely-accepted Darwinian hypothesis. In Darwin's theory, evolution is conceived as passive and mechanical adaptation to the environment, but Nietzsche finds the true meaning of evolution in an aggressive "will to power" to dominate the environment: ". . . The strongest and highest Will to Life does not find expression in a miserable struggle for existence, but in a Will to War, a Will to Power, a Will to Overpower!" There is in evolution no progress towards a goal: each thing in the universe manifests a ceaseless, blind striving for power, shifting back and forth between success and failure in the competition for mastery.

Man's struggle for dominance over his environment is hampered by the teachings of false moralities. The true morality, Nietzsche holds, must build from the immediate sense of power which everyone can feel within himself. Like numerous moralists before him, Nietzsche approves as good whatever conforms to nature, and condemns as bad whatever is contrary to it. But he dismisses as unrealistic the description of nature as a rational or providential order. Nature is essentially the will to power, a brutal and savage contest of strength, characterized by frightfulness and tragedy, bloodshed, suffering, and cruelty. Affirming the values which enhance the will to power, saying "yea" to life as it actually is, constitutes for Nietzsche the true morality.

From the point of view of the Nietzschean morality, all ethical theories which conceal the hard facts of existence and teach the repression of the will to power are insidious. Nietzsche therefore castigates Christians and Jews, Germans and Englishmen, phi-losophers and scientists — and women — for preferring life-deny-ing values. The Judaeo-Christian ethic is singled out as the most pernicious source of anti-natural morality. Its perversion of the will to power is seen in clergymen seeking mastery under cover of hypocritical sermons on meekness, and its repression of the will to power is seen in the "botched and bungled" masses who are taken in by the deceptions of the priests.

The rationalism of traditional philosophy, since it too misrepre-sents reality, is regarded as reinforcing the debilitating influence of Christianity. In holding up the ideal of man as a rational animal, the philosophers mistakenly elevate reason to the preëminent po-sition in human nature. In actuality, the essence of man is not reason, but will — the will to power. In the Nietzschean scheme, the role of reason is to facilitate the functioning of the drive for power by organizing efficiently the conditions of action. Nietzsche uses the Greek gods, Dionysius and Apollo, to dramatize the rela-tionship between the will and the reason. Dionysius, the frenzied and passionate, is revered as the symbol of the undisciplined will to power. Apollo, representing rationality and order, must be the instrument by which the will to power can increase its mastery. With the Apollonian element supporting rather than suppressing the Dionysian, man can defy God and dominate the universe: the moral man "lives dangerously."

· · ·

1. Drawing upon his knowledge of philology and history for evi-dence, Nietzsche contradicts the main currents of the liberal, demo-cratic thought of his time. The cardinal distinction of his ethical theory is that between the "master-morality" of the noble and free spirits and the "slave-morality" of the common run of man.

In a tour through the many finer and coarser moralities which have hitherto prevailed or still prevail on the earth, I found certain traits recurring regularly together, and connected with one an-other, until finally two primary types revealed themselves to me, and a radical distinction was brought to light. There is *master-morality* and *slave-morality;* — I would at once add, however, that in all higher and mixed civilisations, there are also attempts at the reconciliation of the two moralities; but one finds still oftener the confusion and mutual misunderstanding of them, indeed, sometimes their close juxtaposition — even in the same man, within one soul. The distinctions of moral values have either originated in a ruling caste, pleasantly conscious of being different from the ruled — or among the ruled class, the slaves and dependents of all sorts. . . .

The noble type of man regards *himself* as a determiner of values; he does not require to be approved of; he passes the judgment: "What is injurious to me is injurious in itself"; he knows that it is he himself only who confers honour on things; he is a *creator of values*. He honours whatever he recognises in himself: such morality is self-glorification. In the foreground there is the feeling of plenitude, of power, which seeks to overflow, the happiness of high tension, the consciousness of a wealth which would fain give and bestow: — the noble man also helps the unfortunate, but not — or scarcely — out of pity, but rather from an impulse generated by the super-abundance of power. The noble man honours in himself the powerful one, him also who has power over himself, who knows how to speak and how to keep silence, who takes pleasure in subjecting himself to severity and hardness, and has reverence for all that is severe and hard. . . .

It is otherwise with the second type of morality, *slave-morality*. Supposing that the abused, the oppressed, the suffering, the unemancipated, the weary, and those uncertain of themselves, should moralise, what will be the common element in their moral estimates? Probably a pessimistic suspicion with regard to the entire situation of man will find expression, perhaps a condemnation of man, together with his situation. The slave has an unfavourable eye for the virtues of the powerful; he has a scepticism and distrust, a *refinement* of distrust of everything "good" that is there honoured — he would fain persuade himself that the very happiness there is not genuine. On the other hand, *those* qualities which serve to alleviate the existence of sufferers are brought into prominence and flooded with light; it is here that sympathy, the kind, helping hand, the warm heart, patience, diligence, humility, and friendliness attain to honour; for here these are the most useful qualities, and almost the only means of supporting the burden of existence. Slave-morality is essentially the morality of utility. Here is the seat of the origin of the famous antithesis "good" and "evil": — power and dangerousness are assumed to reside in the evil, a certain dreadfulness, subtlety, and strength, which do not admit of being despised. According to slave-morality, therefore, the "evil" man arouses fear; according to master-morality, it is precisely the "good" man who arouses fear and seeks to arouse it, while the bad man is regarded as the despicable being.[b]

2. There are, then, different ethical terms for the two moralities: the distinction between "good" and "bad" is made by the aristocrat, while the opposition of "good" and "evil" is the invention of the slaves. Motivated by resentment, the latter call "evil" those characteristics which the aristocrats most honor in themselves.

The guide-post which first put me on the *right* track was this question — what is the true etymological significance of the various symbols for the idea "good" which have been coined in the various languages? I then found that they all led back to *the same evolution of the same idea* — that everywhere "aristocrat," "noble" (in the social sense), is the root idea, out of which have necessarily developed "good" in the sense of "with aristocratic soul," "noble," in the sense of "with a soul of high calibre," "with a privileged soul" — a development which invariably runs parallel with that other evolution by which "vulgar," "plebeian," "low," are made to change finally into "bad". . . .

The revolt of the slaves in morals begins in the very principle of *resentment* becoming creative and giving birth to values — a resentment experienced by creatures who, deprived as they are of the proper outlet of action, are forced to find their compensation in an imaginary revenge. While every aristocratic morality springs from a triumphant affirmation of its own demands, the slave morality says "no" from the very outset to what is "outside itself," "different from itself," and "not itself": and this "no" is its creative deed.

. . . What respect for his enemies is found, forsooth, in an aristocratic man — and such a reverence is already a bridge to love! He insists on having his enemy to himself as his distinction. He tolerates no other enemy but a man in whose character there is nothing to despise and *much* to honour! On the other hand, imagine the "enemy" as the resentful man conceives him — and it is here exactly that we see his work, his creativeness; he has conceived "the evil enemy," the "evil one," and indeed that is the root idea from which he now evolves as a contrasting and corresponding figure a "good one," himself — his very self!

The method of this man is quite contrary to that of the aristocratic man, who conceives the root idea "good" spontaneously and straight away, that is to say, out of himself, and from that material then creates for himself a concept of "bad"! This "bad" of aristocratic origin and that "evil" out of the cauldron of unsatisfied hatred — the former an imitation, an "extra," an additional nuance; the latter, on the other hand, the original, the beginning, the essential act in the conception of a slave-morality — these two words "bad" and "evil," how great a difference do they mark, in spite of the fact that they have an identical contrary in the idea "good." But the idea "good" is *not* the same: much rather let the question be asked, "Who is really evil according to the meaning of the morality of resentment?" In all sternness let it be answered thus: — *just* the good man of the other morality, just the aristocrat, the powerful one, the one who rules, but who is distorted by the venomous eye of resentfulness, into a new colour, a new signification, a new appearance. This particular point we would be the last to deny: the man who learned to know those "good" ones only as enemies, learned at the same time not to know them only as "*evil enemies*," and the same men who *inter pares* were kept so rigorously in bounds through convention, respect, custom, and gratitude, though much more through mutual vigilance and jealousy *inter pares*, these men who in their relations with each other find so many new ways of manifesting consideration, self-control, delicacy, loyalty, pride, and friendship, these men are in reference to what is outside their circle (where the foreign element, a *foreign* country, begins), not much better than beasts of prey, which have been let loose. They enjoy there freedom from all social control, they feel that in the wilderness they can give vent with impunity to that tension which is produced by enclosure and imprisonment in the peace of society, they *revert* to the innocence of the beast-of-prey conscience, like jubilant monsters, who perhaps come from a ghostly bout of murder, arson, rape, and torture, with bravado and a moral equanimity, as though merely some wild student's prank had been played, perfectly convinced that the poets have now an ample theme to sing and celebrate. It is impossible not to recognise at the core of all these aristocratic races the beast of prey; the magnificent *blonde brute*, avidly rampant for spoil and victory; this hidden core needed an outlet from time to time, the beast must get loose again, must return into the wilderness . . .[c]

3. Nietzsche argues that creativity is the privilege and gift of the aristocratic, i.e., the barbarian, ferocious components of society. Only they, he claims, have accomplished improvements in human nature.

Every elevation of the type "man," has hitherto been the work of an aristocratic society and so it will always be — a society believing in a long scale of gradations of rank and differences of worth among human beings, and requiring slavery in some form or other. Without the *pathos of distance*, such as grows out of the incarnated difference of classes, out of the constant outlooking and downlooking of the ruling caste on subordinates and instruments, and out of their equally constant practice of obeying and commanding, of keeping down and keeping at a distance — that other more mysterious pathos could never have arisen, the longing for an ever new widening of distance within the soul itself, the formation of ever higher, rarer, further, more extended, more comprehensive states, in short, just the elevation of the type "man," the continued "self-surmounting of man," to use a moral formula in a supermoral sense. To be sure, one must not resign oneself to any humanitarian illusions about the history of the origin of an aristocratic society (that is to say, of the preliminary condition for the elevation of the type "man"): the truth is hard. Let us acknowledge unprejudicedly how every higher civilisation hitherto has *originated!* Men with a still natural nature, barbarians in every terrible sense of the word, men of prey, still in possession of unbroken strength of will and desire for power, threw themselves upon weaker, more moral, more peaceful races (perhaps trading or cattle-rearing communities), or upon old mellow civilisations in which the final vital force was flickering out in brilliant fireworks of wit and depravity. At the commencement, the noble caste was always the barbarian caste: their superiority did not consist first of all in their physical, but in their psychical power — they were more *complete* men (which at every point also implies the same as "more complete beasts").[d]

4. The psychical impotence of the "herd" is reflected in the morality it produces. The basic principle of all slave-morality, Nietzsche tells us, is resentment *of the aristocratic spirit. For example, altruism, a typical slave ideal, denies the value of creative egoism which is central to the master-morality.*

The preponderance of an altruistic way of valuing is the result of a consciousness of the fact that one is botched and bungled. Upon examination, this point of view turns out to be: "I am not worth much," simply a psychological valuation; more plainly still: it is the feeling of impotence, of the lack of the great self-asserting impulses of power (in muscles, nerves, and ganglia). This valuation gets translated, according to the particular culture of these classes, into a moral or religious principle (the pre-eminence of religious or moral precepts is always a sign of low culture): it tries to justify itself in spheres whence, as far as it is concerned, the notion "value" hails. The interpretation by means of which the Christian sinner tries to understand himself, is an attempt at justifying his lack of power and of self-confidence: he prefers to feel himself a sinner rather than feel bad for nothing: it is in itself a symptom of decay when interpretations of this sort are used at all. In some cases the bungled and the botched do not look for the reason of their unfortunate condition in their own guilt (as the Christian does), but in society: when, however, the Socialist, the Anarchist, and the Nihilist are conscious that their existence is something for which some one must be *guilty*, they are very closely related to the Christian, who also believes that he can more easily endure his ill ease and his wretched constitution when he has found some one whom he can hold *responsible* for it. The instinct of *revenge* and *resentment* appears in both cases here as a means of enduring life, as a self-preservative measure, as is also the favour shown to *altruistic* theory and practice. The *hatred of egoism*, whether it be one's own (as in the case of the Christian), or another's (as in the case of the Socialists), thus appears as a valuation reached under the predominance of revenge; and also as an act of prudence on the part of the preservative instinct of the suffering, in the form of an increase in their feelings of co-operation and unity . . . At bottom, as I have already suggested, the discharge of resentment which takes place in the act of judging, rejecting, and punishing egoism (one's own or that of others) is still a self-preservative measure on the part of the bungled and the botched. In short: the cult of altruism is merely a particular form of egoism, which regularly appears under certain definite physiological circumstances.

When the Socialist, with righteous indignation, cries for "justice," "rights," "equal rights," it only shows that he is oppressed by his inadequate culture, and is unable to understand why he suffers: he also finds pleasure in crying; — if he were more at ease he would take jolly good care not to cry in that way: in that case he would seek his pleasure elsewhere. The same holds good of the Christian: he curses, condemns, and slanders the "world" — and does not even except himself. But that is no reason for taking him seriously. In both cases we are in the presence of invalids who feel better for crying, and who find relief in slander.[e]

5. Continuing in the same vein, Nietzsche condemns the ideals of peace and universal equality, exposing their life-denying qualities. Exploitation and competition, he argues, characterize all living things, because they are the very essence of the Will to Power.

To refrain mutually from injury, from violence, from exploitation, and put one's will on a par with that of others: this may result in a certain rough sense in good conduct among individuals when the necessary conditions are given (namely, the actual similarity of the individuals in amount of force and degree of worth, and their co-relation within one organisation). As soon, however, as one wished to take this principle more generally, and if possible even as *the fundamental principle of society*, it would immediately disclose what it really is — namely, a Will to the *denial* of life, a principle of dissolution and decay. Here one must think profoundly to the very basis and resist all sentimental weakness: life itself is *essentially* appropriation, injury, conquest of the strange and weak, suppression, severity, obtrusion of peculiar forms, incorporation, and at the least, putting it mildest, exploitation; — but why should one for ever use precisely these words on which for ages a disparaging purpose has been stamped? Even the organisation within which, as was previously supposed, the individuals treat each other as equal — it takes place in every healthy aristocracy — must itself, if it be a living and not a dying organisation, do all that towards other bodies, which the individuals within it refrain from doing to each other: it will have to be the incarnated Will to Power, it will endeavour to grow, to gain ground, attract to itself and acquire ascendency — not owing to any morality or immorality, but because it *lives*, and because life *is* precisely Will to Power. On no point, however, is the ordinary consciousness of Europeans more unwilling to be corrected than on this matter; people now rave everywhere, even under the guise of science, about coming conditions of society in which "the exploiting character" is to be absent: — that sounds to my ears as if they promised to invent a mode of life which should refrain from all organic functions. "Exploitation" does not belong to a depraved, or imperfect and primitive society: it belongs to the *nature* of the living being as a primary organic function; it is a consequence of the intrinsic Will to Power, which is precisely the Will to Life. — Granting that as a theory this is a novelty — as a reality it is the *fundamental fact* of all history: let us be so far honest towards ourselves! [f]

6. *The primary responsibility for the dishonest morality which is exhausting European civilization Nietzsche assigns to Judaism and Christianity.*

I regard Christianity as the most fatal and seductive lie that has ever yet existed — as the greatest and most *impious lie:* I can discern the last sprouts and branches of its ideal beneath every form of disguise, I decline to enter into any compromise or false position in reference to it — I urge people to declare open war with it.

The *morality of paltry people* as the measure of all things: this is the most repugnant kind of degeneracy that civilisation has ever yet brought into existence. And this *kind of ideal* is hanging still, under the name of "God," over men's heads!!

However modest one's demands may be concerning intellectual cleanliness, when one touches the New Testament one cannot help experiencing a sort of inexpressible feeling of discomfort; for the unbounded cheek with which the least qualified people will have their say in its pages, in regard to the greatest problems of existence, and claim to sit in judgment on such matters, exceeds all limits. The impudent levity with which the most unwieldy problems are spoken of here (life, the world, God, the purpose of life), as if they were not problems at all, but the most simple things which these little bigots *know all about!!!* . . .

The *law*, which is the fundamentally realistic formula of certain self-preservative measures of a community, forbids certain actions that have a definite tendency to jeopardise the welfare of that community: it does *not* forbid the attitude of mind which gives rise to these actions — for in the pursuit of other ends the community requires these forbidden actions, namely, when it is a matter of opposing its *enemies*. The moral idealist now steps forward and says: "God sees into men's hearts: the action itself counts for nothing; the reprehensible attitude of mind from which it proceeds must be extirpated . . ." In normal conditions men laugh at such things; it is only in exceptional cases, when a community lives *quite* beyond the need of waging war in order to maintain itself, that an ear is lent to such things. Any attitude of mind is abandoned, the utility of which cannot be conceived.

This was the case, for example, when Buddha appeared among a people that was both peacable and afflicted with great intellectual weariness.

This was also the case in regard to the first Christian community (as also the Jewish), the primary condition of which was the absolutely *unpolitical* Jewish society. Christianity could grow only upon the soil of Judaism — that is to say, among a people that had already renounced the political life, and which led a sort of parasitic existence within the Roman sphere of government. Christianity goes a step *further:* it allows men to "emasculate" themselves even more; the circumstances actually favour their doing so. — *Nature* is *expelled* from morality when it is said, "Love ye your enemies": for *Nature's* injunction, "Ye shall *love* your neighbour and *hate* your enemy," has now become senseless in the law (in instinct); now, even *the love a man feels for his neighbour* must first be based upon something (*a sort of love of God*). *God* is introduced everywhere, and *utility* is withdrawn; the natural *origin* of morality is denied everywhere: the *veneration of Nature*, which lies in *acknowledging a natural morality*, is *destroyed* to the roots . . .

What is it I protest against? That people should regard this paltry and peaceful mediocrity, this spiritual equilibrium which knows nothing of the fine impulses of great accumulations of strength, as something high, or possibly as the standard of all things.ᵍ

7. Nietzsche sums up his case against Judaism and Christianity, stressing their unsuitability for the evolutionary struggle.

Among men, as among all other animals, there is a surplus of
defective, diseased, degenerating, infirm, and necessarily suffering
individuals; the successful cases, among men also, are always the
exception; and in view of the fact that man is *the animal not yet
properly adapted to his environment,* the rare exception. But worse
still. The higher the type a man represents, the greater is the
improbability that he will *succeed;* the accidental, the law of ir-
rationality in the general constitution of mankind, manifests itself
most terribly in its destructive effect on the higher orders of men,
the conditions of whose lives are delicate, diverse, and difficult to
determine. What, then, is the attitude of the two greatest religions
above-mentioned to the *surplus* of failures in life? They endeavour
to preserve and keep alive whatever can be preserved; in fact, as
the religions for *sufferers,* they take the part of these upon principle; they are always in favour of those who suffer from life as
from a disease, and they would fain treat every other experience
of life as false and impossible. However highly we may esteem
this indulgent and preservative care (inasmuch as in applying to
others, it has applied, and applies also to the highest and usually
the most suffering type of man), the hitherto *paramount* religions
— to give a general appreciation of them — are among the principal causes which have kept the type of "man" upon a lower level
— they have preserved too much *that which should have perished.*
One has to thank them for invaluable services; and who is sufficiently rich in gratitude not to feel poor at the contemplation of
all that the "spiritual men" of Christianity have done for Europe
hitherto! But when they had given comfort to the sufferers, courage to the oppressed and despairing, a staff and support to the
helpless, and when they had allured from society into convents
and spiritual penitentiaries the broken-hearted and distracted:
what else had they to do in order to work systematically in that
fashion, and with a good conscience, for the preservation of all
the sick and suffering, which means, in deed and in truth, to
work for *the deterioration of the European race?* To *reverse* all
estimates of value — *that* is what they had to do! And to shatter
the strong, to spoil great hopes, to cast suspicion on the delight

in beauty, to break down everything autonomous, manly, con-
quering, and imperious — all instincts which are natural to the
highest and most successful type of "man" — into uncertainty,
distress of conscience, and self-destruction; forsooth, to invert all
love of the earthly and of supremacy over the earth, into hatred
of the earth and earthly things. . . [h]

*8. The moral philosophers, no less than the priests, teach the denial
of life, and Nietzsche attacks the "superstitions which heretofore have
been fashionable among philosophers." False psychology, faulty
logic, and a misunderstanding of the role of reason serve the philosophers in their hatred of life.*

In the whole of moral evolution, there is no sign of truth: all
the conceptual elements which come into play are fictions; all the
psychological tenets are false; all the forms of logic employed in
this department of prevarication are sophisms. The chief feature
of all moral philosophers is their total lack of intellectual cleanliness and self-control: they regard "fine feelings" as arguments:
their heaving breasts seem to them the bellows of godliness . . .
Moral philosophy is the most suspicious period in the history of
the human intellect . . .

Why everything resolved itself into mummery. — Rudimentary
psychology, which only considered the *conscious* lapses of men (as
causes), which regarded "consciousness" as an attribute of the
soul, and which sought a will behind every action (*i.e.*, an intention), could only answer "*Happiness*" to the question: "*What
does man desire?*" (it was impossible to answer "Power," because
that would have been *immoral*); — consequently behind all men's
actions there is the intention of attaining to happiness by means
of them. Secondly: if man as a matter of fact does not attain to
happiness, why is it? Because he mistakes the means thereto. —
What is the unfailing means of acquiring happiness? Answer: *virtue.* — Why virtue? Because virtue is supreme rationalness, and
rationalness makes mistakes in the choice of means impossible:
virtue in the form of *reason* is the way to happiness. Dialectics is

the constant occupation of virtue, because it does away with passion and intellectual cloudiness.

As a matter of fact, man does *not* desire "happiness." Pleasure is a sensation of power: if the passions are excluded, those states of the mind are also excluded which afford the greatest sensation of power and therefore of pleasure. The highest rationalism is a state of cool clearness, which is very far from being able to bring about that feeling of power which every kind of *exaltation* involves . . .

[They] combat everything that intoxicates and exalts — everything that impairs the perfect coolness and impartiality of the mind. . . . They were consistent with their first false principle: that consciousness was the *highest*, the *supreme* state of mind, the prerequisite of perfection — whereas the reverse is true.

If one should require a proof of how deeply and thoroughly the actually *barbarous* needs of man, even in his present state of tameness and "civilisation," still seek gratification, one should contemplate the "leitmotifs" of the whole of the evolution of philosophy: — a sort of revenge upon reality, a surreptitious process of destroying the values by means of which men live, a *dissatisfied* soul to which the condition of discipline is one of torture, and which takes a particular pleasure in morbidly severing all the bonds that bind it to such a condition.

The history of philosophy is the story of a *secret and mad hatred* of the prerequisites of Life, of the feelings which make for the real values of Life, and of all partisanship in favour of Life. Philosophers have never hesitated to affirm a fanciful world, provided it contradicted this world, and furnished them with a weapon wherewith they could calumniate this world. Up to the present, philosophy has been the *grand school of slander:* and its power has been so great, that even to-day our science, which pretends to be the advocate of Life, has *accepted* the fundamental position of slander . . . What is the hatred which is active here?

I fear that it is still the *Circe of philosophers* — Morality, which plays them the trick of compelling them to be ever slanderers. . . . They believed in moral "truths," in these they thought they had found the highest values; what alternative had they left, save that of denying existence ever more emphatically the more they got to know about it? . . . For this life is *immoral* . . . And it is based upon immoral first principles: and morality says *nay* to Life.[i]

9. *The life-seeking values of cruelty and Homeric deception are rediscovered by Nietzsche in the search for values which will stand right side up before the brute facts of existence.*

. . . Even obvious truths, as if by the agreement of centuries, have long remained unuttered, because they have the appearance of helping the finally slain wild beast back to life again. I perhaps risk something when I allow such a truth to escape; let others capture it again and give it so much "milk of pious sentiment" to drink, that it will lie down quiet and forgotten, in its old corner. — One ought to learn anew about cruelty, and open one's eyes; one ought at last to learn impatience, in order that such immodest gross errors — as, for instance, have been fostered by ancient and modern philosophers with regard to tragedy — may no longer wander about virtuously and boldly. Almost everything that we call "higher culture" is based upon the spiritualising and intensifying of *cruelty* — this is my thesis; the "wild beast" has not been slain at all, it lives, it flourishes, it has only been — transfigured. That which constitutes the painful delight of tragedy is cruelty; that which operates agreeably in so-called tragic sympathy, and at the basis even of everything sublime, up to the highest and most delicate thrills of metaphysics, obtains its sweetness solely from the intermingled ingredient of cruelty. What the Roman enjoys in the arena, the Christian in the ecstasies of the cross, the Spaniard at the sight of the faggot and stake, or of the bullfight, the present-day Japanese who presses his way to the tragedy, the workman of the Parisian suburbs who has a homesickness for bloody revolutions, the Wagnerienne who, with unhinged will, "undergoes" the performance of "Tristan and Isolde" — what all these enjoy, and strive with mysterious ardour to drink in, is the philtre of the great Circe "cruelty". . . . Finally, let us consider that even the seeker of knowledge operates as an artist and glorifier of cruelty, in that he compels his spirit to perceive *against* its own inclination, and often enough against the wishes of his heart: — he forces it to say Nay, where he would like to affirm, love, and adore; indeed, every instance of taking a thing profoundly and fundamentally, is a violation, an intentional injuring of the fundamental will of the spirit, which instinctively aims at appearance and superficiality, — even in every desire for knowledge there is a drop of cruelty.

. . . In this connection, there is the not unscrupulous readiness of the spirit to deceive other spirits and dissemble before them — the constant pressing and straining of a creating, shaping, changeable power: the spirit enjoys therein its craftiness and its variety of disguises, it enjoys also its feeling of security therein — it is precisely by its Protean arts that it is best protected and concealed! — *Counter to* this propensity for appearance, for simplification, for a disguise, for a cloak, in short, for an outside — for every outside is a cloak — there operates the sublime tendency of the man of knowledge, which takes, and *insists* on taking things profoundly, variously, and thoroughly; as a kind of cruelty of the intellectual conscience and taste, which every courageous thinker will acknowledge in himself, provided, as it ought to be, that he has sharpened and hardened his eye sufficiently long for introspection, and is accustomed to severe discipline and even severe words. He will say: "There is something cruel in the tendency of my spirit": let the virtuous and amiable try to convince him that it is not so! In fact, it would sound nicer, if, instead of our cruelty, perhaps our "extravagant honesty" were talked about, whispered about and glorified — we free, *very* free spirits — and some day perhaps *such* will actually be our — posthumous glory! ʲ

10. The ennobling character of suffering can be appreciated only by the aristocrat. Despising as weakness the longing of the "herd" for freedom from pain, the free spirit revels in the elevating power of suffering, for it spurs him on to raise the will to life to an "unconditioned Will to Power."

. . . What they would fain attain with all their strength, is the universal, green-meadow happiness of the herd, together with security, safety, comfort, and alleviation of life for every one; their two most frequently chanted songs and doctrines are called "Equality of Rights" and "Sympathy with all Sufferers" — and suffering itself is looked upon by them as something which must be *done away with*. We opposite ones, however, who have opened our eye and conscience to the question how and where the plant "man" has hitherto grown most vigourously, believe that this has always taken place under the opposite conditions, that for this end the dangerousness of his situation had to be increased enormously, his inventive faculty and dissembling power (his "spirit") had to develop into subtlety and daring under long oppression and compulsion, and his Will to Life had to be increased to the unconditioned Will to Power: — we believe that severity, violence, slavery, danger in the street and in the heart, secrecy, stoicism, tempter's art and devilry of every kind, — that everything wicked, terrible, tyrannical, predatory, and serpentine in man, serves as well for the elevation of the human species as its opposite: — we do not even say enough when we only say *this much;* and in any case we find ourselves here, both with our speech and our science, at the *other* extreme of all modern ideology and gregarious desirability, as their antipodes perhaps? What wonder that we "free spirits" are not exactly the most communicative spirits? that we do not wish to betray in every respect *what* a spirit can free itself from, and *where* perhaps it will then be driven? And as to the import of the dangerous formula, "Beyond Good and Evil," with which we at least avoid confusion, we *are* something else than "*libres-penseurs,*" "*liberi pensatori,*" "free-thinkers," and whatever these honest advocates of "modern ideas" like to call themselves. Having been at home, or at least guests, in many realms of the spirit; having escaped again and again from the gloomy, agreeable nooks in which preferences and prejudices, youth, origin, the accident of men and books, or even the weariness of travel seemed to confine us; full of malice against the seductions of dependency which lie concealed in honours, money, positions, or exaltation of the senses; grateful even for distress and the vicissitudes of illness, because they always free us from some rule, and its "prejudice," grateful to the God, devil, sheep, and worm in us; inquisitive to a fault, investigators to the point of cruelty, with unhesitating fingers for the intangible, with teeth and stomachs for the most indigestible, ready for any business that requires sagacity and acute senses, ready for every adventure, owing to an excess of "free will"; with anterior and posterior souls, into the ultimate intentions of which it is difficult to pry, with foregrounds and backgrounds to the end of which no foot may run; hidden ones under the mantles of light, appropriators, although we resemble heirs and spendthrifts, arrangers and collectors from morning till night, misers of our wealth and our full-crammed drawers, economical in learning and forgetting, inventive in scheming; sometimes proud of tables of categories, sometimes pedants, sometimes night-owls of work even in full day; yea, if necessary, even scarecrows — and it is necessary nowadays, that is to say, inasmuch as we are the born, sworn, jealous friends of *solitude*, of our own profoundest midnight and mid-day solitude: — such kind of men are we, we free spirits! And perhaps *ye* are also something of the same kind, ye coming ones, ye *new* philosophers? ᵏ

11. The philosopher of the future, understanding the values dictated by the will to power, will stand apart from the masses. He will be an aristocrat, not a leveller like the philosophers of the present. True freedom, rather than the false freedom sought by slaves, will be his doctrine.

Will they be new friends of "truth," these coming philosophers? Very probably, for all philosophers hitherto have loved their truths. But assuredly they will not be dogmatists. It must be contrary to their pride, and also contrary to their taste, that their truth should still be truth for every one — that which has hitherto been the secret wish and ultimate purpose of all dogmatic efforts. "My opinion is *my* opinion: another person has not easily a right to it" — such a philosopher of the future will say, perhaps. One must renounce the bad taste of wishing to agree with many people. "Good" is no longer good when one's neighbour takes it into his mouth. And how could there be a "common good"! The expression contradicts itself; that which can be common is always of small value. In the end things must be as they are and have always been — the great things remain for the great, the abysses for the profound, the delicacies and thrills for the refined, and, to sum up shortly, everything rare for the rare.

Need I say expressly after all this that they will be free, *very* free spirits, these philosophers of the future — as certainly also they will not be merely free spirits, but something more, higher, greater, and fundamentally different, which does not wish to be misunderstood and mistaken? But while I say this, I feel under *obligation* almost as much to them as to ourselves (we free spirits who are their heralds and forerunners), to sweep away from ourselves altogether a stupid old prejudice and misunderstanding, which, like a fog, has too long made the conception of "free spirit" obscure. In every country of Europe, and the same in America, there is at present something which makes an abuse of this name: a very narrow, prepossessed, enchained class of spirits, who desire almost the opposite of what our intentions and instincts prompt — not to mention that in respect to the *new* philosophers who are appearing, they must still more be closed windows and bolted doors. Briefly and regrettably, they belong to the *levellers*, these wrongly named "free spirits" — as glib-tongued and scribe-fingered slaves of the democratic taste and its "modern ideas": all of them men without solitude, without personal solitude, blunt, honest fellows to whom neither courage nor honourable conduct ought to be denied; only, they are not free, and are ludicrously superficial, especially in their innate partiality for seeing the cause of almost *all* human misery and failure in the old forms in which society has hitherto existed — a notion which happily inverts the truth entirely![1]

12. The further progress of mankind requires a transvaluation of values *which will give the will to power its rightful place.*

Transvalue values — what does this mean? It implies that all spontaneous motives, all new, future, and stronger motives, are still extant; but that they now appear under false names and false valuations, and have not yet become conscious of themselves.

We ought to have the courage to become conscious, and to affirm all that which has been *attained* — to get rid of the humdrum character of old valuations, which makes us unworthy of the best and strongest things that we have achieved.

Any doctrine would be superfluous for which everything is not already prepared in the way of accumulated forces and explosive material. A transvaluation of values can only be accomplished when there is a tension of new needs, and a new set of needy people who feel all old values as painful, — although they are not conscious of what is wrong.

The standpoint from which my values are determined: is abundance or desire active? . . . Is one a mere spectator, or is one's own shoulder at the wheel — is one looking away or is one turning aside? . . . Is one acting spontaneously, or is one merely reacting to a goad or to a stimulus? . . . Is one simply acting as the result of a paucity of elements, or of such an overwhelming dominion over a host of elements that this power enlists the latter into its service if it requires them? . . . Is one a *problem* one's self or is one a *solution* already? . . . Is one *perfect* through the smallness of the task, or *imperfect* owing to the extraordinary character of the aim? . . . Is one genuine or only an *actor;* is one genuine as an actor, or only the bad copy of an actor? Is one a representative or the creature represented? Is one a personality or merely a rendezvous of personalities? . . . Is one ill from a disease or from surplus health? Does one lead as a shepherd, or as an "exception" (third alternative: as a fugitive)? Is one in need of dignity, or can one play the clown? Is one in search of resistance, or is one evading it? Is one imperfect owing to one's precocity or to one's tardiness? Is it one's nature to say yea, or no, or is one a peacock's tail of garish parts? Is one proud enough not to feel ashamed even of one's vanity? Is one still able to feel a bite of conscience (this species is becoming rare; formerly conscience had to bite too often:

it is as if it now no longer had enough teeth to do so)? Is one still capable of a "duty"? (there are some people who would lose the whole joy of their lives if they were *deprived* of their duty — this holds good especially of feminine creatures, who are born subjects). . . .

It is only a question of power: to have all the morbid traits of the century, but to balance them by means of overflowing, plastic, and rejuvenating power. The *strong* man.^m[m]

13. Before the new philosophy of strength can become effective, there is a task which must be performed: the truth must be shown to those who are fit to receive it. This is the task to which Nietzsche devotes himself.

. . . Meanwhile — for there is plenty of time until then — we should be least inclined to deck ourselves out in such florid and fringed moral verbiage; our whole former work has just made us sick of this taste and its sprightly exuberance. They are beautiful, glistening, jingling, festive words: honesty, love of truth, love of wisdom, sacrifice for knowledge, heroism of the truthful — there is something in them that makes one's heart swell with pride. But we anchorites and marmots have long ago persuaded ourselves in all the secrecy of an anchorite's conscience, that this worthy parade of verbiage also belongs to the old false adornment, frippery, and gold-dust of unconscious human vanity, and that even under such flattering colour and repainting, the terrible original text *homo natura* must again be recognised. In effect, to translate man back again into nature; to master the many vain and visionary interpretations and subordinate meanings which have hitherto been scratched and daubed over the eternal original text, *homo natura;* to bring it about that man shall henceforth stand before man as he now, hardened by the discipline of science, stands before the *other* forms of nature, with fearless Oedipus-eyes, and stopped Ulysses-ears, deaf to the enticements of old metaphysical bird-catchers, who have piped to him far too long: "Thou art more! thou art higher! thou hast a different origin!" — this may be a strange and foolish task, but that it is a *task*, who can deny! [n]

Questions

1. In what sense is Nietzsche the "conscience of his age"?
2. Explain Nietzsche's doctrine of the "transvaluation of values," illustrating his meaning with specific ideals.
3. Contrast the master and slave moralities. What differences in ethical vocabulary are required to express their opposed ethical themes?
4. What are the underlying principles which lead Nietzsche to attack Christianity, pacifism, and democracy?
5. What are Nietzsche's criticisms of traditional moral philosophy? What is his conception of the "true" philosopher?
6. What does "Superman" symbolize in Nietzsche's ethical theory? How does this fit in with his doctrine of "following Nature"?
7. Nietzsche advises us to "live dangerously." What benefits does he anticipate from following this rule of life?
8. Examine critically the Nietzschean theory of the "will to power." Is the conception of nature it involves more or less true to fact than that of such philosophers as Epictetus?
9. What is the relationship between reason and emotion in Nietzsche's ethics? Compare his views with those of the Greek sophists and of Socrates.
10. Adopting Nietzsche's viewpoint, criticize twentieth-century America.

Key to selections:

FRIEDRICH NIETZSCHE, *The Complete Works of Friedrich Nietzsche*, vols. XII, XIII, XVI, Dr. Oscar Levy, ed., New York, Macmillan and Co., 1924. With the kind permission of the publishers.

From *The Will to Power* (tr. A. M. Ludovici)

[a] #54.	[i] #428,
[e] #373.	#434,
[g] #200–201,	#461.
#204,	[m] #1007–1009,
#249.	#1014.

From *The Genealogy of Morals*, First Essay (tr. Horace B. Samuel)

[c] #4,
#10–11.

From *Beyond Good and Evil* (tr. Helen Zimmern)

b #260.	j #229–230.
d #257.	k #44.
f #259.	l #43–44.
h #62.	ʟ #230.

Guide to Additional Reading

INEXPENSIVE EDITIONS:

NIETZSCHE, F., *Beyond Good and Evil*, Great Books Foundation (Regnery).

——, *Thus Spake Zarathustra*, Everyman's Library (Dutton) and Modern Library (Random House).

——, *The Philosophy of Nietzsche*, Modern Library (Random House).

DISCUSSION AND COMMENTARY:

Figgis, J. N., *The Will to Freedom*, New York, Charles Scribner's Sons, 1917.

Kaufmann, W. A., *Nietzsche: Philosopher, Psychologist, Antichrist*, Princeton, Princeton University Press, 1950.

Morgan, G. A., *What Nietzsche Means*, Cambridge, Harvard University Press, 1943.

Salter, W. M., *Nietzsche as Philosopher*, New York, Henry Holt and Company, 1917.

CHAPTER 14

Scientific Method in Ethics

JOHN DEWEY

I n the ninety-two years of his full and active life, John Dewey
(1859–1952) established himself as one of the foremost American
philosophers and educators. Born in Burlington, Vermont, he
spent his life in an environment in which democracy set the key-
note of existence. In his pragmatic philosophy and theory of progressive education, he sought to spell out the ideal of democracy
as not merely a political belief, but also as a way of life, a guiding
principle in education, and a moral ideal. To implement this ideal,
he undertook to remove philosophy and education from the exclusive possession of "ivory tower" specialists by relating the
process of thinking to living social experience.

Each phase of Dewey's academic career provided him with new

interests, activities, and concepts. These he fused into a unified system of ideas, in which philosophy, psychology, and educational theory were combined. As an undergraduate at the University of Vermont, and then at Johns Hopkins University, where he received his Ph.D., Dewey was intensely stimulated by the theory of evolution, German idealistic philosophy, and the theories of the "father of sociology," Auguste Comte. These ideas, new and unorthodox in the 1870's and 1880's, began a liberation of American intellectual life which was appreciably advanced by Dewey's contributions to philosophy and pedagogy.

The personal history of John Dewey was as much a part of his intellectual development as the strictly academic phase of his experience, and he conscientiously kept his theories in close rapport with the actual conditions of his life. His wife, Alice Chipman — whom he married in 1886 — added to her role as wife and mother of a large family that of a welcome influence on Dewey's thinking, through her active participation in intellectual, social, and political affairs. In the course of his long career as a teacher of philosophy — at the University of Michigan, the University of Minnesota, the University of Chicago, and Columbia University — he formed close associations with many distinguished men and women whose original thinking and vigorous social and political activities enriched his own academic and practical experience. One of his most distinctive achievements was the founding of an experimental elementary school at the University of Chicago. From this venture in the application of modern principles of psychology to teaching methods and the integration of thinking and doing in democratically conducted classrooms, he developed his theory of progressive education. At universities in Japan, China, Turkey, and elsewhere abroad, he taught and at the same time learned more fully the importance of democracy and education in promoting individual and social improvement.

A small sample of Dewey's numerous educational and social projects, lectures, articles, and books provides a sufficient indication of his broad interests and great energy. His influence in education was carried abroad through the translation of *The School and*

Society (1900) into twelve languages, and of *Democracy and Education* (1916) into nine. *Reconstruction in Philosophy* (1920), *A Common Faith* (1934), and *Art as Experience* (1934), in their respective branches of philosophy, express essentially the same thesis as the more specialized works in which Dewey places logic and ethics together in the framework of practical experience. Chief among the books devoted to this special concern are *How We Think* (1910), *Human Nature and Conduct* (1922), *Experience and Nature* (1929), *The Quest for Certainty* (1928), and *Logic: The Theory of Inquiry* (1939). Until his death, Dewey continued to write and to take an active interest in philosophy, education, and events in the world about him.

John Dewey attempts to apply the methods of science to the problems of morality. He holds the view that the study of human behavior, especially in regard to moral values, has continued to follow outmoded methods, while the best developed techniques of inquiry have been limited almost entirely to the investigation of the physical world. The resulting discrepancy between our knowledge of physical nature and our knowledge of human nature sets the problem of contemporary ethics:

> . . . The problem of restoring integration and coöperation between man's beliefs about the world in which he lives and his beliefs about the values and purposes that should direct his conduct is the deepest problem of modern life. It is the problem of any philosophy that is not isolated from that life.[a]

Dewey attributes the lag of morality behind technology to the effect of the traditional conception of man as a passive spectator in a fixed and unchanging universe, where truth is absolute and eternal. To bridge the resultant gap between theory and practice, ideas and actions, ideals and behavior, he advocates a thoroughgoing reconstruction of beliefs.

Dewey's ethical theory is built upon the principles of pragmatism, of which the chief elements are scientific method and the conception of the universe as evolutionary.[1] Throughout his writings, he depicts man as a problem-solving organism, constantly making adjustments to the changing conditions which confront him. He classifies human responses to the uncertainties of life situations as *impulsive, habitual,* or *reflective.* Evaluated in terms of effectiveness in solving adjustment problems, impulsive behavior fails because it leads to random reactions, and habitual action fails because it is not adaptable to new conditions. However, reflective thinking, which Dewey equates with scientific inquiry, is a satisfactory method of problem solving, because it is guided to a solution by both past experience and creative ideas. It can thereby "transform a situation in which there is experienced obscurity, doubt, conflict, disturbance of some sort, into a situation that is clear, coherent, settled, harmonious . . ."

The pragmatic criterion of truth is directly related to the outcome of the reflective process. Those ideas which are successful in resolving problematic situations are true, whereas those which do not lead to satisfactory adjustments are false. For the pragmatists, then, truth is relative rather than absolute, changing rather than eternal. The principles of scientific method are readily adapted to the pragmatic position. In science, ideas function as tentative solutions for concrete problems, *i.e.,* as hypotheses, which must be tested by experiment. The empirical verification of hypotheses effects a union of theory and practice. Moreover, through the continuous modification of knowledge which results from the application of scientific method to the solution of the steady stream of problems which characterizes the human scene, knowledge can keep pace with the changing conditions of life and continue to guide it.

As a consequence of his preoccupation with the dynamic aspect of the universe, Dewey produces an ethical theory which "involves

---

[1] Pragmatism was first formulated and named by Charles S. Peirce (1839–1914), a physicist and logician who was influenced in his thinking by the biological theory of evolution. His pragmatism was adopted and modified by William James, John Dewey, and others, chiefly in the United States. Dewey's pragmatism is frequently referred to as "instrumentalism," since it centers about the conception that ideas are "instruments" or plans of action for problem-solving.

nothing less than the problem of the directed reconstruction of economic, political and religious institutions." The conception of what is good must undergo change as society changes and as knowledge of the physical environment increases. The discrepancy between stated ideals and actual behavior in contemporary society can be understood as due in part to the persistence of obsolete values. Dewey maintains that only the use of the methods of science in ethics can secure the continuing adaptation of values to changing human needs. This is tantamount to a recommendation to make active use of intelligence and of the facts of experience in the conduct of the moral life.

• • •

1. Dewey attacks two extremes in ethics, radical empiricism and rationalism. In the former, moral values are identified with subjective experiences of liking and disliking. Dewey regards experiences of this kind as providing only the possibilities *of values. Values as such emerge only after examination of the* conditions *under which liking and disliking occur, and of the* results *to which they lead. The distinction between an experience as such and a valuable experience is given careful and detailed attention.*

The formal statement [of this distinction] may be given concrete content by pointing to the difference between the enjoyed and the enjoyable, the desired and the desirable, the satis*fying* and the satis*factory*. To say that something is enjoyed is to make a statement about a fact, something already in existence; it is not to judge the value of that fact. There is no difference between such a proposition and one which says that something is sweet or sour, red or black. It is just correct or incorrect and that is the end of the matter. But to call an object a value is to assert that it satisfies or fulfills certain conditions. Function and status in meeting conditions is a different matter from bare existence. The fact that something is desired only raises the *question* of its desirability; it does not settle it. Only a child in the degree of his immaturity thinks to settle the question of desirability by reiterated proclamation: "I want it, I want it, I want it." What is objected to in the current empirical theory of values is not connection of them with desire and enjoyment but failure to distinguish between enjoyments of radically different sorts. There are many common expressions in which the difference of the two kinds is clearly recognized. Take for example the difference between the ideas of "satisfying" and "satisfactory." To say that something satisfies is to report something as an isolated finality. To assert that it is satis*factory* is to define it in its connections and interactions. The fact that it pleases or is immediately congenial poses a problem to judgment. How shall the satisfaction be rated? Is it a value or is it not? Is it something to be prized and cherished, *to be* enjoyed? Not stern moralists alone but everyday experience informs us that finding satisfaction in a thing may be a warning, a summons to be on the lookout for consequences. To declare something satis*factory* is to assert that it meets specifiable conditions. It is, in effect, a judgment that the thing "will do." It involves a prediction; it contemplates a future in which the thing will continue to serve; it *will* do. It asserts a consequence the thing will actively institute; it will *do*. That it is satisfying is the content of a proposition of fact; that it is satisfactory is a judgment, an estimate, an appraisal. It denotes an attitude *to be* taken, that of striving to perpetuate and to make secure.[b]

2. The bare facts in which preferences are merely stated are, then, no more than the point of departure for the forming of value judgments. Only through examining the consequences of likings and dislikings can it be decided whether or not they are to be sought after. Otherwise expressed, the facts function as instruments for the construction of value judgments.

Propositions about what is or has been liked are of instrumental value in reaching judgments of value, in as far as the conditions and consequences of the thing liked are thought about. In themselves they make no claims; they put forth no demand upon subsequent attitudes and acts; they profess no authority to direct. If one likes a thing he likes it; that *is* a point about which there can be no dispute: — although it is not so easy to state just *what* is liked as is frequently assumed. A judgment about what is *to be* desired and enjoyed is, on the other hand, a claim on future action; it possesses *de jure* and not merely *de facto* quality. It is a matter of frequent experience that likings and enjoyments are of all kinds, and that many are such as reflective judgments condemn. By way of self-justification and "rationalization," an enjoyment creates a tendency to assert that the thing enjoyed is a value. This assertion of validity adds authority to the fact. It is a decision that the object has a right to exist and hence a claim upon action to further its existence. . . .

Not even the most devoted adherents of the notion that enjoy-ment and value are equivalent facts would venture to assert that because we have once liked a thing we should go on liking it; they are compelled to introduce the idea that *some* tastes are to be cultivated. Logically, there is no ground for introducing the idea of cultivation; liking is liking, and one is as good as another. If enjoyments *are* values, the judgment of value cannot regulate the form which liking takes; it cannot regulate its own conditions. Desire and purpose, and hence action, are left without guidance, although the question of regulation of their formation is the su-preme problem of practical life. Values (to sum up) may be con-nected inherently with liking, and yet not with *every* liking but only with those that judgment has approved, after examination of the relation upon which the object liked depends. A casual liking is one that happens without knowledge of how it occurs nor to what effect. The difference between it and one which is sought because of a judgment that it is worth having and is to be striven for, makes just the difference between enjoyments which are accidental and enjoyments that have value and hence a claim upon our attitude and conduct.[c]

3. Dewey then turns his attention from extreme empiricism to ex-treme rationalism. He criticizes it too from the standpoint of scientific standards. While empiricism fails to go beyond the mere facts of preference, rationalism in ethics is too far removed from the facts to be of practical use. Even in those cases where rationalism proposes concrete values, they are tied to the dead past. The penalty for failure to use scientific method in morals, as it is used in the study of the physical world, is the control of changes in values by arbitrary or accidental forces.

In any case, the alternative rationalistic theory does not afford the guidance for the sake of which eternal and immutable norms are appealed to. The scientist finds no help in determining the probable truth of some proposed theory by comparing it with a standard of absolute truth and immutable being. He has to rely upon definite operations undertaken under definite conditions — upon method. We can hardly imagine an architect getting aid in the construction of a building from an ideal at large, though we can understand his framing an ideal on the basis of knowledge of actual conditions and needs. Nor does the ideal of perfect beauty in antecedent Being give direction to a painter in producing a particular work of art. In morals, absolute perfection does not seem to be more than a generalized hypostatization of the recognition that there is a good to be sought, an obligation to be met — both being concrete matters. Nor is the defect in this respect merely negative. An examination of history would reveal, I am confident, that these general and remote schemes of value actually obtain a content definite enough and near enough to concrete situations as to afford guidance in action only by consecrating some institution or dogma already having social currency. Concreteness is gained, but it is by protecting from inquiry some accepted standard which perhaps is outworn and in need of criticism.

When theories of values do not afford intellectual assistance in framing ideas and beliefs about values that are adequate to direct action, the gap must be filled by other means. If intelligent method is lacking, prejudice, the pressure of immediate circumstance, self-interest and class-interest, traditional customs, institutions of accidental historic origin, are *not* lacking, and they tend to take the place of intelligence. Thus we are led to our main proposition: *Judgments about values are judgments about the conditions and the results of experienced objects; judgments about that which should regulate the formation of our desires, affections and enjoyments.* For whatever decides their formation will determine the main course of our conduct, personal and social. . . .

The time will come when it will be found passing strange that we of this age should take such pains to control by every means at command the formation of ideas of physical things, even those most remote from human concern, and yet are content with haphazard beliefs about the qualities of objects that regulate our deepest interests; that we are scrupulous as to methods of forming ideas of natural objects, and either dogmatic or else driven by immediate conditions in framing those about values. There is, by implication, if not explicitly, a prevalent notion that values are already well known and that all which is lacking is the will to cultivate them in the order of their worth. In fact the most profound lack is not the will to act upon goods already known but the will to know what they are.

It is not a dream that it is possible to exercise some degree of regulation of the occurrence of enjoyments which are of value. Realization of the possibility is exemplified, for example, in the technologies and arts of industrial life — that is, up to a definite limit. Men desired heat, light, and speed of transit and of communication beyond what nature provides of itself. These things have been attained not by lauding the enjoyment of these things and preaching their desirability, but by study of the conditions of their manifestation. Knowledge of relations having been obtained, ability to produce followed, and enjoyment ensued as a matter of course.[d]

4. In physical science, it is realized that knowledge of an object increases as more of its connections and interactions are understood. However, in social science, there is a tendency to ignore the study of the conditions under which values arise, change, and become obsolete. *This is the result of the traditional view that technological skills are inferior to moral skills and of the erroneous assumption that we already know what is valuable.*

With respect to [technological skills] there is no assumption that they can be had and enjoyed without definite operative knowledge. With respect to them it is also clear that the degree in which we value them is measurable by the pains taken to control the conditions of their occurrence. With respect to the latter, it is assumed that no one who is honest can be in doubt what they are; that by revelation, or conscience, or the instruction of others, or immediate feeling, they are clear beyond question. And instead of action in their behalf being taken to be a measure of the extent in which things *are* values to us, it is assumed that the difficulty is to persuade men to act upon what they already know to be good. Knowledge of conditions and consequences is regarded as wholly indifferent to judging what is of serious value, though it is useful in a prudential way in trying to actualize it. In consequence, the existence of values that are by common consent of a secondary and technical sort are under a fair degree of control, while those denominated supreme and imperative are subject to all the winds of impulse, custom and arbitrary authority.

This distinction between higher and lower types of value is itself something to be looked into. Why should there be a sharp division made between some goods as physical and material and others as ideal and "spiritual"? The question touches the whole dualism of the material and the ideal at its root. To denominate anything "matter" or "material" is not in truth to disparage it. It is, if the designation is correctly applied, a way of indicating that the thing in question is a condition or means of the existence of something else. And disparagement of effective means is practically synonymous with disregard of the things that are termed, in eulogistic fashion, ideal and spiritual. For the latter terms if they have any concrete application at all signify something which is a desirable consummation of conditions, a cherished fulfillment of means. The sharp separation between material and ideal good thus deprives the latter of the underpinning of effective support while it opens the way for treating things which should be employed as means as ends in themselves. For since men cannot after all live without some measure of possession of such matters as health and wealth, the latter things will be viewed as values and ends in isolation unless they are treated as integral constituents of the goods that are deemed supreme and final.[e]

5. The transfer of scientific method from the physical sciences to the study of human affairs admittedly involves difficulties. These arise out of the fact that human behavior is more complex than the behavior of physical objects. However, Dewey rejects the view that there is a difference in kind between the physical world and human nature.

But this difference is not a ground for making a sharp division between the two, nor does it account for the fact that we make so little use of the experimental method of forming our ideas and beliefs about the concerns of man in his characteristic social relations. For this separation religions and philosophies must admit some responsibility. They have erected a distinction between a narrower scope of relations and a wider and fuller one into a difference of kind, naming one kind material, and the other mental and moral. They have charged themselves gratuitously with the office of diffusing belief in the necessity of the division, and with instilling contempt for the material as something inferior in kind in its intrinsic nature and worth. Formal philosophies undergo evaporation of their technical solid contents; in a thinner and more viable form they find their way into the minds of those who know nothing of their original forms. When these diffuse and, so to say, airy emanations re-crystallize in the popular mind they form a hard deposit of opinion that alters slowly and with great difficulty.

What difference would it actually make in the arts of conduct, personal and social, if the experimental theory were adopted not as a mere theory, but as a part of the working equipment of habitual attitudes on the part of everyone? It would be impossible, even were time given, to answer the question in adequate detail, just as men could not foretell in advance the consequences for knowledge of adopting the experimental method. It is the nature of the method that it has to be tried. But there are generic lines of difference which, within the limits of time at disposal, may be sketched.

Change from forming ideas and judgments of value on the basis of conformity to antecedent objects, to constructing enjoyable objects directed by knowledge of consequences, is a change from looking to the past to looking to the future. I do not for a moment suppose that the experiences of the past, personal and social, are of no importance. For without them we should not be able to frame any ideas whatever of the conditions under which objects are enjoyed nor any estimate of the consequences of esteeming and liking them. But past experiences are significant in giving us intellectual instrumentalities of judging just these points. They are tools, not finalities. Reflection upon what we have liked and have enjoyed is a necessity. But it tells us nothing about the *value* of these things until enjoyments are themselves reflectively controlled, or, until, as they are recalled, we form the best judgment possible about what led us to like this sort of thing and what has issued from the fact that we liked it.[f]

6. In presenting the underlying assumptions and general frame of reference of ethical experimentalism, Dewey attempts to clarify his attitude towards customary or traditional values. He is not suggesting the sweeping away of time-honored values. Rather, he is recommending the use of intelligent criticism for the sake of integrating values and behavior in the constantly changing context of human experience.

We are not, then, to get away from enjoyments experienced in the past and from recall of them, but from the notion that they are the arbiters of things to be further enjoyed. At present, the arbiter is found in the past, although there are many ways of interpreting what in the past is authoritative. Nominally, the most influential conception doubtless is that of a revelation once had or a perfect life once lived. Reliance upon precedent, upon institutions created in the past, especially in law, upon rules of morals that have come to us through unexamined customs, upon uncriticized tradition, are other forms of dependence. It is not for a moment suggested that we can get away from customs and established institutions. A mere break would doubtless result simply in chaos. But there is no danger of such a break. Mankind is too inertly conservative both by constitution and by education to give the idea of this danger actuality. What there is genuine danger of is that the force of new conditions will produce disruption externally and mechanically: this is an ever present danger. The prospect is increased, not mitigated, by that conservatism which insists upon the adequacy of old standards to meet new conditions. What is needed is intelligent examination of the consequences that are actually effected by inherited institutions and customs, in order that there may be intelligent consideration of the ways in which they are to be intentionally modified in behalf of generation of different consequences.

This is the significant meaning of transfer of experimental method from the technical field of physical experience to the wider field of human life. We trust the method in forming our beliefs about things not directly connected with human life. In effect, we distrust it in moral, political and economic affairs. In the fine arts, there are many signs of a change. In the past, such a change has often been an omen and precursor of changes in other human attitudes. But, generally speaking, the idea of actively adopting experimental method in social affairs, in the matters deemed of most enduring and ultimate worth, strikes most persons as a surrender of all standards and regulative authority. But in principle, experimental method does not signify random and aimless action; it implies direction by ideas and knowledge. The question at issue is a practical one. Are there in existence the ideas and the knowledge that permit experimental method to be effectively used in social interest and affairs? [g]

7. We must recognize that we require new ideas and facts to use the experimental method in ethics. If the uncritical acceptance of traditional values is to end, however, a substitute is needed which can provide sound moral standards. Dewey again turns to scientific method for a solution.

Where will regulation come from if we surrender familiar and traditionally prized values as our directive standards? Very largely from the findings of the natural sciences. For one of the effects of the separation drawn between knowledge and action is to deprive scientific knowledge of its proper service as a guide of conduct — except once more in those technological fields which have been degraded to an inferior rank. Of course, the complexity of the conditions upon which objects of human and liberal value depend is a great obstacle, and it would be too optimistic to say that we have as yet enough knowledge of the scientific type to enable us to regulate our judgments of value very extensively. But we have more knowledge than we try to put to use, and until we try more systematically we shall not know what are the important gaps in our sciences judged from the point of view of their moral and humane use.

For moralists usually draw a sharp line between the field of the natural sciences and the conduct that is regarded as moral. But a moral that frames its judgments of value on the basis of consequences must depend in a most intimate manner upon the conclusions of science. For the knowledge of the relations between changes which enable us to connect things as antecedents and consequences *is* science. The narrow scope which moralists often give to morals, their isolation of some conduct as virtuous and vicious from other large ranges of conduct, those having to do with health and vigor, business, education, with all the affairs in which desires and affection are implicated, is perpetuated by this habit of exclusion of the subject-matter of natural science from a rôle in formation of moral standards and ideals. The same attitude operates in the other direction to keep natural science a technical specialty, and it works unconsciously to encourage its use exclusively in regions where it can be turned to personal and class advantage, as in war and trade.[h]

8. The social implications of experimentalism in ethics are developed through a subtle criticism of subjectivism and egoism in ethical theories. Dewey includes in his criticism theories which are not ordinarily classified as subjective, e.g., philosophical realism, in which values are regarded as independent of human experience. However, Dewey makes the charge of subjectivism because, on such a view, moral improvement is made to depend solely upon changes within individuals; the social context of human activity and its definitive role in modifying values are neglected.

This constant throwing of emphasis back upon a change made in ourselves instead of one made in the world in which we live seems to me the essence of what is objectionable in "subjectivism." Its taint hangs about even Platonic realism with its insistent evangelical dwelling upon the change made within the mind by contemplation of the realm of essence, and its depreciation of action as transient and all but sordid — a concession to the necessities of organic existence. All the theories which put conversion "of the eye of the soul" in the place of a conversion of natural and social objects that modifies goods actually experienced, is a retreat and escape from existence — and this retraction into self is, once more, the heart of subjective egoisms. The typical example is perhaps the other-worldiness found in religions whose chief concern is with the salvation of the personal soul. But other-worldiness is found as well in estheticism and in all seclusion within ivory towers.

It is not in the least implied that change in personal attitudes, in the disposition of the "subject," is not of great importance. Such change, on the contrary, is involved in any attempt to modify the conditions of the environment. But there is a radical difference between a change in the self that is cultivated and valued as an end, and one that is a means to alteration, through action, of objective conditions. The Aristotelian-medieval conviction that highest bliss is found in contemplative possession of ultimate Being presents an ideal attractive to some types of mind; it sets forth a refined sort of enjoyment. It is a doctrine congenial to minds that despair of the effort involved in creation of a better world of daily experience. It is, apart from theological attachments, a doctrine sure to recur when social conditions are so troubled as to make actual endeavor seem hopeless. But the subjectivism so externally marked in modern thought as compared with ancient is either a development of the old doctrine under new conditions or is of merely technical import. The medieval version of the doctrine at least had the active support of a great social institution by means of which man could be brought into the state of mind that prepared him for ultimate enjoyment of eternal Being. It had a certain solidity and depth which is lacking in modern theories that would attain the result by merely emotional or speculative procedures, or by any means not demanding a change in objective existence so as to render objects of value more empirically secure.

The nature in detail of the revolution that would be wrought by carrying into the region of values the principle now embodied in scientific practice cannot be told; to attempt it would violate the fundamental idea that we know only after we have acted and in consequences of the outcome of action. But it would surely effect a transfer of attention and energy from the subjective to the objective. Men would think of themselves as agents not as ends; ends would be found in experienced enjoyment of the fruits of a transforming activity.[i]

9. Thus far, two of the changes that would result from the application of experimentalism to ethics have been sketched, viz., *the change of perspective from past to future and the change of emphasis from the subjective to the objective.*

A third significant change that would issue from carrying over experimental method from physics to man concerns the import of standards, principles, rules. With the transfer, these, and all tenets and creeds about good and goods, would be recognized to be hypotheses. Instead of being rigidly fixed, they would be treated as intellectual instruments to be tested and confirmed — and altered — through consequences effected by acting upon them. They would lose all pretence of finality — the ulterior source of dogmatism. It is both astonishing and depressing that so much of the energy of mankind has gone into fighting for (with weapons of the flesh as well as of the spirit) the truth of creeds, religious, moral and political, as distinct from what has gone into effort to try creeds by putting them to the test of acting upon them. The change would do away with the intolerance and fanaticism that attend the notion that beliefs and judgments are capable of inherent truth and authority; inherent in the sense of being independent of what they lead to when used as directive principles. The transformation does not imply merely that men are responsible for acting upon what they profess to believe; that is an old doctrine. It goes much further. Any belief as such is tentative, hypothetical; it is not just to be acted upon, but is to be *framed* with reference to its office as a guide to action. Consequently, it should be the last thing in the world to be picked up casually and then clung to rigidly. When it is apprehended as a tool and only a tool, an instrumentality of direction, the same scrupulous attention will go to its formation as now goes into the making of instruments of precision in technical fields. Men, instead of being proud of accepting and asserting beliefs and "principles" on the ground of loyalty, will be as ashamed of that procedure as they would now be to confess their assent to a scientific theory out of reverence for Newton or Helmholz or whomever, without regard to evidence.

If one stops to consider the matter, is there not something strange in the fact that men should consider loyalty to "laws," principles, standards, ideals to be an inherent virtue, accounted unto them for righteousness? It is as if they were making up for some secret sense of weakness by rigidity and intensity of insistent attachment. A moral law, like a law in physics, is not something to swear by and stick to at all hazards; it is a formula of the way to respond when specified conditions present themselves. Its soundness and pertinence are tested by what happens when it is acted upon. Its claim or authority rests finally upon the imperativeness of the situation that has to be dealt with, not upon its own intrinsic nature — as any tool achieves dignity in the measure of needs served by it. The idea that adherence to standards external to experienced objects is the only alternative to confusion and lawlessness was once held in science. But knowledge became steadily progressive when it was abandoned, and clews and tests found within concrete acts and objects were employed. The test of consequences is more exacting than that afforded by fixed general rules. In addition, it secures constant development, for when new acts are tried new results are experienced, while the lauded immutability of eternal ideals and norms is in itself a denial of the possibility of development and improvement.[j]

10. In elaborating the change of attitude towards ideals which would result from regarding them as hypotheses, Dewey deals with the question of the relation of means *to* ends. *The observed discrepancies between ideals and actual behavior may be interpreted as a consequence of the persistent separation of means from ends.*

The various modifications that would result from adoption in social and humane subjects of the experimental way of thinking are perhaps summed up in saying that it would place *method and means* upon the level of importance that has, in the past, been imputed exclusively to ends. Means have been regarded as menial, and the useful as the servile. Means have been treated as poor relations to be endured, but not inherently welcome. The very meaning of the word "ideals" is significant of the divorce which has obtained between means and ends. "Ideals" are thought to be remote and inaccessible of attainment; they are too high and fine to be sullied by realization. They serve vaguely to arouse "aspiration," but they do not evoke and direct strivings for embodiment in actual existence. They hover in an indefinite way over the actual scene; they are expiring ghosts of a once significant kingdom of divine reality whose rule penetrated to every detail of life.

It is impossible to form a just estimate of the paralysis of effort that has been produced by indifference to means. Logically, it is truistic that lack of consideration for means signifies that so-called ends are not taken seriously. It is as if one professed devotion to painting pictures conjoined with contempt for canvas, brush and paints; or love of music on condition that no instruments, whether the voice or something external, be used to make sounds. The good workman in the arts is known by his respect for his tools and by his interest in perfecting his technique. The glorification in the arts of ends at the expense of means would be taken to be a sign of complete insincerity or even insanity. Ends separated from means are either sentimental indulgences or if they happen to exist are merely accidental. The ineffectiveness in action of "ideals" is due precisely to the supposition that means and ends are not on exactly the same level with respect to the attention and care they demand.

It is however, much easier to point out the formal contradiction implied in ideals that are professed without equal regard for the instruments and techniques of their realization, than it is to appreciate the concrete ways in which belief in their separation has found its way into life and borne corrupt and poisonous fruits. The separation marks the form in which the traditional divorce of theory and practice has expressed itself in actual life. It accounts for the relative impotency of arts concerned with enduring human welfare. Sentimental attachment and subjective eulogy take the place of action. For there is no art without tools and instrumental agencies. But it also explains the fact that in actual behavior, energies devoted to matters nominally thought to be inferior, material and sordid, engross attention and interest. After a polite and pious deference has been paid to "ideals," men feel free to devote themselves to matters which are more immediate and pressing.[k]

11. An example of the dangers of separating means from ends is found in the contemporary economic scene. The assumption that the pursuit of high ideals is unrelated to a concern for material welfare is a time-honored but dangerous fallacy, Dewey points out. As a consequence of this view, economic activity is deprived of the guidance of moral values and moral values are deprived of their indispensable foundation in material welfare.

It is usual to condemn the amount of attention paid by people in general to material ease, comfort, wealth, and success gained by competition, on the ground that they give to mere means the attention that ought to be given to ends, or that they have taken for ends things which in reality are only means. Criticisms of the place which economic interest and action occupy in present life are full of complaints that men allow lower aims to usurp the place that belongs to higher and ideal values. The final source of the trouble is, however, that moral and spiritual "leaders" have propagated the notion that ideal ends may be cultivated in isolation from "material" means, as if means and material were not synonymous. While they condemn men for giving to means the thought and energy that ought to go to ends, the condemnation should go to them. For they have not taught their followers to think of material and economic activities as *really* means. They have been unwilling to frame their conception of the values that should be regulative of human conduct on the basis of the actual conditions and operations by which alone values can be actualized.

Practical needs are imminent; with the mass of mankind they are imperative. Moreover, speaking generally, men are formed to act rather than to theorize. Since the ideal ends are so remotely and accidently connected with immediate and urgent conditions that need attention, after lip service is given to them, men naturally devote themselves to the latter. If a bird in the hand is worth two in a neighboring bush, an actuality in hand is worth, for the direction of conduct, many ideals that are so remote as to be invisible and inaccessible. Men hoist the banner of the ideal, and then march in the direction that concrete conditions suggest and reward. . . .

The present state of industrial life seems to give a fair index of the existing separation of means and ends. Isolation of economics from ideal ends, whether of morals or of organized social life, was proclaimed by Aristotle. Certain things, he said, are conditions of a worthy life, personal and social, but are not constituents of it. The economic life of man, concerned with satisfaction of wants, is of this nature. Men have wants and they must be satisfied. But they are only prerequisites of a good life, not intrinsic elements in it. Most philosophers have not been so frank nor perhaps so logical. But upon the whole, economics has been treated as on a lower level than either morals or politics. Yet the life which men, women and children actually lead, the opportunities open to them, the values they are capable of enjoying, their education, their share in all the things of art and science, are mainly determined by economic conditions. Hence we can hardly expect a moral system which ignores economic conditions to be other than remote and empty.

Industrial life is correspondingly brutalized by failure to equate it as the means by which social and cultural values are realized. That the economic life, thus exiled from the pale of higher values, takes revenge by declaring that it is the only social reality, and by means of the doctrine of materialistic determinism of institutions and conduct in all fields, denies to deliberate morals and politics any share of causal regulation, is not surprising.

When economists were told that their subject-matter was merely material, they naturally thought they could be "scientific" only by excluding all reference to distinctively human values. Material wants, efforts to satisfy them, even the scientifically regulated technologies highly developed in industrial activity, are then taken to form a complete and closed field. If any reference to social ends and values is introduced it is by way of an external addition, mainly hortatory. That economic life largely determines the conditions under which mankind has access to concrete values may be recognized or it may not be. In either case, the notion that it is the means to be utilized in order to secure significant values as the common and shared possession of mankind is alien and inoperative. To many persons, the idea that the ends professed by morals are impotent save as they are connected with the working machinery of economic life seems like deflowering the purity of moral values and obligations.[1]

12. The relation of means to ends raises again the problem of the lack of integration in contemporary moral life. The "split personality" of present-day ethics may be remedied by bringing together means and ends, theory and practice. What is needed is action guided by intelligent thinking, rather than ineffectual appeals to "good intentions."

Deliberate insincerity and hypocrisy are rare. But the notion that action and sentiment are inherently unified in the constitution of human nature has nothing to justify it. Integration is something to be achieved. Division of attitudes and responses, compartmentalizing of interests, is easily acquired. It goes deep just because the acquisition is unconscious, a matter of habitual adaptation to conditions. Theory separated from concrete doing and making is empty and futile; practice then becomes an immediate seizure of opportunities and enjoyments which conditions afford without the direction which theory — knowledge and ideas — has power to supply. The problem of the relation of theory and practice is not a problem of theory alone; it is that, but it is also the most practical problem of life. For it is the question of how intelligence may inform action, and how action may bear the fruit of increased insight into meaning: a clear view of the values that are worth while and of the means by which they are to be made secure in experienced objects. Construction of ideals in general and their sentimental glorification are easy; the responsibilities both of studious thought and of action are shirked. Persons having the advantage of positions of leisure and who find pleasure in abstract theorizing — a most delightful indulgence to those to whom it appeals — have a large measure of liability for a cultivated diffusion of ideals and aims that are separated from the conditions which are the means of actualization. Then other persons who find themselves in positions of social power and authority readily claim to be the bearers and defenders of ideal ends in church and state. They then use the prestige and authority their representative capacity as guardians of the highest ends confers on them to cover actions taken in behalf of the harshest and narrowest of material ends.[m]

13. In concluding his discussion, Dewey attempts to estimate the responsibility of philosophers and theologians for the lag of ethics behind technology. He looks upon the traditional ethical systems as expressing rather than as creating the preference for values which are placed beyond criticism or modification. In any case, Dewey is convinced that the proved effectiveness of the methods of science makes the traditional approach superfluous.

The social and moral effects of the separation of theory and practice have been merely hinted at. They are so manifold and so pervasive that an adequate consideration of them would involve nothing less than a survey of the whole field of morals, economics and politics. It cannot be justly stated that these effects are in fact direct consequences of the quest for certainty by thought and knowledge isolated from action. For, as we have seen, this quest was itself a reflex product of actual conditions. But it may be truly asserted that this quest, undertaken in religion and philosophy, has had results which have reinforced the conditions which originally brought it about. Moreover, search for safety and consolation amid the perils of life by means other than intelligent action, by feeling and thought alone, began when actual means of control were lacking, when arts were undeveloped. It had then a relative historic justification that is now lacking. The primary problem for thinking which lays claim to be philosophic in its breadth and depth is to assist in bringing about a reconstruction of all beliefs rooted in a basic separation of knowledge and action; to develop a system of operative ideas congruous with present knowledge and with present facilities of control over natural events and energies.[n]

Questions

1. What does Dewey regard as the basic moral problem of modern life? What does he propose as a solution to this critical problem?
2. Explain what is meant by a "value" in Dewey's ethics. How are "values" and "facts" related?
3. What are Dewey's criticisms of (a) extreme empiricism and (b) extreme rationalism? Give examples of theories containing these views.
4. Discuss the distinction Dewey draws between the "desired" and the "desirable." Why does he find it necessary to make this contrast?
5. How does Dewey explain the lag of social science behind physical science? In what ways are traditional philosophies responsible for this situation?
6. What is Dewey's attitude towards customary moral values? How can scientific method affect the selection of ethical standards?
7. Describe the changes which would result from the introduction of experimentalism into ethics.
8. Discuss Dewey's theory of means and ends. How would he judge the belief that "the end justifies the means"?
9. What advantages does Dewey anticipate from the application of scientific method to ethics? Do you agree with him that (a) it is possible to have a scientific theory of ethics, and (b) if it is possible, it would be beneficial?
10. What are the implications of Dewey's theory of value for (a) education, (b) society, and (c) political organization?

Key to selections:

JOHN DEWEY, *The Quest for Certainty*, New York, Minton, Balch and Company, 1929, Chapter X. With the kind permission of the publishers, G. P. Putnam's Sons.

[a] p. 255.	[e] pp. 269–70.
[b] pp. 260–1.	[f] pp. 271–2.
[c] pp. 262–3, 263–4.	[g] pp. 272–3.
	[h] pp. 273–4.
[d] pp. 264–5, 268–9.	[i] pp. 275–6.
	[j] pp. 277–8.

[k] pp. 278–80.   [m] pp. 281–2.
[l] pp. 280–1,   [n] pp. 283–4.
   282–3.

Guide to Additional Reading

INEXPENSIVE EDITIONS:

DEWEY, J., *Human Nature and Conduct*, Modern Library (Random House).

——, *Intelligence in the Modern World: John Dewey's Philosophy*, Modern Library (Random House).

——, *Reconstruction in Philosophy*, Mentor (New American Library).

——, *Theory of Valuation*, Foundations of the Unity of Science (University of Chicago Press).

DISCUSSION AND COMMENTARY:

Bernstein, R., *John Dewey*, New York, Washington Square Press, 1966.

Hook, S., *John Dewey: An Intellectual Portrait*, New York, John Day Company, 1939.

Ratner, J., "Introduction to John Dewey's Philosophy," *Intelligence in the Modern World*, New York, Modern Library, Random House, Inc., 1939.

Schilpp, P. A., (ed.), *The Philosophy of John Dewey*, Library of Living Philosophers, Evanston and Chicago, Northwestern University, 1939.

CHAPTER **15**

The Indefinability of Good

G. E. MOORE

Geoge Edward Moore (1873–1958) was Emeritus Professor of Philosophy at Cambridge University, with which he had been affiliated almost continuously since he entered it as an undergraduate in 1892. His association with his brilliant fellow-student, Bertrand Russell, was a decisive factor in Moore's entering the field of philosophy. He studied under such outstanding teachers of philosophy as Henry Sidgwick, James Ward, and J. E. McTaggart. Honored as one of the most influential of contemporary ethical theorists, Moore was invited to lecture in the United States. He was a visiting professor at Smith College in 1940, and, enjoying his new environment, he remained in the country for several years. He taught at Princeton University, Mills College, and Columbia University and lectured at other major American universities. Between 1921 and 1947, Moore served as editor of the distinguished philosophical journal, *Mind*. His most important works are *Principia Ethica* (1903), *Ethics* (1912), and *Philosophical Studies* (1922).

•

In his *Principia Ethica*, G. E. Moore effects a significant reorientation in ethics and sets the pattern for the modern "analytic movement" in philosophy. Instead of constructing a philosophical system in the traditional way, he starts with an *analysis of the fundamental philosophical questions*. While his conclusions are not shared by all twentieth-century philosophers, there are few who fail to acknowledge the importance of analyzing the basic questions prior to constructing a philosophical system. As Moore puts it:

It appears to me that in Ethics, as in all other philosophical studies, the difficulties and disagreements, of which its history is full, are mainly due to a very simple cause: namely to the attempt to answer questions, without first discovering precisely *what* question it is which you desire to answer. I do not know how far this source of error would be done away, if philosophers would *try* to discover what question they were asking, before they set about to answer it; for the work of analysis and distinction is often very difficult: we may often fail to make the necessary discovery, even though we make a definite attempt to do so. But I am inclined to think that in many cases a resolute attempt would be sufficient to ensure success; so that, if only this attempt were made, many of the most glaring difficulties and disagreements in philosophy would disappear.[a]

Moore points out that traditionally, ethical theorists have taken as primary the unanalyzed question, "What is intrinsically good?" — that is, what is good unconditionally and invariably? By failing to perceive that this is in fact a complex issue, they have given answers which have been for the most part futile and obscure. Moore finds, upon analysis, that the question is in fact two questions, *viz.*, "How is 'good' to be defined?" and "What things are good?" He insists that we must deal with the former before we address ourselves to the latter.

In order to discover whether it is possible to define the term "good," Moore reviews the principal techniques of definition:

(1) definition by example or illustration (*e.g.*, a "conifer" is such a tree as a pine, fir, or hemlock); (2) definition by synonym (*e.g.*, a "spinster" is an "unmarried woman"); and (3) definition by description (*e.g.*, a "tiger" is a large Asiatic carnivorous mammal of the cat family, of a tawny color, transversely striped with black). For the purpose of defining "good," he finds definitions which point to examples or cite illustrations unsatisfactory, since these deal with *things* that are "good," not with the *meaning* of the word. Likewise, definitions which present synonymous expressions for "good" evade the real issue, because they merely substitute one set of words for another without *identifying the property* to which they refer. The final alternative, defining "good" through description, also fails, Moore tells us, because it is not possible to discover any collection of different qualities and properties referred to by the term. Then, since no known mode of definition is satisfactory, and yet the term has meaning, he concludes that "good" is *indefinable*. It follows that the term "good" refers to a simple property of things — *it is a primitive and irreducible quality*. Moore insists, however, that while "good" cannot itself be defined, all other ethical terms can be defined through it.

The conception of the indefinability of the good in Moore's ethical theory is augmented by the doctrine of "ethical realism." According to this doctrine, there are ethical properties which exist independently of human consciousness. For Moore, goodness is such a property. It exists in the real world, apart from the desires and aversions, the pleasures and pains of human beings.

The term "good" refers to a quality which is analogous in some ways to sensory qualities. The philosophical realist maintains that when we speak of a sensory quality, as when we say, "The apple is red," the word "red" is not the name of a particular kind of *experience*, but is the name of an *objectively real property* of the apple. The property, though clearly not the experience, is independent of human perception. In Moore's ethical theory, however, the analogy is not carried beyond this point, because goodness, unlike sensory qualities, cannot be imagined "as existing *by itself* in time." The objective reality of goodness consists in its being *intrinsic, i.e.,* it is *unchanging* and *absolute,* in the sense that "when anything possesses it . . . it would *necessarily* or *must* always, under all circumstances, possess it in exactly the same degree." [1]

Moore regards statements in ethics as essentially of the same kind as any other statements about reality; the certification of their truth or falsity depends upon either *self-evidence* or *external evidence.* Such a statement as "Personal affection is good" is regarded by Moore as self-evidently true. By contrast, he believes that the truth of propositions of the form, "All men desire happiness," can only be established by external evidence. Asserting that the fundamental propositions of ethics are of the former variety, he attempts to clarify the meaning which he attaches to the notion of "self-evidence" in the following manner:

> The expression 'self-evident' means properly that the proposition so called is evident or true, *by itself* alone; that it is not an inference from some proposition other than *itself.* The expression does *not* mean that the proposition is true, because it is evident to you or me or all mankind, because in other words it appears to us to be true. That a proposition appears to be true can never be a valid argument that true it really is. By saying that a proposition is self-evident, we mean emphatically that its appearing so to us, is *not* the reason why it is true: for we mean that it has absolutely no reason.[b]

In sum, the result of Moore's analysis of the primary ethical question, "How is 'good' to be defined?" is: the term "good" is meaningful, yet indefinable; it refers to an independently existent quality, yet it is unlike the natural qualities of the sensory world; and, finally, certain propositions containing the term "good" are true by self-evidence, even though they may not be known by any individual.

· · ·

1. Moore begins his discussion of ethics by rejecting the conception of ethics as an examination of human conduct. He argues that it is "the general enquiry into what is good."

[1] G. E. Moore, *Philosophical Studies,* Kegan Paul, Trench, Trubner Co., Ltd., London, 1922, p. 273.

It is very easy to point out some among our every-day judgments, with the truth of which Ethics is undoubtedly concerned. Whenever we say, 'So and so is a good man,' or 'That fellow is a villain'; whenever we ask, 'What ought I to do?' or 'Is it wrong for me to do like this?'; whenever we hazard such remarks as 'Temperance is a virtue and drunkenness a vice' — it is undoubtedly the business of Ethics to discuss such questions and such statements; to argue what is the true answer when we ask what it is right to do, and to give reasons for thinking that our statements about the character of persons or the morality of actions are true or false. In the vast majority of cases, where we make statements involving any of the terms 'virtue,' 'vice,' 'duty,' 'right,' 'ought,' 'good,' 'bad,' we are making ethical judgments; and if we wish to discuss their truth, we shall be discussing a point of Ethics.

So much as this is not disputed; but it falls very far short of defining the province of Ethics. That province may indeed be defined as the whole truth about that which is at the same time common to all such judgments and peculiar to them. But we have still to ask the question: What is it that is thus common and peculiar? And this is a question to which very different answers have been given by ethical philosophers of acknowledged reputation, and none of them, perhaps, completely satisfactory.

If we take such examples as those given above, we shall not be far wrong in saying that they are all of them concerned with the question of 'conduct' — with the question, what, in the conduct of us, human beings, is good, and what is bad, what is right, and what is wrong. For when we say that a man is good, we commonly mean that he acts rightly; when we say that drunkenness is a vice, we commonly mean that to get drunk is a wrong or wicked action. And this discussion of human conduct is, in fact, that with which the name 'Ethics' is most intimately associated. It is so associated by derivation; and conduct is undoubtedly by far the commonest and most generally interesting object of ethical judgments.

Accordingly, we find that many ethical philosophers are disposed to accept as an adequate definition of 'Ethics' the statement that it deals with the question what is good or bad in human conduct. They hold that its enquiries are properly confined to 'conduct' or to 'practice'; they hold that the name 'practical philosophy' covers all the matter with which it has to do. Now, without discussing the proper meaning of the word (for verbal questions are properly left to the writers of dictionaries and other persons interested in literature; philosophy, as we shall see, has no concern with them), I may say that I intend to use 'Ethics' to cover more than this — a usage, for which there is, I think, quite sufficient authority. I am using it to cover an enquiry for which, at all events, there is no other word: the general enquiry into what is good.

Ethics is undoubtedly concerned with the question what good conduct is; but, being concerned with this, it obviously does not start at the beginning, unless it is prepared to tell us what is good as well as what is conduct. For 'good conduct' is a complex notion: all conduct is not good; for some is certainly bad and some may be indifferent. And on the other hand, other things, beside conduct, may be good; and if they are so, then, 'good' denotes some property, that is common to them and conduct; and if we examine good conduct alone of all good things, then we shall be in danger of mistaking for this property, some property which is not shared by those other things: and thus we shall have made a mistake about Ethics even in this limited sense; for we shall not know what good conduct really is. This is a mistake which many writers have actually made, from limiting their enquiry to conduct. And hence I shall try to avoid it by considering first what is good in general; hoping, that if we can arrive at any certainty about this, it will be much easier to settle the question of good conduct: for we all know pretty well what 'conduct' is. This, then, is our first question: What is good? and What is bad? and to the discussion of this question (or these questions) I give the name of Ethics, since that science must, at all events, include it.[c]

2. Having stated his task in a general way, Moore finds it necessary to remove any remaining misconceptions about the nature of the analysis in which he is engaging. He begins with an examination of the question, "What is good?"

But this is a question which may have many meanings. If, for example, each of us were to say 'I am doing good now' or 'I had a good dinner yesterday,' these statements would each of them be some sort of answer to our question, although perhaps a false one. So, too, when A asks B what school he ought to send his son to, B's answer will certainly be an ethical judgment. And similarly all distribution of praise or blame to any personage or thing that has existed, now exists, or will exist, does give some answer to the question 'What is good?' In all such cases some particular thing is judged to be good or bad: the question 'what?' is answered by 'This.' But this is not the sense in which a scientific Ethics asks the question. Not one, of all the many million answers of this kind, which must be true, can form a part of an ethical system; although that science must contain reasons and principles sufficient for deciding on the truth of all of them. There are far too many persons, things and events in the world, past, present, or to come, for a discussion of their individual merits to be embraced in any science. Ethics, therefore, does not deal at all with facts of this nature, facts that are unique, individual, absolutely particular; facts with which such studies as history, geography, astronomy, are compelled, in part at least, to deal. And, for this reason, it is not the business of the ethical philosopher to give personal advice or exhortation.

But there is another meaning which may be given to the question 'What is good?' 'Books are good' would be an answer to it, though an answer obviously false; for some books are very bad indeed. And ethical judgments of this kind do indeed belong to Ethics; though I shall not deal with many of them. Such is the judgment 'Pleasure is good' — a judgment, of which Ethics should discuss the truth, although it is not nearly as important as that other judgment, with which we shall be much occupied presently — 'Pleasure *alone* is good.' It is judgments of this sort, which are made in such books on Ethics as contain a list of 'virtues' — in Aristotle's 'Ethics' for example.[d]

3. After clarifying the nature of the basic ethical question, Moore emphasizes its primacy for any ethical inquiry.

But our question 'What is good?' may have still another meaning. We may . . . mean to ask, not what thing or things are good, but how 'good' is to be defined. This is an enquiry which belongs only to Ethics . . . and this is the enquiry which will occupy us first.

It is an enquiry to which most special attention should be directed; since this question, how 'good' is to be defined, is the most fundamental question in all Ethics. That which is meant by 'good' is, in fact, except its converse 'bad,' the *only* simple object of thought which is peculiar to Ethics. Its definition is, therefore, the most essential point in the definition of Ethics; and moreover a mistake with regard to it entails a far larger number of erroneous ethical judgments than any other. Unless this first question be fully understood, and its true answer clearly recognised, the rest of Ethics is as good as useless from the point of view of systematic knowledge.[e]

4. Moore discusses the inadequacy of defining "good" by the techniques upon which traditional ethical theorists have relied. He concludes that there is no way to define "good."

What, then, is good? How is good to be defined? Now, it may be thought that this is a verbal question. A definition does indeed often mean the expressing of one word's meaning in other words. But this is not the sort of definition I am asking for. Such a definition can never be of ultimate importance in any study except lexicography. If I wanted that kind of definition I should have to consider in the first place how people generally used the word 'good'; but my business is not with its proper usage, as established by custom. I should, indeed, be foolish, if I tried to use it for something which it did not usually denote: if, for instance, I were to announce that, whenever I used the word 'good,' I must be understood to be thinking of that object which is usually denoted by the word 'table.' I shall, therefore, use the word in the sense

in which I think it is ordinarily used; but at the same time I am
not anxious to discuss whether I am right in thinking that it is
so used. My business is solely with that object or idea, which I
hold, rightly or wrongly, that the word is generally used to stand
for. What I want to discover is the nature of that object or idea,
and about this I am extremely anxious to arrive at an agreement.

But, if we understand the question in this sense, my answer to
it may seem a very disappointing one. If I am asked 'What is
good?' my answer is that good is good, and that is the end of the
matter. Or if I am asked 'How is good to be defined?' my answer
is that it cannot be defined, and that is all I have to say about it.
But disappointing as these answers may appear, they are of the
very last importance. To readers who are familiar with philosophic
terminology, I can express their importance by saying that they
amount to this: That propositions about the good are all of them
synthetic and never analytic; and that is plainly no trivial matter.
And the same thing may be expressed more popularly, by saying
that, if I am right, then nobody can foist upon us such an axiom
as that 'Pleasure is the only good' or that 'The good is the desired' on the pretence that this is 'the very meaning of the word.'

Let us, then, consider this position. My point is that 'good' is a
simple notion, just as 'yellow' is a simple notion; that, just as you
cannot, by any manner of means, explain to any one who does
not already know it, what yellow is, so you cannot explain what
good is. Definitions of the kind that I was asking for, definitions
which describe the real nature of the object or notion denoted by
a word, and which do not merely tell us what the word is used to
mean, are only possible when the object or notion in question is
something complex. You can give a definition of a horse, because
a horse has many different properties and qualities, all of which
you can enumerate. But when you have enumerated them all,
when you have reduced a horse to his simplest terms, then you
can no longer define those terms. They are simply something
which you think of or perceive, and to any one who cannot think
of or perceive them, you can never, by any definition, make their
nature known. It may perhaps be objected to this that we are

able to describe to others, objects which they have never seen or thought of. We can, for instance, make a man understand what a chimaera is, although he has never heard of one or seen one. You can tell him that it is an animal with a lioness's head and body, with a goat's head growing from the middle of its back, and with a snake in place of a tail. But here the object which you are describing is a complex object; it is entirely composed of parts, with which we are all perfectly familiar — a snake, a goat, a lioness; and we know, too, the manner in which those parts are to be put together, because we know what is meant by the middle of a lioness's back, and where her tail is wont to grow. And so it is with all objects, not previously known, which we are able to define: they are all complex; all composed of parts, which may themselves, in the first instance, be capable of similar definition, but which must in the end be reducible to simplest parts, which can no longer be defined. But yellow and good, we say, are not complex: they are notions of that simple kind, out of which definitions are composed and with which the power of further defining ceases.[f]

5. The distinction between the property *designated by the term "good" and* things *which have this property is re-emphasized. Since the term "good" denotes a simple and unanalyzable property, it is indefinable. However, it does not follow from this that objects or activities which "possess" this property cannot be defined. On the contrary, they are complexes, and goodness is one of their specifiable characteristics.*

But I am afraid I have still not removed the chief difficulty which may prevent acceptance of the proposition that good is indefinable. I do not mean to say that *the* good, that which is good, is thus indefinable; if I did think so, I should not be writing on Ethics, for my main object is to help towards discovering that definition. It is just because I think there will be less risk of error in our search for a definition of 'the good,' that I am now insisting that *good* is indefinable. I must try to explain the difference between these two. I suppose it may be granted that 'good' is an adjective. Well 'the good,' 'that which is good,' must therefore be the substantive to which the adjective 'good' will apply: it must be the whole of that to which the adjective will apply, and the adjective must *always* truly apply to it. But if it is that to which the adjective will apply, it must be something different from that adjective itself; and the whole of that something different, whatever it is, will be our definition of *the* good. Now it may be that this something will have other adjectives, beside 'good,' that will apply to it. It may be full of pleasure, for example; it may be intelligent: and if these two adjectives are really part of its definition, then it will certainly be true, that pleasure and intelligence are good. And many people appear to think that, if we say 'Pleasure and intelligence are good,' or if we say 'Only pleasure and intelligence are good,' we are defining 'good.' Well, I cannot deny that propositions of this nature may sometimes be called definitions; I do not know well enough how the word is generally used to decide upon this point. I only wish it to be understood that that is not what I mean when I say there is no possible definition of good, and that I shall not mean this if I use the word again. I do most fully believe that some true proposition of the form 'Intelligence is good and intelligence alone is good' can be found; if none could be found, our definition of *the* good would be impossible. As it is, I believe *the* good to be definable; and yet I still say that good itself is indefinable.[g]

6. *If, as Moore holds, "good" is indefinable, theories which under-take to define it are subject to criticism. He characterizes as the* naturalistic fallacy *any attempt to define "good," whether as "the pleasant," "the desirable," "the rational," "that which is approved," or anything else.*

'Good,' then, if we mean by it that quality which we assert to belong to a thing, when we say that the thing is good, is incapable of any definition, in the most important sense of that word. The most important sense of 'definition' is that in which a definition states what are the parts which invariably compose a certain whole; and in this sense 'good' has no definition because it is simple and has no parts. It is one of those innumerable objects of thought which are themselves incapable of definition, because they are the ultimate terms by reference to which whatever *is* capable of definition must be defined. That there must be an indefinite number of such terms is obvious, on reflection; since we cannot define anything except by an analysis, which, when carried as far as it will go, refers us to something, which is simply different from anything else, and which by that ultimate difference explains the peculiarity of the whole which we are defining: for every whole contains some parts which are common to other wholes also. There is, therefore, no intrinsic difficulty in the contention that 'good' denotes a simple and indefinable quality. There are many other instances of such qualities.

Consider yellow, for example. We may try to define it, by describing its physical equivalent; we may state what kind of light-vibrations must stimulate the normal eye, in order that we may perceive it. But a moment's reflection is sufficient to shew that those light-vibrations are not themselves what we mean by yellow. *They* are not what we perceive. Indeed we should never have been able to discover their existence, unless we had first been struck by the patent difference of quality between the different colours. The most we can be entitled to say of those vibrations is that they are what corresponds in space to the yellow which we actually perceive.

Yet a mistake of this simple kind has commonly been made about 'good.' It may be true that all things which are good are *also* something else, just as it is true that all things which are yellow produce a certain kind of vibration in the light. And it is a fact, that Ethics aims at discovering what are those other properties belonging to all things which are good. But far too many philosophers have thought that when they named those other properties they were actually defining good; that these properties, in fact, were simply not 'other,' but absolutely and entirely the same with goodness. This view I propose to call the 'naturalistic fallacy' . . .[h]

7. Because of its great importance, Moore enlarges upon his discussion of the naturalistic fallacy through illustration.

I do not care about the name: what I do care about is the fallacy. It does not matter what we call it, provided we recognise it when we meet with it. It is to be met with in almost every book on Ethics; and yet it is not recognised: and that is why it is necessary to multiply illustrations of it, and convenient to give it a name. It is a very simple fallacy indeed. When we say that an orange is yellow, we do not think our statements binds us to hold that 'orange' means nothing else than 'yellow,' or that nothing can be yellow but an orange. Supposing the orange is also sweet! Does that bind us to say that 'sweet' is exactly the same thing as 'yellow,' that 'sweet' must be defined as 'yellow'? And supposing it be recognised that 'yellow' just means 'yellow' and nothing else whatever, does that make it any more difficult to hold that oranges are yellow? Most certainly it does not: on the contrary, it would be absolutely meaningless to say that oranges were yellow, unless yellow did in the end mean just 'yellow' and nothing else whatever — unless it was absolutely indefinable. We should not get any very clear notion about things, which are yellow — we should not get very far with our science, if we were bound to hold that everything which was yellow, *meant* exactly the same thing as yellow. We should find we had to hold that an orange was exactly the same thing as a stool, a piece of paper, a lemon, anything you like. We could prove any number of absurdities; but should we be the nearer to the truth? Why, then, should it be different with 'good'? Why, if good is good and indefinable, should I be held to deny that pleasure is good? Is there any difficulty in holding both to be true at once? On the contrary, there is no meaning in saying that pleasure is good, unless good is something different from pleasure. It is absolutely useless, so far as Ethics is concerned, to prove, as Mr. Spencer tries to do, that increase of pleasure coincides with increase of life, unless good *means* something different from either life or pleasure. He might just as well try to prove that an orange is yellow by shewing that it always is wrapped up in paper.[i]

8. Moore elaborates on the essential arbitrariness of all definitions of "good" and illustrates the futility of attempting to resolve arguments in ethics through the agency of definitions. Those who engage in definitional polemics, he charges, are dealing in irrelevancies. Moreover, Moore points out that when an ethical theorist defines "good" as "pleasant," he automatically makes a triviality out of such a statement as, "those acts which produce pleasure are good," since this tells us nothing more than that "those acts which produce pleasure are pleasant."

Let us consider what it is such philosophers say. And first it is to be noticed that they do not agree among themselves. They not only say that they are right as to what good is, but they endeavour to prove that other people who say that it is something else, are wrong. One, for instance, will affirm that good is pleasure, another, perhaps, that good is that which is desired; and each of these will argue eagerly to prove that the other is wrong. But how is that possible? One of them says that good is nothing but the object of desire, and at the same time tries to prove that it is not pleasure. But from his first assertion, that good just means the object of desire, one of two things must follow as regards his proof:

(1) He may be trying to prove that the object of desire is not pleasure. But, if this be all, where is his Ethics? The position he is maintaining is merely a psychological one. Desire is something which occurs in our minds, and pleasure is something else which so occurs; and our would-be ethical philosopher is merely holding that the latter is not the object of the former. But what has that to do with the question in dispute? His opponent held the ethical proposition that pleasure was the good, and although he should prove a million times over the psychological proposition that pleasure is not the object of desire, he is no nearer proving his opponent to be wrong. The position is like this. One man says a triangle is a circle: another replies 'A triangle is a straight line, and I will prove to you that I am right: *for*' (this is the only argument) 'a straight line is not a circle.' 'That is quite true,' the

other may reply; 'but nevertheless a triangle is a circle, and you have said nothing whatever to prove the contrary. What is proved is that one of us is wrong, for we agree that a triangle cannot be both a straight line and a circle: but which is wrong, there can be no earthly means of proving, since you define triangle as straight line and I define it as circle.' — Well, that is one alternative which any naturalistic Ethics has to face; if good is *defined* as something else, it is then impossible either to prove that any other definition is wrong or even to deny such definition.

(2) The other alternative will scarcely be more welcome. It is that the discussion is after all a verbal one. When A says 'Good means pleasant' and B says 'Good means desired,' they may merely wish to assert that most people have used the word for what is pleasant and for what is desired respectively. And this is quite an interesting subject for discussion: only it is not a whit more an ethical discussion than the last was. Nor do I think that any exponent of naturalistic Ethics would be willing to allow that this was all he meant. They are all so anxious to persuade us that what they call the good is what we really ought to do. 'Do, pray, act so, because the word "good" is generally used to denote actions of this nature': such, on this view, would be the substance of their teaching. And in so far as they tell us how we ought to act, their teaching is truly ethical, as they mean it to be. But how perfectly absurd is the reason they would give for it! 'You are to do this, because most people use a certain word to denote conduct such as this.' 'You are to say the thing which is not, because most people call it lying.' That is an argument just as good! — My dear sirs, what we want to know from you as ethical teachers, is not how people use a word; it is not even, what kind of actions they approve, which the use of this word 'good' may certainly imply: what we want to know is simply what *is* good. We may indeed agree that what most people do think good, is actually so; we shall at all events be glad to know their opinions: but when we say their opinions about what *is* good, we do mean what we say; we do not care whether they call that thing which they mean 'horse' or 'table' or 'chair,' 'gut' or 'bon' or 'ἀγαθός'; we want to know

what it is that they so call. When they say 'Pleasure is good,'
we cannot believe that they merely mean 'Pleasure is pleasure'
and nothing more than that.ʲ

9. *He points out that if one does not accept the indefinability of*
"good," one must regard it either as a complex notion or as having no
meaning whatever. Moore insists that neither of these alternatives
fits the facts.

. . . If it is not the case that 'good' denotes something simple
and indefinable, only two alternatives are possible: either it is a
complex, a given whole, about the correct analysis of which there
may be disagreement; or else it means nothing at all, and there is
no such subject as Ethics. In general, however, ethical philosophers have attempted to define good, without recognising what such
an attempt must mean. They actually use arguments which involve one or both of the absurdities considered [in Section 8] . . .
We are, therefore, justified in concluding that the attempt to define good is chiefly due to want of clearness as to the possible nature of definition. There are, in fact, only two serious alternatives
to be considered, in order to establish the conclusion that 'good'
does denote a simple and indefinable notion. It might possibly
denote a complex, as 'horse' does; or it might have no meaning at
all. Neither of these possibilities has, however, been clearly conceived and seriously maintained, as such, by those who presume
to define good; and both may be dismissed by a simple appeal to
facts.

(1) The hypothesis that disagreement about the meaning of
good is disagreement with regard to the correct analysis of a given
whole, may be most plainly seen to be incorrect by consideration
of the fact that, whatever definition be offered, it may be always
asked, with significance, of the complex so defined, whether it is
itself good. To take, for instance, one of the more plausible, because one of the more complicated, of such proposed definitions,
it may easily be thought, at first sight, that to be good may mean
to be that which we desire to desire. Thus if we apply this definition to a particular instance and say 'When we think that A is

good, we are thinking that A is one of the things which we desire to desire,' our proposition may seem quite plausible. But, if we carry the investigation further, and ask ourselves 'Is it good to desire to desire A?' it is apparent, on a little reflection, that this question is itself as intelligible, as the original question 'Is A good?' — that we are, in fact, now asking for exactly the same information about the desire to desire A, for which we formerly asked with regard to A itself. But it is also apparent that the meaning of this second question cannot be correctly analysed into 'Is the desire to desire A one of the things which we desire to desire?': we have not before our minds anything so complicated as the question 'Do we desire to desire to desire to desire A?' Moreover any one can easily convince himself by inspection that the predicate of this proposition — 'good' — is positively different from the notion of 'desiring to desire' which enters into its subject: 'That we should desire to desire A is good' is *not* merely equivalent to 'That A should be good is good.' It may indeed be true that what we desire to desire is always also good; perhaps, even the converse may be true: but it is very doubtful whether this is the case, and the mere fact that we understand very well what is meant by doubting it, shews clearly that we have two different notions before our minds.

(2) And the same consideration is sufficient to dismiss the hypothesis that 'good' has no meaning whatsoever. It is very natural to make the mistake of supposing that what is universally true is of such a nature that its negation would be self-contradictory: the importance which has been assigned to analytic propositions in the history of philosophy shews how easy such a mistake is. And thus it is very easy to conclude that what seems to be a universal ethical principle is in fact an identical proposition; that, if, for example, whatever is called 'good' seems to be pleasant, the proposition 'Pleasure is the good' does not assert a connection between two different notions, but involves only one, that of pleasure, which is easily recognised as a distinct entity. But whoever will attentively consider with himself what is actually before his mind when he asks the question 'Is pleasure (or whatever it may be)

after all good?' can easily satisfy himself that he is not merely wondering whether pleasure is pleasant. And if he will try this experiment with each suggested definition in succession, he may become expert enough to recognise that in every case he has before his mind a unique object, with regard to the connection of which with any other object, a distinct question may be asked. Every one does in fact understand the question 'Is this good?' When he thinks of it, his state of mind is different from what it would be, were he asked 'Is this pleasant, or desired, or approved?' It has a distinct meaning for him, even though he may not recognise in what respect it is distinct. Whenever he thinks of 'intrinsic value,' or 'intrinsic worth,' or says that a thing 'ought to exist,' he has before his mind the unique object — the unique property of things — which I mean by 'good.' Everybody is constantly aware of this notion, although he may never become aware at all that it is different from other notions of which he is also aware. But, for correct ethical reasoning, it is extremely important that he should become aware of this fact; and, as soon as the nature of the problem is clearly understood, there should be little difficulty in advancing so far in analysis.[k]

10. Moore is now in a position to show the detrimental effect of the naturalistic fallacy upon investigation in ethics: it closes inquiry by defining in advance what things will be recognized as good, without shedding any light on the nature of intrinsic goodness. The avoidance of this fallacy is a necessary part of a "Prolegomena to any future Ethics that can possibly pretend to be scientific."

If . . . we once recognise that we must start our Ethics without a definition, we shall be much more apt to look about us, before we adopt any ethical principle whatever; and the more we look about us, the less likely are we to adopt a false one. It may be replied to this: Yes, but we shall look about us just as much, before we settle on our definition, and are therefore just as likely to be right. But I will try to shew that this is not the case. If we start with the conviction that a definition of good can be found, we start with the conviction that good *can mean* nothing else than some one property of things; and our only business will then be to discover what that property is. But if we recognise that, so far as the meaning of good goes, anything whatever may be good, we start with a much more open mind. Moreover, apart from the fact that, when we think we have a definition, we cannot logically defend our ethical principles in any way whatever, we shall also be much less apt to defend them well, even if illogically. For we shall start with the conviction that good must mean so and so, and shall therefore be inclined either to misunderstand our opponent's arguments or to cut them short with the reply, 'This is not an open question: the very meaning of the word decides it; no one can think otherwise except through confusion.' [1]

Questions

1. What new orientation in ethical theory is provided by Moore's *Principia Ethica?* What judgment of traditional ethics would be made if Moore's basic thesis were adopted?

2. Why does Moore maintain that "intrinsic good" is indefinable? Discuss critically his explanation of his position.

3. Give Moore's definition of the "naturalistic fallacy" and cite several illustrations.

4. How does Moore refute the hedonistic doctrine? Do you think his method is an effective one in ethics?

5. Comment upon Moore's view of the nature of self-evident propositions. What would happen to his general ethical theory if there were no self-evident ethical statements?

6. What is meant by "ethical realism"? Would you say that the average man is an ethical realist? Explain your answer, making reference to specific instances of ethical convictions.

7. In what respect can Moore's investigation in ethics be defended as open-minded? Is it logically possible to use his basic method, but reach different conclusions about the nature of ethics?

8. Why is the distinction between "properties of things" and "things having properties" a crucial one for Moore?

9. How would Moore respond to the following assertion of William

James: "There is no *status* for good and evil to exist in, in a purely insentient world."

10. Discuss in detail you opinion as to whether two men, convinced of the validity of Moore's ethical theory, could nevertheless have disputes at the level of practical morality.

Key to selections:

G. E. MOORE, *Principia Ethica*, New York, Cambridge University Press, 1948. With the kind permission of the publishers.

ª Preface, p. vii.	ᵍ pp. 8–9.
ᵇ p. 143.	ʰ pp. 9–10.
ᶜ pp. 1–3.	ⁱ pp. 14–15.
ᵈ pp. 3–4.	ʲ pp. 10–12.
ᵉ p. 5.	ᵏ pp. 15–17.
ᶠ pp. 6–8.	ˡ pp. 20–21.

Guide to Additional Reading

ADDITIONAL SOURCE MATERIAL:

MOORE, G. E., *Ethics*, Home University Library, New York, Henry Holt and Company, 1912.

——, *Philosophical Studies*, New York, Harcourt, Brace and Company, 1922, Chapters VIII, IX, and X.

——, Joseph, H. W. B., and Taylor, A. E., "Is Goodness a Quality?" *Aristotelian Society*, Supplementary vol. II, 1932.

DISCUSSION AND COMMENTARY:

Frankena, W. K., "The Naturalistic Fallacy," *Mind*, XLVIII (October, 1939), 464–67.

Mettrick, E. F., "G. E. Moore and Intrinsic Goodness," *International Journal of Ethics*, XXXVIII (July, 1928), 389–400.

Schilpp, P. A. (ed.), *The Philosophy of G. E. Moore*, Library of Living Philosophers, Evanston and Chicago, Northwestern University, 1939.

Warnock, M., *Ethics since 1900*, London, Oxford University Press, 1960.

Wright, H. W., "The Objectivity of Moral Values," *Philosophical Review* XXXII (July, 1923), 385–400.

CHAPTER 16

Prima Facie Duty

W. D. ROSS

Sir William David Ross (1877–1971) was born in Scotland and educated at both Edinburgh University and Balliol College, Oxford. Ross was not only an authority on Aristotle's philosophy but also a splendid example of Aristotle's "ideal man." Beyond Aristotelian scholarship and original contributions to on-going philosophy, his career included educational leadership at Oxford and roles in public affairs. In short, Ross combined theoretical and practical wisdom. His moral philosophy, found primarily in *The Right and the Good* (1930) and *Foundations of Ethics* (1939), has had lasting influence. He was awarded the Order of the British Empire for his service to Great Britain during World War I, and knighted in 1938.

·

The ethical theory of W. D. Ross resembles that of G. E. Moore in important ways. Both theories hold that intrinsic goodness is an indefinable quality of things; moreover, both theories hold that certain statements about objects being intrinsically good are self-evidently true.

There is a decisive difference between them, however, concerning the status of our concepts of the obligatory: In Moore's system the meanings of such terms as "right," "ought," and "duty" are linked to maximizing intrinsic goodness; in Ross's system there is no such linkage. Ross contends that rightness is a distinct, indefinable characteristic of acts, that it is generally independent of whatever good may result from their occurrence, and that certain statements about the acts being morally right are self-evidently true.[1]

In making his case for ethical intuitionism, Ross insists that the difference between what he terms *"prima facie"* and "actual" duties makes all the difference. He warns that any ethical theory which neglects drawing this distinction in some effective way is systematically directed toward either too much or too little definiteness in its account of obligation. Such a theory fails to fit the beliefs and actions of ordinary morality, beliefs and actions that seem reasonable despite the persuasive attacks against them by ethical theorists.

Consider: It is self-evidently true that if I make a promise to someone, or request and accept assistance from someone, I thereby create a moral claim on myself in that person. I know immediately and without question that I *ought* to keep that promise and that I *ought* to reciprocate in some way. Now Ross terms the kind of act which has the characteristic of generating moral claims as *"prima facie* duty."[2]

As just seen, Ross is an intuitionist in his doctrine of *prima facie* duty. But, as it turns out, this doctrine is more an account of the materials from which we must make a selection than it is an account of our actual obligations. In our daily lives, we are more frequently than not con-

---

[1]Ross was greatly influenced by his teacher H.A. Prichard (1871–1947). The latter maintained that some types of actions are right by their very nature and that one can apprehend when "something ought to be done" by a simple "act of moral thinking."

[2]Ross remarks: "I should make it plain. . .that I am assuming the correctness of some of our main convictions as to *prima facie* duties, or, more strictly, am claiming that we *know* them to be true. To me it seems as self-evident as anything could be, that to make a promise, for instance, is to create a moral claim on us in someone else. Many readers will perhaps say that they do *not* know this to be true. If so, I certainly cannot prove it to them: I can only ask them to reflect again, in the hope that they will ultimately agree that they know it." *The Right and the Good*, Oxford, Clarendon Press, 1930, pp. 20–21 fn.

fronted with conflicting and competing *prima facie* duties. Furthermore, we do not find it to be self-evidently true that one such duty rather than another necessarily has jurisdiction. I ought, for example, to honor my promise to be home early, but I ought also to stay late and speak encouragingly to a friend in distress. Where does my actual duty lie? Notice that we don't deny that there *are* conflicting duties here, but notice also that we want fuller knowledge of the context: Is an important purpose being served by my getting home early? How great is my friend's distress? Aren't other *prima facie* duties involved here? Our *prima facie* duties do not arise in a prearranged harmony of ranked priority nor do they occur singly. Ross contends that a person can only bring his imperfect knowledge of a situation to bear in making his decision, without any guarantee of an objectively correct answer. Our judgments about right action in all but the simplest actual cases are tentative rather than certain. The above-mentioned statement is not intended to deny that, in the abstract, some *prima facie* duties have a greater claim on us that others. As Ross insists, ". . .a great deal of stringency belongs to the duties of 'perfect obligation'–the duties of keeping our promises, of repairing wrongs we have done, and of returning the equivalent of services we have received." Ibid, pp. 41–42.

In the full development of his theory, Ross does deal specifically with the relationship between actual and *prima facie* duty. His answer is what one might expect: The actually right action is the one which "would discharge in the fullest possible measure the various claims or *prima facie* duties that are involved in the situation."[3] It should be noted, however, that, while this answer serves to clarify *what* we seek to realize, it affords little instruction about *how* we are to do so. It remains that the best that we can expect from anyone in a moral situation is a morally informed, carefully assessed judgment which is neither certain nor immediate.

Ross is at his most skillful in arguing that some positions about the nature of actual duties involve serious errors. At one extreme he finds infallible conscience theorists who subscribe to the view that we can always have immediate or direct knowledge of our actual duty. At the other, he finds utilitarians of various sorts who subscribe to the belief that there is only one criterion for determining our actual duty, whatever the

[3]W. D. Ross, *Foundations of Ethics,* Oxford, Clarendon Press, 1939, p. 190.

circumstances. Ross rejects the position of the former on several related grounds: one, it fails to take into account the complexity of the concrete situations in which we must act; two, it fails to face up to the fact that there are honest differences of opinion between men of good faith as to what ought to be done in a given context; three, it simply assumes that there is no problem about selecting one's actual duty from among the variety of moral claims simultaneously incumbent upon a person in a particular situation. He rejects the position of the latter on the ground that the single criterion upon which an actual obligation is supposed to rest—namely, whatever maximizes good—is both too simple for the diverse circumstances we face, and too restricted in its scope.

Ross's insistence that the utilitarian principle is restricted in its scope is of special importance in understanding his position. Put positively, he thinks that there is, indeed, a *prima facie* duty to be beneficent, but he observes that this *prima facie* duty, no less than others, occurs only in connection with certain concrete situations. Thus, there are circumstances in which, just as the utilitarians insist, beneficence takes precedence over all other considerations. By the same token, however, there are also circumstances in which the general welfare is beside the point, while one's honesty or integrity is very much to the point.

·

*1. Ross is convinced that ethical theories such as utilitarianism fail to recognize the complex relations involved in circumstances of obligation. It should be noted that he uses the term "*prima facie *duty" in this analysis to indicate the direction of his own thinking.*

When a plain man fulfils a promise because he thinks he ought to do so, it seems clear that he does so with no thought of its total consequences, still less with any opinion that these are likely to be the best possible. He thinks in fact much more of the past than of the future. What makes him think it right to act in a certain way is the fact that he has promised to do so—that and, usually, nothing more. That his act will produce the best possible consequences is not his reason for calling it right. What lends colour to the theory we are examining, then, is not the actions (which form probably a great majority of our actions) in which some such reflection as 'I have promised' is the only reason we give ourselves for thinking a certain action right, but the exceptional cases in which the consequences of fulfilling a promise (for instance) would be so disastrous to others that we judge it right not to do so. It must of course be admitted that such cases exist. If I have promised to meet a friend at a particular time for some trivial purpose, I should certainly think myself justified in breaking my engagement if by doing so I could prevent a serious accident or bring relief to the victims of one. And the supporters of the view we are examining hold that my thinking so is due to my thinking that I shall bring more good into existence by the one action than by the other. A different account may, however, be given of the matter, an account which will, I believe, show itself to be the true one. It may be said that besides the duty of fulfilling promises I have and recognize a duty of relieving distress, and that when I think it right to do the latter at the cost of not doing the former, it is not because I think I shall produce more good thereby but because I think it the duty which is in the circumstances more of a duty. This account surely corresponds much more closely with what we really think in such a situation. If, so far as I can see, I could bring equal amounts of good into being by fulfilling my promise and by helping some one to whom I had made no promise, I should not hesitate to regard the former as my duty. Yet on the view that what is right is right because it is productive of the most good I should not so regard it. . . .

In fact the theory of 'ideal utilitarianism' . . . seems to simplify unduly our relations to our fellows. It says, in effect, that the only morally significant relation in which my neighbours stand to me is that of being possible beneficiaries by my action. They do stand in this relation to me, and this relation is morally significant. But they may also stand to me in the relation of promisee to promiser, of creditor to debtor, of wife to husband, of child to parent, of friend to friend, of fellow countryman to fellow countryman, and the like; and each of these relations is the foundation of a *prima facie* duty, which is more or less incumbent on me according to the circumstances of the case. When I am in a situation, as perhaps I always am, in which more than one of these *prima facie* duties is incumbent on me, what I have to do is to study the situation as fully as I can until I form the considered opinion (it is never more) that in the circumstances one of them is more incumbent than any other; then I am bound to think that to do this *prima facie* duty is my duty *sans phrase* in the situation.[a]

*2. Ross now defines and clarifies his basic concept "*prima facie *duty." His clarification includes a catalogue of the many types of duty. (He does not claim that his list is exhaustive.)*

I suggest '*prima facie* duty' or 'conditional duty' as a brief way of referring to the characteristic (quite distinct from that of being a duty proper) which an act has, in virtue of being of a certain kind (e.g. the keeping of a promise), of being an act which would be a duty proper if it were not at the same time of another kind which is morally significant. Whether an act is a duty proper or actual duty depends on *all* the morally significant kinds it is an instance of . . . .

There is nothing arbitrary about these *prima facie* duties. Each rests on a definite circumstance which cannot seriously be held to be without moral significance. Of *prima facie* duties I suggest, without claiming completeness or finality for it, the following division.

(1) Some duties rest on previous acts of my own. These duties seem to include two kinds, *(a)* those resting on a promise or what may fairly be called an implicit promise, such as the implicit undertaking not to tell lies which seems to be implied in the act of entering into conversation (at any rate by civilized men), or of writing books that purport to be history and not fiction. These may be called the duties of fidelity. *(b)* Those resting on a previous wrongful act. These may be called the duties of reparation. (2) Some rest on previous acts of other men, i.e. services done by them to me. These may be loosely described as the duties of gratitude. (3) Some rest on the fact or possibility of a distribution of pleasure or happiness (or of the means thereto) which is not in accordance with the merit of the persons concerned; in such cases there arises a duty to upset or prevent such a distribution. These are the duties of justice. (4) Some rest on the mere fact that there are other beings in the world whose condition we can make better in respect of virtue, or of intelligence, or of pleasure. These are the duties of beneficence. (5) Some

rest on the fact that we can improve our own condition in respect of virtue or of intelligence. These are the duties of self-improvement. (6) I think that we should distinguish from (4) the duties that may be summed up under the title of 'not injuring others'. No doubt to injure others is incidentally to fail to do them good; but it seems to me clear that non-maleficence is apprehended as a duty distinct from that of beneficence, and as a duty of a more stringent character. It will be noticed that this alone among the types of duty has been stated in a negative way. An attempt might no doubt be made to state this duty, like the others, in a positive way. It might be said that it is really the duty to prevent ourselves from acting either from an inclination to harm others or from an inclination to seek our own pleasure, in doing which we should incidentally harm them. But on reflection it seems clear that the primary duty here is the duty not to harm others, this being a duty whether or not we have an inclination that if followed would lead to our harming them; and that when we have such an inclination the primary duty not to harm others gives rise to a consequential duty to resist the inclination. The recognition of this duty of non-maleficence is the first step on the way to the recognition of the duty of beneficence; and that accounts for the prominence of the commands, 'thou shalt not kill', 'thou shalt not commit adultery', 'thou shalt not steal', 'thou shalt not bear false witness', in so early a code as the Decalogue. But even when we have come to recognize the duty of beneficence, it appears to me that the duty of non-maleficence is recognized as a distinct one, as *prima facie* more binding. We should not in general consider it justifiable to kill one person in order to keep another alive, or to steal from one in order to give alms to another.

The essential defect of the 'ideal utilitarian' theory is that it ignores, or at least does not do full justice to, the highly personal character of duty. If the only duty is to produce the maximum of good, the question who is to have the good—whether it is myself, or my benefactor, or a person to whom I have made a promise to confer that good on him, or a mere fellow man to whom I stand in no such special relation—should make no difference to my having a duty to produce that good. But we are in fact sure that it makes a vast difference.[b]

3. After arguing that it is a mistake to regard every dutiful act as being so for one and the same reason, he then turns to the distinction between prima facie *and actual or absolute duty.*

. . . I would contend that in principle there is no reason to anticipate that every act that is our duty is so for one and the same reason. Why should two sets of circumstances, or one set of circumstances, *not* possess different characteristics, any one of which makes a certain act our *prima facie* duty? When I ask what it is that makes me in certain cases sure that I have a *prima facie* duty to do so and so, I find that it lies in the fact that I have made a promise; when I ask the same question in another case, I find the answer lies in the fact that I have done a wrong. And if on reflection I find (as I think I do) that neither of these reasons is reducible to the other, I must not on any *a priori* ground assume that such a reduction is possible.

It is necessary to say something by way of clearing up the relation between *prima facie* duties and the actual or absolute duty to do one particular act in particular circumstances. If as almost all moralists except Kant are agreed, and as most plain men think, it is sometimes right to tell a lie or to break a promise, it must be maintained that there is a difference between *prima facie* duty and actual or absolute duty. When we think ourselves justified in breaking, and indeed morally obligated to break, a promise in order to relieve some one's distress, we do not for a moment cease to recognize a *prima facie* duty to keep our promise, and this leads us to feel, not indeed shame or repentance, but certainly compunction, for behaving as we do; we recognize, further, that it is our duty to make up somehow to the promisee for the breaking of the promise. We have to distinguish from the characteristic of being our duty that of tending to be our duty. Any act that we do contains various elements in virtue of which it falls under various categories. In virtue of being the breaking of a promise, for instance, it tends to be wrong; in virtue of being an instance of relieving distress it tends to be right. Tendency to be one's duty may be called a parti-resultant attribute, i.e. one which belongs to an act in virtue of some one component in its nature. *Being* one's duty is a toti-resultant attribute, one which belongs [c] to an act in virtue of his whole nature and of nothing less than this. . . .

4. Ross's ethical intuitionism is exhibited in connection with his doctrine of prima facie *duty: A proposition such as "keeping promises is right" is self-evidently true.*

Something should be said of the relation between our apprehension of the *prima facie* rightness of certain types of act and our mental attitude towards particular acts. It is proper to use the word 'apprehension' in the former case and not in the latter. That an act, *qua* fulfilling a promise, or *qua* effecting a just distribution of good, or *qua* returning services rendered, or *qua* promoting the good of others, or *qua* promoting the virtue or insight of the agent, is *prima facie* right, is self-evident; not in the sense that it is evident from the beginning of our lives, or as soon as we attend to the proposition for the first time, but in the sense that when we have reached sufficient mental maturity and have given sufficient attention to the proposition it is evident without any need of proof, or of evidence beyond itself. It is self-evident just as a mathematical axiom, or the validity of a form of inference, is evident. The moral order expressed in these propositions is just as much part of the fundamental nature of the universe (and, we may add, of any possible universe in which there were moral agents at all) as is the spatial or numerical structure expressed in the axioms of geometry or arithmetic. In our confidence that these propositions are true there is involved the same trust in our reason that is involved in our confidence in mathematics; and we should have no justification for trusting it in the latter sphere and distrusting it in the former. In both cases we are dealing with propositions that cannot be proved, but that just as certainly need no proof. [d]

5. He is not *an intuitionist concerning our actual duties.*

Our judgements about our actual duty in concrete situations have none of the certainty that attaches to our recognition of the general principles of duty. A statement is certain, i.e. is an expression of knowledge, only in one or other of two cases: when it is either self-evident, or a valid conclusion from self-evident premisses. And our judgements about our particular duties have neither of these characters. (1) They are not self-evident. Where a possible act is seen to have two characteristics, in virtue of one of which it is *prima facie* right, and in virtue of the other *prima facie* wrong, we are (I think) well aware that we are not certain whether we ought or ought not to do it; that whether we do it or not, we are taking a moral risk. We come in the long run, after consideration, to think one duty more pressing than the other, but we l o not feel certain that it is so. And though we do not always recognize that a possible act has two such characterstics, and though there *may* be cases in which it has not, we are never certain that any particular possible act has not, and therefore never certain that it is right, nor certain that it is wrong. For, to go no further in the analysis, it is enough to point out that any particular act will in all probability in the course of time contribute to the bringing about of good or of evil for many human beings, and thus have a *prima facie* rightness or wrongness of which we know nothing. (2) Again, our judgements about our particular duties are not logical conclusions from self-evident premisses. The only possible premisses would be the general principles stating their *prima facie* rightness or wrongness *qua* having the different characteristics they do ha 'e; and even if we could (as we cannot) apprehend the extent to which an act will tend on the one hand, for example, to bring about advantages for our benefactors and on the other hand to bring about disadvantages for fellow men who are not our benefactors, there is no principle by which we can draw the conclusion that is on the whole right or on the whole wrong. In this respect the judgement as to the rightness of a particular act is just like the judgement as to the beauty of a particular natural object or work of art. A poem is, for instance, in respect of certain qualities beautiful and in respect of certain others not beautiful; and our judgement as to the degree of beauty it possesses on the whole is never reached by logical reasoning from the apprehension of its particular beauties or particular defects. Both in this and in the moral case we have more or less probable opinions which are not logically justified conclusions from the general principles that are recognized as self-evident.[c]

6. *Ross's most distinctive contribution to ethical theory is found in his answer to the following question: Can one conclude from the fact that our* prima facie

duties are self-evidently true that our actual duties are also self-evidently true?
He answers in the negative. Ross insists that while the properties, for example,
of a given mathematical object such as a triangle are consistent with one another,
the properties of a moral act are not necessarily nor usually consistent.

The general principles of duty are obviously not self-evident from the beginning of our lives. How do they come to be so? The answer is, that they come to be self-evident to us just as mathematical axioms do. We find by experience that this couple of matches and that couple makes four matches, that this couple of balls on a wire and that couple make four balls; and by reflection on these and similar discoveries we come to see that it is of the nature of two and two to make four. In a precisely similar way, we see the *prima facie* rightness of an act which would be the fulfilment of a particular promise, and of another which would be the fulfilment of another promise, and when we have reached sufficient maturity to think in general terms, we apprehend *prima facie* rightness to belong to the nature of any fulfilment of promise. What comes first in time is the apprehension of the self-evident *prima facie* rightness of an individual act of a particular type. From this we come by reflection to apprehend the self-evident general principle of *prima facie* duty. From this, too, perhaps along with the apprehension of the self-evident *prima facie* rightness of the same act in virtue of its having another characteristic as well, and perhaps in spite of the apprehension of its *prima facie* wrongness in virtue of its having some third characteristic, we come to believe something not self-evident at all, but an object of probable opinion, viz. that this particular act is (not *prima facie* but) actually right.

In this respect there is an important difference between rightness and mathematical properties. A triangle which is isosceles necessarily has two of its angles equal, whatever other characteristics the triangle may have—whatever, for instance, be its area, or the size of its third angle. The equality of the two angles is a parti-resultant attribute. And the same is true of all mathematical attributes. It is true, I may add, of *prima facie* rightness. But no act is ever, in virtue of falling under some general description, necessarily actually right; its rightness depends on its whole nature and not on any element in it. The reason is that no mathematical object (no figure, for instance, or angle) ever has two characteristics that tend to give it opposite resultant characteristics, while moral acts often (as every one knows) and indeed always (as on reflection we must admit) have different characteristics that tend to make them at the same time *prima facie* right and *prima facie* wrong; there is probably no act, for instance, which does good to any one without doing harm to some one else, and *vice versa*.[f]

7. *Ross is confident that no reflective person regards the terms "duty" or "right" as synonymous with "productive of the best possible consequences." Moreover, he argues that we do not apprehend in* a priori *fashion or on an empirical basis an invariant relationship between what is dutiful (*prima facie *or actual) and what is productive of the best consequences.*

Supposing it to be agreed, as I think on reflection it must, that no one *means* by 'right' just 'productive of the best possible consequences', or 'optimific', the attributes 'right' and 'optimific' might stand in either of two kinds of relation to each other. (1) They might be so related that we could apprehend *a priori*, either immediately or deductively, that any act that is optimific is right and any act that is right is optimific, as we can apprehend that any triangle that is equilateral is equiangular and *vice versa*. Professor Moore's view is, I think, that the coextensiveness of 'right' and 'optimific' is apprehended immediately. He rejects the possibility of any proof of it. Or (2) the two attributes might be such that the question whether they are invariably connected had to be answered by means of an inductive inquiry. Now at first sight it might seem as if the constant connexion of the two attributes could be immediately apprehended. It might seem absurd to suggest that it could be right for any one to do an act which would produce consequences less good than those which would be produced by some other act in his power. Yet a little thought will convince us that this is not absurd. The type of case in which it is easiest to see that this is so is, perhaps, that in which one has made a promise. In such a case we all think that *prima facie* it is our duty to fulfil the promise irrespective of the precise goodness of the total consequences. And though we do not think it is necessarily our actual or absolute duty to do so, we are far from thinking that any, even the slightest, gain in the value of the total consequences will necessarily justify us in doing something else instead. Suppose, to simplify the case by abstraction, that the fulfilment of a promise to *A* would produce 1,000 units of good for him, but that by doing some other act I could produce 1,001 units of good for *B,* to whom I have made no promise, the other consequences of the two acts being of equal value; should we really think it self-evident that it was our duty to do the second act and not the first? I think not. We should, I fancy, hold that only a much greater disparity of value between the total consequences would justify us in failing to discharge our *prima facie* duty to *A.* After all, a promise is a promise, and is not to be treated so lightly as the theory we are examining would imply. What, exactly, a promise is, is not so easy to determine, but we are surely agreed that it constitutes a serious moral limitation to our freedom of action. To produce the 1,001 units of good for *B* rather than fulfil our promise to *A* would be to take, not perhaps our duty as philanthropists too seriously, but certainly our duty as makers of promises too lightly.ᵍ

8. Ross continues his attack on the foregoing views, paying special attention to the inductive basis. He concludes that considerations about duty are generally independent of our calculations regarding optimific consequences.

The coextensiveness of the right and the optimific is, then, not self-evident. And I can see no way of proving it deductively; nor, so far as I know, has any one tried to do so. There remains the question whether it can be established inductively. Such an inquiry, to be conclusive, would have to be very thorough and extensive. We should have to take a large variety of the acts which we, to the best of our ability, judge to be right. We should have to trace as far as possible their consequences, not only for the persons directly affected but also for those indirectly affected, and to these no limit can be set. To make our inquiry thoroughly conclusive, we should have to do what we cannot do, viz. trace these consequences into an unending future. And even to make it reasonably conclusive, we should have to trace them far into the future. It is clear that the most we could possibly say is that a large variety of typical acts that are judged right appear, so far as we can trace their consequences, to produce more good than any other acts possible to the agents in the circumstances. And such a result falls far short of proving the constant connexion of the two attributes. But it is surely clear that no inductive inquiry justifying even this result has ever been carried through. The advocates of utilitarian systems have been so much persuaded either of the identity or of the self-evident connexion of the attributes 'right' and 'optimific' (or 'felicific') that they have not attempted even such an inductive inquiry as is possible. And in view of the enormous complexity of the task and the inevitable inconclusiveness of the result, it is worth no one's while to make the attempt. What, after all, would be gained by it? If, as I have tried to show, for an act to be right and to be optimific are not the same thing, and an act's being optimific is not even the ground of its being right, then if we could ask ourselves (though the question is really unmeaning) which we ought to do, right acts because they are right or optimific acts because they are optimific, our answer must be 'the former'. If they are optimific as well as right, that is interesting but not morally important; if not, we still ought to do them (which is only another way of saying that they are right acts),and the question whether they are optimific has no importance for moral theory.[h]

9. *In offering an ultimate defense of his theory that our obligations do not reduce to a mere production of good consequences, Ross employs a telling example.*

There is one direction in which a fairly serious attempt has been made to show the connexion of the attributes 'right' and 'optimific'. One of the most evident facts of our noral consciousness is the sense which we have of the sanctity of promises, a sense which does not, on the face of it, involve the thought that one will be bringing more good into existence by fulfilling the promise than by breaking it. It is plain, I think, that in our normal thought we consider that the fact that we have made a promise is in itself sufficient to create a duty of keeping it, the sense of duty resting on remembrance of the past promise and not on thoughts of the future consequences of its fulfilment. Utilitarianism tries to show that this is not so, that the sanctity of promises rests on the good consequences of the fulfilment of them and the bad consequences of their non-fulfilment. It does so in this way: it points out that when you break a promise you not only fail to confer a certain advantage on your promisee but you diminish his confidence, and indirectly the confidence of others, in the fulfilment of promises. . . . It may be suspected . . . that the effect of a single keeping or breaking of a promise in strengthening or weakening the fabric of mutual confidence is greatly exaggerated by the theory we are examining. And if we suppose two men dying together alone, do we think that the duty of one to fulfil before he dies a promise he has made to the other would be extinguished by the fact that neither act would have any effect on the general confidence? Anyone who holds this may be suspected of not having reflected on what a promise is.

I conclude that the attributes 'right' and 'optimific' are not identical, and that we do not know either by intuition, by deduction, or by induction that they coincide in their application, still less that the latter is the foundation of the former. It must be added, however, that if we are ever under no special obligation such as that of fidelity to a promisee or of gratitude to a benefactor, we ought to do what will produce most good; and that even when we are under a special obligation the tendency of acts to promote general good is one of the main factors in determining whether they are right.[i]

Questions

1. What does Ross mean by "*prima facie* duty"?
2. How does Ross, an intuitionist, account for the fact that two men of moral character can disagree about what is actually right in a given situation?
3. How receptive would he be to the Kantian conception of the Categorical Imperative?
4. Wherein do Ross and Moore agree and differ concerning their ethical intuitionism? How important is their disagreement?
5. Give an example which tends to support Ross in his criticism of utilitarianism. Explain.
6. How would Ross argue against those who claim that one's actual duty in any situation depends entirely upon how the person feels about it?
7. Do you think that Ross's theory comes close to capturing the moral convictions of the average man? Discuss.
8. Is it self-evidently true that when I make a promise, all things being equal, I ought to keep it or is it merely a matter of one's cultural background?
9. Do you agree with Ross's contention that it is false to subsume all duties under the duty of beneficence?

10. In a situation in which there are several claims incumbent upon us simultaneously, is Ross's account capable of determining which course of action is right? Does each *prima facie* duty impose as great a claim upon us as any other?

Key to selections:

W. D. Ross, *The Right and the Good,* Oxford University Press, 1930. Reprinted by permission of the publisher.

[a] pp. 17–19.	[f] pp. 32–34.
[b] pp. 19–22.	[g] p. 34.
[c] pp. 24–28.	[h] pp. 36–37.
[d] pp. 29–30.	[i] pp. 37–39.
[e] pp. 30–31.	

GUIDE TO ADDITIONAL READING

ADDITIONAL SOURCE MATERIAL:

Ross, W. D., *Foundations of Ethics,* Oxford, Clarendon Press, 1939.
———, *Kant's Ethical Theory,* Oxford, Clarendon Press, 1934.

DISCUSSION AND COMMENTARY:

Blanshard, B., *Reason and Goodness,* London, G. Allen, 1961, Ch. 6.
Johnson, A. O., *Rightness and Goodness,* The Hague, Martinus Nijhoff, 1959.
McCloskey, H. J. "Ross and the Concept of *Prima Facie* Duty," *Australasian Journal of Philosophy,* 41 (1964), 336–345.
Strawson, P. F., "Ethical Intuitionism," *Philosophy,* 24 (1949), 23–33.

CHAPTER **17**

Ethics
as Emotive
Expression

A. J. AYER

Professor Alfred J. Ayer (1910–   ), Professor of Mind and
Logic at the University of London, was a scholar at Eton College
and Christ Church, Oxford. He lectured at Christ Church from
1932 to 1935, and from 1935 to 1944 was a research scholar there,
receiving his M.A. in 1936. From 1944 to 1946, Professor Ayer
was a Fellow of Wadham College, Oxford, and Dean of Wadham
in 1945–46. During the second World War, he served in the Welsh
Guards and performed intelligence duties. Also, in 1945, he was
an attaché to the British Embassy in Paris. His appointment as
Grote Professor of Philosophy at the University of London came
in 1946; the academic year 1948–49 Professor Ayer spent as a
visiting professor at New York University. One of the clearest
expositors of logical positivism, Professor Ayer has written, besides a number of articles, *Language, Truth and Logic* (1936, revised in 1946), and *The Foundations of Empirical Knowledge*
(1940).

C. L. STEVENSON

Professor Charles L. Stevenson (1908–1979), of the Department of Philosophy of the University of Michigan, received his A.B. from Yale University in 1930, his B.A. from Cambridge University in 1933, and his Ph.D. from Harvard in 1935. From 1934 to 1939, he was at Harvard doing graduate work and teaching, and from 1939 to 1946, he was an assistant professor at Yale, joining the staff at the University of Michigan in 1946. During the academic year 1945–46, Professor Stevenson was a Guggenheim Memorial Foundation Fellow. His chief work in ethics, *Ethics and Language,* was published in 1944, and he wrote a number of articles for British and American journals.

•

The ethical theories of Ayer and Stevenson are understandable only in terms of the narrowed role which philosophy plays for the logical positivists.[1] Looking upon the methods of science and

[1] As a philosophical movement, logical positivism received its initial impetus from the work of Moritz Schlick (1882–1936), Rudolf Carnap (1891–   ), and other members of the "Vienna Circle" in the early 1920's.

mathematics as the only means by which reliable knowledge can be obtained, they assign to philosophy a subordinate position among the theoretical disciplines. Once esteemed as the "queen of the sciences," philosophy becomes, on their view, the "hand-maiden of the sciences." It is defined as *logical* or *linguistic analysis*, and its primary function is the clarification of the meanings of scientific statements.

Viewed as analysis, philosophy deals with the language used in speaking about actual objects, and not with the objects themselves: it operates on the level of language rather than experience. Philosophers have frequently speculated about reality and have made judgments about it which they put forward as factually true. Admittedly, some of these judgments have been found to be true, *e.g.*, Democritus' theory, later restated by Newton as the first law of motion, that the motion of a body will persist unless opposed; however, many of them turn out to be false, *e.g.*, Aristotle's theory that the heavenly bodies are unchanging and indestructible. But what is to the point, the decision as to which judgments were in keeping with fact and which were false was reached only when the method of science was brought to bear upon them. Philosophical speculation, the positivists have concluded, is a vain way to discover facts. However, philosophers have made valuable contributions through their analyses of scientific concepts, judgments, and language. The positivists, therefore, propose that philosophers leave the discovery of facts to the scientists and devote themselves exclusively to the analysis and improvement of the language used to communicate facts.

In their analysis of language, the positivists maintain that only two kinds of sentences are meaningful and therefore genuine, *empirical* or *synthetic* statements [2] and *analytic* statements. An empirical statement, *e.g.*, "Some metals expand when heated," is one which can be confirmed to a high degree of probability by *observation and experiment*. An analytic statement, *e.g.*, "All

[2] Not all philosophers use the terms "synthetic" and "empirical" interchangeably in their classification of statements.

spinsters are unmarried," or "All circles are squares," is one which can be established as true or false by an examination of the *definitions* of its terms. Utterances which are neither empirical nor analytic are termed "literal nonsense," *i.e.*, even though they may seem to, they do not really assert or deny any confirmable fact, nor are they true or false by definition. They are therefore relegated to the status of pseudo-statements or "metaphysical" sentences. Expressions like, "Everything has a purpose in the natural order," and "Disease is caused by the presence of evil spirits in the body," are typical of this class of expression. Although the logical positivists maintain that pseudo-statements have no literal or logical meaning, they believe that some of them possess *emotive meaning*, *i.e.*, they express or evoke feelings.

The distinction between meaningful and literally nonsensical sentences — between genuine and pseudo-statements — is brought to bear upon ethics. Statements which are *descriptive* of moral behavior, *i.e.*, those which have literal meaning, are regarded as belonging to the social sciences, even though traditional ethical theorists include them in their theories. Normative sentences, *i.e.*, those which say what "ought" to be done, are the special province of ethics. However, being neither confirmable by experience nor true by definition, they must be looked upon as literally meaningless expressions; if they have *any* meaning, as they seem to have, it must be an *emotive* meaning.[3]

The positivists are agreed that ethics, because it is normative, cannot be a science. In its extreme form, the positivistic position excludes ethics from the realm of systematic inquiry, on the grounds that it has no factual content. A. J. Ayer, however, takes the stand that the ethical theorist has a legitimate function, namely, *the logical analysis of ethical (normative) terms, e.g.,*

---

[3] Although there is general agreement among the logical positivists that ethical sentences are emotive, different interpretations have arisen regarding the type of emotive meaning involved. For example, the sentence, "Cheating is wrong," may be taken to mean: (1) "Don't cheat!" (imperative); (2) "I wish you wouldn't cheat." (optative); (3) "Cheating!!!" in a tone of disgust (exclamatory); and (4) "I disapprove of cheating — you should disapprove as well!" (persuasive).

"good" and "evil," "right" and "wrong," as they are actually used in ethical discourse. Through his examination of the symbols of ethical language and their logical relations, he substantiates the positivistic contention that normative terms are different in kind from descriptive terms, since they do not have referents. Ayer concludes that the ethical theorist's task is completed when he has shown that normative sentences are purely emotive and therefore merely pseudo-statements.

The conception of ethics developed by C. L. Stevenson — one which in more recent years has gained popularity with many of the positivists — extends the boundaries of the legitimate limits of ethical inquiry. He argues that Ayer, like the extreme positivists who deny ethics has any place as an intellectual enterprise, fails to take account sufficiently of the significant role played by emotive meaning in human behavior. Even though emotive expressions do not themselves convey knowledge, they have great importance in the ethical decisions men must make and should not be ignored:

> . . . It is certainly mandatory that the term "emotive" . . . be kept as a tool for use in careful study, not as a device for relegating the nondescriptive aspects of language to limbo.[4]

Consequently, Stevenson carries his analysis beyond ethical statements to include ethical situations, and, in particular, ethical disagreements.

• • •

1. Ayer develops his position from the assumption that a strictly philosophical treatment of ethics can be concerned only with definitions of ethical terms. *It cannot deal with moral exhortations, descriptions of moral experiences, or actual value judgments, in the manner of traditional ethical systems. Moreover, the inclusion of*

---

[4] C. L. Stevenson, *Ethics and Language*, New Haven, Yale University Press, 1944, p. 79.

pseudo-statements in an ethical theory obscures its logical structure,
creating needless discussion and controversy.

The ordinary system of ethics, as elaborated in the works of
ethical philosophers, is very far from being a homogeneous whole.
Not only is it apt to contain pieces of metaphysics, and analyses
of non-ethical concepts: its actual ethical contents are themselves
of very different kinds. We may divide them, indeed, into four
main classes. There are, first of all, propositions which express
definitions of ethical terms, or judgements about the legitimacy or
possibility of certain definitions. Secondly, there are propositions
describing the phenomena of moral experience, and their causes.
Thirdly, there are exhortations to moral virtue. And, lastly, there
are actual ethical judgements. It is unfortunately the case that
the distinction between these four classes, plain as it is, is commonly ignored by ethical philosophers; with the result that it is
often very difficult to tell from their works what it is that they are
seeking to discover or prove.

In fact, it is easy to see that only the first of our four classes,
namely that which comprises the propositions relating to the definitions of ethical terms, can be said to constitute ethical philosophy. The propositions which describe the phenomena of moral experience, and their causes, must be assigned to the science of
psychology, or sociology. The exhortations to moral virtue are not
propositions at all, but ejaculations or commands which are designed to provoke the reader to action of a certain sort. Accordingly, they do not belong to any branch of philosophy or science.
As for the expressions of ethical judgements, we have not yet determined how they should be classified. But inasmuch as they are
certainly neither definitions nor comments upon definitions, nor
quotations, we may say decisively that they do not belong to
ethical philosophy. A strictly philosophical treatise on ethics
should therefore make no ethical pronouncements. But it should,
by giving an analysis of ethical terms, show what is the category
to which all such pronouncements belong. And this is what we are
now about to do.

A question which is often discussed by ethical philosophers is whether it is possible to find definitions which would reduce all ethical terms to one or two fundamental terms. But this question, though it undeniably belongs to ethical philosophy, is not relevant to our present enquiry. We are not now concerned to discover which term, within the sphere of ethical terms, is to be taken as fundamental; whether, for example, "good" can be defined in terms of "right" or "right" in terms of "good," or both in terms of "value." What we are interested in is the possibility of reducing the whole sphere of ethical terms to non-ethical terms. We are enquiring whether statements of ethical value can be translated into statements of empirical fact.

2. Ayer is critical of "subjectivists" and "utilitarians," who define value expressions in terms of such psychological states as "feelings of approval" or "pleasure." Although they can thus convert ethical statements into factual ones, Ayer points out that their definitions of ethical terms do not follow normal linguistic usage. For example, the subjectivist may define "good" as "what is approved." However, our language permits us to say without contradiction, "This act is at the same time really bad but is nevertheless approved." The subjectivist is led to the linguistic absurdity of regarding such a statement as self-contradictory.

That [statements of ethical value can be translated into statements of empirical fact] is the contention of those ethical philosophers who are commonly called subjectivists, and of those who are known as utilitarians. For the utilitarian defines the rightness of actions, and the goodness of ends, in terms of the pleasure, or happiness, or satisfaction, to which they give rise; the subjectivist, in terms of the feelings of approval which a certain person, or group of people, has towards them. Each of these types of definition makes moral judgements into a sub-class of psychological or sociological judgements; and for this reason they are very attractive to us. For, if either was correct, it would follow that ethical assertions were not generically different from the factual assertions which are ordinarily contrasted with them . . .

Nevertheless we shall not adopt either a subjectivist or a utilitarian analysis of ethical terms. We reject the subjectivist view that to call an action right, or a thing good, is to say that it is generally approved of, because it is not self-contradictory to assert that some actions which are generally approved of are not right, or that some things which are generally approved of are not good. And we reject the alternative subjectivist view that a man who asserts that a certain action is right, or that a certain thing is good, is saying that he himself approves of it, on the ground that a man who confessed that he sometimes approved of what was bad or wrong would not be contradicting himself. And a similar argument is fatal to utilitarianism. We cannot agree that to call an action right is to say that of all the actions possible in the circumstances it would cause, or be likely to cause, the greatest happiness, or the greatest balance of pleasure over pain, or the greatest balance of satisfied over unsatisfied desire, because we find that it is not self-contradictory to say that it is sometimes wrong to perform the action which would actually or probably cause the greatest happiness, or the greatest balance of pleasure over pain, or of satisfied over unsatisfied desire. And since it is not self-contradictory to say that some pleasant things are not good, or that some bad things are desired, it cannot be the case that the sentence "x is good" is equivalent to "x is pleasant," or to "x is desired." And to every other variant of utilitarianism with which I am acquainted the same objection can be made. And therefore we should, I think, conclude that the validity of ethical judgements is not determined by the felicific tendencies of actions, any more than by the nature of people's feelings; but that it must be regarded as "absolute" or "intrinsic," and not empirically caculable.

If we say this, we are not, of course, denying that it is possible to invent a language in which all ethical symbols are definable in non-ethical terms, or even that it is desirable to invent such a language and adopt it in place of our own; what we are denying is that the suggested reduction of ethical to non-ethical statements is consistent with the conventions of our actual language. That is, we reject utilitarianism and subjectivism, not as proposals to replace our existing ethical notions by new ones, but as analyses of our existing ethical notions. Our contention is simply that, in our language, sentences which contain normative ethical symbols are not equivalent to sentences which express psychological propositions, or indeed empirical propositions of any kind.

3. Having denied that value sentences can be translated into factual statements, Ayer turns his attention to the analysis of normative sentences. He points out that certain terms or symbols may be used either normatively or descriptively. For example, in the sentence "x (killing, stealing, etc.) is wrong," the term "wrong" is used descriptively if it refers to an actual attitude found in a particular society. On the other hand, "x is wrong" is a normative expression when the term "wrong" is intended to express a value judgment about some type of behavior. Because the same words may be employed in the formation of a normative or a descriptive sentence, it is necessary to exercise caution and single out the normative symbols with which this analysis is concerned.

It is advisable here to make it plain that it is only normative ethical symbols, and not descriptive ethical symbols, that are held by us to be indefinable in factual terms. There is a danger of confusing these two types of symbols, because they are commonly constituted by signs of the same sensible form. Thus a complex sign of the form "*x* is wrong" may constitute a sentence which expresses a moral judgement concerning a certain type of conduct, or it may constitute a sentence which states that a certain type of conduct is repugnant to the moral sense of a particular society. In the latter case, the symbol "wrong" is a descriptive ethical symbol, and the sentence in which it occurs expresses an ordinary sociological proposition; in the former case, the symbol "wrong" is a normative ethical symbol, and the sentence in which it occurs does not, we maintain, express an empirical proposition at all. It is only with normative ethics that we are at present concerned; so that whenever ethical symbols are used in the course of this argument without qualification, they are always to be interpreted as symbols of the normative type.

4. Since normative ethical terms cannot be reduced to factual terms, the "absolutist" in ethics may claim that ethical expressions can be grasped only by "intuition." Because he does not accept intuition as a reliable test of truth or falsity, Ayer finds this position untenable. Having already rejected the subjectivist and utilitarian views, which claim that value statements are genuinely synthetic — i.e., that they are genuine factual statements — it may be asked what other possibilities exist.

In admitting that normative ethical concepts are irreducible to empirical concepts, we seem to be leaving the way clear for the "absolutist" view of ethics — that is, the view that statements of value are not controlled by observation, as ordinary empirical propositions are, but only by a mysterious "intellectual intuition." A feature of this theory, which is seldom recognized by its advocates, is that it makes statements of value unverifiable. For it is notorious that what seems intuitively certain to one person may seem doubtful, or even false, to another. So that unless it is possible to provide some criterion by which one may decide between conflicting intuitions, a mere appeal to intuition is worthless as a test of a proposition's validity. But in the case of moral judgements, no such criterion can be given. Some moralists claim to settle the matter by saying that they "know" that their own moral judgements are correct. But such an assertion is of purely psychological interest, and has not the slightest tendency to prove the validity of any moral judgement. For dissentient moralists may equally well "know" that their ethical views are correct. And, as far as subjective certainty goes, there will be nothing to choose between them. When such differences of opinion arise in connection with an ordinary empirical proposition, one may attempt to resolve them by referring to, or actually carrying out, some relevant empirical test. But with regard to ethical statements, there is, on the "absolutist" or "intuitionist" theory, no relevant empirical test. We are therefore justified in saying that on this theory ethical statements are held to be unverifiable. They are, of course, also held to be genuine synthetic propositions.

Considering the use which we have made of the principle that a synthetic proposition is significant only if it is empirically verifiable, it is clear that the acceptance of an "absolutist" theory of ethics would undermine the whole of our main argument. And as we have already rejected the "naturalistic" theories which are commonly supposed to provide the only alternative to "absolutism" in ethics, we seem to have reached a difficult position. We shall meet the difficulty by showing that the correct treatment of ethical statements is afforded by a third theory, which is wholly compatible with our radical empiricism.

5. The theory by which Ayer intends to establish the status of normative terms starts with the assumption that basic ethical terms are pseudo-symbols which cannot be analyzed into component parts. Consequently, ethical statements made up of such terms are emotive expressions, not genuine propositions having factual meaning.

We begin by admitting that the fundamental ethical concepts are unanalysable, inasmuch as there is no criterion by which one can test the validity of the judgements in which they occur. So far we are in agreement with the absolutists. But, unlike the absolutists, we are able to give an explanation of this fact about ethical concepts. We say that the reason why they are unanalysable is that they are mere pseudo-concepts. The presence of an ethical symbol in a proposition adds nothing to its factual content. Thus if I say to someone, "You acted wrongly in stealing that money," I am not stating anything more than if I had simply said, "You stole that money." In adding that this action is wrong I am not making any further statement about it. I am simply evincing my moral disapproval of it. It is as if I had said, "You stole that money," in a peculiar tone of horror, or written it with the addition of some special exclamation marks. The tone, or the exclamation marks, adds nothing to the literal meaning of the sentence. It merely serves to show that the expression of it is attended by certain feelings in the speaker.

If now I generalize my previous statement and say, "Stealing money is wrong," I produce a sentence which has no factual meaning — that is, expresses no proposition which can be either true or false. It is as if I had written "Stealing money!!" — where the shape and thickness of the exclamation marks show, by a suitable convention, that a special sort of moral disapproval is the feeling which is being expressed. It is clear that there is nothing said here which can be true or false. Another man may disagree with me about the wrongness of stealing, in the sense that he may not have the same feelings about stealing as I have, and he may quarrel with me on account of my moral sentiments. But he cannot, strictly speaking, contradict me. For in saying that a certain type of action is right or wrong, I am not making any factual statement, not even a statement about my own state of mind. I am merely expressing certain moral sentiments. And the man who is ostensibly contradicting me is merely expressing his moral sentiments. So that there is plainly no sense in asking which of us is in the right. For neither of us is asserting a genuine proposition.

6. *For the further development of this view, several qualifications are made: first, "expression" is reserved for the "emotive," and "assertion" for the "cognitive" elements of language; second, ethical terms may not only express feelings, but they may also evoke feelings in others; and third, the distinction between "expression of feeling" and "assertion of feeling" is employed by Ayer in order to distinguish his position from that of orthodox subjectivism.*

What we have just been saying about the symbol "wrong" applies to all normative ethical symbols. Sometimes they occur in sentences which record ordinary empirical facts besides expressing ethical feelings about those facts: sometimes they occur in sentences which simply express ethical feeling about a certain type of action, or situation, without making any statement of fact. But in every case in which one would commonly be said to be making an ethical judgement, the function of the relevant ethical word is purely "emotive." It is used to express feeling about certain objects, but not to make any assertion about them.

It is worth mentioning that ethical terms do not serve only to express feeling. They are calculated also to arouse feeling, and so to stimulate action. Indeed some of them are used in such a way as to give the sentences in which they occur the effect of commands. Thus the sentence "It is your duty to tell the truth." may be regarded both as the expression of a certain sort of ethical feeling about truthfulness and as the expression of the command "Tell the truth." The sentence "You ought to tell the truth" also involves the command "Tell the truth," but here the tone of the command is less emphatic. In the sentence "It is good to tell the truth" the command has become little more than a suggestion. And thus the "meaning" of the word "good," in its ethical usage, is differentiated from that of the word "duty" or the word "ought." In fact we may define the meaning of the various ethical words in terms both of the different feelings they are ordinarily taken to express, and also the different responses which they are calculated to provoke.

We can now see why it is impossible to find a criterion for determining the validity of ethical judgements. It is not because they have an "absolute" validity which is mysteriously independent of ordinary sense-experience, but because they have no objective validity whatsoever. If a sentence makes no statement at all, there is obviously no sense in asking whether what it says is true or false. And we have seen that sentences which simply express moral judgements do not say anything. They are pure expressions of feeling and as such do not come under the category of truth and falsehood. They are unverifiable for the same reason as a cry of pain or a word of command is unverifiable — because they do not express genuine propositions.

Thus, although our theory of ethics might fairly be said to be radically subjectivist, it differs in a very important respect from the orthodox subjectivist theory. For the orthodox subjectivist does not deny, as we do, that the sentences of a moralizer express genuine propositions. All he denies is that they express propositions of a unique non-empirical character. His own view is that they express propositions about the speaker's feelings. If this were so, ethical judgements clearly would be capable of being true or false. They would be true if the speaker had the relevant feelings, and false if he had not. And this is a matter which is, in principle, empirically verifiable. Furthermore they could be significantly contradicted. For if I say, "Tolerance is a virtue," and someone answers, "You don't approve of it," he would, on the ordinary subjectivist theory, be contradicting me. On our theory, he would not be contradicting me, because, in saying that tolerance was a virtue, I should not be making any statement about my own feelings or about anything else. I should simply be evincing my feelings, which is not at all the same thing as saying that I have them.

7. Once the distinction between expressing and having an emotion is recognized, Ayer argues, it becomes apparent that a genuine dispute in ethics has to be on a factual level. This is so because value sentences, being expressions of feelings, cannot be true or false: one man's emotions cannot "contradict another man's emotions.

The distinction between the expression of feeling and the assertion of feeling is complicated by the fact that the assertion that one has a certain feeling often accompanies the expression of that feeling, and is then, indeed, a factor in the expression of that feeling. Thus I may simultaneously express boredom and say that I am bored, and in that case my utterance of the words, "I am bored," is one of the circumstances which make it true to say that I am expressing or evincing boredom. But I can express boredom without actually saying that I am bored. I can express it by my tone and gestures, while making a statement about something wholly unconnected with it, or by an ejaculation, or without uttering any words at all. So that even if the assertion that one has a certain feeling always involves the expression of that feeling, the expression of a feeling assuredly does not always involve the assertion that one has it. And this is the important point to grasp in considering the distinction between our theory and the ordinary subjectivist theory. For whereas the subjectivist holds that ethical statements actually assert the existence of certain feelings, we hold that ethical statements are expressions and excitants of feeling which do not necessarily involve any assertions.

We have already remarked that the main objection to the ordinary subjectivist theory is that the validity of ethical judgements is not determined by . . . their author's feelings. And this is an objection which our theory escapes. For it does not imply that the existence of any feelings is a necessary and sufficient condition of the validity of an ethical judgement. It implies, on the contrary, that ethical judgements have no validity.

There is, however, a celebrated argument against subjectivist theories which our theory does not escape. It has been pointed out by Moore that if ethical statements were simply statements about the speaker's feelings, it would be impossible to argue about questions of value. To take a typical example: if a man said that thrift was a virtue, and another replied that it was a vice, they would not, on this theory, be disputing with one another. One would be saying that he approved of thrift, and the other that *he* didn't; and there is no reason why both these statements should not be true. Now Moore held it to be obvious that we do dispute about questions of value, and accordingly concluded that the particular form of subjectivism which he was discussing was false.

It is plain that the conclusion that it is impossible to dispute about questions of value follows from our theory also. For as we hold that such sentences as "Thrift is a virtue" and "Thrift is a vice" do not express propositions at all, we clearly cannot hold that they express incompatible propositions. We must therefore admit that if Moore's argument really refutes the ordinary subjectivist theory, it also refutes ours. But, in fact, we deny that it does refute even the ordinary subjectivist theory. For we hold that one really never does dispute about questions of value.

This may seem, at first sight, to be a very paradoxical assertion. For we certainly do engage in disputes which are ordinarily regarded as disputes about questions of value. But, in all such cases, we find, if we consider the matter closely, that the dispute is not really about a question of value, but about a question of fact. When someone disagrees with us about the moral value of a certain action or type of action, we do admittedly resort to argument in order to win him over to our way of thinking. But we do not attempt to show by our arguments that he has the "wrong" ethical feeling towards a situation whose nature he has correctly apprehended. What we attempt to show is that he is mistaken about the facts of the case. We argue that he has misconceived the agent's motive: or that he has misjudged the effects of the action, or its probable effects in view of the agent's knowledge; or that he has failed to take into account the special circumstances in which the agent was placed. Or else we employ more general arguments about the effects which actions of a certain type tend to produce, or the qualities which are usually manifested in their performance. We do this in the hope that we have only to get our opponent to agree with us about the nature of the empirical facts for him to adopt the same moral attitude towards them as we do. And as the people with whom we argue have generally received the same moral education as ourselves, and live in the same social order, our expectation is usually justified.

8. If two parties to an ethical dispute have similar moral backgrounds, they may resolve their differences once they agree upon the facts of the case. However, when the parties to the dispute have different moral standards, their disagreements spring from differences in the disputants' emotional attitudes, even if they agree on matters of fact. As a result, the dispute is only an exchange of derogatory remarks, which express emotions. Since legitimate arguments can occur only on the factual level, Ayer concludes "that ethics, as a branch of knowledge, is nothing more than a department of psychology and sociology."

But if our opponent happens to have undergone a different process of moral "conditioning" from ourselves, so that, even when he acknowledges all the facts, he still disagrees with us about the moral value of the actions under discussion, then we abandon the attempt to convince him by argument. We say that it is impossible to argue with him because he has a distorted or undeveloped moral sense; which signifies merely that he employs a different set of values from our own. We feel that our own system of values is superior, and therefore speak in such derogatory terms of his. But we cannot bring forward any arguments to show that our system is superior. For our judgement that it is so is itself a judgement of value, and accordingly outside the scope of argument. It is because argument fails us when we come to deal with pure questions of value, as distinct from questions of fact, that we finally resort to mere abuse.

In short, we find that argument is possible on moral questions only if some system of values is presupposed. If our opponent concurs with us in expressing moral disapproval of all actions of a given type *t*, then we may get him to condemn a particular action A, by bringing forward arguments to show that A is of type *t*. For the question whether A does or does not belong to that type is a plain question of fact. Given that a man has certain moral principles, we argue that he must, in order to be consistent, react morally to certain things in a certain way. What we do not and cannot argue about is the validity of these moral principles. We merely praise or condemn them in the light of our own feelings.

If anyone doubts the accuracy of this account of moral disputes, let him try to construct even an imaginary argument on a question of value which does not reduce itself to an argument about a question of logic or about an empirical matter of fact. I am confident that he will not succeed in producing a single example. And if that is the case, he must allow that its involving the impossibility of purely ethical arguments is not, as Moore thought, a ground of objection to our theory, but rather a point in favour of it.

Having upheld our theory against the only criticism which appeared to threaten it, we may now use it to define the nature of all ethical enquiries. We find that ethical philosophy consists simply in saying that ethical concepts are pseudo-concepts and therefore unanalysable. The further task of describing the different feelings that the different ethical terms are used to express, and the different reactions that they customarily provoke, is a task for the psychologist. There cannot be such a thing as ethical science, if by ethical science one means the elaboration of a "true" system of morals. For we have seen that, as ethical judgements are mere expressions of feeling, there can be no way of determining the validity of any ethical system, and, indeed, no sense in asking whether any such system is true. All that one may legitimately enquire in this connection is, What are the moral habits of a given person or group of people, and what causes them to have precisely those habits and feelings? And this enquiry falls wholly within the scope of the existing social sciences.

9. Having transferred all the factual statements of ethics to the social scientists and relegated all the normative expressions of ethics to the limbo of emotive utterances, Ayer regards his task as an analyst completed. Stevenson agrees in general with Ayer's analysis of ethical language. However, in his judgment, ethical inquiry must be extended to include an examination of the role of emotive expressions in ethical disputes. Stevenson begins by pointing out that ethical arguments involve both factual and value elements. Although there is a complex interplay of attitudes and beliefs, ethical disagreement is primarily a matter of disagreement in attitude, *and secondarily of* disagreement in belief. *He approaches the subject of ethical disagreement through a question as to the method of resolving disputes.*

When people disagree about the value of something — one saying that it is good or right, and another that it is bad or wrong — by what methods of argument or inquiry can their disagreement be resolved? Can it be resolved by the methods of science, or does it require methods of some other kind, or is it open to no rational solution at all?

The question must be clarified before it can be answered. And the word that is particularly in need of clarification, as we shall see, is the word "disagreement."

Let us begin by noting that "disagreement" has two broad senses: In the first sense it refers to what I shall call "disagreement in belief." This occurs when Mr. A believes p, when Mr. B believes not-p, or something incompatible with p, and when neither is content to let the belief of the other remain unchallenged. Thus doctors may disagree in belief about the causes of an illness; and friends may disagree in belief about the exact date on which they last met.

In the second sense, the word refers to what I shall call "disagreement in attitude." This occurs when Mr. A has a favorable attitude to something, when Mr. B has an unfavorable or less favorable attitude to it, and when neither is content to let the other's attitude remain unchanged . . . This second sense can be illustrated in this way: Two men are planning to have dinner together. One is particularly anxious to eat at a certain restaurant, but the other doesn't like it. Temporarily, then, the men cannot "agree" on where to dine. Their argument may be trivial, and perhaps only half serious; but in any case it represents a disagreement *in attitude*. The men have divergent preferences, and each is trying to redirect the preference of the other . . .

The difference between the two senses of "disagreement" is essentially this: the first involves an opposition of beliefs, both of which cannot be true, and the second involves an opposition of attitudes, both of which cannot be satisfied.

10. The distinction between disagreement in belief and disagreement in attitude is the basis of Stevenson's analysis of ethical dis-

agreements. He is opposed to the doctrine that all genuine ethical disputes are primarily matters of belief; he contends that the distinguishing feature of ethical disagreement is the underlying disagreement in attitude.

Let us apply this distinction to a case that will sharpen it. Mr. A believes that most voters will favor a proposed tax, and Mr. B disagrees with him. The disagreement concerns attitudes — those of the voters — but note that A and B are *not* disagreeing in attitude. Their disagreement is *in belief about* attitudes. It is simply a special kind of disagreement in belief, differing from disagreement in belief about head colds only with regard to subject matter. It implies not an opposition of the actual attitudes of the speakers, but only of their beliefs about certain attitudes. Disagreement *in* attitude, on the other hand, implies that the very attitudes of the speakers are opposed. A and B may have opposed beliefs about attitudes without having opposed attitudes, just as they may have opposed beliefs about head colds without having opposed head colds. Hence we must not, from the fact that an argument is concerned with attitudes, infer that it necessarily involves disagreement *in* attitude.

We may now turn more directly to disagreement about values, with particular reference to normative ethics. When people argue about what is good, do they disagree in belief, or do they disagree in attitude? A long tradition of ethical theorists strongly suggest, whether they always intend to or not, that the disagreement is one *in belief*. Naturalistic theorists, for instance, identify an ethical judgment with some sort of scientific statement, and so make normative ethics a branch of science. Now a scientific argument typically exemplifies disagreement in belief, and if an ethical argument is simply a scientific one, then it too exemplifies disagreement in belief. . . . Disagreement about what is good is disagreement *in belief* about attitudes; but we have seen that that is simply one sort of disagreement in belief, and by no means the same as disagreement *in* attitude. Analyses that stress disagreement *in* attitude are extremely rare.

If ethical arguments, as we encounter them in everyday life, involved disagreement in belief exclusively — whether the beliefs were about attitudes or about something else — then I should have no quarrel with the ordinary sort of naturalistic analysis. Normative judgments could be taken as scientific statements, and amenable to the usual scientific proof. But a moment's attention will readily show that disagreement in belief has not the exclusive role that theory has so repeatedly ascribed to it. It must be readily granted that ethical arguments usually involve disagreement in belief; but they *also* involve disagreement in attitude. And the conspicuous role of disagreement in attitude is what we usually take, whether we realize it or not, as the distinguishing feature of ethical arguments. For example:

Suppose that the representative of a union urges that the wage level in a given company ought to be higher — that it is only right that the workers receive more pay. The company representative urges in reply that the workers ought to receive no more than they get. Such an argument clearly represents a disagreement in attitude. The union is *for* higher wages; the company is *against* them, and neither is content to let the other's attitude remain unchanged. *In addition* to this disagreement in attitude, of course, the argument may represent no little disagreement in belief. Perhaps the parties disagree about how much the cost of living has risen, and how much the workers are suffering under the present wage scale. Or perhaps they disagree about the company's earnings, and the extent to which the company could raise wages and still operate at a profit. Like any typical ethical argument, then, this argument involves both disagreement in attitude and disagreement in belief.

11. Stevenson enlarges upon his thesis that ethical disagreements are chiefly matters of attitude by showing two ways in which they function in actual situations. First, the conflicting attitudes determine what disagreements in belief are relevant to an argument, and second, they determine whether or not the argument has been settled.

In the first place, disagreement in attitude determines what beliefs are *relevant* to the argument. Suppose that the company affirms that the wage scale of fifty years ago was far lower than it is now. The union will immediately urge that this contention, even though true, is irrelevant. And it is irrelevant simply because information about the wage level of fifty years ago, maintained under totally different circumstances, is not likely to affect the present attitudes of either party. To be relevant, any belief that is introduced into the argument must be one that is likely to lead one side or the other to have a different attitude, and so reconcile disagreement in attitude. Attitudes are often functions of beliefs. We often change our attitudes to something when we change our beliefs about it; just as a child ceases to *want* to touch a live coal when he comes to *believe* that it will burn him. Thus in the present argument, any beliefs that are at all likely to alter attitudes, such as those about the increasing cost of living or the financial state of the company, will be considered by both sides to be relevant to the argument. Agreement in belief on these matters may lead to agreement in attitude toward the wage scale. But beliefs that are likely to alter the attitudes of neither side will be declared irrelevant. They will have no bearing on the disagreement in attitude, with which both parties are primarily concerned.

In the second place, ethical argument usually terminates when disagreement in attitude terminates, even though a certain amount of disagreement in belief remains. Suppose, for instance, that the company and the union continue to disagree in belief about the increasing cost of living, but that the company, even so, ends by favoring the higher wage scale. The union will then be content to end the argument, and will cease to press its point about living costs. It may bring up that point again, in some future argument of the same sort, or in urging the righteousness of its victory to the newspaper columnists; but for the moment the fact that the company has agreed in attitude is sufficient to terminate the argument. On the other hand: suppose that both parties agreed on all beliefs that were introduced into the argument, but even so continued to disagree in attitude. In that case neither party would feel that their dispute had been successfully terminated. They might look for other beliefs that could be introduced into the argument. They might use words to play on each other's emotions. They might agree (in attitude) to submit the case to arbitration, both feeling that a decision, even if strongly adverse to one party or the other, would be preferable to a continued impasse. Or, perhaps, they might abandon hope of settling their dispute by any peaceable means.

12. The presuppositions of positivism result necessarily in the conclusion that normative ethics cannot be a science. *Stevenson, as a positivist, shares this view, but at the same time recognizes normative ethics as a vital* human activity, *in which science can — in favorable circumstances — contribute materially to the resolution of ethical (attitudinal) disagreements. As a human activity, ethics has its own characteristic functions and methods for the treatment of moral issues,* i.e., *issues involving "personal and social decisions about what is to be approved." To sum up, ethics is not itself a science, though science may be of major importance in the resolution of ethical problems.*

It will be obvious that to whatever extent an argument involves disagreement in belief, it is open to the usual methods of the sciences. If these methods are the *only* rational methods for supporting beliefs — as I believe to be so, but cannot now take time to discuss — then scientific methods are the only rational methods for resolving the disagreement in *belief* that arguments about values may include.

But if science is granted an undisputed sway in reconciling beliefs, it does not thereby acquire, without qualification, an undisputed sway in reconciling attitudes. We have seen that arguments about values include disagreement in attitude, no less than disagreement in belief, and that in certain ways the disagreement in attitude predominates. By what methods shall the latter sort of disagreement be resolved?

The methods of science are still available for that purpose, but only in an indirect way. Initially, these methods have only to do with establishing agreement in belief. If they serve further to establish agreement in attitude, that will be due simply to the psychological fact that altered beliefs may cause altered attitudes. Hence scientific methods are conclusive in ending arguments about values only to the extent that their success in obtaining agreement in belief will in turn lead to agreement in attitude.

In other words, the extent to which scientific methods can bring about agreement on values depends on the extent to which a commonly accepted body of scientific beliefs would cause us to have a commonly accepted set of attitudes.

How much is the development of science likely to achieve, then, with regard to values? To what extent *would* common beliefs lead to common attitudes? It is, perhaps, a pardonable enthusiasm to *hope* that science will do everything — to hope that in some rosy future, when all men know the consequences of their acts, they will all have common aspirations, and live peaceably in complete moral accord. But if we speak not from our enthusiastic hopes, but from our present knowledge, the answer must be far less exciting. We usually *do not know*, at the beginning of any argument about values, whether an agreement in belief, scientifically established, will lead to an agreement in attitude or not. It is logically possible, at least, that two men should continue to disagree in attitude even though they had all their beliefs in common, and even though neither had made any logical or inductive error, or omitted any relevant evidence. Differences in temperament, or in early training, or in social status, might make the men retain different attitudes even though both were possessed of the complete scientific truth. Whether this logical possibility is an empirical likelihood I shall not presume to say; but it is unquestionably a possibility that must not be left out of account.

To say that science can always settle arguments about value, we have seen, is to make this assumption: Agreement in attitude will always be consequent upon complete agreement in belief, and science can always bring about the latter. Taken as purely heuristic, this assumption has its usefulness. It leads people to discover the discrepancies in their beliefs, and to prolong enlightening argument that *may* lead, as a matter of fact, from commonly accepted beliefs to commonly accepted attitudes. It leads people to reconcile their attitudes in a rational, permanent way, rather than by rhapsody or exhortation. But the assumption is *nothing more*, for present knowledge, than a heuristic maxim. It is wholly without any proper foundation of probability. I conclude, therefore, that scientific methods cannot be guaranteed the definite rôle in the so-called "normative sciences" that they may have in the natural sciences . . .

Insofar as normative ethics draws from the sciences, in order to change attitudes *via* changing people's beliefs, it *draws* from *all* the sciences; but a moralist's peculiar aim — that of *redirecting* attitudes — is a type of activity, rather than knowledge, and falls within no science. Science may study that activity, and may help indirectly to forward it; but it is not *identical* with that activity.

Questions

1. How does Ayer describe the basic task of the ethical theorist?
2. According to Ayer, what is the difference between "normative ethical symbols" and "descriptive ethical symbols"? What function does this distinction have in his theory of ethics?
3. What characteristics does Ayer assign to ethical statements? How does his view of their nature affect the evaluation of traditional ethical theories?
4. Assuming that Ayer's position is correct, is there need for any further work to be done in ethics? If so, whose task would it be?
5. What is the difference between "disagreement in belief" and "disagreement in attitude," according to Stevenson's usage?
6. In what respect does Stevenson believe "disagreement in attitude" to be basic to ethics? What relationship is there between disagreement in attitude and in belief, in ethical disputes?
7. What grounds does Stevenson provide for his conclusion that ethics is not a branch of science? Is his position completely opposed to that of John Dewey, or are there significant areas of agreement between pragmatists and positivists?

8. Compare the positivism of Ayer with that of Stevenson, pointing out the respects in which they are similar and the respects in which they are different.
9. Compare the analytic approach of G. E. Moore with that of the positivists. How can you account for the fact that these two theories reach widely different conclusions, despite the essential similarity of their method and conception of ethical theory?
10. What do you believe are the implications for morality of a positivistic ethical theory?

Key to selections:

A. J. AYER, *Language, Truth and Logic*, Chapter VI, pp. 103–112. Reprinted with the kind permission of the publishers, Dover Publications, Inc., New York 19 ($2.25 clothbound, $1.25 paperbound). Canadian circulation by permission of Victor Gollancz, Ltd., publishers.

C. L. STEVENSON, "The Nature of Ethical Disagreement," *Sigma*, vols. 1–2, nos. 8–9, 1947–48. With the kind permission of the author and of the *Centro di Metodologia*, Milan, Italy, the publishers.

Guide to Additional Reading

ADDITIONAL SOURCE MATERIAL:

AYER, A. J., "On the Analysis of Moral Judgements," *Horizon*, XX (September, 1949), 171–184.
FRANKENA, W. K., *Ethics*, Englewood Cliffs, Prentice-Hall, Inc., 1963.
SCHLICK, M., *Problems of Ethics*, tr. David Rynin, New York, Prentice-Hall, Inc., 1939.
STEVENSON, C. L., *Ethics and Language*, New Haven, Yale University Press, 1946.
——, "The Emotive Meaning of Ethical Terms," *Mind*, XLVI (January, 1937), 14–31.
——, "Ethical Judgments and Avoidability," *Mind*, XLVII (January, 1938), 45–57.
——, "Meaning: Descriptive and Emotive," *Philosophical Review*, LVII (April, 1948), 127–144.
——, "The Emotive Conception of Ethics and Its Cognitive Implications," *Philosophical Review*, LIX (July, 1950), 291–394.

CHAPTER 18

Ethics as Radical Freedom

SIMONE
DE BEAUVOIR

Simone de Beauvoir (1908–   ) is a French philosopher, novelist, and dramatist of note. She won the Prix Goncourt for *The Mandarins* in 1954. Best known as a contributor to French existentialism through her literary works, she is also an important, clear exponent of existentialism in her philosophical writings. *The Ethics of Ambiguity*, 1948, is a particularly efficacious exposition of what is frequently referred to as Sartrean existentialism. De Beauvoir's close relationship to Jean-Paul Sartre as a fellow student and as a colleague in the French intellectual world through the years makes it difficult and, perhaps unnecessary, to distinguish between their separate contributions to ethics.

•

Søren Kierkegaard (1813-1855), who may be considered as the father of modern existentialism, interpreted the Socratic dictum, "know thyself," in an untraditional way. It has most frequently been taken to mean that man should regard himself as the primary object of rational investigation. While Kierkegaard regards the dictum as stressing the importance of man understanding himself, he warns that it does not justify our assimilating the study of man to the patterns employed in the formal, physical or social sciences. His objection — and the objection of all existentialists — to making human beings the object of rational inquiry is extreme: to presume that a person is able to be classified under such definitions or stated essences as "rational animal" or "animal with a conscience," or, again, that he is accurately and wholly described by such a collection of concepts as "honest," "friendly," "cowardly," etc., is to deny his uniqueness. The existentialist admonishes us to realize that, in contrast to a chair, tree, molecule, or even God, a human being cannot be reduced to a set of concepts.

The opposition of existentialism to the rational tradition can scarcely be exaggerated. Kierkegaard and all other existentialists insist that any attempt to impose rational categories on an intrinsically absurd universe is paradoxical in two senses: in the first place, as the rationalist employs the familiar dichotomies of freedom and responsibility, object and subject, being and nonbeing, existence and essence, he fails to meet his own standard of logical consistency; in the second, he forever precludes himself from encountering reality.

It is the hallmark of existentialism to speak of the human condition or situation as one in which man is radically free. But this thesis leads the existentialist immediately into the paradox of saying that freedom is man's essential characteristic, that man is the slave of the concept of freedom. The existentialist counters that the term "freedom," when properly used, refers to the *condition of human existence* rather than to a characteristic of man's nature. Man's freedom is manifested in his creative endeavors, in his spontaneous actions, and most of all, in his making decisions. It falls to the individual alone to commit himself at every moment to one of a limitless range of possibilities. Furthermore, according to existential doctrine, neither reason, nor social convention, nor God's will can relieve a person of the burden and responsibility of having to make choices. Moreover, none of these factors can assure the superiority of one choice over another. The human circumstance is agonizing and admits of no palliatives. The French contemporary existentialist, Jean-Paul Sartre (1905–   ), perhaps best describes the consequences of facing up to this true state of affairs:

> If existence really does precede essence, there is no explaining things away by reference to a fixed and given human nature. In other words, there is no determinism, man is free, man is freedom. On the other hand, if God does not exist, we find no values or commands to turn to which legitimize our conduct. So in the bright realm of values, we have no excuse behind us, nor justification before us. We are alone, with no excuses.[1]

Thus, existentialism holds that *what* a man is, is a function of the choices he makes, not that the choices he makes are a function of what he is. The everpresent danger for the individual in our highly organized society is that he will lose his uniqueness through submitting to external forces. It is difficult, however, to envision anyone choosing freely against the immense number of determinative pressures — social, political, economic, religious and intellectual — which sanction and demand mere conformity. Is not the pathetic weakness of the individual sufficient in itself to justify his moving with the mainstream? The existentialist remonstrates that such a plea is a mere pretense for shirking responsibility. The question is not, whether like a hero of one's imagination, a person can overcome tremendous odds, but rather, whether he has the courage to live *authentically*. To claim that one has no choice because of all the external pressures that can be brought to bear is to exchange the human situation for that of an automaton — to sacrifice being a genuine subject in favor of becoming a mere object. Furthermore, even if such an exchange occurs, the choice bringing it about and the responsibility for the resulting renunciation of individuality is still one's own. In brief, at no time or place can an individual plead that what he is has been shaped by any factor other than himself.

[1]Jean-Paul Sartre, *Existentialism*, New York, Philosophical Library, 1947, p. 27.

Even though the existentialist will admit that a person's decisions may have a profound impact upon others, he is still confronted with the dreadful realization that there are no universal principles to guide or sanctify his conduct. Between one individual and another, there are no assured bonds. Social order, like natural order, is a fabrication, an avoidance of the fact of man's total isolation. The virtue of the authentic or genuine man consists in his honest recognition of this fact. He alone has integrity; his reward in an admittedly unique sense of the word is that he does not suffer self-alienation.

Although classifying existentialists is both difficult and risks error, it can be pointed out that some among them show a decidedly religious orientation, while others steadfastly reject religion in any of its forms. Kierkegaard is clearly a member of the first group, and Sartre and his associate, Simone de Beauvoir, belong to the second. Kierkegaard does not claim any objective knowledge of God; nevertheless he believes, after the manner of a Christian mystic, that however absurd and paradoxical it seems, the individual can establish rapport with the eternal God by a "leap of Faith." Sartre and de Beauvoir, on the other hand, warn that it is as self-deceptive for human beings to escape the burden of responsibility for their actions through an appeal to supernatural belief as it is to avoid responsibility by subsuming one's actions under natural laws. From birth to death, Sartrean man is bound only by the ideals and obligations which, in his freedom, he creates for himself.

• • •

1. Simone de Beauvoir begins by pointing out that although mortality does not distinguish men from other creatures, the fact that they know their death is imminent does. Such knowledge is tragic: on the one hand, to face honestly the bleak prospect of certain death is almost unbearable, while on the other, to attempt any form of escape is self-deceptive.

"The continous work of our life," says Montaigne, "is to build death." He quotes the Latin poets: *Prima, quae vitam dedit, hora corpsit.* And again: *Nascentes morimur.* Man knows and thinks this tragic ambivalence which the animal and the plant merely undergo. A new paradox is thereby introduced into his destiny. "Rational animal," "thinking reed," he escapes from his natural condition without, however, freeing himself from it. He is still a part of this world of which he is a consciousness. He asserts himself as a pure internality against which no external power can take hold, and he also experiences himself as a thing crushed by the dark weight of other things. At every moment he can grasp the non-temporal truth of his existence. But between the past which no longer is and the future which is not yet, this moment when he exists is nothing. This privilege, which he alone possesses, of being a sovereign and unique subject amidst a universe of objects, is what he shares with all his fellow-men. In turn an object for others, he is nothing more than an individual in the collectivity on which he depends.

As long as there have been men and they have lived, they have all felt this tragic ambiguity of their condition, but as long as there have been philosophers and they have thought, most of them have tried to mask it. They have striven to reduce mind to matter, or to reabsorb matter into mind, or to merge them within a single substance. Those who have accepted the dualism have established a hierarchy between body and soul which permits of considering as negligible the part of the self which cannot be saved. They have denied death, either by integrating it with life or by promising to man immortality. Or, again they have denied life, considering it as a veil of illusion beneath which is hidden the truth of Nirvana.

And the ethics which they have proposed to their disciples has always pursued the same goal. It has been a matter of eliminating the ambiguity by making oneself pure inwardness or pure externality, by escaping from the sensible world or by being engulfed in it, by yielding to eternity or enclosing oneself in the pure moment. Hegel, with more ingenuity, tried to reject none of the aspects of man's condition and to reconcile them all. According to his system, the moment is preserved in the development of time; Nature asserts itself in the face of Spirit which denies it while assuming it; the individual is again found in the collectivity within which he is lost; and each man's death is fulfilled by being canceled out into the Life of Mankind. One can thus repose in a marvelous optimism where even the bloody wars simply express the fertile restlessness of the Spirit.[a]

2. The existentialists charge that most ethical thinkers fail to ground their theories in the human condition of ambiguity, the condition wherein the awareness of life is the awareness of death.

. . . . Let us try to assume our fundamental ambiguity. It is in the knowledge of the genuine conditions of our life that we must draw our strength to live and our reason for acting.

From the very beginning, existentialism defined itself as a philosophy of ambiguity. It was by affirming the irreducible character of ambiguity that Kierkegaard opposed himself to Hegel, and it is by ambiguity that, in our own generation, Sartre, in *Being and Nothingness*, fundamentally defined man, that being whose being is not to be, that subjectivity which realizes itself only as a presence in the world, that engaged freedom, that surging of the for-oneself which is immediately given for others. But it is also claimed that existentialism is a philosophy of the absurd and of despair. It encloses man in a sterile anguish, in an empty subjectivity. It is incapable of furnishing him with any principle for making choices. Let him do as he pleases. In any case, the game is lost. Does not Sartre declare, in effect, that man is a "useless passion," that he tries in vain to realize the synthesis of the for-oneself and the in-oneself, to make himself God? It is true. But it is also true that the most optimistic ethics have all begun by emphasizing the element of failure involved in the condition of man; without failure, no ethics; for a being who, from the very start, would be an exact co-incidence with himself, in a perfect plenitude, the notion of having-to-be would have no meaning. One does not offer an ethics to a God. It is impossible to propose any to man if one defines him as nature, as something given. The so-called psychological or empirical ethics manage to establish themselves only by introducing surreptitiously some flaw within the man-thing which they have first defined.[b]

3. Something of the Sartrean human condition is captured by the folk maxim that "it is better to have loved and lost than never to have loved at all." The crux of the existentialist thesis is that a man discloses his existence mainly through willing to be what he is not, even though he knows his efforts to have being *are doomed to failure.*

Man, Sartre tells us, is "a being who *makes himself* a lack of being *in order that there might be* being." That means, first of all, that his passion is not inflicted upon him from without. He chooses it. It is his very being and, as such, does not imply the idea of unhappiness. If this choice is considered as useless, it is because there exists no absolute value before the passion of man, outside of it, in relation to which one might distinguish the useless from the useful. The word "useful" has not yet received a meaning on the level of description where *Being and Nothingness* is situated. It can be defined only in the human world established by man's projects and the ends he sets up. In the original helplessness from which man surges up, nothing is useful, nothing is useless. It must therefore be understood that the passion to which man has acquiesced finds no external justification. No outside appeal, no objective necessity permits of its being called useful. It *has* no reason to will itself. But this does not mean that it can not justify itself, that it can not *give itself* reasons for being that it does not *have.* And indeed Sartre tells us that man makes himself this lack of being *in order that* there might be being. The term *in order that* clearly indicates an intentionality. It is not in vain that man nullifies being. Thanks to him, being is disclosed and he desires this disclosure. There is an original type of attachment to being which is not the relationship "waiting to be" but rather "wanting to disclose being." Now, here there is not failure, but rather success. This end, which man proposes to himself by making himself lack of being, is, in effect, realized by him. By uprooting himself from the world, man makes himself present to the world and makes the world present to him. I should like to be the landscape which I am contemplating, I should like this sky, this quiet water to think themselves within me, that it might be I whom they express in flesh and bone, and I remain at a distance. But it is also by this distance that the sky and the water exist before me. My contemplation is an excruciation only because it is also a joy. I can not appropriate the snow field where I slide. It remains foreign, forbidden, but I take delight in this very effort toward an impossible possession. I experience it as a triumph, not as a defeat. This means that man, in his vain attempt to *be* God, makes himself exist *as* man, and if he is satisfied with this existence, he coincides exactly with himself. It is not granted him to exist without tending toward this being which he will never be. But it is possible for him to want this tension even with the failure which it involves. His being is lack of being, but this lack has a way of being which is precisely existence.[c]

4. One consequence of the existentialist thesis, viz., that human existence requires the denial of being an object, is that the individual is the sole source of values. Freedom, non-being, and values are interdependent; but if man sets up values outside himself, he is consenting to be a thing, not a person.

The first implication of such an attitude is that the genuine man will not agree to recognize any foreign absolute. When a man projects into an ideal heaven that impossible synthesis of the for-itself and the in-itself that is called God, it is because he wishes the regard of this existing Being to change his existence into being; but if he agrees not to be in order to exist genuinely, he will abandon the dream of an inhuman objectivity. He will understand that it is not a matter of being right in the eyes of a God, but of being right in his own eyes. Renouncing the thought of seeking the guarantee for his existence outside of himself, he will also refuse to believe in unconditioned values which would set themselves up athwart his freedom like things. Value is this lacking-being of which freedom *makes itself* a lack; and it is because the latter makes itself a lack that value appears. It is desire which creates the desirable, and the project which sets up the end. It is human existence which makes values spring up in the world on the basis of which it will be able to judge the enterprise in which it will be engaged. But first it locates itself beyond any pessimism, as beyond any optimism, for the fact of its original springing forth is a pure contingency. Before existence there is no more reason to exist than not to exist. The lack of existence can not be evaluated since it is the fact on the basis of which all evaluation is defined. It can not be compared to anything for there is nothing outside of it to serve as a term of comparison. This rejection of any extrinsic justification also confirms the rejection of an original pessimism which we posited at the beginning. Since it is unjustifiable from without, to declare from without that it is unjustifiable is not to condemn it. And the truth is that outside of existence there is nobody. Man exists. For him it is not a question of wondering whether his presence in the world is useful, whether life is worth the trouble of being lived. These questions make no sense. It is a matter of knowing whether he wants to live and under what conditions.[d]

5. It appears to be a corollary of the absence of all objective value that the individual is free to create values arbitrarily. Is a person not free to act capriciously? De Beauvoir argues painstakingly that existentialism does not support such moral irresponsibility; on the contrary, she argues that it expresses the truly human principle of responsibility.

But if man is free to define for himself the conditions of a life which is valid in his own eyes, can he not choose whatever he likes and act however he likes? Dostoievsky asserted, "If God does not exist, everything is permitted." Today's believers use this formula for their own advantage. To re-establish man at the heart of his destiny is, they claim, to repudiate all ethics. However, far from God's absence authorizing all license, the contrary is the case, because man is abandoned on the earth, because his acts are definitive, absolute engagements. He bears the responsibility for a world which is not the work of a strange power, but of himself, where his defeats are inscribed, and his victories as well. A God can pardon, efface, and compensate. But if God does not exist, man's faults are inexpiable. If it is claimed that, whatever the case may be, this earthly stake has no importance, this is precisely because one invokes that inhuman objectivity which we declined at the start. One can not start by saying that our earthly destiny *has* or *has not* importance, for it depends upon us to give it importance. It is up to man to make it impotrant to be a man, and he alone can feel his success or failure. And if it is again said that nothing forces him to try to justify his being in this way, then one is playing upon the notion of freedom in a dishonest way. The believer is also free to sin. The divine law is imposed upon him only from the moment he decides to save his soul. In the Christian religion, though one speaks very little about them today, there are also the damned. Thus, on the earthly plane, a life which does not seek to ground itself will be a pure contingency. But it is permitted to wish to give itself a meaning and a truth and it then meets rigorous demands within its own heart.[e]

6. De Beauvoir argues that in the first place, it does not follow from the fact that each man is the source of his own values that there can be no agreement about norms. In the second place, she points out, any quest for a universal morality which arises out of the presumption of a "universal man" amounts to an attempt to found morality on myth.

However, even among the proponents of secular ethics, there are many who charge existentialism with offering no objective content to the moral act. It is said that this philosophy is subjective, even solipsistic. If he is once enclosed within himself, how can man get out? But there too we have a great deal of dishonesty. It is rather well known that the fact of being a subject is a universal fact and that the Cartesian *cogito* expresses both the most individual experience and the most objective truth. By affiming that the source of all values resides in the freedom of man, existentialism merely carries on the tradition of Kant, Fichte, and

Hegel, who, in the words of Hegel himself, "have taken for their point of departure the principle according to which the essence of right and duty and the essence of the thinking and willing subject are absolutely identical." The idea that defines all humanism is that the world is not a given world, foreign to man, one to which he has to force himself to yield from without. It is the world willed by man, insofar as his will expresses his genuine reality. . . .

And, indeed, we are coming to the real situation of the problem. But to state it is not to demonstrate that it can not be resolved. On the contrary, we must here again invoke the notion of Hegelian "displacement." There is an ethics only if there is a problem to solve. And it can be said, by inverting the preceding line of argument, that the ethics which have given solutions by effacing the fact of the separation of men are not valid precisely because there *is* this separation. An ethics of ambiguity will be one which will refuse to deny *a priori* that separate existants can, at the same time, be bound to each other, that their individual freedoms can forge laws valid for all.[f]

7. De Beauvoir next explicates what is meant by the existential insistence that "willing oneself free" is the absolute precondition of morality. She contrasts willing oneself not free, which is contradictory, with *choosing not to will oneself free. The fact that one may choose not to be free does not remove one from the moral sphere.*

As for us, whatever the case may be, we believe in freedom. Is it true that this belief must lead us to despair? Must we grant this curious paradox: that from the moment a man recognizes himself as free, he is prohibited from wishing for anything?

On the contrary, it appears to us that by turning toward this freedom we are going to discover a principle of action whose range will be universal. The characteristic feature of all ethics is to consider human life as a game that can be won or lost and to teach man the means of winning. Now, we have seen that the original scheme of man is ambiguous: he wants to be, and to the extent that he coincides with this wish, he fails. All the plans in which this will to be is actualized are condemned; and the ends circumscribed by these plans remain mirages. Human transcendence is vainly engulfed in those miscarried attempts. But man also wills himself to be a disclosure of being, and if he coincides with this wish, he wins, for the fact is that the world becomes present by his presence in it. But the disclosure implies a perpetual tension to keep being at a certain distance, to tear oneself from the world, and to assert oneself as a freedom. To wish for the disclosure of the world and to assert oneself as freedom are one and the same movement. Freedom is the source from which all significations and all values spring. It is the original condition of all justification of existence. The man who seeks to justify his life must want freedom itself absolutely and above everything else. At the same time that it requires the realization of concrete ends, of particular projects, it requires itself universally. It is not a ready-made value which offers itself from the outside to my abstract adherence, but it appears (not on the plane of facility, but on the moral plane) as a cause of itself. It is necessarily summoned up by the values which it sets up and through which it sets itself up. It can not establish a denial of itself, for in denying itself, it would deny the possibility of any foundation. To will oneself moral and to will oneself free are one and the same decision. . . . . .

Every man is originally free, in the sense that he spontaneously casts himself into the world. But if we consider this spontaneity in its facticity, it appears to us only as a pure contingency, an upsurging as stupid as the clinamen of the Epicurean atom which turned up at any moment whatsoever from any direction whatsoever. And it was quite necessary for the atom to arrive somewhere. But its movement was not justified by this result which had not been chosen. It remained absurd. Thus, human spontaneity always projects itself toward something. The psychoanalyst discovers a meaning even in abortive acts and attacks of hysteria. But in order for this meaning to justify the transcendence which discloses it, it must itself be founded, which it will never be if I do not choose to found it myself. Now, I can evade this choice. We have said that it would be contradictory deliberately to will oneself not free. But one can choose not to will himself free. In laziness, heedlessness, capriciousness, cowardice, impatience, one contests the meaning of the project at the very moment that one defines it. The spontaneity of the subject is then merely a vain living palpitation, its movement toward the object is a flight, and itself is an absence. To convert the absence into presence, to convert my flight into will, I must assume my project positively. It is not a matter of retiring into the completely inner and, moreover, abstract movement of a given spontaneity, but of adhering to the concrete and particular movement by which this spontaneity defines itself by thrusting itself toward an end. It is through this end that it sets up that my spontaneity confirms itself by reflecting upon itself. Then, by a single movement, my will, establishing the content of the act, is legitimized by it. I realize my escape toward the other as a freedom when, assuming the presence of the object, I thereby assume myself before it as a presence. But this justification requires a constant tension. My project is never founded; it founds itself. To avoid the anguish of this permanent choice, one may attempt to flee into the object itself, to engulf one's own presence in it. In the servitude of the serious, the original spontaneity strives to deny itself. It strives in vain, and meanwhile it then fails to fulfill itself as moral freedom.[g]

8. Freedom of the will has always posed a serious problem for ethical theorists. Many have felt that to deny it in favor of determinism is to deny morality itself. Those who accept it, however, are faced with a set of perplexing problems, not the least of which is accommodating the reality of evil. De Beauvoir points out that the existentialist solves this particular problem through the account of genuine freedom as the capacity to will evil as well as good.

It can be seen that, on the one hand, freedom can always save itself, for it is realized as a disclosure of existence through its very failures, and it can again confirm itself by a death freely chosen. But, on the other hand, the situations which it discloses through its project toward itself do not appear as equivalents. It regards as privileged situations those which permit it to realize itself as indefinite movement; that is, it wishes to pass beyond everything which limits its power; and yet, this power is always limited. Thus, just as life is identified with the will-to-live, freedom always appears as a movement of liberation. It is only by prolonging itself through the freedom of others that it manages to surpass death itself and to realize itself as an indefinite unity. Later on we shall see what problems such a relationship raises. For the time being it is enough for us to have established the fact that the words "to will oneself free" have a positive and concrete meaning. If man wishes to save his existence, as only he himself can do, his original spontaneity must be raised to the height of moral freedom by taking itself as an end through the disclosure of a particular content.

But a new question is immediately raised. If man has one and only one way to save his existence, how can he choose not to choose it in all cases? How is a bad willing possible? We meet with this problem in all ethics, since it is precisely the possibility of a perverted willing which gives a meaning to the idea of virtue. We know the answer of Socrates, of Plato, of Spinoza: "No one is willfully bad." And if Good is a transcendent thing which is more or less foreign to man, one imagines that the mistake can be explained by error. But if one grants that the moral world is the world genuinely willed by man, all possibility of error is eliminated. Moreover, in Kantian ethics, which is at the origin of all ethics of autonomy, it is very difficult to account for an evil will. As the choice of his character which the subject makes is achieved in the intelligible world by a purely rational will, one can not understand how the latter expressly rejects the law which it gives to itself. But this is because Kantism defined man as a pure positivity, and it therefore recognized no other possibility in him than coincidence with himself. We, too, define morality by this adhesion to the self; and this is why we say that man can not positively decide between the negation and the assumption of his freedom, for as soon as he decides, he assumes it. He can not positively will not to be free for such a willing would be self-destructive. Only, unlike Kant, we do not see man as being essentially a positive will. On the contrary, he is first defined as a negativity. He is first at a distance from himself. He can coincide with himself only by agreeing never to rejoin himself. There is within him a perpetual playing with the negative, and he thereby escapes himself, he escapes his freedom. And it is precisely because an evil will is here possible that the words "to will oneself free" have a meaning. Therefore, not only do we assert that the existentialist doctrine permits the elaboration of an ethics, but it even appears to us as the only philosophy in which an ethics has its place. For, in a metaphysics of transcendence, in the classical sense of the term, evil is reduced to error; and in humanistic philosophies it is impossible to account for it, man being defined as complete in a complete world. Existentialism alone gives — like religions — a real role to evil, and it is this, perhaps, which make its judgments so gloomy. Men do not like to feel themselves in danger. Yet, it is because there are real dangers, real failures and real earthly damnation that words like victory, wisdom, or joy have meaning. Nothing is decided in advance, and it is because man has something to lose and because he can lose that he can also win.

Therefore, in the very condition of man there enters the possibility of not fulfilling this condition. In order to fulfill it he must assume himself as a being who "makes himself a lack of being so that there might be being." But the trick of dishonesty permits stopping at any moment whatsoever. One may hesitate to make oneself a lack of being, one may withdraw before existence, or one may falsely assert oneself as being, or assert oneself as nothingness. One may realize his freedom only as an abstract independence, or, on the contrary, reject with despair the distance which separates us from being. All errors are possible since man is a negativity, and they are motivated by the anguish he feels in the face of his freedom. Concretely, men slide incoherently from one attitude to another.[h]

9. *In an effort to draw together the features of the existentialist view and to show its plausibility for us as concrete individuals,*

de Beauvoir portrays existentialism as a moral philosophy in which individualism is fundamental. It is one which, in its realism, is neither pessimistic nor optimistic.

Is this kind of ethics individualistic or not? Yes, if one means by that that it accords to the individual an absolute value and that it recognizes in him alone the power of laying the foundations of his own existence. It is individualism in the sense in which the wisdom of the ancients, the Christian ethics of salvation, and the Kantian ideal of virtue also merit this name; it is opposed to the totalitarian doctrines which raise up beyond man the mirage of Mankind. But it is not solipsistic, since the individual is defined only by his relationship to the world and to other individuals; he exists only by transcending himself, and his freedom can be achieved only through the freedom of others. He justifies his existence by a movement which, like freedom, springs from his heart but which leads outside of him.

This individualism does not lead to the anarchy of personal whim. Man is free; but he finds his law in his very freedom. First, he must assume his freedom and not flee it; he assumes it by a constructive movement: one does not exist without doing something; and also by a negative movement which rejects oppression for oneself and others. In construction, as in rejection, it is a matter of reconquering freedom on the contingent facticity of existence, that is, of taking the given, which, at the start, *is there* without any reason, as something willed by man. A conquest of this kind is never finished; the contingency remains, and, so that he may assert his will, man is even obliged to stir up in the world the outrage he does not want. But this element of failure is a very condition of his life; one can never dream of eliminating it without immediately dreaming of death. This does not mean that one should consent to failure, but rather one must consent to struggle against it without respite.

Yet, isn't this battle without victory pure gullibility? It will be argued that this is only a ruse of transcendence projecting before itself a goal which constantly recedes, running after itself on an endless treadmill; to exist for Mankind is to remain where one is, and it fools itself by calling this turbulent stagnation progress; our whole ethics does nothing but encourage it in this lying enterprise since we are asking each one to confirm existence as a value for all others; isn't it simply a matter of organizing among men a complicity which allows them to substitute a game of illusions for the given world?

We have already attempted to answer this objection. One can formulate it only by placing himself on the grounds of an inhuman and consequently false objectivity; within Mankind men may be fooled; the word "lie" has a meaning by opposition to the truth established by men themselves, but Mankind can not fool itself completely since it is precisely Mankind which creates the criteria of true and false. In Plato, art is mystification because there is the heaven of Ideas; but in the earthly domain all glorification of the earth is true as soon as it is realized. Let men attach value to words, forms, colors, mathematical theorems, physical laws, and athletic prowess; let them accord value to one another in love and friendship, and the objects, the events, and the men immediately *have* this value; they have it absolutely. It is possible that a man may refuse to love anything on earth; he will prove this refusal and he will carry it out by suicide. If he lives, the reason is that, whatever he may say, there still remains in him some attachment to existence; his life will be commensurate with this attachment; it will justify itself to the extent that it genuinely justifies the world.

This justification, though open upon the entire universe through time and space, will always be finite. Whatever one may do, one never realizes anything but a limited work, like existence itself which tries to establish itself through that work and which death also limits. It is the assertion of our finiteness which doubtless gives the doctrine which we have just evoked its austerity and, in some eyes, its sadness. As soon as one considers a system abstractly and theoretically, one puts himself, in effect, on the plane of the universal, thus, of the infinite. That is why reading the Hegelian system is so comforting. . . .[i]

10. Existentialism rejects the delusory, negative comfort of traditional philosophy, preferring the austerity of the "truth of life." De Beauvoir urges that the existentialist ethic offers the only course modern man can follow to achieve salvation in the world as it actually is.

. . . I remember having experienced a great feeling of calm on reading Hegel in the impersonal framework of the Bibliotheque Nationale in August 1940. But once I got into the street again, into my life, out of the system, beneath a real sky, the system was no longer of any use to me: what it had offered me, under a show of the infinite, was the consolations of death; and I again wanted to live in the midst of living men. I think that, inversely, existentialism does not offer to the reader the consolations of an abstract evasion: existentialism proposes no evasion. On the contrary, its ethics is experienced in the truth of life, and it then appears as the only proposition of salvation which one can address to men. Taking on its own account Descartes' revolt against the evil genius, the pride of the thinking reed in the face of the universe which crushes him, it asserts that, despite his limits, through them, it is up to each one to fulfill his existence as an absolute. Regardless of the staggering dimensions of the world about us, the density of our ignorance, the risks of catastrophies to come, and our individual weakness within the immense collectivity, the fact remains that we are absolutely free today if we choose to will our existence in its finiteness, a finiteness which is open on the infinite. And in fact, any man who has known real loves, real revolts, real desires, and real will knows quite well that he has no need of any outside guarantee to be sure of his goals; their certitude comes from his own drive. There is a very old saying which goes: "Do what you must, come what may." That amounts to saying in a different way that the result is not external to the good will which fulfills itself in aiming at it. If it came to be that each man did what he must, existence would be saved in each one without there being any need of dreaming of a paradise where all would be reconciled in death.[j]

Questions

1. Discuss the role of death in existentialist ethics. Is it fair to say that the existentialist is preoccupied with his mortality?

2. What would be de Beauvoir's defense of non-theistic existentialist ethics against the implications of Dostoievsky's maxim, "If God does not exist, everything is permitted."?

3. How does the denial of *being* facilitate affirmation of *existence*? What is "the disclosure of existence"?

4. What are the principal theses of the "ethics of ambiguity"? Do they hold together in a consistent system?

5. What is the significance for ethics of the denial of objectivity as a human characteristic?

6. What are the chief characteristics of man as a moral being in de Beauvoir's view?

7. Elaborate the contrast between "willing oneself not free" and "not willing oneself free." What is the significance of this contrast in the existentialist ethics?

8. How does de Beauvoir account for evil? What significance is given to the possibility of "bad willing"?

9. What problems of social morality are posed by the radical subjectivity of existential ethics? Are the solutions proposed by de Beauvoir adequate to assure social order?

10. Deweyan pragmatism and Sartrean existentialism share the premise that values are created by men, that they are not given as conditions of life. Contrast the implications of this premise as developed in the two systems of ethics with respect to: (1) the role of science in human affairs, (2) the nature of relationships between the individual and society, and (3) the meaning of freedom of will and its ethical significance. Are there other significant points of agreement or contrast?

Key to selections:

Simone de Beauvoir, *The Ethics of Ambiguity*, New York, The Citadel Press, 1964. Reprinted with the kind permission of the Philosophical Library, New York.

ᵃ pp. 7–8	ᶠ pp. 16–18
ᵇ pp. 9–10	ᵍ pp. 23–26
ᶜ pp. 11–13	ʰ pp. 32–34
ᵈ pp. 14–15	ⁱ pp. 156–158
ᵉ pp. 15–16	ʲ pp. 158–159

Guide to Additional Reading

ADDITIONAL SOURCE MATERIAL:

JASPERS, KARL, *Existentialism and Humanism*, trans. E. B. Ashton, New York, R. F. Moore Co., 1952.

KIERKEGAARD, SØREN A., *The Concept of Dread*, trans. Walter Lowrie, Princeton, Princeton University Press, 1944 (2nd. ed. 1957).

——, *Concluding Unscientific Postscript*, trans. David F. Swenson, Princeton University Press, 1941.

MARCEL, GABRIEL, *The Existential Background of Human Dignity*, Cambridge, Harvard University Press, 1963.

DISCUSSION AND COMMENTARY:

Barrett, William, *Irrational Man: A Study in Existential Philosophy*, Garden City, New York, Doubleday, 1958.

Blackham, Harold J., *Six Existentialist Thinkers*, New York, Harper, 1959.

Breisach, Ernst, *Introduction to Modern Existentialism*, New York, Grove Press, 1962.

Grene, Marjorie, *Dreadful Freedom, A Critique of Existentialism*, Chicago, University of Chicago Press, 1948.

CHAPTER 19

Good Reasons in Ethics

KURT BAIER

K urt Baier (1917–   ), an Austrian by birth, received his advanced philosophical training at Oxford University, England. He began his professional life in Australia and New Zealand where he taught at such institutions as the University of Melbourne and Canberra University College. Prior to coming to the United States in 1962, he served as President of the Australian Association of Philosophy. Professor Baier is presently Chairman of the Department of Philosophy at the University of Pittsburgh, In addition to his chief work in ethics, *The Moral Point of View.* he has contributed numerous articles to philosophical journals.

•

Baier is a prominent member of a group of ethical theorists frequently referred to as "prescriptivists," a group which emphasizes the directive or guiding function of moral judgments in arriving at moral decisions. These philosophers are not primarily concerned with challenging the analyses of ethical language insisted on by Ayer, Stevenson, and others — analyses wherein moral judgments are regarded as essentially emotive in meaning. Rather, they conceive of themselves as embarking on what they consider to be the more traditional and relevant task of analyzing the role that moral judgments play in our quest for solutions to concrete and vital moral problems.

According to Baier, moral investigation begins with the question "What shall I do?", or more precisely, "What is the best thing to do?", or to be more precise still, "What course of action is supported by the best reasons?" When he uses the term "best reasons," he is thinking of a class of *good reasons* — facts which can play a part in effecting a decision for one course of action rather than another — some of which are superior to others. Baier's evidence that there are good reasons is simply that people actually do believe that certain kinds of facts will guide them in making proper decisions. For most of us, learning that if we do A rather than B, we will be doing something detrimental to society, counts, in and of itself, as a good reason for not doing A; or, again, learning that doing C rather than D will produce pleasure rather than pain for someone constitutes, in and of itself, a good reason for doing C. In brief, he is content to work from the psycho-sociological fact that men do have "consideration-making beliefs" without attempting to settle the ultimate philosophical status of such beliefs.

As we have indicated, Baier does not regard good reasons as either all of a kind or on the same level. Just as John Stuart Mill insisted that some pleasures are superior to others, so too Baier insists that some reasons are superior to others. Again, just as Mill ultimately defends his hierarchy by an appeal to "competent judges," so too Baier submits the matter to those who can appreciate the entire range of reasons. He declares that, in general, selfish reasons are superior to reasons of immediate pleasure, and that moral reasons outweigh selfish reasons.

An examination of the nature of an ethical dispute will illustrate the role of the hierarchy of good reasons. Suppose A struck B in anger, but now both are calm enough to debate the morality of the action. B claims that A broke a rule of gentlemanly behavior. A objects that rules are made to be broken when they fail to serve our private interests. B counters that if the rules of conduct are abandoned, society will degenerate into a human jungle. This interchange of "good reasons" points up the fact that there are various justifications for rules of behavior — we typically offer various kinds of reasons for behavior. After B pointed out that a rule of conduct had been transgressed, A offered a justification or good reason for breaking the rule, namely, promotion of personal interest, while B responded with a justification in terms of social welfare. The question now becomes one of finding a viewpoint from which the disputants can determine fairly and effectively the superiority of one kind of reason over another. Baier holds that there is such a viewpoint: "the moral point of view."

The only standpoint from which we can judge between the kinds of good reasons is one which fulfills two conditions: first, it must, as Kant emphasized, be one in which everyone is regarded as subject to the same rules; second, it must be one which is for the good of everyone alike. The essence of the second condition is simply that a given action be such that an individual would find it acceptable, whether he was related to it either as an active agent or as a passive recipient. Only when we adopt a genuinely impartial viewpoint in which no one is morally exempt, and no one is morally neglected, can we carry out the judicial function of deciding how to rank good reasons. Any other viewpoint is unsatisfactory because, being less than perfectly impartial, rank has not been taken into account. When we avail ourselves of "the moral point of view," we are "looking at the world from the point of view of anyone" and for the good of everyone. In brief, then, Baier offers a theory which assures us that good reasons can be ranked in such a way that they provide us with an effective basis for moral decisions.

1. Baier raises a question which has been central to the history of ethics: Is there a distinction between the moral point of view and that of self-interest?

Throughout the history of philosophy, by far the most popular candidate for the position of the moral point of view has been self-interest. There are obvious parallels between these two standpoints. Both aim at the good. Both are rational. Both involve deliberation, the surveying and weighing of reasons. The adoption of either yields statements containing the word 'ought.' Both involve the notion of self-mastery and control over the desires. It is, moreover, plausible to hold that a person could not have a reason for doing anything whatsoever unless his behavior was designed to promote his own good. Hence, if morality is to have the support of reason, moral reasons must be self-interested, hence the point of view of morality and self-interest must be the same. On the other hand, it seems equally obvious that morality and self-interest are very frequently opposed. Morality often requires us to refrain from doing what self-interest recommends or to do what self-interest forbids. Hence morality and self-interest cannot be the same points of view.[a]

2. By drawing a distinction within a distinction, Baier isolates the view of "enlightened self-interest" so that it presents the most plausible case for asserting that morality and egoism coincide. This plausibility is enhanced by the limited support of the notable commentator on ethics, Henry Sidgwick. However, Baier points out that far from being "the moral viewpoint," it would substitute chaos for moral order, if universally practiced.

Can we save the doctrine that the moral point of view is that of self-interest? One way of circumventing the difficulty just mentioned is to draw a distinction between two senses of 'self-interest,' shortsighted and enlightened. The shortsighted egoist always follows his short-range interest without taking into consideration how this will affect others and how their reactions will affect him. The enlightened egoist, on the other hand, knows that he cannot get the most out of life unless he pays attention to the needs of others on whose good will he depends. On this view, the standpoint of (immoral) egoism differs from that of morality in that it fails to consider the interests of others even when this costs little or nothing or when the long-range benefits to oneself are likely to be greater than the short-range sacrifices.

This view can be made more plausible still if we distinguish between those egoists who consider each course of action on its own merits and those who, for convenience, adopt certain rules of thumb which they have found will promote their long-range interest. Slogans such as 'Honesty is the best policy,' 'Give to charity rather than to the Department of Internal Revenue,' 'Always give a penny to a beggar when you are likely to be watched by your acquaintances,' 'Treat your servants kindly and they will work for you like slaves,' 'Never be arrogant to anyone — you may need his services one day,' are maxims of this sort. They embody the "wisdom" of a given society. The enlightened long-range egoist may adopt these as rules of thumb, that is, as *prima-facie* maxims, as rules which he will observe unless he has good evidence that departing from them will pay him better than abiding by them. It is obvious that the rules of behavior adopted by the enlightened egoist will be very similar to those of a man who rigidly follows our own moral code.

Sidgwick appears to believe that egoism is one of the legitimate "methods of ethics," although he himself rejects it on the basis of an "intuition" that it is false. He supports the legitimacy of egoism by the argument that everyone could consistently adopt the egoistic point of view. "I quite admit that when the painful necessity comes for another man to choose between his own happiness and the general happiness, he must as a reasonable being prefer his own, i.e. it is right for him to do this on my principle." The consistent enlightened egoist satisfies the categorical imperative, or at least one version of it, 'Act only on that maxim whereby thou canst at the same time will that it should become a universal law.'

However, no "intuition" is required to see that this is not the point of view of morality, even though it can be universally adopted without self-contradiction. In the first place, a consistent egoist adopts for all occasions the principle 'everyone for himself' which we allow (at most) only in conditions of chaos, when the normal moral order breaks down. Its adoption marks the return to the law of the jungle, the state of nature, in which the "softer," more "chivalrous" ways of morality have no place.[b]

3. He further argues that self-interested views, whether short-range or enlightened, are logically self-defeating.

. . . It can be shown that those who adopt consistent egoism cannot make moral judgments. Moral talk is impossible for consistent egoists. But this amounts to a *reductio ad absurdum* of consistent egoism.

Let B and K be candidates for the presidency of a certain country and let it be granted that it is in the interest of either to be elected, but that only one can succeed. It would then be in the interest of B but against the interest of K if B were elected, and vice versa, and therefore in the interest of B but against the interest of K if K were liquidated, and vice versa. But from this it would follow that B ought to liquidate K, that it is wrong for B not to do so, that B has not "done his duty" until he has liquidated K; and vice versa. Similarly K, knowing that his own liquidation is in the interest of B and therefore anticipating B's attempts to secure it, ought to take steps to foil B's endeavors. It would be wrong for him not to do so. He would "not have done his duty" until he had made sure of stopping B. It follows that if K prevents B from liquidating him, his act must be said to be both wrong and not wrong — wrong because it is the prevention of what B ought to do, his duty, and wrong for B not to do it; not wrong because it is what K ought to do, his duty, and wrong for K not to do it. But one and the same act (logically) cannot be both morally wrong and not morally wrong. Hence in cases like these morality does not apply.

This is obviously absurd. For morality is designed to apply in just such cases, namely, those where interests conflict. But if the point of view of morality were that of self-interest, then there could *never* be moral solutions of conflicts of interest. However, when there are conflicts of interest, we always look for a "higher" point of view, one from which such conflicts can be settled. Consistent egoism makes everyone's private interest the "highest court of appeal." But by 'the moral point of view' we *mean* a point of view which is a court of appeal for conflicts of interest. Hence it cannot (logically) be identical with the point of view of self-interest . . .ᶜ

4. Having asserted that ethical disputes are insoluble unless we can show some reasons to be superior to others, he turns his attention to the way in which the hierarchy of reasons is established. He begins with a ranking or comparison of self-regarding reasons and other regarding reasons with respect to pleasure.

How can we establish rules of superiority? It is a prima-facie reason for me to do something not only that I would enjoy it if *I* did it, but also that *you* would enjoy it if *I* did it. People generally would fare better if this fact were treated as a pro, for if this reason were followed, it would create additional enjoyment all around. But which of the two prima-facie reasons is superior when they conflict? How would we tell?

At first it would seem that these reasons are equally good, that there is nothing to choose between them, that no case can be made out for saying that people generally would fare better if the one or the other were treated as superior. But this is a mistake.

Suppose I could be spending half an hour in writing a letter to Aunt Agatha who would enjoy receiving one though I would not enjoy writing it, or alternatively in listening to a lecture which I would enjoy doing. Let us also assume that I cannot do both, that I neither enjoy writing the letter nor dislike it, that Aunt Agatha enjoys receiving the letter as much as I enjoy listening to the lecture, and that there are no extraneous considerations such as that I deserve especially to enjoy myself there and then, or that Aunt Agatha does, or that she has special claims against me, or that I have special responsibilities or obligations toward her.

In order to see which is the better of these two reasons, we must draw a distinction between two different cases: the case in which someone derives pleasure from giving pleasure to others and the case where he does not. Everyone is so related to certain other persons that he derives greater pleasure from doing something together with them than doing it alone because in doing so he is giving them pleasure. He derives pleasure not merely from the game of tennis he is playing but from the fact that in playing he is pleasing his partner. We all enjoy pleasing those we love. Many of us enjoy pleasing even strangers. Some even enjoy pleasing their enemies. Others get very little enjoyment from pleasing their fellow men.

We must therefore distinguish between people with two kinds of natural make-up: on the one hand, those who need not always choose between pleasing themselves and pleasing others, who can please themselves *by* pleasing others, who can please themselves more by not merely pleasing themselves, and, on the other hand, those who always or often have to choose between pleasing themselves and pleasing others, who derive no pleasure from pleasing others, who do not please themselves more by pleasing not merely themselves.

If I belong to the first kind, then I shall derive pleasure from pleasing Aunt Agatha. Although writing her a letter is not enjoyable in itself, as listening to the lecture is, I nevertheless derive enjoyment from writing it because it is a way of pleasing her and I enjoy pleasing people. In choosing between writing the letter and listening to the lecture, I do not therefore have to choose between pleasing her and pleasing myself. I have merely to choose between two different ways of pleasing myself. If I am a man of the second kind, then I must choose between pleasing myself and pleasing her. When we have eliminated all possible moral reasons, such as standing in a special relationship to the person, then it would be strange for someone to prefer pleasing someone else to pleasing himself. How strange this is can be seen if we substitute for Aunt Agatha a complete stranger.

I conclude from this that the fact that I would enjoy it if *I* did x is a better reason for doing x than the fact that you would enjoy it if I did x. Similarly in the fact that I would enjoy doing x if I did it I have a reason for doing x which is better than the reason for doing y which I have in the fact that you would enjoy doing y as much as I would enjoy doing x. More generally speaking, we can say that self-regarding reasons are better than other-regarding ones. Rationally speaking, the old quip is true that everyone is his own nearest neighbor.[d]

5. Again and quite surprisingly, Baier suggests that generally speaking, when self-interested reasons and altruistic reasons are pitted against each other, the former properly takes precedence.

This is more obvious still when we consider the case of self-interest. Both the fact that doing x would be in my interest and the fact that it would be in someone else's interest are excellent prima-facie reasons for me to do x. But the self-interested reason is better than the altruistic one. Of course, interests need not conflict, and then I need not choose. I can do what is in both our interests. But sometimes interests conflict, and then it is in accordance with reason (prima facie) to prefer my own interest to someone else's. That my making an application for a job is in *my* interest is a reason for me to apply, which is better than the reason against applying, which I have in the fact that my not applying is in *your* interest.

There is no doubt that this conviction is correct for all cases. It is obviously better that everyone should look after his own interest than that everyone should neglect it in favor of someone else's. For whose interest should have precedence? It must be remembered that we are considering a case in which there are no special reasons for preferring a particular person's interests to one's own, as when there are no special moral obligations or emotional ties. Surely, in the absence of any *special* reasons for preferring someone else's interests, *everyone's* interests are best served if *everyone* puts his own interests first. For, by and large, everyone is himself the best judge of what is in his own best interest, since everyone usually knows best what his plans, aims, ambitions, or aspirations are. Moreover, everyone is more diligent in the promotion of his own interests than that of others. Enlightened egoism is a possible, rational, orderly system of running things, enlightened altruism is not. Everyone can look after himself, no one can look after everyone else. Even if everyone had to look after only two others, he could not do it as well as looking after himself alone. And if he has to look after only one person, there is no advantage in making that person some one other than himself. On the contrary, he is less likely to know as well what that person's interest is or to be as zealous in its promotion as in that of his own interest.[e]

6. He is unwilling to concede, however, that reasons of self-interest are the highest. He then presents a case for the superiority of moral reasons.

Are moral reasons really superior to reasons of self-interest as we all believe? Do we really have reason on our side when we follow moral reasons against self-interest? What reasons could there be for being moral? Can we really give an answer to 'Why should we be moral?' It is obvious that all these questions come to the same thing. When we ask, 'Should we be moral?' or 'Why should we be moral?' or 'Are moral reasons superior to all others?' we ask to be shown the reason for being moral. What is this reason?

Let us begin with a state of affairs in which reasons of self-interest are supreme. In such a state everyone keeps his impulses and inclinations in check when and only when they would lead him into behavior detrimental to his own interest. Everyone who follows reason will discipline himself to rise early, to do his exercises, to refrain from excessive drinking and smoking, to keep good company, to marry the right sort of girl, to work and study hard in order to get on, and so on. However, it will often happen that peoples' interests conflict. In such a case, they will have to resort to ruses or force to get their own way. As this becomes known, men will become suspicious, for they will regard one another as scheming competitors for the good things in life. The universal supremacy of the rules of self-interest must lead to what Hobbes called the state of nature. At the same time, it will be clear to everyone that universal obedience to certain rules overriding self-interest would produce a state of affairs which serves everyone's interest much better than his unaided pursuit of it in a state where everyone does the same. Moral rules are universal rules designed to override those of self-interest when following the latter is harmful to others. 'Thou shalt not kill,' 'Thou shalt not lie,' 'Thou shalt not steal' are rules which forbid the inflicting of harm on someone else even when this might be in one's interest.

The very *raison d'être* of a morality is to yield reasons which overrule the reasons of self-interest in those cases when everyone's following self-interest would be harmful to everyone. Hence moral reasons are superior to all others.ᶠ

7. But can we convince a defender of enlightened self-interest that moral reasons are superior? Baier responds to this challenge by pointing out that, in the first place, the typical argument for self-interest is circular and therefore fallacious, and, in the second place, that although the moral theorist may be tempted to respond with an equally circular counterargument, he need not do so: he can propose a viewpoint from which a decision about the two types of reasons can be rendered — a decision which favors moral reasons.

"But what does this mean?" it might be objected. "If it merely means that we do so regard them, then you are of course right, but your contention is useless, a mere point of usage. And how could it mean any more? If it means that we not only do so regard them, but *ought* so to regard them, then there must be *reasons* for saying this. But there could not be any reasons for it. If you offer reasons of self-interest, you are arguing in a circle. Moreover, it cannot be true that it is always in my interest to treat moral reasons as superior to reasons of self-interest. If it were, self-interest and morality could never conflict, but they notoriously do.

It is equally circular to argue that there are moral reasons for saying that one ought to treat moral reasons as superior to reasons of self-interest. And what other reasons are there?"

The answer is that we are now looking at the world from the point of view of *anyone*. We are not examining particular alternative courses of action before this or that person; we are examining two alternative worlds, one in which moral reasons are always treated by everyone as superior to reasons of self-interest and one in which the reverse is the practice. And we can see that the first world is the better world, because we can see that the second world would be the sort which Hobbes describes as the state of nature.

This shows that I ought to be moral, for when I ask the question 'What ought I to do?' I am asking, 'Which is the course of action supported by the best reasons?' But since it has just been shown that moral reasons are superior to reasons of self-interest, I have been given a reason for being moral, for following moral reasons rather than any other, namely, they are better reasons than any other.[g]

8. Through an analysis of Hobbesian political and ethical theory, Baier both clarifies a portion of his own position and provides an answer to the question: "Do we have a reason for being moral, whatever the conditions we find ourselves in?"

... Could there not be situations in which it is not true that we have reasons for being moral, that, on the contrary, we have reasons for ignoring the demands of morality? Is not Hobbes right in saying that in a state of nature the laws of nature, that is, the rules of morality, bind only *in foro interno?*

Hobbes argues as follows.

(i) To live in a state of nature is to live outside society. It is to live in conditions in which there are no common ways of life and, therefore, no reliable expectations about other people's behavior other than that they will follow their inclination or their interest.

(ii) In such a state reason will be the enemy of co-operation and mutual trust. For it is too risky to hope that other people will refrain from protecting their own interests by the preventive elimination of probable or even possible dangers to them. Hence reason will counsel everyone to avoid these risks by preventive action. But this leads to war.

(iii) It is obvious that everyone's following self-interest leads to a state of affairs which is desirable from no one's point of view. It is, on the contrary, desirable that everybody should follow rules overriding self-interest whenever that is to the detriment of others. In other words, it is desirable to bring about a state of affairs in which all obey the rules of morality.

(iv) However, Hobbes claims that in the state of nature it helps nobody if a single person or a small group of persons begins to follow the rules of morality, for this could only lead to the extinction of such individuals or groups. In such a state, it is therefore contrary to reason to be moral.

(v) The situation can change, reason can support morality, only when the presumption about other people's behavior is reversed. Hobbes thought that this could be achieved only by the creation of an absolute ruler with absolute power to enforce his laws. We have already seen that this is not true and that it is quite different if people live in a society, that is, if they have common ways of life, which are taught to all members and somehow enforced by the group. Its members have reason to expect their fellows generally to obey its rules, that is, its religion, morality, customs, and law, even when doing so is not, on certain occasions, in their interest. Hence they too have reason to follow these rules.

Is this argument sound? One might, of course, object to step (i) on the grounds that this is an empirical proposition for which there is little or no evidence. For how can we know whether it is true that people in a state of nature would follow only their inclinations or, at best, reasons of self-interest, when nobody now lives in that state or has ever lived in it?

However, there is some empirical evidence to support this

claim. For in the family of nations, individual states are placed very much like individual persons in a state of nature. The doctrine of the sovereignty of nations and the absence of an effective international law and police force are a guarantee that nations live in a state of nature, without commonly accepted rules that are somehow enforced. Hence it must be granted that living in a state of nature leads to living in a state in which individuals act either on impulse or as they think their interest dictates. For states pay only lip service to morality. They attack their hated neighbors when the opportunity arises. They start preventive wars in order to destroy the enemy before he can deliver his knockout blow. Where interests conflict, the stronger party usually has his way, whether his claims are justified or not. And where the relative strength of the parties is not obvious, they usually resort to arms in order to determine "whose side God is on." Treaties are frequently concluded but, morally speaking, they are not worth the paper they are written on. Nor do the partners regard them as contracts binding in the ordinary way, but rather as public expressions of the belief of the governments concerned that for the time being their alliance is in the interest of the allies. It is well understood that such treaties may be canceled before they reach their predetermined end or simply broken when it suits one partner. In international affairs, there are very few examples of *Nibelungentreue*, although statesmen whose countries have profited from keeping their treaties usually make such high moral claims.[h]

9. The implications for international affairs are further examined, and considerations are uncovered to indicate the hierarchy of good reasons on a moral rather than a self-interested basis.

It is, moreover, difficult to justify morality in international affairs. For suppose a highly moral statesman were to demand that his country adhere to a treaty obligation even though this meant its ruin or possibly its extinction. Suppose he were to say that treaty obligations are sacred and must be kept whatever the consequences. How could he defend such a policy? Perhaps one might argue that someone has to make a start in order to create mutual confidence in international affairs. Or one might say that setting a good example is the best way of inducing others to follow suit. But such a defense would hardly be sound. The less skeptical one is about the genuineness of the cases in which nations have adhered to their treaties from a sense of moral obligation, the more skeptical one must be about the effectiveness of such examples of virtue in effecting a change of international practice. Power politics still govern in international affairs.

We must, therefore, grant Hobbes the first step in his argument and admit that in a state of nature people, as a matter of psychological fact, would not follow the dictates of morality. But we might object to the next step that knowing this psychological fact about other people's behavior constitutes a reason for behaving in the same way. Would it not still be immoral for anyone to ignore the demands of morality even though he knows that others are likely or certain to do so, too? Can we offer as a justification for morality the fact that no one is entitled to do wrong just because someone else is doing wrong? This argument begs the question whether it *is* wrong for anyone in this state to disregard the demands of morality. It cannot be wrong to break a treaty or make preventive war if we have no reason to obey the moral rules. For to say that it is wrong to do so is to say that we ought not to do so. But if we have no reason for obeying the moral rule, then we have no reason overruling self-interest, hence no reason for keeping the treaty when keeping it is not in our interest, hence it is not true that we have a reason for keeping it, hence not true that we ought to keep it, hence not true that it is wrong not to keep it.

I conclude that Hobbes's argument is sound. Moralities are systems of principles whose acceptance by everyone as overruling the dictates of self-interest is in the interest of everyone alike, though following the rules of a morality is not of course identical with following self-interest. If it were, there could be no conflict between a morality and self-interest and no point in having moral rules overriding self-interest. Hobbes is also right in saying that the application of this system of rules is in accordance with reason only in social conditions, that is, when there are well-established ways of behavior.

The answer to our question 'Why should we be moral?' is therefore as follows. We should be moral because being moral is following rules designed to overrule self-interest whenever it is in the interest of everyone alike that everyone should set aside his interest. It is not self-contradictory to say this, because it may be in one's interest *not* to follow one's interest at times. We have already seen that enlightened self-interest acknowledges this point. But while enlightened self-interest does not require any genuine sacrifice from anyone, morality does. In the interest of the possibility of the good life for everyone, voluntary sacrifices are sometimes required from everybody. Thus, a person might do better for himself by following enlightened self-interest rather than morality. It is not possible, however, that *everyone* should do better for himself by following enlightened self-interest rather than morality. The best possible life *for everyone* is possible only by everyone's following the rules of morality, that is, rules which quite frequently may require individuals to make genuine sacrifices.

It must be added to this, however, that such a system of rules has the support of reason only where people live in societies, that is, in conditions in which there are established common ways of behavior. Outside society, people have no reason for following such rules, that is, for being moral. In other words, outside society, the very distinction between right and wrong vanishes.[i]

10. Even if we admit that some types of reasons are qualitatively superior to others, it can still be asked why we should follow reason at all. Baier approaches this question by first clarifying what it means to act "contrary to reason."

What is it to follow reason? . . . It involves two tasks, the theoretical, finding out what it would be in accordance with reason to do in a certain situation, what contrary to reason, and

the practical task, to act accordingly. . . . We must remind ourselves that there are many different ways in which what we do or
believe or feel can be contrary to reason. It may be *irrational*, as
when, for no reason at all, we set our hand on fire or cut off our
toes one by one, or when, in the face of conclusive evidence to the
contrary, someone *believes* that her son killed in the war is still
alive, or when someone is *seized by fears* as a gun is pointed at him
although he knows for certain that it is not loaded. What we do,
believe, or feel is called irrational if it is the case not only that
there are conclusive or overwhelming reasons against doing,
believing, or feeling these things, but also that we must know there
are such reasons and we still persist in our action, belief, or feeling.

Or it may be *unreasonable*, as when we make demands which
are excessive or refuse without reason to comply with requests
which are reasonable. We say of demands or requests that they
are excessive if, though we are entitled to make them, the party
against whom we make them has good reasons for not complying,
as when the landlord demands the immediate vacation of the
premises in the face of well-supported pleas of hardship by the
tenant.

Being unreasonable is a much weaker form of going counter to
reason than being irrational. The former applies in cases where
there is a conflict of reasons and where one party does not acknowledge the obvious force of the case of the other or, while acknowledging it, will not modify his behavior accordingly. A person is
irrational only if he flies in the face of reason, if, that is, all reasons
are on one side and he acts contrary to it when he either acknowledges that this is so or, while refusing to acknowledge it, has no
excuse for failing to do so.

Again, someone may be *inconsistent*, as when he refuses a Jew
admission to a club although he has always professed strong
positive views on racial equality. Behavior or remarks are inconsistent if the agent or author professes principles adherence
to which would require him to say or do the opposite of what he
says or does.

Or a person may be *illogical*, as when he does something which, as anyone can see, cannot or is not at all likely to lead to success. Thus when I cannot find my glasses or my fountain pen, the logical thing to do is to look for them where I can remember I had them last or where I usually have them. It would be illogical of me to look under the bed or in the oven unless I have special reason to think they might be there. To say of a person that he is a logical type is to say that he always does what, on reflection, anyone would agree is most likely to lead to success. Scatterbrains, people who act rashly, without thinking, are the opposite of logical.[j]

11. With some understanding of what it would mean to reject reason as a guide, he indicates that, in one sense at least, the question "Why follow reason?" is a trivial exercise in rhetoric.

When we speak of following reason, we usually mean 'doing what is supported by the best reasons because it is so supported,' or perhaps 'doing what we think (rightly or wrongly) is supported by the best reasons because we think it is so supported.' It might, then occur to someone to ask, 'Why should I follow reason?' During the last hundred years or so, reason has had a very bad press. Many thinkers have sneered at it and have recommended other guides, such as the instincts, the unconscious, the voice of the blood, inspiration, charisma, and the like. They have advocated that one should not follow reason but be guided by these other forces.

However, in the most obvious sense of the question 'Should I follow reason?' this is a tautological question like 'Is a circle a circle?'; hence the advice 'You should not follow reason' is as nonsensical as the claim 'A circle is not a circle.' Hence the question 'Why should I follow reason?' is as silly as 'Why is a circle a circle?' We need not, therefore, take much notice of the advocates of unreason. They show by their advocacy that they are not too clear on what they are talking about.

How is it that 'Should I follow reason?' is a tautological question like 'Is a circle a circle?' Questions of the form 'Shall I do this?'

or 'Should I do this?' or 'Ought I to do this?' are . . . requests to someone (possibly oneself) to deliberate on one's behalf. That is to say, they are requests to survey the facts and weigh the reasons for and against this course of action. These questions could therefore be paraphrased as follows. 'I wish to do what is supported by the best reasons. Tell me whether this is so supported.' As already mentioned, 'following reason' means 'doing what is supported by the best reasons.' Hence the question 'Shall (should, ought) I follow reason?' must be paraphrased as 'I wish to do what is supported by the best reasons. Tell me whether doing what is supported by the best reasons is doing what is supported by the best reasons.' It is, therefore, not worth asking.

The question '*Why* should I follow reason?' simply does not make sense. Asking it shows complete lack of understanding of the meaning of 'why questions.' 'Why should I do this?' is a request to be given the reason for saying that I should do this. It is normally asked when someone has already said, 'You should do this' and answered by giving the reason. But since 'Should I follow reason?' means 'Tell me whether doing what is supported by the best reasons is doing what is supported by the best reasons,' there is simply no possibility of adding 'Why?' For the question now comes to this, 'Tell me the reason why doing what is supported by the best reasons is doing what is supported by the best reasons.' It is exactly like asking, 'Why is a circle a circle?'ᵏ

12. Baier does acknowledge, however, that the question "Why follow reason?" is meaningful, but only in the sense in which it pertains to reason in its theoretical rather than practical role. Somewhat reminiscent of Epictetus nineteen centuries earlier, Baier points out that any effort to displace the authority of reason depends upon the very authority of that which it would displace.[1]

However, it must be admitted that there is another possible interpretation to our question according to which it makes sense and can even be answered. 'Why should I follow reason?' may

[1]See p. 2. (*Great Traditions in Ethics*).

not be a request for a reason in support of a tautological remark, but a request for a reason why one should enter on the theoretical task of deliberation. . . . Following reason involves the completion of two tasks, the theoretical and the practical. The point of the theoretical is to give guidance in the practical task. We perform the theoretical only because we wish to complete the practical task in accordance with the outcome of the theoretical. On our first interpretation, 'Should I follow reason?' means 'Is the practical task completed when it is completed in accordance with the outcome of the theoretical task?' And the answer to this is obviously 'Yes,' for that is what we mean by 'completion of the practical task.' On our second interpretation, 'Should I follow reason?' is not a question about the practical but about the theoretical task. It is not a question about whether, given that one is prepared to perform both these tasks, they are properly completed in the way indicated. It is a question about whether one should enter on the whole performance at all, whether the "game" is worth playing. And this is a meaningful question. It might be better to "follow inspiration" than to "follow reason," in this sense: better to close one's eyes and wait for an answer to flash across the mind.

But while, so interpreted, 'Should I follow reason?' makes sense, it seems to me obvious that the answer to it is 'Yes, because it pays.' Deliberation is the only reliable method. Even if there were other reliable methods, we could only tell whether they were reliable by checking them against this method. Suppose some charismatic leader counsels, 'Don't follow reason, follow me. My leadership is better than that of reason'; we would still have to check his claim against the ordinary methods of reason. We would have to ascertain whether in following his advice we were doing the best thing. And this we can do only by examining whether he has advised us to do what is supported by the best reasons. His claim to be better than reason can in turn only be supported by the fact that he tells us precisely the same as reason does.

Is there any sense, then, in his claim that his guidance is preferable to that of reason? There may be, for working out what is supported by the best reasons takes a long time. Frequently, the best thing to do is to do something quickly now rather than the most appropriate thing later. A leader may have the ability to "see," to "intuit," what is the best thing to do more quickly than it is possible to work this out by the laborious methods of deliberation. In evaluating the qualities of leadership of such a person, we are evaluating *his ability to perform correctly the practical task of following reason* without having to go through the lengthy operations of the theoretical. Reason is required to tell us whether anyone has qualities of leadership better than ordinary, in the same way that pencil and paper multiplications are required to tell us whether a mathematical prodigy is genuine or a fraud. . . .[1]

Questions

1. What types of "good reasons" does Baier distinguish, and how does he arrange them in hierarchical order? Can you think of any types of good reason that might be added?
2. In what ways is Baier's ethical theory dependent on the moral philosophy of John Stuart Mill? of Immanuel Kant? Include consideration of the purposes of moral philosophy.
3. What distinctions does Baier make among types of self-interest? What value is assigned to self-interest among good reasons?
4. Outline Baier's demonstration of the illogical character of egoistic theories.
5. Apply Baier's method of moral decision-making to the problem of cheating on examinations; to one or more actual moral problems in your own experience.
6. What is Baier's evaluation of altruistic reasons? Do you agree or disagree and why?
7. What does Baier mean by "moral reasons"? How does he explain their superiority to other good reasons?
8. What is the function of Baier's detailed examination of Hobbes' theory?
9. Discuss Baier's analysis of international morality. Does he provide adequate support for the analogy between individual and international morality?

10. (a) Discuss and evaluate Baier's distinction between "irrational," "unreasonable," and "inconsistent." Does the contrast hold for the positive forms?
(b) What answers does Baier give to the question, "Why follow reason?" Of what importance is the answer in his ethical theory?

Key to selections:

KURT BAIER, *The Moral Point of View*, Copyright 1958 Cornell University Used by permission of Cornell University Press.

^a pp. 187–188	^g pp. 309–310
^b pp. 188–189	^h pp. 310–313
^c pp. 189–190	ⁱ pp. 313–315
^d pp. 304–306	^j pp. 315–317
^e pp. 306–307	^k pp. 317–318
^f pp. 308–309	^l pp. 318–320

Guide to Additional Reading

ADDITIONAL SOURCE MATERIAL:

HARE, R. M., *The Language of Morals*, New York, Oxford University Press, 1964.
NOEL-SMITH, P. H., *Ethics*, Baltimore, Penguin Books, 1954.
TOULMIN, S., *Reason in Ethics*, Cambridge, Cambridge University Press, 1960.

DISCUSSION AND COMMENTARY:

Frankena, W. K., *Ethics*, Englewood Cliffs, Prentice-Hall, 1963.
Baier, K., "Good Reasons," *Philosophical Studies*, IV(1953), 1–15.
——, "Proving a Moral Judgement," *Philosophical Studies*, IV(1953), 33–44.
Kerner, G., *The Revolution in Ethical Theory*, New York, Oxford University Press, 1966.

CHAPTER 20

Ethics and Social Justice

JOHN RAWLS

P rofessor John Rawls (1921–   ) received his Ph.D. in philosophy from Princeton University in 1950. From 1953 to 1959, he taught at Cornell University, and while there he served as co-editor of the *Philosophical Review* for one year. From 1960 to 1962, he was Professor of Philosophy at Massachusetts Institute of Technology, and since 1962 he has been teaching at Harvard University. His chief work in ethics, *A Theory of Justice*, was published in 1971; in addition, he has written numerous articles for philosophical journals.

•

John Rawls' *A Theory of Justice* has received widespread public attention. This is an unusual reception for a lengthy, fully-argued philosophical treatise, and it is, perhaps, indicative of a view which may become the mark of our historical period: Socio-political institutions are themselves proper subjects for moral assessment. With the resolution of a Plato, Rawls insists that social morality is neither merely a matter of personal morality nor of institutional efficiency. Rawls is not Platonistic, however, in his approach to social and normative problems. In this regard, he belongs to the tradition of Hobbes, Locke, and Rousseau — the tradition of social-contract theorists.

Adopting the thesis that the ultimate basis of society is a set of tacit agreements, Rawls identifies his initial problem to be that of discovering the conditions which such agreements must satisfy. To the end of indicating his conclusions about this, an examination of accounts which he would judge to be unsuccessful becomes instructive. Thus he would argue that Hobbes' explication of the social contract cannot be basic. Hobbes insists that it is solely because of our self-serving desire for security that we agree to subordinate ourselves completely to an absolute sovereign power. But, this done, and the benefit of a measure of security achieved through the power of the sovereign, would we remain bound by the agreements made? It does not seem likely. On the Hobbesian account, for example, if a citizen in a relatively secure state desires to commit an illegal act and is confident that he can avoid detection, there is no reason in theory or practice for him to feel morally constrained from acting on that desire. If there is no fear, there is no obligation. Rawls is led by considerations of this sort to recognize that *basic social* agreements must be such that they are acceptable in perpetuity, that is, they are not conditional upon the happenstance of one's position in a society at a given time.

Consider another account of a social principle. In presenting an ideal state (*The Republic*), Plato invokes the notion that, on occasions, the leaders must manipulate some citizens. through the device of a "Noble Lie" in order to achieve a well-ordered state. Rawls would contend that no man, of his own volition, will agree to a social principle which reduces him to a mere means. An example of this sort isolates an additional criterion which social agreements must satisfy, namely, compacts must be such that if they were made public, all men would continue to support them. In Plato's case, however, publicity would surely work toward the disaffection of those being lied to. Strangely enough, this would be the case even if such men acknowledged their inferior abilities.

Rawls, therefore, isolates what he takes to be two important conditions for anyone entering into social agreements. Put negatively, the first is that the commitment to them does not depend upon the vagaries of an individual's circumstances; the second is that the commitment to them does not depend upon the individual's ignorance of their precise nature. Put positively, the first requirement is that everyone can make this commitment in perpetuity; the second is that everyone's commitment to the social principles involved increases as his understanding of them grows.

In line with the foregoing analysis, Rawls introduces the notion of an *ideal observer*. In this capacity, we must systematically ignore the happenstance of our special talents and inclinations, relative social status, political ideology, and all other accidental features of our life. From this vantage point, we are deliberately operating under a "veil of ignorance"; operating, that is, as free and rational persons with all factors of inequality eliminated. Rawls maintains that we have now arrived at the "original position" in which we can formulate the principles of social justice. These are the principles "agreed to in an initial situation that is fair": (1) each person in a society has an equal right to the maximum liberty compatible with the same amount of liberty for everyone else (equal liberty principle); (2) inequality is permissible to the extent that (a) it serves everyone's advantage, and (b) it arises under conditions of equal opportunity (difference principle).[1] These two principles are not correlative for Rawls. While a person under desperate economic and human circumstances would agree to a great loss of personal liberty in order to survive at a minimal level, he would not do so under less stringent conditions.

---

[1] In the full development of his viewpoint, which appears in *A Theory of Justice* [Cambridge, Harvard University Press, 1971, p. 302], Rawls gives his most technical formulation of the principles:

> "*First Principle.* Each person is to have an equal right to the most extensive total system of equal basic liberties compatible with a similar system of liberty for all. *Second Principle.* Social and economic inequalities are to be arranged so that they are both: (a) to the greatest benefit of the least advantaged, consistent with the just savings principle, and (b) attached to offices and positions open to all under conditions of fair equality of opportunity."

Since Rawls' second principle is reminiscent of the utilitarian ideal of promoting "the greatest happiness for the greatest number," it is appropriate to ask whether his view is merely classical utilitarianism in modern, sophisticated form.[2] Rawls' answer to this question would be that their divergence is much greater than a utilitarian suspects. As has just been pointed out, if the difference principle conflicts with the equal liberty principle, the latter takes priority unless we are faced with a condition of stark survival. On the other hand, according to the utilitarian or neo-Benthamite, Rawls' concern about the liberty of individuals is taken care of by the second principle. For, experience shows that, in the long run, gains in equal liberty have indeed been a fundamental and significant means for the promotion of social well-being. Rawls' objection to this prudential appeal is categorical: The ultimate justification of equal liberty in society is not that of a mere means to an end; rather, the principle of equal liberty is logically prior to the difference principle. Unfortunately the utilitarian perceives the relationship between liberty and social well-being as a mere matter of contingency. This position leaves open unjust possibilities, such as a benign slavery. No basis is provided for objecting to the loss of personal dignity in a conceivable context in which animal wants and needs are amply met.

The point Rawls is making is that any principle which allows for the possibility of such a case is unacceptable once it is understood. His message is clear: "Each person possesses an inviolability founded on justice that even the welfare of society as a whole cannot override. . . . Therefore . . . the rights secured by justice are not subject to political bargaining or to the calculus of social interests."[3]

The selections which follow are drawn from Rawls' article, "Justice as Reciprocity," which constitutes a brief survey of some salient features contained in *A Theory of Justice*.

• • •

[2] *Great Traditions in Ethics*, ch. XI, especially with respect to Bentham, pp. 229–230.
[3] Rawls, *A Theory of Justice*, p. 4.

1. Rawls sets for himself the task of analyzing that virtue of social institutions termed justice. *He supplies the distinctions between justice and fairness which are required for bringing the concepts into focus.*

It might seem at first sight that the concepts of justice and fairness are the same, and that there is no reason to distinguish between them. To be sure, there may be occasions in ordinary speech when the phrases expressing these notions are not readily interchangeable, but it may appear that this is a matter of style and not a sign of important conceptual differences. I think that this impression is mistaken, yet there is, at the same time, some foundation for it. Justice and fairness are, indeed, different concepts, but they share a fundamental element in common, which I shall call the concept of reciprocity. They represent this concept as applied to two distinct cases: very roughly, justice to a practice in which there is no option whether to engage in it or not, and one must play; fairness to a practice in which there is such an option, and one may decline the invitation. In this paper I shall present an analytic construction of the concept of justice from this point of view, and I shall refer to this analysis as the analysis of justice as reciprocity.

Throughout I consider justice as a virtue of social institutions only, or of what I have called practices. Justice as a virtue of particular actions or of persons comes in at but one place, where I discuss the prima facie duty of fair play. . . . Further, the concept of justice is to be understood in its customary way as representing but one of the many virtues of social institutions; for these institutions may be antiquated, inefficient, or degrading, or any number of other things, without being unjust. Justice is not to be confused with an all-inclusive vision of a good society, or thought of as identical with the concept of right. It is only one part of any such conception, and it is but one species of right. I shall focus attention, then, on the usual sense of justice in which it means essentially the elimination of arbitrary distinctions and the establishment within the structure of a practice of a proper share, balance, or equilibrium between competing claims. The principles of justice serve to specify the application of "arbitrary" and "proper," and they do this by formulating restrictions as to how practices may define positions and offices, and assign thereto powers and liabilities, rights and duties. While the definition of the sense of justice is sufficient to distinguish justice as a virtue of institutions from other such virtues as efficiency and humanity, it does not provide a complete conception of justice. For this the associated principles are needed. The major problem in the analysis of the concept of justice is how these principles are derived and connected with this moral concept, and what is their logical basis; and further, what principles, if any, have a special place and may properly be called the principles of justice. The argument is designed to lay the groundwork for answering these questions.[a]

2. Rawls introduces the two basic principles associated with the concept of justice. According to to his reasoning, they apply to the practices of persons. *By* persons *he means either particular human beings or collective agencies, and by* practices *he means "any form of activity specified by a system of rules which defines offices and roles, rights and duties."*

The conception of justice which I want to consider has two principles associated with it. Both of them, and so the conception itself, are extremely familiar; and, indeed, this is as it should be, since one would hope eventually to make a case for regarding them as the principles of justice. It is unlikely that novel principles could be candidates for this position. It may be possible, however, by using the concept of reciprocity as a framework, to assemble these principles against a different background and to look at them in a new way. I shall now state them and then provide a brief commentary to clarify their meaning.

First, each person participating in a practice, or affected by it, has an equal right to the most extensive liberty compatible with a like liberty for all; and second, inequalities are arbitrary unless it is reasonable to expect that they will work out to everyone's advantage, and provided that the positions and offices to which they attach, or from which they may be gained, are open to all. These principles express justice as a complex of three ideas: liberty, equality, and reward for services contributing to the common good.

A word about the term "person." This expression is to be construed variously depending on the circumstances. On some occasions it will mean human individuals, but in others it may refer to nations, provinces, business firms, churches, teams, and so on. The principles of justice apply to conflicting claims made by persons of all of these separate kinds. There is, perhaps, a certain logical priority to the case of human individuals: it may be possible to analyze the actions of so-called artificial persons as logical constructions of the actions of human persons, and it is plausible to maintain that the worth of institutions is derived solely from the benefits they bring to human individuals. Nevertheless an analysis of justice should not begin by making either of these assumptions, or by restricting itself to the case of human persons; and it can gain considerably from not doing so. As I shall use the term "person," then, it will be ambiguous in the manner indicated.[b]

3. Rawls clarifies and qualifies equal liberty, *the first principle of justice.*

The first principle holds, of course, only if other things are equal: that is, while there must always be a justification for departing from the initial position of equal liberty (liberty being defined by reference to the pattern of rights and duties, powers and liabilities, established by a practice), and the burden of proof is placed on him who would depart from it, nevertheless, there can be, and often there is, a justification for doing so. Now, that similar particular cases, as defined by a practice, should be treated similarly as they arise, is part of the very concept of a practice; in accordance with the analysis of justice as regularity, it is involved in the notion of an activity in accordance with rules, and expresses the concept of equality in one of its forms: that is, equality as the impartial and equitable administration and application of the rules whatever they are, which define a practice. The first principle expresses the concept of equality in another form, namely, as applied to the definition and initial specification of the structure of practices themselves. It holds, for example, that there is a presumption against the distinctions and classifications made by legal systems and other practices to the extent that they infringe on the original and equal liberty of the persons participating in them, or affected by them. The second principle defines how this presumption may be rebutted.

It might be argued at this point that justice requires only that there be an equal liberty. If, however, a more extensive liberty were possible for all without loss or conflict, then it would be irrational to settle upon a lesser liberty. There is no reason for circumscribing rights unless their exercise would be incompatible, or would render the practice defining them less effective. Where such a limitation of liberty seems to have occurred, there must be some special explanation. It may have arisen from a mistake or misapprehension; or perhaps it persists from a time past when it had a rational basis, but does so no longer. Otherwise, such a limitation would be inexplicable; the acceptance of it would conflict with the premise that the persons engaged in the practice want the things which a more extensive liberty would make possible. Therefore no serious distortion of the concept of justice is likely to follow from associating with it a principle requiring the greatest equal liberty. This association is necessary once it is supposed, as I shall suppose, that the persons engaged in the practices to which the principles of justice apply are rational.[c]

4. Rawls continues with the clarification and qualification of the difference principle.

The second principle defines what sorts of inequalities are permissible; it specifies how the presumption laid down by the first principle may be put aside. Now by inequalities it is best to understand not any differences between offices and positions, but differences in the benefits and burdens attached to them either directly or indirectly, such as prestige and wealth, or liability to taxation and compulsory services. Players in a game do not protest against there being different positions, such as that of batter, pitcher, catcher, and the like, nor to there being various privileges and powers specified by the rules. Nor do citizens of a country object to there being the different offices of government such as that of president, senator, governor, judge, and so on, each with its special rights and duties. It is not differences of this kind that are normally thought of as inequalities, but differences in the resulting distribution established by a practice, or made possible by it, of the things men strive to attain or to avoid. Thus they may complain about the pattern of honors and rewards set up by a practice (e.g., the privileges and salaries of government officials) or they may object to the distribution of power and wealth which results from the various ways in which men avail themselves of the opportunities allowed by it (e.g., the concentration of wealth which may develop in a free price system allowing large entrepreneurial or speculative gains).

It should be noted that the second principle holds an inequality is allowed only if there is a reason to believe that the practice with the inequality, or resulting in it, will work for the advantage of *every* person engaging in it. Here it is important to stress that every person must gain from the inequality. Since the principle applies to practices, it implies then that the representative man in every office or position defined by a practice, when he views it as a going concern, must find it reasonable to prefer his condition and prospects with the inequality to what they would be under the practice without it. The principles exclude, therefore, the justification of inequalities on the grounds that the disadvantages of those in one position are outweighed by the greater advantages of those in another position. This rather simple restriction is the main modification I wish to make in the utilitarian principle as usually understood. When coupled with the notion of a practice, it is a restriction of consequence, and one which some utilitarians, notably

Hume and Mill, have used in their discussions of justice without realizing apparently its significance, or at least without calling attention to it.

Further, it is also necessary that the various offices to which special benefits or burdens attach are open to all. It may be, for example, to the common advantage, as just defined, to attach special benefits to certain offices. Perhaps by doing so the requisite talent can be attracted to them and encouraged to give its best efforts. But any offices having special benefits must be won in a fair competition in which contestants are judged on their merits. If some offices were not open, those excluded would normally be justified in feeling unjustly treated, even if they benefited from the greater efforts of those who were allowed to compete for them. Moreover, they would be justified in their complaint not only because they were excluded from certain external emoluments of office, but because they were barred from attaining the great intrinsic goods which the skillful and devoted exercise of some offices represents, and so they would be deprived, from the start, of one of the leading ways to achieve a full human life.[d]

5. Having presented the principles of justice, Rawls next considers how they are derived. Although he does not dismiss the possibility that the equal liberty principle is self-evident, he offers instead a set of assumptions from which both principles seem to follow: He assumes that men are mutually self-interested; rational; and similar in needs, interests, and capacities.

I want to bring out how they [the principles of justice] are generated by imposing the constraints of having a morality upon persons who confront one another on those occasions when questions of justice arise.

In order to do this, it seems simplest to present a conjectural account of the derivation of these principles as follows. Imagine a society of persons amongst whom a certain system of practices is already well established. Now suppose that by and large they are mutually self-interested; their allegiance to their established practices is normally founded on the prospect of their own advantage. One need not, and indeed ought not, to assume that, in all senses of the term "person," the persons in this society are mutually self-interested. If this characterization holds when the line of division is the family, it is nevertheless likely to be true that members of families are bound by ties of sentiment and affection and willingly acknowledge duties in contradiction to self-interest. Mutual self-interestedness in the relations between families, nations, churches, and the like, is commonly associated with loyalty and devotion on the part of individual members. If this were not so the conflicts between these forms of association would not be pursued with such intensity and would not have such tragic consequences. If Hobbes' description of relations between persons seems unreal as applied to human individuals, it is often true enough of the relations between artificial persons; and these relations may assume their Hobbesian character largely in consequence of that element which that description professedly leaves out, the loyalty and devotion of individuals. Therefore, one can form a more realistic conception of this society if one thinks of it as consisting of mutually self-interested families, or some other association. Taking the term "person" widely from the start prepares one for doing this. It is not necessary to suppose, however, that these persons are mutually self-interested under all circumstances, but only in the usual situations in which they participate in their common practices concerning which the question of justice arises.

Now suppose further that these persons are rational: they know their own interests more or less accurately; they realize that the several ends they pursue may conflict with each other, and they are able to decide what level of attainment of one they are willing to sacrifice for a given level of attainment of another; they are capable of tracing out the likely consequences of adopting one practice rather than another, and of adhering to a course of action once they have decided upon it; they can resist present temptations and the enticements of immediate gain; and the bare knowledge or perception of the difference between their condition and that of others is not, within certain limits and in itself, a source of great dissatisfaction. Only the very last point adds anything to the standard definition of rationality as it appears say in the theory of price; and there is no need to question the propriety of this definition given the purposes for which it is customarily used. But the notion of rationality, if it is to play a part in the analysis of justice should allow, I think, that a rational man will resent or will be dejected by differences of condition between himself and others only where there is an accompanying explanation: that is, if they are thought to derive from injustice, or from some other fault of institutions, or to be the consequence of letting chance work itself out for no useful common purpose. At any rate, I shall include this trait of character in the notion of rationality for the purpose of analyzing the concept of justice. The legitimacy of doing so will, I think, become clear as the analysis proceeds. So if these persons strike us as unpleasantly egoistic in their relations with one another, they are at least free in some degree from the fault of envy.

Finally, assume that these persons have roughly similar needs, interests, and capacities, or needs, interests, and capacities in various ways complementary, so that fruitful cooperation amongst them is possible; and suppose that they are sufficiently equal in power and the instruments thereof to guarantee that in normal circumstances none is able to dominate the others. This condition (as well as the other conditions) may seem excessively vague; but in view of the conception of justice to which the argument leads, there seems to be no reason for making it more exact at this point.[4]

Since these persons are conceived as engaging in their common practices, which are already established, there is no question of our supposing them to come together to deliberate as to how they will set up these practices for the first time. Yet we can imagine that from time to time they discuss with one another whether any

---

[4] In this description of the situation of the persons, I have drawn on Hume's account of the circumstances in which justice arises, see *A Treatise of Human Nature*, bk. III, pt. II, sec. II, and *An Enquiry Concerning the Principles of Morals*, sec. III, pt. I. It is, in particular, the scarcity of good things and the lack of mutual benevolence that leads to conflicting claims, and which gives rise to the "cautious, jealous virtue of justice," a phrase from the *Enquiry*, ibid., par. 3.

of them has a legitimate complaint against their established institutions. This is only natural in any normal society. Now suppose
that they have settled on doing this in the following way. They
first try to arrive at the principles by which complaints and so
practices themselves are to be judged. That is, they do not begin
by complaining; they begin instead by establishing the criteria by
which a complaint is to be counted legitimate. Their procedure for
this is to let each person propose the principles upon which he
wishes his complaints to be tried with the understanding that, if
acknowledged, the complaints of others will be similarly tried;
and moreover, that no complaints will be heard at all until everyone is roughly of one mind as to how complaints are to be judged.
Thus while each person has a chance to propose the standards he
wishes, these standards must prove acceptable to the others before
his charges can be given a hearing. They all understand further
that the principles proposed and acknowledged on this occasion
are binding on future occasions. So each will be wary of proposing
a principle which would give him a peculiar advantage in his
present circumstances, supposing it to be accepted (which is, perhaps, in most cases unlikely). Each person knows that he will be
bound by it in future circumstances the peculiarities of which cannot be known, and which might well be such that the principle is
then to his disadvantage. The basic idea in this procedure is that
everyone should be required to make in advance a firm commitment to acknowledge certain principles as applying to his own
case and such that others also may reasonably be expected to
acknowledge them; and that no one be given the opportunity to
tailor the canons of a legitimate complaint to fit his own special
conditions, and then to discard them when they no longer suit his
purpose. Hence each person will propose principles of a general
kind which will, to a large degree, gain their sense from the various
applications to be made of them, the particular circumstances of
these applications being as yet unknown. These principles will
express the conditions in accordance with which each person is the
least unwilling to have his interests limited in the design of practices, given the competing interests of the others, on the supposition that the interests of others will be limited likewise. The

restriction[s] which would so arise might be thought of as those a person would keep in mind if he were designing a practice in which his enemy were to assign him his place.ᵉ

6. *When men are impartial, that is, when they operate under a Rawlsian "veil of ignorance," the appropriateness of the two principles of justice is manifest.*

. . . Given all the conditions as described in the conjectural account, it would be natural if the two principles of justice were to be jointly acknowledged. Since there is no way for anyone to win special advantages for himself, each would consider it reasonable to acknowledge equality as an initial principle. There is, however, no reason why they should regard this position as final. If there are inequalities which satisfy the conditions of the second principle, the immediate gain which equality would allow can be considered as intelligently invested in view of its future return. If, as is quite likely, these inequalities work as incentives to draw out better efforts, the members of this society may look upon them as concessions to human nature: they, like us, may think that people ideally should want to serve one another. But as they are mutually self-interested, their acceptance of these inequalities is merely the acceptance of the relations in which they actually stand, and a recognition of the motives which lead them to engage in their common practices. Being themselves self-interested, they have no title to complain of one another. And so provided the conditions of the principle are met, there is no reason why they should not allow such inequalities. Indeed, it would be short-sighted of them not to do so, and could result, in most cases, only from their being dejected by the bare knowledge, or perception, that others are better situated. Each person will, however, insist on an advantage to himself, and so on a common advantage, for none is willing to sacrifice anything for the others.⁵

---

⁵ A similar argument is given by F. Y. Edgeworth in "The Pure Theory of Taxation," *Economic Journal* 7 (1897). Reprinted in *Classics in the Theory of Public Finance*, ed. Musgrave and Peacock, New York: St. Martin's, 1958, pp. 120ff.

These remarks are not offered as a rigorous proof that persons conceived and situated as the conjectural account supposes, and required to adopt the procedure described, would settle on the two principles of justice stated and commented upon. . . . For this a much more elaborate and formal argument would have to be given. I shall not undertake a proof in this sense. In a weaker sense, however, the argument may be considered a proof, or as a sketch of a proof, although there still remain certain details to be filled in, and various alternatives to be ruled out.[f]

7. As developed earlier by Rawls, the concepts of fairness and justice are distinguishable. Fairness applies to "practices where persons are cooperating with or competing against one another and which allow a choice whether or not to do so." Justice applies to those "practices in which there is no such choice whether or not to participate." It is to be recalled as well, however, that both concepts have "a fundamental element in common," namely, the concept of reciprocity. Turning his attention to the importance of reciprocity for his social thesis, Rawls argues that unless justice is founded upon the "mutual acknowledgment of principles by free and equal persons," it becomes subject to the contingencies of force and circumstance."

That the principles of justice may be regarded as associated with the sense of justice in the manner described illustrates some important facts about them. For one thing it suggests the thought that justice is the first moral virtue in the sense that it arises once the concept of morality is imposed on mutually self-interested persons who are similarly situated; it is the first moral concept to be generated when one steps outside the bounds of rational self-interest. More relevant at the moment, the conjectural derivation emphasizes that fundamental to both justice and fairness is the concept of reciprocity. In the sense in which I shall use this concept, the question of reciprocity arises when free persons, who have no moral authority over one another and who are engaging in or who find themselves participating in a joint activity, are amongst themselves settling upon or acknowledging the rules which define it and which determine their respective shares in its benefits and burdens. The principle of reciprocity requires of a practice that it satisfy those principles which the persons who participate in it could reasonably propose for mutual acceptance under the circumstances and conditions of the hypothetical account. Persons engaged in a practice meeting this principle can then face one another openly and support their respective positions, should they appear questionable, by reference to principles which it is reasonable to expect each to accept. A practice will strike the parties as conforming to the notion of reciprocity if none feels that, by participating in it, he or any of the others are taken advantage of or forced to give in to claims which they do not accept as legitimate. But if they are prepared to complain this implies that each has a conception of legitimate claims which he thinks it reasonable for all to acknowledge. If one thinks of the principles of justice as arising in the manner described, then they specify just this sort of conception.

It is this requirement of the possibility of mutual acknowledgment of principles by free and equal persons who have not authority over one another which makes the concept of reciprocity fundamental to both justice and fairness. Only if such acknowledgment is possible can there be true community between persons in their common practices; otherwise their relations will appear to them as founded to some degree on force and circumstance.ᵍ

8. Additional clarification of the concept of justice as reciprocity is achieved by contrasting its principles with those of classical utilitarianism on the issue of slavery.

One may begin by noticing that classical utilitarianism permits one to argue that slavery is unjust on the grounds that the advantages to the slaveholder as slaveholder do not counterbalance the disadvantages to the slave and to society at large, burdened by a comparatively inefficient system of labor. Now the conception of justice as reciprocity, when applied to the practice of slavery with its offices of slaveholder and slave, would not allow one to consider the advantages of the slaveholder in the first place. As that office is not in accordance with principles which could be mutually acknowledged, the gains accruing to the slaveholder, assuming them to exist, cannot be counted as in any way mitigating the injustice of the practice. The question whether these gains outweigh the disadvantages to the slaves and to society cannot arise, since in considering the justice of slavery these gains have no weight at all which requires that they be overridden. Where the conception of justice as reciprocity applies, slavery is always unjust.

I am not, of course, suggesting the absurdity that the classical utilitarians approved of slavery.[6] I am only rejecting a type of argument which their view allows them to use in support of their disapproval of it. The conception of justice as derivative from efficiency implies that judging the justice of a practice is always, in principle at least, a matter of weighing up advantages and disadvantages, each having an intrinsic value or disvalue as the satisfaction of interests, irrespective of whether or not these interests necessarily involve acquiescence in principles which could not mutually be acknowledged. Utilitarianism cannot account for the fact that slavery is always unjust, nor for the fact that it would be recognized as irrelevant in defeating the accusation of injustice for one person to say to another, engaged with him in a common practice and debating its merits, that nevertheless it allowed of the greatest satisfaction of desire. The charge of injustice cannot be rebutted in this way. If justice were derivative from a higher order executive efficiency, this would not be so.

But now, even if it is taken as established that, so far as the ordinary conception of justice goes, slavery is always unjust (that is, slavery by definition violates commonly recognized principles of justice), the classical utilitarian would surely reply that these principles, like other moral principles subordinate to that of utility, are only generally correct. It is simply for the most part true

---

[6] To the contrary, Bentham argued very powerfully against it. See *A Fragment of Government*, ch. II, par. 34, footnote 2; *The Principles of Morals and Legislation*, ch. XVI, par. 44, footnote; ch. XVII, par. 4, footnote; *The Theory of Legislation*, pt. III, ch. II.

that slavery is less efficient than other institutions; and while common sense may define the concept of justice in such a way that slavery is proved unjust, nevertheless, where slavery would lead to the greatest satisfaction of desire, it is not wrong. Indeed, it is then right, and for the very same reason that justice, as ordinarily understood, is usually right. If, as ordinarily understood, slavery is always unjust, to this extent the utilitarian conception of justice might be admitted to differ from that of moral opinion. Still the utilitarian would want to hold that, as a matter of moral principle, his view is correct in giving no special weight to considerations of justice beyond that allowed for by the general presumption of effectiveness. And this, he claims, is as it should be. The everyday opinion is morally in error, although, indeed, it is a useful error, since it protects rules of generally high utility.

The question, then, relates not simply to the analysis of the concept of justice as common sense defines it, but the analysis of it in the wider sense as to how much weight considerations of justice, as defined, are to have when laid against other kinds of moral considerations. Here again I wish to argue that reasons of justice have a special weight for which only the conception of justice as reciprocity can account. Moreover, it belongs to the concept of justice that they do have this special weight. While Mill recognized that this was so, he thought that it could be accounted for by the special urgency of the moral feelings which naturally support principles of such high utility. But it is a mistake to resort to the urgency of feeling; as with the appeal to intuition, it manifests a failure to pursue the question far enough. The special weight of considerations of justice can be explained from the conception of justice as reciprocity. It is only necessary to elaborate a bit what has already been said, as follows.

If one examines the circumstances in which a certain tolerance of slavery is justified, or perhaps better, excused, it turns out that these are of a rather special sort. Perhaps slavery exists as an inheritance from the past and it proves necessary to dismantle it piece by piece; at times slavery may conceivably be an advance on previous institutions. Now while there may be some excuse for slavery in special conditions, it is never an excuse for it that it is sufficiently advantageous to the slaveholder to outweigh the disadvantages to the slave and to society. A person who argues in this way is not perhaps making a wildly irrelevant remark; but he is guilty of a moral fallacy. There is disorder in his conception of the ranking of moral principles. For the slaveholder, by his own admission, has no moral title to the advantages which he receives as a slaveholder. He is no more prepared than the slave to acknowledge the principle upon which is founded the respective positions in which they both stand. Since slavery does not accord with principles which they could mutually acknowledge, they each may be supposed to agree that it is unjust: it grants claims which it ought not to grant and in doing so denies claims which it ought not to deny. Amongst persons in a general position who are debating the form of their common practices, it cannot, therefore, be offered as a reason for a practice that, in conceding these very claims that ought to be denied, it nevertheless meets existing interests more effectively. By their very nature the satisfaction of these claims is without weight and cannot enter into any tabulation of advantages and disadvantages.

Furthermore, it follows from the concept of morality that, to the extent that the slaveholder recognizes his position vis-à-vis the slave to be unjust, he would not choose to press his claims. His not wanting to receive his special advantages is one of the ways in which he shows that he thinks slavery is unjust. It would be fallacious for the legislator to suppose, then, that it is a ground for having a practice that it brings advantages greater than disadvantages, if those for whom the practice is designed and to whom the advantages flow, acknowledge that they have no moral title to them and do not wish to receive them.

For these reasons the principles of justice have a special weight; and with respect to the principle of the greatest satisfaction of desire, as cited in the general position amongst those discussing the merits of their common practices, the principles of justice have an absolute weight. In this sense they are not contingent; and this is why their force is greater than can be accounted for by the general presumption (assuming that there is one) of the effectiveness, in the utilitarian sense, of practices which in fact satisfy them.[h]

9. Drawing his accounts together, Rawls sums up, in a positive way, his concept of justice in terms of the social contract.

If, however, the argument above regarding slavery is correct, granting these assumptions as moral and political principles makes no difference. To view individuals as equally fruitful lines for the allocation of benefits, even as a matter of moral principle, still leaves the mistaken notion that the satisfaction of desire has value in itself irrespective of the relations between persons as members of a common practice, and irrespective of the claims upon one another which the satisfaction of interests represents. To see the error of this idea one must give up the conception of justice as an executive decision altogether and refer to the notion of justice as fairness: that participants in a common practice be regarded as having an original and equal liberty and that their common practices be considered unjust unless they accord with principles which persons so circumstanced and related could freely acknowledge before one another, and so could accept as fair. Once the emphasis is put upon the concept of the mutual recognition of principles by participants in a common practice the rules of which are to define their several relations and give form to their claims on one another, then it is clear that the granting of a claim the principle of which could not be acknowledged by each in the general position (that is, in the position in which the parties propose and acknowledge principles before one another) is not a reason for adopting a practice. Viewed in this way, the background of the claim is seen to exclude it from consideration; that it can represent a value in itself arises from the conception of individuals as separate lines for the assignment of benefits, as isolated persons who stand as claimants on an administrative or benevolent largesse. Occasionally persons do so stand to one another; but this is not the general case, nor, more importantly, is it the case when it is a matter of the justice of practices themselves in which participants stand in various relations to be appraised in accordance with standards which they may be expected to acknowledge before one another. Thus, however mistaken the notion of the social contract may be as history, and however far it may overreach itself as a general theory of social and political obligation, it does express, suitably interpreted, an essential part of the concept of justice.[i]

Questions

1. How sharp a distinction does Rawls draw between the concepts of justice and fairness? Can you suggest some circumstances in which the terms *justice* and *fairness* might be used interchangeably and some circumstances in which they could not? How is the concept of reciprocity related to the above-mentioned concepts?

2. State the principle of equal liberty and illustrate its meaning by providing a situation to which it might apply.

3. State the principle of difference and illustrate its meaning by providing a situation to which it might apply.

4. Sometimes Rawls emphasizes the priority of the equal liberty principle to the difference principle. Why is this order of priority important?

5. Would Rawls'contract theory be undermined if one assumed that men were *not* mutually self-interested; rational; and similar in needs, interests, and capacities? Discuss the theoretical significance of the assumption that men have these traits.

6. Must Rawls deny Hobbes' depiction of the state of nature as "a time of war, where every man is enemy to every man"? Discuss.

7. What meaning does Rawls' metaphor "veil of ignorance" convey? In your dealings with others, are you ever willing to place yourself under the veil of ignorance?

8. Rawls charges that utilitarianism does not necessarily preclude slavery as a theoretical possibility. Does his discussion unduly emphasize the difference between theory and practice? Develop.

9. According to Rawls, it is a mistaken notion that "the satisfaction of desire has value in itself irrespective of the relations between persons as members of a common practice." By insisting on this point, does

Rawls ally himself more nearly with Kant than with Mill? Defend your answer.
10. Suppose that one fully accepts the Rawlsian social theory. Would a person be free to adopt an individual morality such as Epicurus proposes? Or Spinoza? Or Nietzsche?

Key to selections:

JOHN RAWLS, "Justice as Reciprocity," from John Stuart Mill, *Utilitarianism*, Samuel Gorovitz, ed., Indianapolis, The Bobbs-Merrill Company, 1971. Reprinted with the kind permission of the publisher.

[a] pp. 242–243.
[b] pp. 244–245.
[c] pp. 245.
[d] pp. 245–247.
[e] pp. 248–250.

[f] pp. 251–252.
[g] pp. 255–256.
[h] pp. 264–265.
[i] pp. 266–267.

Guide to Additional Reading

ADDITIONAL SOURCE MATERIAL:

Rawls, J., "Justice as Fairness," *Philosophical Review*, LXVII (1958), 164–194.
——, "Two Concepts of Rules," *Philosophical Review*, LXIV (1955), 3–32.
——, *A Theory of Justice*, Cambridge, Harvard University Press, 1971.

DISCUSSION AND COMMENTARY:

Barry, B., *The Liberal Theory of Justice*, Oxford, Clarendon Press, 1973.
Arrow, K., "Some Ordinalist-Utilitarian Notes on Rawls's Theory of Justice," *Journal of Philosophy*, LXX (1973), 245–263.
Feinberg, J., "Duty and Obligation in the Non-Ideal World," *Journal of Philosophy*, LXX (1973), 263–275.
Gordon, S., "John Rawls's Difference Principle, Utilitarianism, and the Optimum Degree of Inequality," *Journal of Philosophy*, LXX (1973), 275–280.

Epilogue

Because human experience does not come analyzed for us, ethical theorizing persists as a vital enterprise. And because life is a complex matrix in which a wide variety of perspectives is formed, we cannot expect to find unanimity in ethics, save perhaps in the general, if sometimes unacknowledged, homage to the power of reason. From the diversity of tradition, circumstance, and personality have come alternative and even conflicting moral ideals: the Stoic devotion to self-discipline, as well as the Epicurean preference for the pleasant life; Saint Augustine's fervent love of God and Nietzsche's God-defying Superman; the Kantian model of the duty-bound individual and the socially conscious Utilitarian, seeking the happiness of the greatest number.

No matter how far away from life ethical speculation may go — and moral philosophy is as notable for its abstruse qualities as for its penetrating analyses and systematic development of ideas — it is, in the last analysis, from life itself that the ethical theorist acquires the raw materials upon which he must work. It is to life again that he intends his theories to apply at some stage in the interaction of belief and behavior. Not by haphazard or arbitrary eclecticism, but under the guidance of reason can we cull what is valuable from ethical theory and dismiss what is without significance. The ability to evaluate alternative ethical principles and to understand the connection between theory and the living moral situation calls for mental maturity and independence of a high degree — wisdom is not easily come by.

Acquaintance with the various theories of ethics is only a first step towards understanding the complexities of the moral life. Temporarily at least, it may lead us in a direction counter to our accustomed ways of thinking. We are born into a culture where definite moral practices and ideas are already fixed by custom and tradition. Consequently, the notion that morality is so clear-cut and final that reflection about it is unnecessary is probably more comfortable than the exertion of theorizing.

The attitude that whatever is, is right, and the accompanying preference for a moral theory which leaves the familiar order undisturbed, conceal a narrow dogmatism. It assumes unwittingly that there exists only one "correct" theory, the one that is in operation here and now. The dogmatist all too often fears that if he does not have on tap quick and certain answers for every moral question, if he cannot be sure that he has the one and only valid ethical theory, he will be in a state of ineffectual confusion, incapable of decisive moral action. But this entails a misunderstanding of the nature of ethical theory with which some people may enter the study of ethics; it should not be the view with which they leave the subject.

William James held that, "To know the chief rival attitudes towards life as the history of thinking has developed them, and to have heard some of the reasons they can give for themselves ought to be considered an essential part of liberal education." The fact that philosophers of equal intelligence and integrity have come out on opposite sides of the same moral issues is no argument against the study of ethics. On the contrary, it is the very point and value of the discipline that active disagreement should be maintained and encouraged. The study of different ethical theories is an antidote for provincialism, an invitation to openmindedness. Even if we retain the same moral principles with which we began our inquiry, we can enjoy enlightened, enriched belief. The naïveté of judging issues in terms of black-or-white can be replaced by the sophistication of considered judgments and refined distinctions. The reflective man can hold his views with conviction, secure in the knowledge that he has examined alternatives and reasoned his way to his position. Basing his preference on rational, rather than on emotional grounds, he can both respect his own philosophy and appreciate the reasonableness and feasibility of others'.

Reflection on moral matters enhances the individual's ability to think things through. It is the *autonomy of mind* — the capacity to think for oneself — which unites all those who enter upon the philosophic enterprise. Moreover, the effect of the reflective attitude is to make audible the "still small voice that murmurs 'fiddlesticks'" to superficial moral beliefs. The diversity born of intellectual integrity is probably the strongest force that has kept ethical inquiry alive and productive for thousands of years and keeps it astir today. The last ethical theory has not yet been written, the last ethical insight has not yet been recorded. *To think maturely on moral matters is the desideratum and value of the study of ethics.*

Index

455

Picture Credits